D1328342

The Cry of Home

CULTURAL NATIONALISM AND THE MODERN WRITER

The Cry
of Home

CULTURAL NATIONALISM

AND THE MODERN WRITER

---

edited by H. Ernest Lewald

THE UNIVERSITY OF TENNESSEE PRESS

AN OFFICIAL PROJECT OF THE

Modern Language Association of America

·

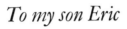

To my son Eric

Preface

The interaction of nationalism, culture, and literature has received far less attention from scholars than the subject merits. Scholarly research on the topic as reflected in published work has been both scanty and uneven, yet in some ways this thrust by a wide array of contemporary writers to interpret, perpetuate, and sometimes glorify the nationalistic essence of their cultures should overshadow our interest in related areas that have already claimed attention: the fields of political nationalism and romanticism, for instance, which have been viewed as generating forces for political activities from Napoleon to Hitler. Perhaps the answer to the question of imbalance lies in the difficulty of finding a common denominator for the disparate "cries of home." Certainly, contemporary writers whose works can be said to exhibit cultural nationalism do not together constitute a "movement," for the character and intensity of this ill-defined spirit vary greatly from one nation or people to another and, hence, so do the literary and artistic expressions of that spirit. Nevertheless, despite the cataloguing difficulty, the time is overdue to take a look, and preferably a comparative look, at a driving force that can be observed in some of our finest contemporary literature.

The foregoing expression of need was articulated originally in 1968 at the Modern Language Association session (General Topics 6) devoted to "Literature and Society," a session presided over by the editor of the present volume. It was at this meeting that the foundation was laid for exploring the quite complex theme with such scholars as Germaine Brée, Rima Drell Reck, and Lewis P. Simpson, all actively involved with the Literature and Society section in recent years. Subsequently, the venture to commission original essays for inclusion in a single collection on the subject was endorsed as an official project of the MLA.

As might be expected, an accord on the components of cultural nationalism could not be reached by the study group without some compromising. The consensus seemed to be that cultural nationalism is a spiritual force composed of the ethos, language, and socio-political interests of a people that finds genuine expression on an artistic, social, and political level. On the positive side it allows the individual, and most certainly the artist or writer, to act as an integral part of a social organism that, enriched by his contributions, will transcend his limited experience and endure after him. In this sense cultural nationalism also allows minority cultures to survive within a larger organism without being absorbed by the latter. On the negative side, however, cultural nationalism has led time and again to xenophobia, ethnocentrism, and the annihilation of cultures and peoples.

The original difficulty of defining cultural nationalism was matched, ultimately, by the editor's problem of how to arrange the essays to best aid the reader in his comparison and synthesis of the contents. One possible approach is that taken in the introduction where cultural nationalism is examined in terms of four different relationships: Nationalism and Politics, Nationalism and Culture, Nationalism and Language, and Nationalism and Literature. Such a grouping is obviously impractical for the essays, however, because the relationships are not mutually exclusive; they more often appear as concurrent overlapping threads in the same work. Thus, the present division of the contributions into Europe, North America, and Third World—a grouping somewhat by geographical source but to some extent by culture also—was settled upon as the nearest approach possible to a useful arrangement. As can be seen in the seventeen essays here included, the mature and technologically advanced countries of the Western World seem to be undergoing a process of losing some national essence, while the younger and underdeveloped nations of the so-called Third World are still destined to search for a national identity; and the various minority cultures, old as well as emergent, continue to draw on their cultural resources in an effort to avoid social absorption.

Inevitably, a collection that can only sample world literature in one volume will have gaps. The method of choosing languages and literatures was eclectic but in part determined by the interest of the individual scholars. As well, the confluence of quite a number of languages and literatures dictated certain editorial procedures. Many references that would be known to the specialist in any one field have been explained to the reader who, after all, cannot be versed in seventeen areas. Titles have been translated by the editor even when no official English version seemed to exist. The bibliographies have been kept in the respective original languages, although the Roman alphabet was used in the case of Slavic and Semitic titles. The use and emphasis concerning the bibliographies as well as footnotes vary according to the contributors' focus and predilection, and no attempt has been made to curtail individual presentations.

I wish to acknowledge with sincere appreciation the splendid cooperation of each of the essayists. Their scholarly contributions are in my judgment needed and significant. My special thanks go also to Dr. Yulan Washburn and Claire Furr for their help and suggestions, and all of us of course were gratified by the decision of the Publications Committee of the Modern Language Association to lend its official support to this book. It is hoped that the essays and the bibliographies will be informative as well as useful as a reference to those interested in the relationship between the modern writer and the *Cry of Home.*

H. E. L.

Contents

The Cry of Home

CULTURAL NATIONALISM AND THE MODERN WRITER

Introduction

NATIONALISM AND POLITICS

Political scientists as well as historians for some time have made it their business to define and analyze nationalism—but not always with consensus results. The definitions vary widely, and this is quite understandable, for the ramifications of nationalism reach deeply into the realm of psychological forces, social patterns, and cultural symbols, creating an extremely complex totality. Even so, the existing definitions when considered together make up a fairly complete picture. Hans Kohn, acknowledged authority on the subject, defines nationalism as "first and foremost a state of mind" and as "a community in behavior." Carlton Hayes in his *Essays on Nationalism* sees nationalism as an historical process that is channeled into a political consciousness revolving around a national state, but he also notes that "nationality is an attribute of human culture and civilization," having the effect of creating an emotional fusion of the group mind. For Eugen Lemberg, nationalism constitutes an ideology to be shared by a society, a political expression at the service of a culture.

Obviously, then, nationalism as a political force can be viewed as the consequence of fundamental social relations within a community of material and spiritual interests—embracing morals, customs, and traditions that join to create what has so often been called a "common destiny," "soul of the people," or, to employ the term used by Jacques Cotnam, one of the essayists in this volume, a *vouloir-vivre collectif*.

Historians tell us that political nationalism emerged in eighteenth-century Europe, spread throughout the Continent in the nineteenth century, and penetrated into the areas of the world where new nations emerged from crumbling colonial empires. No doubt the rise of the modern nation-state in Europe created a shining political surface that floated on deep cultural waters; but the cultural-organic forces holding up the political stratum deserve close attention since they preceded the Age of Nationalism and in our present era are again dynamic enough to alter the composition of the national spirit, at least in technologically advanced states. The political trajectory from clan to nation to state represents the history of a struggle to make political boundaries coincide with cultural ones, which often involves subordinating national concepts to a state's ideology. Within this framework we can easily place the elusive process of welding different cultural, ethnic, regional, and linguistic groups—frequently minorities or subcultures—into a grand total for political purposes. The examples are abundant: the political verification of Spain began under the Castilian rule in the fifteenth century at the expense of the Catalan, Asturian, and Basque nations—a rule still resisted by these minority cultures under Franco's regime. The unification of Italy's linguistic and cultural regions that began with Garibaldi and the Risorgimento still continues. England's political creation, Great Britain, has never assimilated the national concepts still valid today in Wales, Scotland, or Ireland. On the largest imaginable scale, Russia's control of a number of Soviet republics continues an expansionary policy that dates from early tsarist days, and it remains to be seen if Marxist ideology is sufficient to create a common emotive basis for so many independent cultural, ethnic, and linguistic nations.

History has seldom been kind to smaller nations or minorities. In Europe, for instance, they were often condemned to play the role of agents, pawns, or victims in the power struggle that constantly reshaped political boundaries. It seems axiomatic that politically coerced minorities—cultural organisms within an alien framework—develop a heightened sense of national uniqueness as part of a self-preservation process. Political dictates that ignore cultural frontiers have sown the seeds of future strife or disunity. The artificial creation of Belgium through a British policy to contain the French in the post-Napoleonic era laid the groundwork for a continued confrontation of a Protestant-Flemish and Catholic-French culture. The fragmentation of the Austrian empire (Donaumonarchie) in 1919 left in its wake nations that failed to recognize their cultural needs or identities within the newly formed states. The Sudeten Germans served as a pawn for Hitler's expansionistic adventures; and in 1919 as well as in 1945 the complicated map of the Balkans was redrawn creating new minority groups—such as the Hungarians in neighboring states—that were and are being repressed in their efforts to retain their cultural identity. That point is developed very clearly in this volume in the essay by George Gömöri; and Germaine Brée's contribution shows us that the political boundaries of present-day Africa still resemble in many ways the lines carved by the colonial powers, which often do not coincide with the realities of tribal or linguistic demography. In Latin America, as will be seen in the editor's own essay, the fragmentation process also ignored cultural and linguistic ties, at the same time creating new states that are too small, too isolated, or too bereft of any resources to function effectively.

The modern state harboring several nations or minority groups and thus lacking a homogeneous society or *Kulturgemeinschaft* is faced with the problem of allegiance. From the state's point of view, it must promote the allegiance of its disparate parts—a major problem because the members of the minority nation will fail to identify with the state's goals whenever policies appear that are damaging to the minority's interests. Yet from the vantage point of the minority culture, it must, in order to survive, resist absorption by the main cultural organism. The latter is difficult, for even minorities such as the Chicanos, who can draw cultural support from their original homeland across the border, feel the gravitational pull exerted by the social and economic practices of the dominant culture of California or New Mexico. Doubtlessly the most dramatic and continued example of an exiled culture is represented by the history of the Diaspora. Only in this century has Zionism paved the way toward the creation of a Jewish state; and it remains to be seen to what extent the Jews of the Diaspora are willing to identify their composite culture with that of the newly founded state of Israel, which is a theme developed in the essay by Gila Ramras–Rauch. How far the Zionists will be tested in their conflict of interests between the new Jewish state and their respective host cultures is another facet of the question, and Allen Guttmann's article on Jewish culture in America points precisely to this division of cultural identity. Similarly, the black citizen of the United States is suffering from an identification crisis. De–Africanized after his forced arrival in the New World as to tribal culture and language, the American black finds his present–day quest for black identity to be the result of ethnic, not cultural rejection. The recent Congress of African People held in Atlanta, Georgia, indicates the willingness of black American leaders to point toward Africa as their spiritual and even political homeland. But attaining Africanhood would prove much more difficult culturally than politically, since the black American's culture is today but a subculture of the American one. He would have to relearn his lost heritage unless he is willing to accept his black Americanism as a genuine cultural vehicle. Such is the plight of several main characters examined by O. B. Emerson in his essay on black literature.

It is interesting to speculate about the correlations between the intensity of nationalism and the survival quotient of a culture. Irish or Welsh nationalism flourishes while the English counterpart does not. Nations such as Estonia, Poland, or Hungary maintain a traditionally strong national spirit, probably due to their recurrent struggle to survive as states and nations. Presently affluent states such as Sweden, France, or Italy show a relatively low degree of national fervor while in the underdeveloped nations of Africa or Latin America the economic and political dependence on their former colonial masters or on the big industrial powers has created a compensatory reaction that makes abundant use of the emotive powers inherent in national feeling.

NATIONALISM AND CULTURE

Looking at the broad spectrum that places the individual at one end and the modern state at the other, we note that the interplay between the individual's self-interest and his anonymous fate within a political structure that regulates the existence of millions will determine the degree of national cohesion. More specifically, the political apparatus cannot function without a corresponding cultural system that provides national unity and goals. If, for instance, the forlorn inhabitants of the overpopulated areas in our industralized countries begin to feel an increasing sense of alienation and anomie at the expense of cultural cohesion, their awareness of a national identity as well as their allegiance to the state will continue to diminish.

Probably the perfect homogeneous spirit was provided by a clan, which gave the individual a measurable social extension of himself and his family. It was a spirit continually reinforced by the sharing of physical and ecological characteristics—terrain, climate, fauna, flora, and living conditions—which in turn influenced cultural expressions. Norms, beliefs, and conduct evolved from man's ecological adaptation and continued to evolve in a natural fashion until extraneous social agents began to create a more heterogeneous culture. Perhaps the key word here is *natural*, since it represents the direct interaction between nature and the socialized human being. It was this interaction that led the romantics to this search for the true cultural and literary expression of a national feeling, a *Volksgeist*. The preromantic Herder, modifying Montesquieu's concept of the factors shaping a people's uniqueness in his famous *L'esprit des lois* (1748), took nationality to be basically an organization regulated by natural law. Nineteenth-century romanticism accepted nature as a great determining force, a concept that the French critic Hippolyte Taine redefined late in the century with the formula "moment, milieu, race" and a concept that novelists like Maurice Barrès in more recent times have used in urging that man avoid severing his ties with the land that shelters the spirit of his forefathers.

There can be, in our times, however, no facile recapturing of a "moment, milieu, race" that would allow us to "verify" culture as being derived from natural forces. What was survival for a clan becomes a saga in the romantic age; an early people's history becomes historicity; what was sacred changes into mythology or theology; and communal expression is now studied as poetry. There might well exist a cultural axiom that states that the strength of a national feeling within a homogeneous society is determined by an inverse relation to the number of its members and its physical extension. It is no longer possible to break down the sum total of a culture and trace its components to the source. Yet we do know that the cultural *persona* of, say, the present-day Finns, Poles, or Irish represents a continuity whose initial stages are not accounted for and that the present culture reflects the influence of many adaptations.

The modern state or nation acknowledges this continuity and tries to reinforce its social cohesiveness, now for the sake of the state or nation. Thus we have national shrines, holy rivers, places of pilgrimage, revered names, and sacred objects. Schoolchildren must undergo the daily ritual of pledging loyalty to symbolic emblems, memorizing the epic deeds of historic figures, and in general absorbing a national essence from a variety of literary, pictorial, folkloric, or musical patterns. Holidays, parades, and official acts reinforce the national cohesion by manipulating myths, symbols, and rituals; and heroes are established as national models if their exploits happen to fit the dynamics of a culture. The Cid has survived as an embodiment of a Christian Spain that fought the infidels for eight hundred years; Alexander Nevsky can still be pertinent as the defender of the sacred Russian soil against Mongols and Teutonic invaders alike; and Charles Lindbergh represents the triumph of the American dream that amalgamated the pioneer spirit with good old American know-how in the machine age.

By their nature, Philip Wheelright tells us in *The Burning Fountain*, myths are collective and communal and bind people's psychological or spiritual activities by spurring the collective imagination. The collective aspect of the myth impact obviously serves as a vital ingredient in fashioning a national psyche. Mythical imagination suspends the exercise of reason and appeals to the irrational in mankind, according to Ernst Cassirer, and whatever emerges as being heroic or sacred will exert a form of magic sway over the national psyche. Thus a few bars of music identified as a national anthem still produce a strong emotional response in civic crowds, and individuals destroying a simple piece of painted cloth designated a national flag are severely punished, and the killing of persons labeled enemies is still rewarded in any modern state.

But, in our industrial societies the heroes are tired and myths have paled. Even the recent moon walks have been interpreted as a triumph of technical teamwork that left no room for the mythical imagination. As the urbanized dweller is channeled through his daily elevator shafts, subway tunnels, windowless offices, factories, and apartment buildings and is confronted with synthetic experiences presented through electronic equipment, his overwhelmingly technological existence denaturalizes him and the countless millions who crowd the cities and suburbs in modern nations. Free in an ontological sense but rootless in their individuation, modern urban dwellers come to represent the opposite of a primitive man who lived close to nature and was alert to its life-giving and life-taking moods. Northrop Frye did well to point out that myths—truly a union of memory and rituals—are inextricably involved in the prelogical and preverbal synchronization of a culture with the rhythm of its natural environment.

The process of denaturalization that is rendering the metaphysics of a regional and national spirit largely nonfunctional has reached the stage of changing citizen-identity to consumer-identity, a clear shift from the political to the economic mode. The advantages of the European Common Market attract the consumer rather than the citizen. Reinhold Grimm and H. G. Hüttich bear out this trend in their essay, analyzing the extremely low yield of cultural nationalism in postwar West German letters. A similar case can be made for the other member nations of the economic community. G. S. Fraser in his article expresses the belief that the absorption into the Common Market will hasten the end of "a traditional pattern of English life" sustained by a class spirit that is already dissolving into "nostalgia, hope, depression and resentment," as can be verified in the major English prose works since the Second World War. France and Italy, today caught in the growing pains of technocracies, registered their mark on the scale of nationalism in their respective literatures following invasions and occupations by foreign troops during the Second World War. Thereafter the writer's search for his ties to a national heritage became highly personalized, as Rima Drell Reck and Sarah D'Alberti show in their essays.

Culture as a live organism responds to actions endangering its existence, and nationalism is the fever with which the organism shakes the body politic. Political nationalism is thus nourished by a cultural counterpart. As Salih J. Altoma's study of the modern Arab novel indicates, Pan-Arabism is a religious and social commodity that expands greatly when inflamed by war. Professor Ramras-Rauch makes a comparative case in his analysis of the Israeli novel of today. Irish and Welsh nationalism is not sustained by political crises but instead by cultural constants that for a long time have acted as deterrents to the gravitational pull of English culture and language. Of course, for culture to be responsive to national stimulus it must retain the cohesion built into a *Kulturgemeinschaft* that has not lost too much rapport with the organic life cycle.

NATIONALISM AND LANGUAGE

Anthropologists never cease to point out that culture shapes linguistic expression, while linguists continue to explore the impact of linguistic structure on thought patterns. Without entering here into speculations on this academic dispute, it suffices to note that either alternative establishes a close interaction between culture and language. The German romantics in their search for the genuine expression of the *génie d'un peuple* attempted to reach into the remotest past to find a primordial language (*Ursprache*) as well as a communal existence bound together by a common speech (*Sprach-*

gemeinschaft). Haman, Herder, or the Brothers Grimm certainly furnish examples of such attempts.

The evocative and connotative powers of a word or a phrase are shared by those who participate in a given language, dialect, or speech form; and the phonetic treatment of the word will have similar effects. Shared speech patterns create social cohesion; at the same time, they exclude those who do not or cannot utilize them. A foreigner is a person who might or might not communicate with the members of a *Sprachgemeinschaft* with a fair degree of fluency, but because of his cultural formation he is assumed to see life differently. Quite understandably, linguist Edward Sapir states that language is *the* medium of expression of a given society, almost a philosophy, that contributes greatly to the cultural uniqueness of a society.

A unique verbal symbolization of natural phenomena or social behavior is certainly tantamount to a relativistic but fixed *Weltanschauung*. Anthropologist Clyde Kluckhohn mentions, for instance, that some American Indian languages allow the speaker to modulate an account in five basic ways, depending on such factors as hearsay, direct observation, and three degrees of plausibility. Professor Kluckhohn's colleagues always delight in telling literary people that Britons and Americans still suffer from the common delusion that they speak the same language.

Like cultural organisms, a language seems to be subject to the laws governing dynamic and static conditions: languages evolve with the dynamics of a heterogeneous society but become static when separated from their parent body. It is the fate of minority languages, created by shifting political boundaries or migrations, that they become archaic with the passage of time. As a cultural island, a national identity cemented by a common tongue isolates as it unifies. Yet, as on the level of cultural evolution, it is indeed utopian—using Karl Mannheim's interpretation of the term—to expect a "separate but equal" status for the minority cultures and their languages. Left to generate its own national identity quotient, the host culture will operate on an organic level and try to absorb any foreign body within its sphere of influence. Thus European language pockets in America have suffered their decline and fall. Even Yiddish, the lingua franca of the Jews in Europe and America since the Reformation days and based on sixteenth-century German dialect, is in danger of dissolution in spite of its inextricable ties to Jewish culture in exile. Interestingly, however, the present black America quest for its own cultural identity is producing a parallel development on the linguistic level. The aforementioned Pan-African conference held in Atlanta in the summer of 1970 showed the determination of the participants —artists, writers, politicians, and simply black citizens—to act within a framework of an African ethos and language. Quite obviously Imamu Amiri Baraka (formerly LeRoi Jones) and the conventioneers using Swahili vocabulary realize that the conscious creation of a minority culture must include a corresponding language in order to succeed.

NATIONALISM AND LITERATURE

Cultural symbolization is an integral part of literary expression and few writers would fail to be conscious of their roles as interpreters of human experience and of their mission to recapture it by means of a style that draws from language nuances so subtle that the impressions and connotations thereby created usually fail to survive in translation. The French poet Paul Valéry, aware that he followed in the footsteps of such illustrious countrymen as Montesquieu and Taine, paraphrased their literary tenets in stating that literature is the inevitable product of a matrix formed by race, land, memories, and national unity.

Since the beginning of literature, its practitioners have had to be guardians of their people's culture and singers of its themes. It must have been easier in the beginning, when literature worked and reworked myths and rituals that bound a group of people together with the aid of symbols and sounds, creating the magic spell which made men rush into battle, defy death, and accept an impending fate. It was a literature of full participation in the life cycle of a clan or nation, embodying archetypal themes of survival, decay, and rebirth; of vitality and pollution; and of the hero's self-sacrifice to save his people. This literature constantly kindled the folk imagination. Aeneas, Beowulf, or Roland shouldered the heavy responsibility of carrying out their mission within a national framework. The *Iliad*, the *Eddas*, or the *Kalevala* constitute "expressions of a profound sense of togetherness"—to quote Philip Wheelwright—in which "human activity is energized into a spiritual force."

The role of romanticism in creating political nationalism in the nineteenth century has already been discussed. Quite clearly the romantic spirit in search of a people's primordial speech and thought had been capable of producing a national literature that showed at least the intent to conjure up a far-removed essence: McPherson's pseudo-epic *Ossian,* Gogol's *Taras Bulba,* Hernández's *Martín Fierro,* Leopardi's *All'Italia,* or Eichendorff's poems.

But as romanticism became politicized, producing a Heine, Byron, Lamartine, or Espronceda, a nationalistic mode began to supplant the ontological search for a spiritual contact with an essence from the past. Not that a quite openly nationalistic strain was not visible in Shakespeare's *Henry V* or Tolstoi's *War and Peace,* but toward the turn of the twentieth century the writer began to visualize his dual role as the pure artist and a social being. Thomas Mann recognized this duality as a confrontation of the bohemian and the bourgeois elements, largely drawn from his own experiences. Maurice Barrès felt compelled to popularize the tragedy of losing one's identity with the native soil by drifting into the lure of an easy cosmopolitanism in the French capital, in a sense a theme that was precursor to the alienated existence in the big city that developed decades later. But perhaps William Butler Yeats, one of the authors discussed by Robert Tracy in his contribution to this volume, best exemplified the ordeal of the artist forced to distinguish between a national vision and nationalistic means. His reluctance, after having written *Cathleen Ni Houlihan,* to produce further plays with a political texture for the Irish National theater shows the artist's awareness of the dangers in surrendering his craft to a nonartistic cause, in Yeats's case to put to use his world of myth, symbols, and language for a nationalistic purpose: a political solution for Ireland.

While the "detached" writer—a Faulkner, Céline, or Hamsun—is free to draw from the accumulated layers of national or regional culture in order to create a personal and organically conceived glimpse at life, the nationalistic writer uses his national culture for ideological reasons. Professor Drell Reck's account of the political dominance over nationalistic prose in France from Barrès to Bardèche, spanning the first half of this century, points precisely to this phenomenon.

It is understandable that wars, invasions, occupations, or territorial mutilations produce a corresponding emotive reaction on the part of the writer as cultural guardian. Professor Gömöri's essay shows that novels dealing with Nazi occupation and heroic resistance still make the rounds in Central European nations; and Professors Ramras-Rauch and Altoma in their contributions find it natural that the Arab-Israeli conflict would be expressed on a fictional plane. The emerging states, as a direct consequence of entering the postcolonnial era, seem to be undergoing a period of consolidation, often from a tribal to a national personality, that would demand the collaboration of the artist and writer caught in the spirit of a nation-in-becoming, as witnessed by Professor Brée's analysis of President Senghor's writings. The most extreme example of nationalistic literature belongs, of course, to the category of didactic-propagandistic writing that is prompted, abetted, and decreed by the various ministries of culture in totalitarian states for the purpose of purveying "constructive" emotions for the masses. E. J. Czerwinski's essay, focusing on the subservience of the arts to ideologies or political cohesion in Soviet literature, illustrates this problem explicitly. And as Seymour Menton points out in his discussion of revolutionary writing in the Cuba of today, Fidel Castro's recent chastising of the "bourgeois" literati in Cuba constitutes a fairly predictable development within the context of literature as a means for socio-political ends.

As to the literature of minority cultures, its fate is closely tied to the survival of the minority's language and life patterns. Two basic positions seem to be open for the writer in a minority culture. On the one hand, as Professor Cotnam illustrates in his essay on French-Canadian fiction, the writer can remain within the confines of a carefully preserved but static way of life, as happens with the Yiddish literature emanating from the Russian *stetl* or the New York sidewalks, or as expressed by Québécois "provincialism," both of which are based on a *joual* culture. But taking the other position, the writer can also choose an open confrontation with the dominant or host culture, in which case the static but safe homogeneity of his minority culture will break down and in the final instance be consumed by the generated friction. Here the Cotnam and Guttmann examples of French-Canadian and American Jewish novelists come to mind, especially Godin and Godbout among the more recent Québécois writers, and Saul Bellow and Philip Roth in American Jewish fiction.

The reduction of a minority culture to its smallest denominator is the literature of the exiled. In a self-imposed or, more often, politically decreed exile, the writer can but draw from a language and experience that are usually alien to his milieu; he draws upon and perpetuates a past that is finally shared only by a handful of other cultural islands. Such is the fate of the writer belonging to the ever-diminishing circles of White Russians, Baltic nationals, Spanish Republicans, German-Jewish refugees, and Eastern Germans after 1945. The voluntarily exiled writer can and usually does go home and stay a while. The famous American expatriates of the twenties did not remain in Paris; none of them absorbed enough Gallic language or spirit to write in French or about French life; and their Gay Paree was not the Paris of Barrès or even Proust. Kessel Schwartz in his exploration of the contemporary Spanish novel focuses, unavoidably, on the refugees from Franco's Spain: Ramón Sender and Francisco Ayala, possibly the most talented and prolific Spanish novelists in exile, could not go home; and their works deal largely with Spain before and during that most tragic Civil War, although they have taught and lived in the United States for the last thirty years. Probably the best and certainly most unique example of exile literature is furnished by Vladimir Nabokov. During his first stage he wrote a number of novels and stories in his native language while immersed in a still huge colony of White Russians in Berlin. During his American cycle he dared to write in English and chose stylistically and thematically to challenge the American culture that surrounded him in his academic experiences at Wellesley and Cornell. Although he was hailed as a great American novelist, the outstanding male characters he created in Humbert Humbert, Professor Pnin, and the false Professor Kinbote reflect unmistakably the culturally estranged and bewildered author who observes the U. S. A. as would an anthropologist watching the coming of age in Samoa. His Professor Pnin stopped reading *Life* because he could not tell which colored pages were ads. Nabokov's *Memory, Speak* is in a sense the grimmest admission of the exile whose cultural time and place will soon be extinguished. It should not surprise anyone that after being elevated to the rank of Great American Novelist, Nabokov turned to translate Pushkin, Russia's national poet.

While the exile's cultural isolation makes him receptive to a national consciousness that survives in and through him, the writer and, of course, the reader in modern mass society experience an oversaturation of commercial or didactic signifiers that deaden their capacity to react to the symbolization of basic shared experiences. As Lewis P. Simpson observes in his essay interpreting the spirit of Southern letters and in particular of Faulkner, the most gifted Southern writers, observing with horror a dehumanized consumer society, denounced the apocalypse of modern civilization and thus revealed their role as prophets who fashion words in agony and tears.

Ours is not a literary age of prophetic voices but rather one that produces anti-novels and countercultures, which are in essence not only anti-bourgeois and anti-technocratic but anti-intellectual as well. So far the de-nationalized scientific world federation of tomorrow has been popularized only by disenchanted humanists with a gift for prose and some time ago at that. On the road to an assured Brave New World we will, however, witness repeated signs of rebellion by the writer and the artist who can create universally only by drawing upon the stream of life that springs from his native land.

H. E. L.

Europe
THE MERGING CULTURES

I

Contributors to Part I

GEORGE SUTHERLAND FRASER, a native of Glasgow, is Reader of Modern English Literature at the University of Leicester, England. During the 1930s and 1940s his fame was based upon several volumes of poetry. From 1945 to 1958 he was a free-lance writer and in 1950–1951 served as cultural adviser to the U. K. Liaison Mission in Japan. His literary criticisms have appeared in the *Times Literary Supplement, Observer, New Statesman, Partisan Review,* and other magazines. Among his several books are *The Modern Writer and His World, Vision and Rhetoric,* and monographs on Dylan Thomas, W. B. Yeats, and Ezra Pound.

ROBERT TRACY was born in an American town crowded with exiled Aran Islanders. Most of his ancestors lived and died in Ireland; one appears briefly in Yeats's *Autobiographies,* where the poet describes her dreams and mythological visions. Tracy completed his graduate studies at Harvard, taught at Carleton College, Minnesota, and has been a member of the English department at the University of California, Berkeley, since 1960. In 1965–1966 he was Bruern Fellow at the University of Leeds, teaching American literature there, and he spent 1971–1972 as Leverhulme Fellow at Trinity College, Dublin, lecturing on Anglo-Irish literature. He has edited Synge's *The Aran Islands and Other Writings* (1962) and has written on Joyce's interest in Sinn Fein, Ireland's nationalist movement, and the echoes of this interest in *Ulysses.*

GEORGE GÖMÖRI was born in Budapest. He did his university studies in his home town and at Oxford; he taught at the University of California at Berkeley, did research at Harvard, and is at present a Fellow of Darwin College, Cambridge, and teaches Polish language and literature at the University of Cambridge. Most of his publications have to do with East European literature, mainly modern Polish and Hungarian writers. His publications include a book, *Polish and Hungarian Poetry, 1945–1956* (Oxford, 1966); *New Writings of East Europe*, coedited with Charles Newman, and a number of essays and articles that appeared in such journals as *Books Abroad, Tri-Quarterly, Mosaic*, and *The Slavonic and East European Review*.

E. J. CZERWINSKI's specialization centers on comparative studies in Slavic literatures with an emphasis on fiction and drama. He has combined this interest with his own cultural observations in Eastern Europe. Over the last few years he has made trips to the Soviet Union and the Balkan nations; he spent two years (1962–1964) in Poland as a Kosciuszko Foundation scholar, one year (1968–1969) in Yugoslavia on a Fulbright research grant, and six months (1969) in Czechoslovakia. He is presently professor of Slavic literature at the Stony Brook campus of the State University of New York. He has been active as a contributor to such journals as *Books Abroad, Comparative Drama, Canadian Slavic Studies*, the *Polish Review*, and the *Slavic and East European Journal*. He recently published a book, *The Soviet Invasion of Czechoslovakia: Its Effects on East Europe*, and prepared a program on "Nationalism: An Emerging Theme in Slavic Drama" for the Northeast Slavic Conference in 1971.

SARAH D'ALBERTI holds a doctoral degree from the University of Palermo and a Ph.D. in Italian literature from New York University. She has taught at Hunter and Queens College and is presently associate professor at York College of the City University of New York. Among her publications the following books can be singled out: a critical edition of Tasso's *Aminta, Pirandello romanziere*, which was published in Italy, and *Giuseppe Antonio Borgese*.

RIMA DRELL RECK received her B.A. from Brandeis University, won a Fulbright scholarship to France, and was awarded a Ph.D. at Yale in 1960. She has taught at Tulane University and in 1961 joined the faculty of Louisiana State University in New Orleans where she is presently professor of comparative literature and associate editor of *The Southern Review*.

She has published numerous articles on modern literature in journals and quarterlies such as *PMLA, French Review, Yale French Studies, Modern Drama, Forum*, and *Modern Language Quarterly*. She also edited *Explorations in Literature* (1966) and is coauthor of *Bernanos, Confrontations* (1966). Her most recent book, *Literature and Responsibility: The French Novelist in the Twentieth Century*, appeared in 1969. She is presently working on a volume on French collaborationist writers, and has been awarded a Guggenheim Fellowship for 1972–73 to complete her new book.

REINHOLD GRIMM received his Ph.D. at the University of Erlangen. He has taught at his alma mater as well as the University of Frankfurt in his native Germany and was visiting professor at Columbia and New York University. Since 1967 he has been Alexander Hohlfeld Professor of German at the University of Wisconsin in Madison. His publications include *Bertolt Brecht: Die Struktur seines Werkes,* now in its sixth edition, *Bertolt Brecht und die Weltliteratur,* and *Strukturen: Essays zur deutschen Literatur.* He specializes in the fields of contemporary German literature and comparative literature studies.

H. G. HÜTTICH, coauthor of this essay, is at present writing a doctoral dissertation at the University of Wisconsin entitled "Cultural Politics and the East German Theater."

KESSEL SCHWARTZ earned his M.A. from the University of Missouri and his Ph.D. from Columbia. He has been Director of Cultural Centers in Nicaragua and Ecuador and taught at Hofstra, Hamilton, Colby, the University of Vermont, and Arkansas. Since 1962 he has been professor of Hispanic literature at the University of Miami. His publications are many and show his knowledge of both Spanish Peninsular as well as Spanish American literature. Outside of some sixty articles that appeared in such journals as *Hispania, Romance Notes,* or *Romanic Review,* he has written a number of books. The most prominent are *A New History of Spanish Literature* (with Raymond Chandler), *Introduction to Modern Spanish Literature, Vicente Aleixandre,* and *The Meaning of Existence in Contemporary Hispanic Literature.* In 1972 his *A New History of Spanish American Fiction* was published.

Cultural Nationalism
in the Recent English Novel

G. S. FRASER

I

In 1939, when the Second World War broke out, Great Britain was no longer quite the leading power she had been throughout the nineteenth century. But a lot of the map was still painted red; she was still an imperial power. And though there had been two Labour Governments since the end of the First World War, and though the National Government which ruled Great Britain throughout most of the 1930s included National Unionists, National Liberals, and National Labour party members, it still contained in positions of central authority many people who belonged to the older English aristocracy or gentry, like Anthony Eden and Duff Cooper, or who, like Stanley Baldwin and Neville Chamberlain, belonged to the mercantile or manufacturing classes, whom in the nineteenth century the public schools or Oxford or Cambridge, or both, had turned into very satisfying simulacra of the older gentry.

There were still clear distinctions between the upper classes, tradespeople, and the workers. There was still an assumption, in spite of Hunger Marches, in spite of the fascination with Communist ideas of younger sons of the ruling classes, like Isherwood or Auden or Spender or Day-Lewis, and in spite of the tendency of some of them to sentimentalize the working man, an assumption that, whatever kind of government ruled the country, its members would be drawn from what has since loosely been called the Establishment. Unemployment, the rise of Hitler, the Peace Pledge Movement, Sir Oswald Mosley's New party (attracting at first men who were to become leaders of the Left, like John Strachey, and men inherently liberal and humane in principle, like Sir Harold Nicolson) that was soon to become a kind of equivalent—in its black shirts—of the Nazis or the Fascists; the Peace Pledge Union and the League of Nations Covenant; the ideas of Keynes about national finance; the Webbs's book on the Soviet Union; all these things (like the Left Book Club, and the much feebler Right Book Club) suggested that among intellectuals, but primarily it should be noted among intellectuals of the ruling classes, there was a ferment of worry and discontent about the way the country was going.

Among novelists of talent there had been a feeling of guilt about the empire, from E. M. Forster's *A Passage to India* of 1924 to George Orwell's *Burmese Days* (his best novel *qua* novel) of the mid-1930s. But what should be noticed is that, with a few exceptions, of those who were not primarily political novelists, like James Hanley, no strikingly talented novelists sprang from either the working classes or the lower-middle classes. The revolutionaries, the radicals, the sharp novelistic critics of the status quo sprang from what, in the early 1950s, Henry Fairlie, giving a new word an old twist, was to call "the Establishment." The best reviewers on the most intelligent radical weekly in the country, the *New Statesman*, were members or connections of the Bloomsbury coterie, or, like Cyril Connolly, old Etonians with what at times were called "bolshie" views. England remained, almost in the sense of Plato's *Republic*, a tripartite society; and it remained, as was shown by the national spirit of unity when the First World War broke out, a society, perhaps because rather than in spite of these firm traditional divisions, with an extraordinary underlying sense of unity, of community. The old clichés about losing every battle but the last, keeping a stiff upper lip, finding foreigners funny, muddling through, lingered on.

I served through that war myself, as a volunteer, from 1939 to 1946, in the ranks rising (after an abortive attempt to get a commission) from the rank of private to that of quarter-master sergeant. I felt declassed, since my father had been a captain in the First World War, and, as he was a university graduate, of old Highland blood, and had been town clerk of Aberdeen, was the kind of Scotsman who is counted by English standards a gentleman (though a town clerk from England, with a grammar school education, would not have ranked in the same way: Scotsmen in England, if literate and well mannered, are like people with just a little Negro blood, that does not show, in the United States: they can "pass").

As a poet of some reputation, in those days, I was not very much hampered by my rank and had many close friends—among officers, like John Waller; among civilian writers and poets like Bernard Spencer, Lawrence Durrell, Terence Tiller; and among fellow rankers, like Erik de Mauny, a corporal of the New Zealand Army and now BBC correspondent in Paris—who were all, like myself, very much excited by the idea that they were the new generation of important young British writers. There was also a wonderful old eccentric—actually only three or four years older than myself, though he seemed incredibly battered—John Gawsworth; and there were John Spiers, the fine disciple of Leavis, and his beautiful wife, Ruth. Within the firm outer framework of rank and status, a poet was automatically counted as a kind of gentleman. I knew not so well, though I was later to help John Waller to edit his collected poems, the very fine poet Keith Douglas, who had run away from a safe staff job in Cairo to fight, as a captain, with his old tank regiment in the western desert.

The point I am making is that, though I repined at being officially at the bottom end of it, I never, I think, resented the tripartite system as such. The concept of a gentleman was not at all a disagreeable one to me; only the concept that, not being an officer, I was not quite one myself. This did not mean that I was a reactionary; like most other serving soldiers in the ranks, I voted for the Labour party, by post, in the 1945 general election, and, when I got home to join my mother and sister in Chelsea, my great wish was to achieve some sort of literary career that would put the humiliations behind me. I lectured to fellow soldiers on poetry, on Auden and Spender and these other figures of the 1930s; I had long and friendly arguments with little Communist groups, but it seemed to me in 1945 that the establishment of a welfare state solved all my problems. There was going to be full employment, free medical service, just rationing for all of us in what was going to remain a siege economy; the welfare state, in short, and I could get ahead with my own individual literary ambitions and meet all the London poets without expecting that any other really drastic social changes would be necessary.

I remember Richard Hoggart, when I met him first casually in the late 1940s, being very shocked by this attitude of mine; I remember also the Scottish poet Hugh MacDiarmid, when I took him home to dinner with my mother in Chelsea, again some time in the 1930s, saying to me, "You know I am a Communist." "Oh," I said—not consciously echoing, I hope, "Many of my best friends are Jews"— "we know lots of Communists, and get on with them perfectly well."

In the queer sort of interregnum of first Crippsian austerity and then Butskellism between 1945 and 1957, the year of Suez and Hungary, in that literary London world which I knew fairly well, a man's politics were thought of as a private matter of his own concern, like his religion. I liked the poet Roy Campbell and used to explain to people that he was not really a Francoist, but an old-fashioned Royalist, a Carlist; I, and a number of friends, were perhaps old-fashioned Royalists too. I remember, on Coronation Day (we were all pretty drunk) weeping over the Queen's broadcast speech on television and saying, "We have not done enough for her."

There was a kind of general good-will for a number of years, springing from a pride in having weathered out the war, in having borne our period of austerity decently without an important black market, in perpetually remeeting people one had met in the war. And of course I did not (nor did a friend like Erik de Mauny) write the novel about our Cairo days we had been intending to write. We were living in a vacuum, though a quite agreeable one. "Your whole generation," I remember William Empson saying to me, "seems to me to have been, as it were, *slugged*."

I was in Japan in 1950 and 1951, at the time of the outbreak of the Korean war, and I remember what a shock that was; it was one, but only one, of the factors that induced a nervous breakdown, on account of which I had to be flown home. But after six months of humane and sensitive treatment in one of the great London teaching mental hospitals, the Maudsley, I was well enough to get out again and pick up my threads of reviewing, broadcasting, and literary criticism. And I must have remained naïve, because it was after that that I blubbered over Coronation Day, as I had earlier blubbered over VJ Day. The Korean war had come to an end, the Cold War seemed very cold (not likely to fuse and blow up), and the group of friends made during the war—the "old chums' league," none of them, like myself, quite fulfilling their early literary promise—were still around the pubs.

I had been helped and encouraged while I was ill mainly by friends who nearly all could be taken as belonging in some ways to the Establishment: Alan Pryce Jones (an extraordinarily kindly and perceptive man, as all old Etonians I have known have been), Janet Adam Smith of the *New Statesman*, Manya Harari (the translator of Pasternak) of the Harvill Press. But around 1953 to 1955, new voices began to be heard in fiction, as also in poetry and drama: Kingsley Amis, John Wain, John Braine, Iris Murdoch, Philip

Larkin; in poetry others also, Thom Gunn, Elizabeth Jennings, Ted Hughes, D. J. Enright, the group sometimes called the Movement; in drama, notably John Osborne, John Arden (the best of these new dramatists, and the least commercially successful), Arnold Wesker (the most open, sincere, vulnerable, and weakest, I think). The late 1950s were also the period of books like Raymond Williams's *The Long Revolution* and Richard Hoggart's *The Uses of Literacy*, theoretical statements of the kind of cultural radicalism which the new novelists (and I have forgotten one genuinely working-class novelist, Alan Sillitoe) also seemed to be expressing. I think it was in the late 1950s, also, that Alfred Alvarez, in an anthology of recent verse for Penguin Books, launched a ferocious attack against what he called the "gentility principle." As a reviewer, broadcaster, and an anonymous leader writer for a very important literary weekly, I was brought in contact with these new movements and personally with some of these new people; I was awakened, a little, from my dogmatic slumbers and realized that there was another nation—as in Disraeli's phrase about "the two nations"—which was, around 1953 or so, first finding its voice.

II

Kingsley Amis's *Lucky Jim* and John Wain's *Hurry on Down* were different novels in many ways, *Lucky Jim* much more a unified construction, *Hurry On Down* more in a picaresque tradition, but their novelty was in questioning the whole assumption of classical English fiction from Fielding through Thackeray onward: that what a young man of some talent, uncertain prospects, and dimmish background wants is (besides a happy marriage, and all that) an accepted place in the upper reaches of the community, and that he will go out of his way to be pleasant to his elders and betters.

Both novels questioned whether the elders were better; they asked whether British society on the whole was not so riddled with pretentiousness and snobbery that the best thing perhaps for a young man might not be to opt out. In a more metaphysical way, Iris Murdoch's *Under the Net* asked the same sort of question. They were not radically revolutionary novels (Amis, after being a mild Fabian, has become in some ways, in recent years, very much a man of the Right).

Reading both these novels today, though they are as amusing as ever, it is strange to remember how much indignation they created.

One of the funniest passages in *Lucky Jim*, where Jim Dixon, logged with beer, has burned holes in his sheet in the house of the awful Professor Welch with his even more awful gorgon of a wife, guiltily turns the sheet upside down and is helped in his subterfuge by the heroine, caused friends of mine to grow red with rage: no *gentleman* would behave like that. And was Wain's hero, running away from one job to another and finally settling down as a gagman to a team of comedians, not simply opting out of his responsibilities to society? Amis's underestimated second novel, *That Uncertain Feeling*, with its wonderful picture of the squalors of provincial marriage and the amount of intrigue and wire-pulling involved in getting a job in a library in Wales, worried people in a different way. It was at moments wildly farcical. It seemed as if it were going to treat adultery in a Restoration comedy sort of way. But it came down in the end to saying that adultery whether or not wrong is messy and likely to create unhappiness and trouble. And the hero, a weak but likable man (Amis's heroes, with a few exceptions, like the lustful, wrathful, but in the end pitiable hero of *One Fat Englishman*, tend to be this) opts in the end for his wife and his children and for not letting the (suddenly, at a key moment, unexpectedly formidable) rich man he was cuckolding maneuver him into a better job, not for his own sake, but to spite somebody else.

There is an odd kind of residual, perhaps Nonconformist religiousness in Amis. In what I think is one of his best novels, *Take a Girl Like You*, the hero, Patrick, who lives for parties and sexual pleasure and who sometimes thinks remorsefully that if he had pulled himself together he could be a considerable Latin scholar, feels not only a sense of social shame (his best friend, his code hero, despises him for unsporting conduct) but a sense of sin when he has more or less raped poor, obstinately innocent, or at least *demi-vierge*, Jenny Bun when she is all out after having drunk too much at a party. Even Jim Dixon, created much more in a climate of satirical farce, feels guilty about ditching the neurotic, minimally pretty Margaret for a much nicer girl, until a friend assures him, coming into the structure of the novel to do so just a thought too conveniently, that Margaret does not really need him: she does not want love or marriage, she is really sufficient to herself, and neurotically she will find somebody else to batten on.

The sexual urgencies which beset the heroes of Amis's novels (and, to a rather lesser degree, some of Wain's) are mixed up with a very complicated feeling that it is natural but it is not right. This attitude toward sex has a good deal in common with the working-class attitudes described by Richard Hoggart in *The Uses of Literacy*. Hoggart tells me that he cut and bowdlerized this material a great deal because, having shown the manuscript to middle-class friends, he found that it shocked them a great deal.

Wain and Amis were, in fact, giving highbrow critics or critics in what Jimmy Porter in *Look Back in Anger* calls the "posh Sundays" a frank look at a kind of provincial life where both emotion and impulse are less controlled than they are in upper-class English life but where, on the other hand, conscience and doubt nag more. They were also questioning the "high culture," Bloomsbury, the visual arts, connoisseurship, Renaissance music on the recorders; Amis toward the end of *Lucky Jim* compares two of his more unpleasant characters in appearance and manner to Lytton Strachey and André Gide. They were also suggesting that there are new weapons by which intelligent young men, reasonably well educated, of the lower-middle classes, cannot break into the upper classes—why should they want to?—but can break through the wire-mesh of its defenses, the most notable being deliberate rudeness.

Allan Sillitoe's and John Braine's background was different; both were genuinely working class, neither had done brilliantly at school, or gone to Oxford, like Wain and Amis, and taken first-class degrees there. Braine is not so good a writer as either Amis or Wain, but his first novel, *Room at the Top*, was a very frightening picture of the corrupting effect of a purely businessman's city (a city without a cultural elite, without a patriciate, in the sense of old and distinguished local families which had some other values than cash values) on a fairly bright and fairly decent lad whose father in the 1930s had been a militant trade unionist and had suffered from it.

Joe Lampton is obsessed by money. He grades cars, clothes, women as Grade 1, 2, or 3, and what he especially lusts after is a Grade 1 woman. He gets a job in the local town hall, which puts him on the fringes of gentility, joins the local amateur dramatic society, seduces a woman who is genuinely sensitive and intelligent but who is, alas, thirty-five (an attractive age in a woman, but Joe is in his twenties and notices the little crow's-feet at the corners of her eyes). His working-class puritanism comes out; he is furious when he learns that his mistress has allowed herself to be painted in the nude (it is, I think, if I have read my Hoggart and my Orwell—on British seaside postcards—a mark of British working-class culture that sex can be naughty, dirty, oo-la-la, funny, as in Frankie Howard's jokes in *Up Pompei*, but there is a strong sense of shame and awkwardness about the naked human body; it could not possibly be considered detachedly, though with an erotic aura to the detachment, as "beautiful": D. H. Lawrence, the daddy of a lot of this stuff, thought one should only make love in the dark, and David Holbrook, a great English neo-puritan, neo-nationalist in a sort of way, neo-snooper into his neighbors' sexual practices, is always inveighing against the *eye*, against the esthetically detached erotic imagination, against what he calls *voyeurism*). Lampton ditches his possibly educative older mistress and gets the silly, bunnyish daughter of a local magnate pregnant. The mistress kills herself in a car crash, not quite accident, not quite suicide, a Freudian unconsciously intended accident.

Lampton remorsefully goes around pubs looking for somebody to beat him up, but nobody obliges (he is a decent young chap!). He is a smart young chap, also, and the father of the girl he has impregnated allows the marriage and takes Joe into the firm. I thought this novel was a terrible attack on the values of a purely commercial society, but when, shortly after its publication, Braine came down from the north to Leicester (Lear's Castrum, the dead center of England, where I teach) he said it was essentially a fairy tale, about the princess who marries the swineherd. A sequel, *Life at the Top*, showed Joe being two-timed by his bunny-princess but happy enough to be in among the money. Braine was born a Catholic, was rumored at one time to have Marxist sympathies, is now a High Tory (if "high," except in the English sense of hung game, is at all appropriate for any modern type of conservatism) wanting to de-liberalize the last twenty-five years of British legislation, to restore capital punishment, for instance. Amis, an infinitely more intelligent man, once a mild Fabian, as I said, now spends a lot of his correspondence space getting at "Lefties" (give him his due, I think he means crypto-neo-Stalinists, rather than Lib-Lab people like myself, whose imagination is often, in George Eliot's phrase on the first page of *Scenes from Clerical Life*, "doing a little quiet Toryism on the sly").

III

Allan Sillitoe is a different case altogether, and a much more respectable one. He is the essential rebel, but what one might call the Nietzschean, unconsciously Nietzschean, rather than the Marxist rebel. His heroes are all loners, risking everything. In his first (and I think his only good) novel, *Saturday Night and Sunday Morning*, the hero is a rogue male, working too hard on his piecework in a Nottingham bicycle factory to please his mates. He does this to have money for the week-ends, to spend on the rogue male's pleasures, "fishin' and screwin'." He is having it off with two girls at once, who are, so far as I remember, sisters; one has to have an abortion in a bath with a bottle of gin to help; the husband of the other, who is in the army, sends a couple of chums up to Nottingham to beat the hero up. He survives this, as he has survived many things, and, after going through a period of slight depression, cheers up at a party where a lively wife smashes a glass on her nagging husband's forehead. Our last glimpse of him is rather like that of the Fisher King of Eliot or Prince Ferdinand, "fishing beside the dull canal."

The effect of this novel on me was to make me think that one tends to look for individualism among one's academic colleagues, for various kinds of conformism among the working classes; Sillitoe suggested that English working class life, at least in Nottingham, at least in the not quite defined period he was writing about, was a creative anarchy.

His short stories are possibly better than his novels. The most famous of them, "The Loneliness of the Long Distance Runner," is about a Borstal boy who is a loner, who hates all authority, and whose sole gift and pleasure is for long-distance running. Borstals, I should explain perhaps to American readers, are training and corrective centers for youthful or adolescent delinquents, run rather on the lines of the tougher English public schools (which Americans, again, would call private schools). They compete in games and athletics, just as public schools do. The governor of this Borstal in the story wants the hero to win a long-distance race in an inter-Borstal competition—partly for the sake of the hero's morale, partly for what one might call the sake of the "old school."

The boy, against all the inclinations of his mind and body, forces himself to lose the race, not out of petty personal spite against the governor, but as a gesture of independence, a gesture against authority in general, and perhaps, in a rather inchoately conceived way, as a class gesture. One should add, perhaps, that the other stories in the volume to which this story gives its title by no means idealize working-class life; they are bitter little sketches of frustration and misery, not so much economic in its roots (the characters all earn enough to pay the rent, to smoke, to go to football matches, to drink, often, pint after pint of beer) but psychological. A small boy watches curiously a lonely man preparing to hang himself, asks intelligent questions, and goes away. A lonely middle-aged working man, who has been a semi-alcoholic, makes friends casually with a couple of schoolgirls and gets in the habit of taking them out to afternoon tea. The police get track of this, think he is a dirty old man, and warn him to leave the girls alone. He is lonely, he needs affection, his feeling for the girls is a perfectly innocent one. He goes back to morose solitary boozing in the pubs. In another story, a working man whose sole emotional commitment is to his local football team comes back home in such a foul mood after it has lost a home match that his wife, a long-suffering but not particularly attractive person, walks out on him for good. Sillitoe's portrait, I would say, of the English working classes in the post-1945 era is a portrait of a group of people who are not violent, not committed to revolution, but full of a bitter and stoical resentment. They are aware not so much of a class enemy as of a kind of meaninglessness, lack of emotional nourishment, group purpose in their lives. Everything is sour.

IV

It might be interesting to contrast with these writers of, broadly, lower-middle class or working-class origins a number of other writers: one, Lord Snow, C. P. Snow, is of fairly humble Leicester origins but has certainly, like an Arnold Bennett "Card," "made it." Angus Wilson, for long an official in the British Museum Reading Room, who only gave up that job in his middle forties when it became clear that he could support himself by writing (he also does some part-time teaching in one of the newer universities), is a member of the literate and academic middle classes. Anthony Powell, whose long serial novel *The Music of Time* is one of the most consistently distinguished achievements in postwar English fiction, is very firmly, like his hero Nicholas Jenkins, a member of the minor Anglo-Welsh gentry, but so firmly such a member that, unlike his Oxford contemporary Evelyn Waugh, he feels no need to romanticize that class (which was Waugh's class, I think, adoptively, rather than quite by birth and ancestry). These three all overlap a bit in the areas of English life they cover; their characters all might have met each other, but it is hard to know what they would have had to say to each other. Snow has been terribly lambasted by F. R. Leavis, not only for his lecture, *The Two Cultures*, but for his novels, which Dr. Leavis finds more or less a set of cardboard cut-outs with the characters speaking in an extraordinarily dead way.

Snow, moving from a scholarship from Leicester University College (as it was in the 1930s) to Cambridge, from working with Rutherford at Cambridge, from a high civil service post during the Second World War, on to a peerage and minor ministerial rank in Harold Wilson's last government, has stepped steadily up the ladder of power but has never perhaps asked himself whether it was really worth climbing. I think Leavis was extraordinarily unfair to Snow, who is concerned in a broad, blunt way about essential human problems (even the problem of human survival) and who writes very accurately about how committees make decisions, sometimes redress injustices, and choose people for top jobs. All this is terribly *practically* important, but it tends to transform itself into obviously accurate but slightly flat fiction. But one is left asking questions: is the career open to talents, or even the chance of the impersonal intelligence to acquire power to deal with administrative or political crises, as essential for fictional art as all that?

I have a very great personal liking and respect for Snow, but I have sometimes an odd feeling that he has succeeded in life in a very public-spirited, hard-working, and respectable way, but has never in a sense *lived*. One will not pull the country together by proving, what is perfectly true, that England is now a meritocracy rather than an aristocracy, that a clever young man can get on, and that people in power try, on the whole, to be fair. It would be crude to say that Snow lacks vision; but I think it is true to say that a depiction, however accurate, of the machinery by which a government, or a civil service department, or an Oxbridge college may, with luck, be on the whole more often right than wrong in its decisions is not heart-warming, is not a substitute, say, for Blake's vision of the giant Albion. Of course, the thing works. But what is it for? To that question Snow has decent but minimal answers. As a young man he did not see visions, and as an old man he does not dream dreams. A dreadful dryness in contemporary British life is reflected in his novels, though, I think, wholly unconsciously.

Angus Wilson is a writer of completely different temperament, scratchy and malicious (Snow is almost excessively fair to all his characters), even spiteful, Dickensianally exaggerative, not an Establishment man, as Snow essentially is, but a liberal, a progressive, a social and personal nonconformist, who has the most piercing sense of the dangers of humbug and self-deception involved in his own attitudes, as well as in more obviously vulnerable ones of a reactionary or sentimental kind.

Wilson, I think, is specially important for a study of this sort because what he is centrally concerned with is the corruption of consciousness in contemporary English society, the refusal of so many of us to look the facts of our parlous national situation in the face. One of Wilson's main literary devices is to take the role-playing, the fitting into a given social situation, which is part of the British character, and show, by parody, by exaggeration, in how many ways, in an awkward and uncomfortable transitional society, how many of us deceive ourselves and attempt to deceive others about what we really are.

Wilson is Dickensian not only in his sense of the wide, prevailing burgeoning of the great traditional English vice of hypocrisy, but also in his sense, sometimes melodramatically expressed, of the existence of what can only be called raw evil, cruelty, lust, brutality, meanness, nastiness. Yet he has a Dickensian sense also of a certain basic or minimal decency which characters who often seem on the surface either dull, ordinary, or dislikable can struggle for. He has a range in some ways outside Dickens's, which is not to say that he is half or quarter as great a novelist. But he knows, for instance, the English academic world, of which *Anglo-Saxon Attitudes* is perhaps the best-informed study; the strange atmosphere of polite dislike which does not always prevent colleagues from cooperating fruitfully; the various ways in which the proper urge or impulse of the scholar can relapse into sloth or deviate into fantasy. His novels are, and are meant to be, uncomfortable reading, and yet they are in a sense patriotic novels.

Wilson does not love his fellow men much, I think, as individuals, but he has a general concern about them, of a puritanical, nontheistic, neo-Calvinist sort; he admires such decencies as they are occasionally capable of, and has a kind of tired pity for their inevitable lapses and vices. I am not sure whether Wilson, any more than Snow, has what could be called a Platonic vision of the Good; life, for him, is something to be endured rather than enjoyed; but he has a very genuine Augustinian vision of Evil, and a strenuous sense of our need to struggle continually and strenuously against Evil, though with the possibility, usually, of winning only small victories on small fronts.

If too many of Snow's characters are happy men because they are successful men, too many of Wilson's characters are unhappy because they have a false consciousness which they cannot turn into a true consciousness. I said that in one sense Snow's characters could be said never to have lived, nor he himself to have done so: Wilson's characters live, he lives, in an atmosphere which has never touched simple joy, the calm of reciprocated love, poetry—things outside his range. He has not a style quite good enough for its purposes. When he parodies Virginia Woolf, for instance, one realizes that the parody fails because he cannot write as well as she can. Happiness and beauty are not his things, but perhaps these are not only unattainable, and as ideal aims liable to rot into sentimentality, but positively wrong things to aim at in our at-risk society. I find Wilson tonic but chilling, thus probably proving that, within the limits of his personal possibilities, he is a good novelist.

Anthony Powell covers more or less the same period of time as Snow and Wilson, but he is more often compared to his Oxford contemporary, and friendly acquaintance rather than intimate friend, Evelyn Waugh. Waugh's solidest achievement in fiction is probably his trilogy on the Second World War, *The Sword of Honour* (comparable, also, in many ways to Ford Madox Ford's Tietjens tetralogy of the 1920s). This trilogy is the nearest that Waugh got to a "straight" novel, and the most penetrating among his fictions in its implied, and at crucial moments, explicitly expressed self-criticisms of his own often romantically snobbish and antiquarianly social-climbing religious and social attitudes. But the trilogy could not properly be called an expression of cultural nationalism. Man, says an old German proverb, begins at the rank of baron; baron, Spanish *varon*, is of course the equivalent of the Latin *vir*. For Waugh, *homo* as contrasted to *vir*, the common human creature in his general condition of misery and dependence, of being a target rather than a gun, a source rather than a channel, did not quite exist. Prickly and assertive though Waugh's patriotism no doubt was, he cannot quite be called a cultural nationalist. His novels are essentially—the title of the first, *Decline and Fall*, is significant—a prolonged farcical-tragical "decline and fall," the lapse into vacuousness and desuetude, of a traditional European ruling class.

Anthony Powell is different: he was educated at Eton, whereas Waugh was educated at a comparatively minor public school, Lancing; Powell was the son of a professional soldier, whereas Waugh was the son of a London publisher. (Evelyn Waugh was also not a very good literary critic and was the younger brother of another novelist, Alec, the author of *The Loom of Youth*, who from his youth had an embarrassingly second-rate literary success.) In Powell's novels before 1939, apparently similar in many ways to Waugh's earlier novels, Powell was essentially a novelist of the "dry mock," of intelligent dislike and dry observation, whereas Waugh was always a novelist of romantic farce, whose characters are larger and simpler than life, and whose typical heroes are "holy fools."

Powell, in short, was from the start a disabused belonger, where the English upper classes were concerned, while Waugh was a satirical but glamorized observer and arriver. Waugh had a far more energetic and poetic creative gift; his most memorable characters are people whom one would not expect to meet in real life, though one recognizes them, joyously, as representative archetypes. Powell's characters on the other hand are laboriously actual, and in his postwar sequence *The Music of Time*, he has given us an extraordinarily detailed, vivid, and exact account of what should not be called an Establishment, but rather a casual yet determinative network of connections: school connections, university connections, business connections, connections on the fringes of the arts, music, and literature in which his narrator, Nicholas Jenkins, is caught up. Everything seems to happen haphazardly and yet also by the centripetal necessity established by a field of force. New characters are drawn into that field of force like flies into a spider's web (except that there is no personal spider, rather as one might say that there is no personal devil or God) or iron filings toward a powerful magnet. Nothing seems purposeful, yet everything is part of a pattern, of what Virginia Woolf called a great city's "hum and buzz of implications."

Powell, unlike Waugh, could not be thought of as writing an elegy. His most likable characters are often not the best born; a brilliant failure, like the alcoholic Stringham, is treated with a certain tenderness that is not extended to the obtuse, egocentric, and yet, apart from the blunders of his personal life, growingly successful Widmerpool, and yet Widmerpool is also treated with a certain detached justice. Though Powell's characters are shown as basically simple people, with a ruling passion that shapes their interests (though it does not always determine their fates) from childhood on, there is always something about them that neither the reader nor Nicholas Jenkins, the narrator, fully understands. In a kind of dry and often laborious show-motion comedy, Powell gives us a sense, which perhaps neither Snow nor Wilson gives us, of the essential mysteriousness of people, but essentially of English people. In an interview in the Saturday supplement of the *Times* in 1970, he remarked that he had in the 1930s spent several months in the United States visiting Hollywood, meeting Scott Fitzgerald, whom he liked, and then traveling rather adventurously in Central America; but he realized even then that these experiences, exciting and colorful in themselves, could be of no use to him as a novelist. He is the last representative in the novel of the English passion for anecdote; it is interesting that he has edited John Aubrey's *Brief Lives* and written a biography of Aubrey. England, with its passion for memory and for what can seem trivial and irrelevant detail, is the only place where his imagination works.

V

The pattern I have sketched out is not a clear one, even to myself. But it might be roughly true to say that since about 1945, novelists have been subconsciously aware that a traditional pattern of English life has come to an end, a pattern of fairly rigid hierarchy, though with a certain social mobility for the talented, and of imperial power. Younger novelists have been aware that this pattern gave them, and their class, no proper place or role; older novelists have watched the rack or wrack dislimned. The cultural nationalism, so far as it has existed, has been a kind of perturbed disconcertedness. The young Wain and Amis and Braine say, "We were never invited to the party." Wilson asks whether the party was ever worth going to. Powell and Waugh in different ways see that the party is over. Snow only, incorrigibly optimistic, feels that it is still on, and that his committee-men are the life and soul of it. Nostalgia, hope, depression, and resentment have perhaps been the main motivating forces. All this will no doubt change when and if Great Britain joins the Common Market and becomes part of a "Europe of Europeans." And the new young novelists of the 1960s, the Margaret Drabbles and Edna O'Briens and A. S. Byatts, have in a sense lost this interest and have become concerned mainly with the problems of the personal life. A novelist of greater stature than these, Iris Murdoch, moves, whatever her scene, into a world which is partly one of fantasy and to concerns which are universal and metaphysical.

It can be said at least of cultural nationalism in the postwar English novel that it is much less sour and rancorous, much less ultimately despairing, than it might have been. The English scene is pretty grim, many of them seem to say, many English people are dim or awful, but in the end, where else would one want to live? As a Scotsman, settled since 1945 in England, but having traveled or taught in a variety of other places—the Middle East during the war, South America shortly afterward, Japan, France and Greece on trips, the United States on a year's visiting exchange, Belgium, Holland, Luxembourg on British Council tours—I think I agree with them on the whole. Not that all these other places have not their own special incitements and excitements to offer: but where else permanently (in the short permanence of one's mortal life) than England would one want to live?

BIBLIOGRAPHY

Allen, Walter. *Tradition and Dream*. London: Phoenix House, 1964.

Alvarez, Alfred. *The New Poetry: An Anthology*. Middlesex: Penguin, 1962.

Amis, Kingsley. *Lucky Jim*. Garden City, N. Y.: Doubleday, 1954.

———. *One Fat Englishman*. New York: Harcourt, 1963.

———. *Take A Girl Like You*. New York: Harcourt, 1960.

———. *That Uncertain Feeling*. New York: Harcourt, 1956.

Bergonzi, Bernard. *The Situation of the Novel*. London: Macmillan, 1970.

Bradbury, Malcolm. *Evelyn Waugh*. Writers and Critics 39. Edinburgh: Oliver and Boyd, 1964.

Braine, John. *Life at the Top*. Boston: Houghton, 1962.

———. *Room at the Top*. Boston: Houghton, 1957.

Burgess, Anthony. *The Novel Now*. New York: Norton, 1967.

Byatt, A. S. *Degrees of Freedom: The Novels of Iris Murdoch*. New York: Barnes and Noble, 1965.

Carens, James F. *The Satiric Art of Evelyn Waugh*. Seattle: University of Washington Press, 1966.

Fraser, G. S. *The Modern Writer and His World*. Rev. ed. New York: Praeger, 1965.

Gindin, James. *Post-War British Fiction*. Berkeley: University of California Press, 1962.

Halio, Jay L. *Angus Wilson*. Writers and Critics 37. Edinburgh: Oliver and Boyd, 1964.

Hoggart, Richard. *The Uses of Literacy*. London: Chatto and Windus, 1957.

Karl, Frederick R. *A Reader's Guide to the Contemporary English Novel*. London: Thames and Hudson, 1963.

Kettle, Arnold. *An Introduction to the English Novel*. Vol. II. London: Arrow Books, 1963.

McCormick, John. *Catastrophe and Imagination: An Interpretation of the Recent English and American Novel*. London: Longmans, 1957.

Murdoch, Iris. *Under the Net.* New York: Viking, 1954.

Powell, Anthony. *Dance to the Music of Time.* 2 vols. Boston: Little, 1963–64.

Sillitoe, Alan. *Saturday Night and Sunday Morning.* New York: Knopf, 1962.

Snow, Sir Charles Percy. *The Two Cultures.* Cambridge, England: University of Cambridge Press, 1964.

Stopp, F. J. *Evelyn Waugh: Portrait of an Artist.* London: Chapman and Hall, 1958.

Wain, John. *Hurry on Down.* London: Secker and Warburg, 1955.

Waugh, Evelyn. *Decline and Fall.* Boston: Little, 1946.

———. *The Sword of Honour.* London: Butler & Tanner Ltd., 1965.

Williams, Raymond. *The Long Revolution.* New York: Columbia University Press, 1961.

Ireland: The Patriot Game

ROBERT TRACY

*Cosmopolitan literature is, at best, but a poor bubble, though a
big one. Creative work has always a fatherland... there is no fine
nationality without literature, and... the converse also,... there is
no fine literature without nationality.*

—W. B. Yeats

> *Romantic Ireland's dead and gone,
> It's with O'Leary in the grave.*
> —W. B. Yeats, "September 1913"

*I have never ridiculed my Faith, but as regards my Fatherland
the first duty of a writer is to let his Fatherland down, otherwise he
is no writer. In the name of Jesus, how the hell can a writer attack
anyone else's Fatherland if he doesn't attack his own?*
—Brendan Behan, *Confessions of an Irish Rebel* (1965)

The three passages which I have quoted above represent the three
decisive stages in the relationship between modern Irish nationalism and modern Irish literature. Yeats made his remarks about
literature and nationality only a few months after the fall of Parnell
(1890) had destroyed all hope of bringing about Irish Home Rule by
legal parliamentary methods. Yeats believed that writers must now
take the lead in the struggle for independence and proceed by other
than political means, by creating among Irishmen an intense national
spirit. This would be accomplished by arranging for the publication
and distribution of nineteenth-century literary works which could
be justified both on literary and patriotic grounds, portraying the
Irish scene without caricaturing Irish life. At the same time Yeats
himself and other young writers would create new works out of

the heroic legends of ancient Ireland and offer the people "images" of heroism so that they, "Looking upon those images, might bear / Triumphant children." [1]

When he came to write "September 1913," Yeats had begun to suspect that his dream of a heroic Ireland was threatened less by British rule than by the huckster mentality of the Irish middle class. The occasion for the poem was the controversy over Hugh Lane's offer of modern paintings to form a Dublin Municipal Gallery, which activated all the Dublin middle class's suspicion of art and artists and made Yeats understand how wide a gap lay between his vision of the future Ireland and theirs and how unmoved they were likely to be by poetic invitations to heroism. Yeats gradually moved to the aristocratic position of his later years, which saw the true Ireland as a place of gallant and cultured lords, humorous and loyal peasants, and with this position he abandoned any real hope of relating literature to political nationalism. The majority of modern Irish writers have been unwilling to abandon the struggle entirely, but there has been little in the way of new ideas about the subject since Yeats's time. Brendan Behan, however, who began as a political activist rather than as a writer, has suggested a new function though hardly an original one, that of sarcastically criticizing the slogans and pretensions of political nationalism. In Ireland this criticizing function is traditional for poets—the ancient bards were allowed a fair amount of political power and respect in ancient Ireland, not because of their ability to celebrate in appropriate language the deeds of kings but because of their notorious powers of satire.

The myth about modern Irish literature and modern Irish nationalism is that the present-day Irish Republic owes its existence as an independent polity to literature. As with all myths, this one contains a very strong measure of truth, and in addition had, in Yeats, a gifted and enthusiastic propagandist. Yeats and many of his contemporaries consciously set to work to create the sense of national identity which they believed a necessary preamble to political action, and they were able to argue that in the nineteenth century the songs of Thomas Moore (1779–1852)and the heroic poems of Standish O'Grady (1846–1928) were as influential in recreating a national consciousness among the long-repressed Irish as were the mass meetings and parliamentary strategies used by the "Liberator,"

[1] *The King's Threshold* (1904), ll. 131-32, in *The Collected Plays of W. B. Yeats* (New York, 1953), 73.

Daniel O'Connell (1775–1847), and Charles Stewart Parnell (1846–1891). The poets played an even more important function by creating interest and sympathy for the Irish cause outside Ireland, since English public opinion and American money were both essential for the achievement of independence. When Yeats helped to found the Irish Literary Theatre in 1899 (it did not become the Abbey Theatre until 1904), he was interested both in using ancient Irish heroic material and in exploring the possibilities of modern verse drama in English, but he also seems to have been aware of how immediate an impact such plays could have in creating a national consciousness. In retrospect, at least, he was able to convince himself that he and Lady Gregory had founded the theater primarily for nationalist purposes. J. M. Synge, who attended the first performance in 1899, wrote soon afterward that he had "sensed that the spirit of a nation had hovered for an instant in the room." [2] Yeats knew that the Abbey's greatest success was his *Cathleen Ni Houlihan* (1902), a nationalist play which brought onto the stage an emblematic figure for Ireland, the Poor Old Woman who mourns her lost lands, who draws the young men out to fight for her, and who, at the news of rebellion against the English, turns into "a young girl, and she had the walk of a queen." Cathleen was played by Maud Gonne (1866–1953), a fiery and beautiful young revolutionary agitator who had already become in her own right a kind of emblematic figure for the Irish cause, and who was able to suggest, as she moved about the stage, the resilient young body beneath the appearance of decrepit old age. Yeats was in love with Maud Gonne, and he wrote the play for her. His involvement with the nationalist cause was thus highly personal and poetic as well as political, but there is little doubt that *Cathleen Ni Houlihan* played some part in arousing a sense of ntaional identity. At the end of his life, thinking of the abortive Easter Rising of 1916, when Padraic Pearse (1879–1916) and James Connolly (1870–1916) seized Dublin's General Post Office and proclaimed the Irish Republic from its steps, only to be defeated and executed by the British, Yeats could ask in "The Man and the Echo" (1939), "Did that play of mine send out / Certain men the English shot?" The expected answer is, presumably, a qualified "yes." Among the leaders of the Rising, as Yeats catalogues them in

[2] "The Irish Literary Movement," *L'Européen* (Paris), 31 May 1902, reprinted in J. M. Synge, *The Aran Islands and Other Writings*, ed. Robert Tracy (New York, 1962).

"Easter 1916" ("I write it out in a verse—/ MacDonagh and MacBride / And Connolly and Pearse"), Pearse, who "rode our wingèd horse," and his "helper and friend" MacDonagh were both poets. Terence MacSwiney (1879–1920), an Abbey playwright who became Lord Mayor of Cork and protested the destruction of his city by British troops, died in a British prison after a protest fast of seventy days, fasting as the poet Seanchan fasts in Yeats's play *The King's Threshold* (1903). The close ties between the Irish Literary Movement, the Gaelic Revival (an attempt to restore spoken Gaelic as the national language), and political nationalism were acknowledged after the establishment (1922) of the Irish Free State, when Yeats was appointed to the Senate; later, the first president of Eire was Dr. Douglas Hyde (1860–1949), folklorist, poet, translator from Gaelic (*Love Songs of Connacht*, 1893), historian of the Irish Literary Movement, author of poems and stories in Gaelic and of the first play ever written in that language, *The Twisting of the Rope* (*Casadh an Tsúgáin*, 1901), adapted from a short story by Yeats and acted by the Irish Literary Theatre.

Yet, despite these close ties between literature and the nationalist movement, from the very beginning there was a clear divergence between the writers and their activist allies. Joyce, who avoided any involvement with politics, and especially any involvement with Irish politics, acutely defined the problem of the artist in politics in a conversation in 1918. "As an artist I am against every state," he declared. "The state is concentric, man is eccentric. Thence arises an eternal struggle."[3] Yeats and the other Abbey Theatre playwrights very quickly found themselves being denounced by the political nationalists for not being sufficiently positive and didactic. Maud Gonne and the journalist Arthur Griffith (1872–1922), who later served as De Valera's lieutenant and as president (1922) of Dail Eireann, were eager for more plays like *Cathleen Ni Houlihan*, but they scorned anything less overtly propagandistic. Griffith led the furious attacks on J. M. Synge's *In the Shadow of the Glen* (1903) and *The Playboy of the Western World* (1907), plays which he considered subversive because in them Irish peasants were depicted as behaving immorally or foolishly. He was quick to point out that not Irishmen but Anglo-Irishmen (defined by Brendan Behan as "a Protestant with a horse"[4]) controlled the Abbey and

[3] Joyce in conversation with Georges Borach, 21 Oct. 1918, quoted in Richard Ellmann, *James Joyce* (New York, 1959), 460.

[4] *The Hostage* (New York, 1958), Act I, p. 11.

wrote its plays. For Yeats the experience seems to have strengthened his already strong tendency to despise politics and to seek in the form of the Japanese Noh play an exclusively aristocratic art form, in an idealized view of the Anglo-Irish Ascendancy, an aristocratic tradition which he could celebrate in verse and prose. In the auto-biographical essay "Estrangement" (1926), he remarks that when a sensitive man "throws himself into the work of some league he succeeds just in so far as he puts aside all delicate and personal gifts . . . I can only wish that a young Irishman of talent and culture may spend his life, from eighteen to twenty-five, outside Ireland." [5] He goes on, "the Irish town mind will by many channels, public and private, press its vulgarity upon us. . . ." [6] "Ireland has grown sterile, because power has passed to men who lack the training which requires a certain amount of wealth to ensure continuity from generation to generation, and to free the mind in part from other tasks." [7]

This disillusioned attitude, repeatedly and bitterly expressed by Yeats in the twenties and thirties, still shapes the work of many recent Irish writers. There is a repeated sense that something precious has been lost in the extinction, cultural as well as political, of the old Ascendancy. This persists even though the historical evidence for the Ascendancy's devotion to cultural matters is very slender indeed, once the names of "Goldsmith and the Dean, Berkeley and Burke" [8] have been intoned, and the Ascendancy's much-vaunted chivalric virtues were chiefly displayed outside Ireland, in extending the British Empire. Modern writers repeatedly follow Yeats by express-ing their disdain for the middle-class political and social life of the Irish Republic, and by suggesting that the true national spirit can be found only among those peasants who dwell far from the corrupting and Anglicized cities and speak Irish. The struggles of the Revolu-tion and the Civil War (1922–1923) appear as brutal rather than heroic, and as having brought about little real change, only a chance for the "gombeen men," small-town hucksters, to rise to the top. In "A Country Walk" (1962) the poet Thomas Kinsella (b. 1928) speaks of "the phantom hag, / Tireless Rebellion," but also scorns

---

[5] W. B. Yeats, *Autobiographies* (London, 1956), 476.
[6] *Ibid.*, 484.
[7] *Ibid.*, 489.
[8] Yeats, "Blood and the Moon" (1928), *The Collected Poems of W. B. Yeats* (New York, 1953), 233.

the survivors who "have exchanged / A trenchcoat playground for a gombeen jungle" in a parody of Yeats's "Easter 1916":

> Around the corner, in an open square,
> I come upon the sombre monuments
> That bear their names: MacDonagh & McBride,
> Merchants; Connolly's Commercial Arms....[9]

The career of the most important Irish writer of recent times clearly illustrates how marked this disillusionment is, though Brendan Behan (1923–1964) worked out some interesting personal variations on Yeats's model. Behan grew up in a radical working-class family. His relatives had fought for the Revolution for nationalist reasons, but they were also socialists and hoped that freedom from English rule would bring about a redistribution of wealth and a better life. Behan's maternal uncle, Peadar Kearney (d. 1942), wrote "The Soldier's Song," now the Republic's national anthem. Behan's family had been politically disenchanted by the results of Revolution, however. They disapproved of the Free State government, set up in 1922, because the treaty establishing the Free State had accepted the separation of the six counties of Northern Ireland from the rest and left the Catholic population of those six counties under Anglo-Irish Protestant rule. Brendan Behan himself joined the IRA (Irish Republican Army), an organization dedicated to reuniting the six counties to the rest of Ireland under a single government. Membership in the IRA has been illegal since 1922. Behan's membership, as he tells us in the autobiographical *Borstal Boy* (1959), led to his arrest in Liverpool in 1939, where he had gone to strike a blow against England by planting gelignite bombs in Cammell Laird's shipyard (his grandmother and two aunts had been arrested earlier on another operation, having gone to England to set up a hideout for IRA men on active service.[10] The activists' theory was the old Irish adage that "England's trouble is Ireland's opportunity"—any weakening of the British war effort might weaken Britain's ability to retain control over the six counties. "My name is Brendan Behan," he declared to the arresting officers. "I came over here to fight for the Irish Workers' and Small Farmers' Republic, for a full and free life, for my countrymen, North and South, and for the removal of the baneful influence of British Imperialism from Irish affairs. God save Ireland."

[9] Thomas Kinsella, Douglas Livingstone, and Anne Sexton, *Poems* (New York, 1968), 23.

[10] Dominic Behan, *My Brother Brendan* (London, 1965), 31, 49.

The wording of this declaration deliberately announced his membership in the socialist left wing of the IRA. "The left-wing element in the movement would be delighted," he remarks, "and the others, the craw-thumpers [practicing Catholics], could not say anything against me, because I was a good Volunteer, captured carrying the struggle to England's doorstep—but they would be hopping mad at me giving everyone the impression that the IRA was Communistic." [11]

Too young for prison, Behan was placed in a Borstal school, a British reformatory for juveniles. Later (1942) he was deported to Ireland, where he was immediately rearrested and imprisoned (1942–1946) as an IRA member. He seems to have emerged from this set of experiences prepared to distrust all political or nationalistic slogans and myths. His first play, *The Quare Fellow* (1954; two earlier plays are unpublished), was written and is set in an Irish prison. The play was originally written in Gaelic, and its original title was *The Twisting of Another Rope (Casadh Tsúgáin Eile)*[12] in ironic tribute to Hyde's *Casadh an Tsúgáin*, which had been culturally and politically so important to Irish nationalism. The subject is an execution by hanging in an Irish prison, for which an English hangman has been imported—a grotesque situation after independence from England has been achieved, and in the play made more grotesque by the alleged explanation of why the Irish government has no official executioner of its own: there is a requirement that all civil servants in the Republic pass an examination in written and spoken Gaelic, by law the national language, and no candidate for the executioner's post has been able to do this. Behan is able to ridicule this requirement, dictated by a political adaptation of cultural nationalism, and at the same time he is able to hint that a real knowledge of the Gaelic language, that is, the natural use of it in serious situations rather than the mere study of it to pass a state examination, implies some share in the true values of the folk, a natural sense of compassion for the criminal rather than the artificial and legalistic notion that he deserves to be punished. Synge has defined this attitude in *The Aran Islands* (1907), his impressionistic account of life among the Gaelic-speaking islanders off the west coast of Ireland:

> This impulse to protect the criminal is universal in the west. It seems partly due to the association between justice and the hated

[11] *Borstal Boy* (New York, 1959), 7.
[12] Brendan Behan, *Confessions of an Irish Rebel* (London, 1965), 242.

English jurisdiction, but more directly to the primitive feeling of these people ... that a man will not do wrong unless he is under the influence of a passion which is as irresponsible as a storm on the sea. If a man has killed his father, and is already sick and broken with remorse, they can see no reason why he should be dragged away and killed by the law.

Such a man, they say, will be quiet all the rest of his life, and if you suggest that punishment is needed as an example, they ask, "Would any one kill his father if he was able to help it?" [13]

In Behan's play the sympathetic prison guards are Gaelic speakers, and their values are those of the country people. One of them, Regan, argues continually against capital punishment as cruel and unnatural, and describes the prisoner going to execution as "surrounded by a crowd of bigger bloody ruffians than himself, if the truth were but told." [14] The presence of the two kind guards and their statements imply a system of basic national values quite independent of any political regime or political slogans, a system preserved among those who speak the Irish language naturally rather than to satisfy some civil service requirement, and who approach a criminal with compassion rather than legalisms. Political changes, even the struggle for national independence, are irrelevant in this play. An Irish prison is just like a British one. "The Free State didn't change anything more than the badge on the warders' caps," [15] one old prisoner remarks, echoing a statement Behan attributes to his grandmother—the mother of four sons who fought for Ireland in 1916—in his *Confessions of an Irish Rebel* (1965):

"Do you know the difference between having an Irish Republic and being a section of the British Empire?"
"No," says I, "what is it?"
"You'll get an eviction order written in Irish with a harp, rather than one written in English with the lion and the unicorn." [16]

Or, as Yeats cynically put it in his two-line poem "Parnell" (1938):

Parnell came down the road, he said to a cheering man:
"Ireland shall get her freedom and you still break stone."

In *The Hostage* (1958), also first written in Gaelic, Behan launches a far more savage attack on the political use of national myths. These myths can become weapons with which the old destroy the young. In the play, the IRA captures a young English soldier in

---

[13] *The Aran Islands and Other Writings*, 61.
[14] *The Quare Fellow* (New York, 1956), 63.
[15] *Ibid.*, 21.
[16] Behan, *Confessions of an Irish Rebel*, 134.

Northern Ireland and holds him as hostage for an IRA member about to be executed in Belfast jail. The soldier is held captive in a Dublin brothel owned by "Monsewer," an Anglo-Irishman who has become "more Irish than the Irish." Monsewer refuses to respond to any English form of address, wears kilts, speaks in Gaelic whenever possible (though his Irish companions know nothing of that language), and has led Irish revolutionary soldiers "on the back of his white horse at the head of his regiment, the cross of Christ held high in his right hand like Brian Boru in the battle of Clontarf leading his men to war and glory." [17] Monsewer and his assistant Pat, who fought with him through the Revolution and Civil War and lost a leg "at Mullingar, on the field of battle," [18] are both kind enough to the hostage, but it is their insistence on seeing the world only in terms of old slogans, old loyalties, that brings about his death. To risk death for political causes, or to encourage others to do so, is immoral, Behan proclaims, a trick old men play upon young ones. In a world where an atom bomb can obliterate everything, the border separating the six counties from the rest of Ireland is not worth fighting about, and the IRA is a dangerous anachronism—as is the persistence in old national rivalries which might bring about an atomic war. "It's such a big bomb it's after making me scared of little bombs," says Pat. "The I.R.A. is out of date and so is the R.A.F. So is the Swiss Guard and the Foreign Legion, the Red Army, the United States Marines, the Free State Army.... The Coldstream Guards, the Scots Guards, the Welsh Guards, the Grenadier Guards...."[19] When the Irish police raid the brothel, at the end of the play, the hostage is killed. "Don't cry, Teresa," Pat says to the girl who loved him, "and don't blame anybody for it. Nobody meant to kill him." "But he's dead," she answers.

> PAT. And so is the boy in Belfast jail.
> TERESA. Ah, it was not Belfast Jail or the six counties that was bothering you—but your lost youth and your crippled leg....[20]

The play's repudiation of political nationalism and its rallying cries are pointedly brought home by an absurdist technique, for after Teresa's speech the dead hostage rises to his feet and sings to the audience a song beginning, "The bells of hell / Go ting-a-ling-a-ling / For you but not for me." The auditors are reminded that the

---

[17] *The Hostage*, 12.
[18] *Ibid.*, 68.
[19] *Ibid.*, 4.
[20] *Ibid.*, 92.

hostage's death is only part of a play, while they will go out of the theater into a real world ruled by ancient rivalries and slogans, which can really snuff out their lives. Behan made his own repudiation of nationalism in general, and Irish nationalism in particular, explicit in *Confessions of an Irish Rebel*: "I really could not see why two small Islands off the coast of Europe ... required four capitals. One is enough, and we should live off the better one, which is in England." [21] His brother Dominic Behan (b. 1924) has expressed the same disenchantment with the nationalist cause and its slogans in his play *Posterity Be Damned* (1960) and in his song "The Patriot Game," which commemorates a young IRA man shot by the Northern Irish authorities, commemorating him not by repeating the clichés of patriotic oratory but by suggesting how these clichés have been a trap:

> Come all young rebels and list while I sing
> How love of one's land is a terrible thing.
> It banishes fear with the speed of a flame,
> And makes us all part of the Patriot Game.[22]

Given their background, the Behans could hardly romanticize the Anglo-Irish Ascendancy, as Yeats had done after he became disenchanted about Irish nationalism, but in other respects their theme of disillusion with the reality of Irish political freedom resembles his. In recent Irish novels it is possible to discern an even closer adherence to Yeats's view of things. The fine comic writer Mervyn Will (b. 1908) expressed some of his bitterness at present-day Ireland's clerical domination and puritanism in *The Unfortunate Fursey* (1947) and *The Return of Fursey* (1948), two stories about a tenth-century monk troubled by devils and witches, but when he came to portray the modern scene in *Leaves for the Burning* (1952) and *No Trophies Raise* (1956) his mood approaches despair. In *Leaves for the Burning* only one character has found peace and dignity in modern Ireland, by settling in Connemara and devoting her time to fostering cottage industries. Her solution is a return to that real world of the Gaeltacht—the Gaelic-speaking area of Ireland—that Behan senses as underlying the political nation—the real Ireland, with all its compassionate values intact, perceived beneath the official Ireland, as in C. S. Lewis's *That Hideous Strength* the realm of

[21] *Ibid.*, 134.
[22] *My Brother Brendan*, 37.

Logres with its heroic virtues can be perceived beneath modern Britain, or as Dostoevsky can see the true Slavic soul of peasant Russia beneath the government's "Westernized" nineteenth-century façade. Wall emphasizes his point by giving this character the name of Conroy, an inevitable reminder of Gabriel Conroy, Joyce's hero in "The Dead," and his deferred "journey westward" to the sources of ethnic and psychic life. No one else in *Leaves for the Burning* can find any kind of peace, and Wall has carefully placed the events of the novel in the week preceding Yeats's "official" funeral in 1948 (the poet was buried in France in 1939; nine years later his body was carried to Sligo on an Irish corvette, and buried as he had requested, in Drumcliffe churchyard). By doing so he is able to stress the unromantic quality of life in modern Ireland and to contrast it with the differently romantic dreams of Yeats and of the rebels of 1916. They represent a past that is generous, heroic, poetic, moved by other considerations than money. Wall's hero, Lucian Burke, is a minor official buried in a country village. He tries to save an old castle, the site of a great Irish love story, which is to be demolished for road-building material, but he fails—there is no interest in this heroic and romantic past. As he sits with Miss Conroy in Connemara he thinks of the forthcoming Yeats funeral:

> Somewhere far out beyond those headlong seas a corvette was forcing its way towards Ireland, and the coffin of W. B. Yeats was on board lashed to the rainswept deck. They were bringing the poet back to bury him among the people he knew, but who did not know him. It would be a shabby affair. It had begun badly with a secondhand corvette, bought cheap from the British who had no further use for it. There would probably be a band with monstrous yokels of six-and-a-half feet blowing their souls into fifes while small boys walked alongside hammering drums. There would be a mob of small townspeople pushing and straining to see the show, not one of them aware of the mental size of the man they were burying. And the small literati would be there in force .... It would be a very shoddy affair; its only excuse that it was native.[23]

The IRA appears, as a couple of shabby gunmen who hold up Lucian's office and wound him when he resists, but they too are shown as incapable of heroism. Modern Ireland is represented by Senator Trefoil, who fought through the Revolution for the cause but has now realized it can be turned to profit. "The politicians had come here before they were politicians," Lucian muses in Connemara,

[23] *Leaves for the Burning* (New York, 1952), 188.

the men who were now County Managers and Senator Trefoils; and, drunk with the sheer beauty of the scene, with the rugged peasant life and with the strange words of a dying language, had made a national revolution. That had been in their generous youth before they had become politicians, and before they had learnt the satisfaction of power and of great possessions.[24]

Trefoil himself has a rare moment of self-awareness. "Our rebellion in 1916 and our whole national movement was started by fools who expected nothing out of it for themselves," he tells his crony, the County Manager.

> "Men of vision, I would rather call them," said the County Manager softly.
> "Men of vision me eye," ejaculated the Senator, "fellows that wrote poetry and the like . . . . We're the men of vision. We're the ones that did well for ourselves out of their sacrifice . . . ."[25]

Ireland is portrayed as a desolate, hopeless, and gloomy place, where only drink can relieve the despair. For Miss Conroy there is folk crafts, for Lucian a vague trust in "breeding" and tradition. "Perhaps you and I and our kind are not so ineffective as I have thought," one of Lucian's friends writes him after the shooting.

> Perhaps our pride and the tradition in which we were brought up, the houses which taught us little but at least never taught us a pliant knee, have given us something which we can contribute to the life of to-day, so that another voice may continue to be heard alongside the cry of the huckster which sounds from every corner of the land. How I hate that importunate tradesman's cry, the chorus of big and little business: "We have something for sale, for sale!"[26]

But Yeats, like O'Leary, is in his grave. Gentle or peasant, wise or simple, there is little that the traditionalist can do except cling to his own self-respect and hope for better days. Wall returns to the same theme, with even greater despair, in *No Trophies Raise*, where genuine worth is put down by those who profess to value the best of the old traditions but pervert those traditions into slogans and then use those slogans for personal profit.

John Montague (b. 1929), best known as a poet, makes a similar point in several of the short stories contained in his collection *Death of a Chieftain* (1964). Montague has no romantic illusions about life in small-town and rural Ireland. But in the title story he creates an

---

[24] *Ibid.*, 187.
[25] *Ibid.*, 207.
[26] *Ibid.*, 212–13.

Ascendancy hero, drunken, impoverished, "more Irish than the Irish" like Behan's Monsewer, and obsessively seeking in Central America for tumuli on the Celtic model, which will prove that there once existed a worldwide Celtic civilization. Despite his shabbiness, he is recognized as a true chieftain by the local Indians and ceremonially murdered. In "A Change of Management" Montague indicts the new Ireland. His entrepreneur, Clohessy, remarks that Ireland has "had a lot of patriots," and when his companion agrees, goes on,

> "But what it has never had are a group of practical, hard-headed people who would try to put it back on its feet, like any business.... One would have to give up a lot, of course.... But there would be the satisfaction of being one of the first in a new line of well-trained —eh—"
> "Patriots," finished O'Shea.
> "Yes." [27]

O'Shea overcomes his doubts, but the drunken poet Cronin explains to him what is happening:

> "...*The bastards are on the march*.... Since this country was founded we've had two waves of chancers. The first were easy to spot; the gunmen turned gombeen: they were so ignorant that they practically ruined themselves. But this second lot are a tougher proposition. In fifty years they'll have made this country just like every place else.... Factories owned by Germans, posh hotels catering to the grey flannel brigade, computers instead of decent pen-pushers: do you call that progress? Well, by Jesus, I don't, and I'll fight it tooth and nail. If this country becomes a chancer's paradise, it will be over my dead body...." [28]

Behan, Wall, and Montague concentrate on contemporary Ireland, and its apparent betrayal of national characteristics and of the romantic ideals of the poets who dreamed of an independent Ireland. But two of the most celebrated novels of the past few years return to the presumed heroic age, when the present-day Irish Republic was being formed, only to find there the beginnings of today's disillusionment. Michael Farrell's *Thy Tears Might Cease* (1963) and James Plunkett's *Strumpet City* (1969) are both extremely ambitious novels. They are both old-fashioned novels. Neither writer seems to be aware of any advances in the technique of the novel after the death of Trollope. They are competent story-tellers working within

[27] "A Change of Management," in *Death of a Chieftain and Other Stories* (London, 1964), 109.
[28] *Ibid.*, 113.

the nineteenth-century tradition. They have been compared by some enthusiastic reviewers to Tolstoi, to Pasternak, and to the Prince di Lampedusa, because of their ability to handle an enormous cast of characters, to cover a significant historical event which brings about a change in the nature of life in their country, to give a convincing account of how such an event affects private lives and relationships, and above all to suggest the "feel" of a particular historical time and place.

Michael Farrell (1899–1962) was an executive of Radio Eireann, the Irish equivalent of the BBC. He spent many years in writing *Thy Tears Might Cease*, a vast panoramic novel which eventually ran to some 320,000 words, but he could not bring himself to publish it, probably because the book had literally become his life—most of the hero's adventures and traits are Farrell's, and the writing of the book had occupied twenty-five of his adult years. As a novel, even as posthumously published after Monk Gibbon had shortened it by nearly a third, *Thy Tears Might Cease* is disappointing, but its very weaknesses reveal some of the fascinatingly ambiguous attitudes with which a modern Irish author approaches the Irish Revolution, what it created and what it destroyed.

Farrell gives his hero, Martin Matthew Reilly, a divided background, so that his political and emotional loyalties are divided as well. Reilly's dead father was Irish, Catholic, and a Home Ruler, one who hoped for an orderly progress toward a legal Home Rule granted by vote of the British Parliament. His dead mother was Anglo-Irish, Protestant, and her background was Unionist and so unalterably opposed to any type of Home Rule. Reilly himself is an unbearable snob. He glories in an aristocratic Catholic ancestor who fought at Fontenoy (1745) in Louis XV's Irish Brigade, and his response to Pearse's proclamation of the Irish Republic in 1916 is to exclaim, "But Ireland was always a kingdom! It was the Fleur-de-Lis and the Green Flag that my ancestor Colonel Reilly fought for." [29] He is profoundly moved on a visit to his Ascendancy relatives in 1914, when all stand to sing "God Save the King" before closing up the big house forever and sending the men off to France, yet it is not long before Martin himself is fighting the king with the rebel army, only to feel profound disgust when his associates talk in Irish and burn the great house of his mother's people to the ground. Farrell's real theme is the Revolution as a break with the past. Martin

[29] *Thy Tears Might Cease* (New York, 1964), 301.

talks of his own past constantly, and carries around a box full of letters, diaries, and other memorabilia, including a mysterious letter which will eventually tell him all about his dead parents. But in the turmoil of Revolution he loses the box, and his precious past with it. Though Farrell concedes that the Revolution was a necessary assertion of political independence and national values, he emphasizes the tremendous cost of the nation's loss of much of the past. The old gentleman class, with its gracious traditions, are romantically depicted here in a way that owes more to Yeats's dreams of the Ascendancy than to historical fact. Revolution destroys these gentlemen, and their places are taken by those who find patriotic slogans a useful smokescreen for repression, personal profit, and the paying off of old personal scores. Keelard, the great house of Martin's mother's family, is burned down by rebels from the neighborhood not because it is a military objective or a symbol of repression but because a local politician can do a deal with the empty land. Through Reilly's eyes his childhood in Edwardian Ireland is seen as a golden age, and his personal tragedy lies in the way in which the revolutionary cause he fights for completely destroys this romantic past and the traditional order which nourishes him. The buildings that housed his childhood, the people who surrounded him, are all swept away. The Revolution demands great bravery of him, but its results will probably be petty—the fighters for freedom set up their own police patrols in Dublin, not to harass the government's police but to threaten prostitutes and "indecent" chorus girls. The old Ascendancy past will be destroyed, but it will not be replaced by freedom and justice. It will be replaced by the Ireland Mervyn Wall portrays, a paradise for the professional puritan and the gombeen man:

> after we have won . . . Conroy's police will have a green uniform and a green flag. The lamp-posts will be painted green, the street names will be in Irish, which no one understands. That is all. No, not all! Those people over there in the car [middle-class people] will have climbed into the saddle. They will be *all*-powerful . . . .[30]

In *Strumpet City*, James Plunkett (b. 1920) writes not about the Revolution but about the 1913 General Strike in Dublin which preceded it. In the strike he sees a situation as heroic and as seminal for modern Ireland as "the Troubles." The leaders of the strike, James Larkin and James Connolly (the Connolly of the 1916 Rising and Yeats's poem), were socialists who dreamed both of freedom from

[30] *Ibid.*, 413.

British rule and of social justice and realized that mere political independence would be meaningless. Their principles are implicit in Brendan Behan's identification of himself to the Liverpool police as a soldier of "the Irish Workers' and Small Farmers' Republic." Bernadette Devlin and other members of the People's Democracy party in Northern Ireland today are their political heirs.

Practically speaking, the General Strike was a failure. The employers formed an association and received help from English employers, while the strikers found that the British Trade Unions were not much interested in helping Irishmen. After many bitter months, the beaten workers returned to their jobs, their demands unmet. Plunkett clearly admires Larkin and his dream of an Irish Workers' Republic under the "Plough and the Stars"—the flag of Irish socialism. He sees the smashing of the strike as a decisive moment, the one that insured that an independent Ireland would be governed by conservative Catholic middle-class values, afraid to complete its nationalist revolution by rethinking the nature of the state and its duties. Only the warders' cap badges were to change.

As a novel, *Strumpet City* is not very interesting, except for the collector of literary-nationalistic clichés. There is a great deal about Rashers Tierney, who begs, scavenges, and plays the tin-whistle in the streets of Dublin with a wearisomely cocky cheerfulness. The Irish like to sing and dance, and would like watermelons if they grew in Ireland. The rest of the characters are stereotypes of sentimental novels and plays about Ireland—brave and dedicated leaders, poor but honest women, sturdy workingmen, scrupulously clean little rooms in the slums, a stern puritanical priest, a boisterous drunken priest. Plunkett avoids the acid tones which Behan and Sean O'Casey often use when discussing the mores of the Dublin slum-dweller. There are some moments of honesty—the fastidious Father O'Connor deliberately seeks a slum parish but is revolted by the poor, while the drunken Father Giffley is compassionate enough to realize that justice is on the workers' side but cannot help in any effective way and drowns his realization in drink. The death of Rashers Tierney in his cellar, where his body rots and is partly eaten by his dog, is as sordid as any theorist of the proletarian novel could wish. But Plunkett fails to make his social attitudes and his story-telling techniques into a unified whole, and the impact of *Strumpet City* is consequently blurred.

From these five authors, then, it is possible to discern the role of cultural nationalism in modern Irish writing—or, to be precise, in modern Irish writing *in English,* for there is, of course, a whole literary world of writers writing in Gaelic, whose work I have not discussed and who maintain that only in the true Irish language can the spirit of the people be portrayed. Brendan Behan, Mervyn Wall, John Montague, Michael Farrell, James Plunkett are agreed in their disappointment with life in the modern Irish Republic and in seeing that life as a political and moral betrayal of the poets and dreamers who led the Revolution. They resent the perversion of the nationalist ideal into mere political slogans. Wall and Farrell blame this betrayal on the "chancers" or gombeen men who turned the Revolution to personal profit, elbowed the gentlemen out of any position of leadership, and supported an obscurantist and puritanical form of Catholicism as a bulwark against any serious efforts to achieve social justice. John Montague is in general agreement, but, looking to the future, he sees in the emergence of a new managerial class devoted to efficiency an even greater threat to traditional values. Behan and Plunkett do not accept the Yeatsian theory that the gentry are the nation's natural leaders and that their disappearance has been a disaster. Both portray "gentlemen" sardonically. They suggest that the Revolution was not so much betrayed as never really begun, for it never properly defined the ideal of independence in terms of social justice for all, nor even considered what social justice in Irish terms could mean. All five of these writers search for a national identity that manifests itself in other than political ways. For all five, in their disillusion with the reality of modern Ireland, the words of the Irish poet, journalist, and visionary Æ (George William Russell, 1867–1935) define the inevitable nature of the writer's involvement with nationalism: "There are no nations to whom the entire and loyal allegiance of man's spirit could be given," he wrote. "It can only go out to the ideal empires and nationalities in the womb of time, for whose coming we pray."

BIBLIOGRAPHY

Behan, Brendan. *Borstal Boy.* New York: Knopf, 1959.
——. *Confessions of an Irish Rebel.* London: Hutchinson, 1965.
——. *The Hostage.* New York: Grove Press, 1958.
——. *The Quare Fellow.* New York: Grove Press, 1956.
Farrell, Michael. *Thy Tears Might Cease.* New York: Knopf, 1964.
Gregory, Isabella Augusta, Lady. *Cuchulain of Muirthelmne.* London: Murray, 1902.

Gregory, Isabella Augusta, Lady. *Gods and Fighting Men*. London: Murray, 1904.
———. *Our Irish Theatre*. New York: Putnam's, 1914.
Kinsella, Thomas. *Poems* by Thomas Kinsella, Douglas Livingstone, and Anne Sexton. New York: Oxford University Press, 1968.
Montague, John. *Death of a Chieftain and Other Stories*. London: Mac-Gibbon and Kee, 1964.
———. *Forms of Exile*. Dublin: Dolmen Press, 1958.
———. *Poisoned Lands, and Other Poems*. Philadelphia: DuFour Editions, 1963.
Plunkett, James. *Strumpet City*. New York: Delacorte Press, 1969.
Synge, John Millington. *The Aran Islands and Other Writings*, ed. Robert Tracy. New York: Vintage, 1962.
———. *The Complete Plays of John M. Synge*. New York: Vintage, 1960.
Wall, Mervyn. *Leaves for the Burning*. New York: Devin-Adair, 1952.
———. *No Trophies Raise*. London: Methuen, 1956.
———. *The Return of Fursey*. London: Pilot Press, 1948.
———. *The Unfortunate Fursey*. New York: Crown, 1947.
Yeats, W. B. *Autobiographies*. London: Macmillan, 1956.
———. *The Collected Plays of W. B. Yeats*. New York: Macmillan, 1953.
———. *The Collected Poems of W. B. Yeats*. New York: Macmillan, 1953.
———. *Essays and Introductions*. London: Macmillan, 1961.
———. *Explorations*. New York: Macmillan, 1962.
———. *Mythologies*. New York: Macmillan, 1959.

OTHER REFERENCES

Arnold, Matthew. *On the Study of Celtic Literature* (1867). Long Acre, 1910.
Behan, Dominic. *My Brother Brendan*. London, 1965.
Brooke, Stopford A., and T. W. Rolleston. *A Treasury of Irish Poetry*. London, 1900; rpt. 1932.
Carney, James. *Studies in Irish History and Literature*. Dublin, 1955.
Clarke, Austin. *Poetry in Modern Ireland*. Dublin, 1951.
Colum, Padraic (ed.). *A Treasury of Irish Folklore*. New York, 1954.
Corkery, Daniel. *Synge and Anglo-Irish Literature*. London, 1931.
Davitt, Michael. *The Fall of Feudalism in Ireland*. London, 1904.
Dillon, Myles. *Early Irish Literature*. Chicago, 1948.
Duffy, Sir Charles Gavan, G. H. Sigerson, and Douglas Hyde. *The Revival of Irish Literature*. London, 1894.
Ellis-Fermor, Una. *The Irish Dramatic Movement*. London, 1954.
Farren, Robert. *The Course of Irish Verse in English*. New York, 1947.
Flanagan, Thomas. *The Irish Novelists, 1800–1850*. New York, 1959.
Flower, Robin. *The Irish Tradition*. Oxford, 1947.
Greene, D. H., and E. M. Stephens. *J. M. Synge*. New York, 1959.
Gregory, Isabella Augusta, Lady. *Journals, 1916–1930*. Ed. Lennox Robinson. New York, 1947.
Healy, T. M. *Letters and Leaders of My Day*. 2 vols. London, 1928.

Howarth, Herbert. *The Irish Writers, 1880–1940.* New York, 1958.

Hyde, Douglas. *Beside the Fire: A Collection of Irish Gaelic Folk Stories.* London, 1890.

———. *A Literary History of Ireland.* London, 1899.

———. *The Love Songs of Connacht.* London, 1893; rpt. New York, 1969.

———. *The Religious Songs of Connacht.* London, 1906.

Kiely, Benedict. *Modern Irish Fiction.* London, 1950.

Loftus, R. J. *Nationalism in Modern Irish Poetry.* Madison, Wis., 1964.

Massachusetts Review, 5, no. 4 (Winter, 1964), 249–380. Special Irish Issue.

Mercier, Vivian. *The Irish Comic Tradition.* Oxford, 1962.

O'Connor, Frank. *A Book of Ireland.* London, 1959.

———. *A Short History of Irish Literature.* New York, 1967.

O'Faolain, Sean. *The Irish.* London, 1947.

O'Farachain, Robert. See Farren.

Price, Allan. *Synge and Anglo-Irish Drama.* London, 1961.

Weygandt, Cornelius. *Irish Plays and Playwrights.* Boston, 1913.

Dominant Themes in Contemporary
East European Fiction

GEORGE GÖMÖRI

POLISH FICTION

National stereotypes change slowly and die hard everywhere. Images and notions of a nation, any nation, about herself are even more ingrained in the collective mind and only on rare occasions are subject to revision. In Eastern Europe where in the last two centuries the writer's historical role has been defined as that of a prophet, of a political leader, or of an educator of the backward masses, where the poet was called upon to become an "organizer of the national consciousness," this revision of the national self-image has been done more often by writers and intellectuals than by professional politicians. The lack of independent and democratic political institutions greatly enhanced the importance of the written word in these countries and led to expectations which East European writers find increasingly hard to fulfill. Nevertheless, the treatment of a central theme in Polish, Czech and Slovak, and Hungarian literature can often be very informative, telling us more about the real problems and emotions of the people than tons of florid or tedious political oratory.

One of the central, if not the central, themes of contemporary Polish literature has been the Second World War, which in Polish minds falls into two parts: the September catastrophe and the German occupation. The war years not only gave every Pole his fair share of terrifying experiences, they left their imprint on the Polish national psyche. On the one hand, the occupation and the Warsaw uprising of 1944 reactivated certain latent national stereotypes restoring the validity of Polish martyrology born in the nineteenth-century struggles for independence. The mass extermination of the Jews and the incredible hecatomb of the Warsaw Uprising, on the other hand, created an atmosphere in which almost everyone who survived could feel guilty for not being able to save others from annihilation. Before 1939 Polish literature did not know the problem of guilt; the hero of the Polish novel was always a victim of circumstances; there was always someone else, usually a foreigner, to be blamed for his errors and failure. The occupation gave the "first chance of psychological frankness," [1] for it burdened the most serious Polish writers with a powerful guilt complex on account of the massacre of the Jews and also on account of the many young men and women dying at the barricades. The guilt complex arising from the enormity of Jewish suffering is strongest in the works of Jerzy Andrzejewski and the Catholic writer Jerzy Zawieyski, but it even permeates the postwar stories of writers of Jewish origin such as Adolf Rudnicki and Stanislaw Wygodzki.

Yet all those books written in the first decade after the war could not fully capture the complex, treacherous, cliff-hanging reality of the German occupation. This could not be done for a number of reasons of which, apart from the nearness in time, the requirements and restrictions of Stalinist communism were the most important. No one in Poland could write the truth, even his subjective version of the truth, about the AK, the nationalist Home Army which, though obeying orders of the Polish government in exile, fought bravely against the Germans but was suppressed for anti-Russian activities in 1945. When Andrzejewski published *Ashes and Diamonds* (1948), it became a popular success partly because of his ambiguous attitude toward the young men from the AK who keep fighting even after the Germans have been driven out. In the somewhat malicious opinion of the critic Sandauer, Andrzejewski's novel, intended as a condemnation of the postwar conspiracy, showed in reality that the author was fascinated by it.[2] In fact, both the murdered Communist functionary and his young murderer Maciej enjoy the writer's sympathy. But if *Ashes and Diamonds* managed to strike an uneasy balance between the political exigencies of the day and the personal loyalty of Poles to the Home Army, this was an exception; most postwar novels would prefer to keep silent about the AK or to parrot the official line about "treason" and "provocation" serving Western "imperialist" interests.

[1] Andrzej Kijowski, *Arcydzieło nieznane* (Cracow, 1964), 48.
[2] Artur Sandauer, *Dla każdego coś przykrego* (Cracow, 1966), 100.

It was only in the fullness of the Thaw, in 1956 and 1957, that the controversial subject of the Home Army and the Warsaw Uprising could be raised once again. This gave a chance to some writers, ex-members of the Home Army, to tell their part of the story. The most popular and probably the best of these was Roman Bratny's *The Columbus Boys Born in 1920* (*Kolumbowie rocznik 20*) (1957) which has seen eleven printings. Bratny's story follows the conspiratorial career of his young heroes ("Columbus" being the pseudonym of one of them) from the barricades of burning Warsaw and German POW camps up to the birth of "People's Poland." Only then is it that their roads diverge in a tragic way. Some ex-conspirators take to the woods, others never return from the West, and still others whose main ambition is "to come to an understanding" with Poland's new masters are viewed with suspicion by the authorities. In some ways, this last category is in the worst situation: these ex-soldiers of the AK do not really belong anywhere; they are forced to operate on a political no-man's-land and often fall victim (like Jerzy in Bratny's novel) to the revenge of their former comrades.

Although fairly traditional in its artistic method and scrupulously realistic in its description of actual events, *The Columbus Boys* had a therapeutic effect on the Polish reader. For the first time since the war he could relive and reenact in his mind the glory and the tragic fall of a whole generation; moreover, some grievances of Polish society against the Russians and the new regime could be aired or at least alluded to in Bratny's book: the massacre of the Polish military officers at Katyń, the Russian inactivity during the Warsaw Uprising, the fake elections of 1947. Although Bratny's aim was not to vindicate those AK groups which continued fighting against the new Polish authorities after 1945, he was anxious to explain the feelings of those members of the Home Army who did not adhere to any particular political party or ideology but were united in a "vague oppositionism" against the Russian-sponsored regime. For this they could not be entirely blamed. Even if their political expectations were unrealistic, many of them tried to find a place in the new society, but society failed to integrate them. Apart from Bratny, others, such as J. S. Stawiński, recalled the Warsaw Uprising in their strongly autobiographical fiction. Three of Stawiński's stories, among them *Canal* (*Kanał*), became rather popular and were used as film scenarios in coming years.

The partial rehabilitation of the Home Army and the resulting flood of publications, some scholarly, some autobiographical, filled a gap, satisfying a very real social demand. However, once the facts were established, the myth surrounding the AK could be slowly demolished and the experiences of conspiracy and partisan life gradually revalued. Two main approaches could be adopted toward this end: the grotesque and the moralistic. Before Stawiński's *Hungarians* (*Węgrzy*), no other work would deal with the 1944 uprising on a comic level. Stawiński's hero is a typical *cwaniak*, an engaging rogue and a black-marketeer who somehow gets involved in the uprising and ends up carrying messages between a Home Army command and a Hungarian unit stationed near Warsaw ready to support the uprising under certain conditions. The negotiations between the AK and the Hungarians fail to bring positive results, but Stawiński portrays the odyssey of his unwilling hero between the Polish and the German lines with a rare talent for the grotesque. Politically, the story gives a good opportunity to criticize the AK high command which has absolutely no contact with the Russians biding their time on the other side of the Vistula.

A different approach is taken by J. J. Szczepański, whose novel on the September catastrophe, *Polish Autumn*, a painstakingly exact description of the wanderings of an artillery unit across the Polish countryside in 1939, is thought to be one of the best works of fiction on the subject. Szczepański's short stories, published after 1956, are based mostly on his own experiences "from the woods," where he had fought in a partisan unit of the Home Army. Among these sad, psychologically motivated stories there is one, *Boots*, which subjects the legend of the Home Army to a serious revision. When Germany's defeat is becoming clear to all, some Vlasovites [3] come over to the Polish partisan unit. This creates a problem: they cannot be acknowledged as allies by the AK; neither can they be treated as proper prisoners. The "solution" desired by some partisans is carried out upon orders from the local commander of the AK battalion; the ex-Vlasovites are all shot and their excellent boots distributed among the poorly equipped partisans. Although Lieutenant Szary, the author's mouthpiece in the story, is aware of the fact that these Vlasovites (mostly Kalmuks) have committed atrocities against the Polish population, their treacherous annihilation weighs heavily on his conscience. For, in fact, these wretched strangers are shot to the last man not so much because of their probable war crimes, but

[3] General Vlasov was commander of troops formed by the Germans from Russian and other "Soviet" prisoners of war and used against the Red Army but also for "police actions" in occupied territories.

because their German-supplied boots are in such a good condition.

Though the stereotype of the German that was firmly imprinted in the Polish consciousness during the war did not change much after the fall of Berlin, with the passing of time his simplified image (with subtypes such as the haughty Prussian officer, the coldly murdering SS-man, and the bestial *Kapo* of the concentration camp) gave way to a less emotional treatment which made room for individual exceptions. There is Ahlgrim, the young Wehrmacht officer in *The Columbus Boys*, a chance acquaintance and almost a friend of Jerzy, who hates the war but dares not to desert. He sympathizes with the Polish resistance and, ironically, is fatally shot by an insurgent when taken prisoner during the Warsaw Uprising. As for German anti-Fascists and Communists, they appeared in Polish prose soon after the war in the stories of Tadeusz Borowski, probably the most effective chronicler of the dehumanizing effect of Auschwitz on the survivors; but one needed Borowski's experiences to be able to forgive yesterday's jailers and tormentors.

Another interesting example of Polish attitudes toward the Germans is Andrzej Brycht's *Dance in Hitler's Quarters* (*Dancing w kwaterze Hitlera*), first published in 1966. In Brycht's story a young man meets a girl while on a bicycle tour round the Mazovian lakes. They visit Hitler's wartime living quarters and air raid shelter at Kętrzyn (now a museum), and it is there that they meet their "friendly" German. He is a somewhat unlikely figure: he speaks fluent Polish and has an impeccable anti-Fascist record; he was a political prisoner during the war, taking part in the building of Hitler's air raid shelter at Kętrzyn; and, on top of it all, he is the proud owner of a shiny new Mercedes. Until now Brycht's youthful hero has had only vague ideas about the war and the occupation; now the German's gruesome reminiscences suddenly revive the nightmare of Hitler's New Order. The shock makes the young man physically ill, and in the meantime the friendly German takes Anka, his girlfriend, for a ride. Brycht cannot hate the German politically; all the same, he feels a passionate resentment against him. He has survived the war and even sports a Mercedes! Here Brycht (a rather second-rate writer otherwise) puts his finger on a sensitive spot of many Poles who regard the economic success of West Germany as a personal insult. After what they did to other nations, the Germans managed to reach a living standard which is beyond the most optimistic expectation of an ordinary citizen of People's Poland. Part of Brycht's sudden popularity derived from the fact that in his *Dance in Hitler's Quarters*, while registering some change in the Polish national stereotype of the Germans, he nevertheless reaffirmed the emotional content of this well-justified but increasingly anachronistic resentment.

Tadeusz Nowakowski complains in one of his essays about the striking Polonocentrism of Polish prose since the war. A few passages later he adds: "So far no work of art commensurate with what Poles lived through in the course of the last twenty years has been created and we don't know whether there will ever be such a work." [4] By and large, this is true, yet since 1956 there were some at least partly successful efforts to grasp and express this mass of accumulated experience. The literature of the Thaw, with its self-searching quest for the truth, coupled with accents of strong social criticism and satire, or "black literature," produced less Polonocentric and, on the whole, more universal models than the literature of the September campaign or that of the occupation. This is not to say, however, that the problems raised by the most prominent writers of this period were unconnected with the specific conditions of postwar Poland.

No single novel or story made such impact on public opinion as Adam Ważyk's famous *Poem for Adults;* but some successful prose works examining the effects of Stalinism were produced by three writers: Kazimierz Brandys, Marek Hłasko, and Andrzejewski. Strangely enough, it was the most moderate of the three, Brandys, whose *The Defense of "Granada,"* published in January 1956, provoked the loudest controversy. The theme of this long story is the disillusionment of the young generation, whose collective experience was characterized by the author in these words: "They belonged to a nation that might have perished. Nothing was left to them save a strong will to live." [5] As to their psychology, "they trusted none but themselves and were suspicious of everyone who had lived through the war differently than they had." [6] At the same time these young people were suffering from an "orphan-complex" and had a strong, though secret, craving for authority. Brandys recounts an ambitious venture of a group of these ex-fighters: they set up an experimental theater named "Granada" where they want to stage real, that is, revolutionary plays by authors like Bertold Brecht and Vladimir Mayakovski. Before long their ambitions clash with "higher inter-

[4] *Aleja dobrych znajomych* (London, 1968), 142.
[5] *Contemporary Polish Short Stories* (Warsaw, 1960), 71.
[6] *Ibid.,* 73.

ests" and their revolutionary zeal is shattered by institutional rigidity. The party's strategy and their own ideological mistakes are
explained to the actors by a certain Doctor Foul, a functionary in
the cultural department. Obeying his instructions leads first to bouts
of self-criticism and a tightening of discipline, later to frustration,
and still later to complete apathy; no artist can serve two masters at
the same time. After Stalin's death the actors realize that they were
indeed fooled by Doctor Foul, the Great Dialectician, since under
his—or the party's—influence they betrayed their friends, their art,
everything. There is nobody to blame and, anyway, "the Revolution
demands sacrifices," says Doctor Foul. Brandys gives the story a
fairly optimistic ending, but he leaves the main question unanswered:
were those sacrifices really necessary? Once such a question is asked,
it undermines the psychological fundamentals of Stalinism. Herein
lies the importance of *The Defense of "Granada."* Stalinist practices,
especially arbitrary arrests and imprisonments of Communists, were
condemned in Brandys's next book, *Matka Królów* (the English title
was changed to *Sons and Comrades*), though in this skillfully constructed novel as well as in his story about the "Granada," Brandys
took great care to stay within the limits of criticism sanctioned by
the new course of the Polish United Workers party (PUWP) and
Gomułka's speeches of 1956 and 1957. The main hero of *Matka
Królów* may find his arrest incomprehensible and his imprisonment
unjust but he never ceases to be a Communist, implicitly trusting the
party which, he believes, at one point will surely correct its mistakes.

This was not the view of Marek Hłasko, the angriest young man
of the Polish Thaw, whose grim and savage short stories, interlaced
with the humor and poetry of the Warsaw suburbs, were welcomed
by readers who were bored to tears by "production novels" meant
to be an authentic slice of Polish reality. Although some of his
shorter novels, e.g., *Next Stop—Paradise*, were criticized for their
crude sensationalism and hastily sketched characters,[7] his novel about
Stalinist Poland called *The Graveyard* belongs to the most characteristic and, for many, the most memorable writings of the period.
Unpublishable in Poland even in the relatively permissive atmosphere of 1957, it was eventually published in Paris in 1958. *The
Graveyard* is a charcoal sketch of a totalitarian society where human
life lost its meaning, and where people have lost their faith or integrity, or both. Thus the graveyards are the people themselves who

[7] Sandauer, 38.

buried their hopes, expectations, and—decency. At the same time, *The Graveyard* is a funny book, for Hłasko sees Polish reality as a farce. People get into jail, lose their jobs, or get sacked from the party for grotesque reasons; discussions and speeches at party meetings are so ludicrous that they are actually exhilarating. Hłasko's conclusions, implicit in the framework of the book, could be summed up roughly as follows: (a) this is a system that operates with humanistic slogans but actually dehumanizes everybody, (b) the only defense against it is complete cynicism, expressed in the anarchistic-individual revolt of "opting out." "I don't like *it*," says Kowalski to the policeman at the end, "it" meaning the system. Hłasko was actually consistent in carrying his revolt to the last conclusion. In 1958 he "opted out" himself, staying in the West where he wrote, among other things, a sort of autobiography, *Beautiful Twenty-year Olds* (*Piękni, dwudziestoletni*), a curious portrayal of a very impulsive young Pole who has played the role of the "noble bandit" all his life and made his exit as unexpectedly as he first had burst into the Polish literary scene in the mid-fifties.[8]

If Brandys's dilemma was typical for many Marxist intellectuals of the middle generation and Hłasko expressed the despair of young workers and students, Andrzejewski's development defies social classification of this kind. Andrzejewski, a Catholic moralist before the war—Georges Bernanos and Joseph Conrad are quoted as his models—became a chronicler of the *condition humaine* during the occupation which he witnessed in Warsaw. His vision of a new and more just social order resulted in *Ashes and Diamonds* which, in spite of its sympathy for the Maciejs of the AK, pleaded for peace and for the dissolution of the Underground. During the following years, between 1949 and 1954, Andrzejewski reached the nadir of his literary career: his masochistic "love-affair" with the party, culminating in his public advocacy of Zhdanov's Socialist Realism, wilted his creative powers. In retrospect, this seems to have been inevitable, for Andrzejewski's talent predestines him to a peculiar, indeed romantic, practitioner of existentialism. If, as Kijowski says, the central problem of Andrzejewski's writing is that of individual redemption,[9] it is clear that no ritualistic flagellation would ever have made a Socialist Realist out of Andrzejewski. The historical transition of the Thaw, on the other hand, gave him the opportunity for gradual de-

---

[8] Hłasko died in 1969 in Wiesbaden from an overdose of sleeping pills.
[9] Kijowski, 93.

tachment from his Marxist *persona* and return to his old themes. Faith and power, the delusions of faith and the illusion of power, became the center of his interest in and after 1956.

This phase produced two historical parables: *The Inquisitors* (*Ciemności kryją ziemię*) and *The Gates of Paradise*. The first of these novels is set in Spain in the heyday of the Inquisition, with such ideologically motivated protagonists as a Dominican monk and Torquemada. The Chief Inquisitor understandably believes in the "educational value" of fear as well as torture and manages to convince the deeply religious monk, Diego, that without discovering newer and newer heresies, the faith cannot be upheld in its purity. Diego joins the Inquisition and distinguishes himself in its service, only to understand much later the vulnerability of his faith and the futility of his sacrifice. *The Gates of Paradise* is an elegant, short, and ambiguous novel about the Children's Crusade of the thirteenth century. According to Andrzejewski, the motives of the children starting and joining in the crusade were not at all religious but stemmed from physical desire, envy, and jealousy; their driving force was not devotion but libido. Jerusalem, the tomb of Christ to be delivered "from the infidel Turk," stands here as the symbol of unattainable happiness and it might be interpreted as a symbol of all utopias, including communism. Artistically, *The Gates of Paradise* is more perfect than *The Inquisitors*, but its message is similar: excessive faith should not be trusted, because it either disguises a craving for power, or it will be terribly misused by the powers that be. Both books can be read as an indirect protest against ideological manipulation. They are good examples of the kind of pseudo-historical novel which has become popular since 1956: the setting is historical but the conflicts and their evaluation are thoroughly contemporary. Apart from Andrzejewski the possibilities of this genre have been successfully explored by Parnicki and Bocheński.

In 1968 Andrzejewski published a short but significant novel devoted to specific Polish problems. The central character in *Appeal* [10] is a psychopath undergoing treatment in a mental hospital. The characters of *Ashes and Diamonds* were exaggerated or idealized, but the general tenor of the book counseled moderation and appealed to sanity. Twenty years later Andrzejewski's development came to a full circle: now he diagnoses and describes the symptoms of Polish

---

[10] Andrzejewski sent his manuscript to the best Polish emigré publisher; his book stood no chance of being published in Poland. This is why *Appeal* was first published in Paris as *Apelacja* by the Instytut Literacki in 1968.

insanity. Marian Konieczny whose reminiscences and lengthy memorandum addressed to the first secretary of the Polish United Workers' party make up the larger part of the book is a paranoiac, suffering from a mania of persecution. His tortuously meandering autobiography (which is a fairly typical biography of a man of his generation) provides the clue to his madness. He was a partisan during the war in the AK and a policeman in the first few years following liberation. He was arrested by the security police in 1948 (and forced to testify in a political case against his girlfriend), and he became an employee in a state enterprise after his release. Here he worked devotedly, even too devotedly, for socialism. He kept personal files on his colleagues which by 1956 made him very unpopular. He lost his job and found a new one only after great difficulties. In a word, he was a man who had to fight for survival all his life, sometimes as a hunter, sometimes as one of the hunted. This predicament proves too much for him in the end, and he imagines a plot directed against himself by the counter-intelligence which obtains information from a mysterious electronic brain. In Konieczny's mind almost everyone is an agent of sinister powers, including the doctors who are trying to cure him. His only hope lies in the first secretary of the party; only he can give absolution and smash the ring of agents around the persecuted man. The tone of his letter to Gomułka is revealing: "I am thanking you, Citizen, the First Secretary, from the depths of my heart and I am making a solemn vow that I shall try to serve People's Poland and the Government with all my strength, with devotion and efficiency, in the name of the Father and Son and the Holy Ghost. Amen." [11]

Andrzejewski's book would read like a parody, if it were not so true to reality. Unfortunately, his psychopath symbolizes and, to a certain extent, expresses the state of Polish society in 1968. This is more than mere disillusionment in the workings of power, a constant theme in Polish literature since the mid-fifties. Konieczny's thoughts vacillate between fear and incomprehension: he had fought against the Germans, trying all his life to be a good patriot and a faithful executor of the state's will; and yet, no one seems to like or understand him. He is alienated from the world of normal human beings. It is his alienation more than anything else that causes this breakdown and drives him to a state of paranoia. He cannot understand for what he is being punished. It is immaterial that he calls his imag-

[11] Andrzejewski, *Apelacja*, 102.

inary persecutors "counter-intelligence"—they could be called
Freemasons, Jews, or revisionists as well; what is important is his
unshakable belief in a myth, that of a colossal plot of "agents," of
sinister elements. The crisis year of the Gomułka regime was 1968.
Although the regime weathered the crisis, the compromise on which
it was based has been badly shaken, if not destroyed. Andrzejewski
knows that at least a part of Polish society accepted the official version of events of March 1968 and that no rational argument would
appeal to people who are capable of accepting half-truths and distor-
tions of such magnitude. Konieczny feels that he is not alone in being wronged: "the injustice committed against me is not just the
private case of an individual, it has a broader aspect." [12] In our opinion, Andrzejewski's psychopath stands for the paranoic fears and
incomprehension affecting large segments of the party apparatus as
well as that of society. This general state is connected with the
question of responsibility for economic mismanagement and for social inequality in present-day Poland, so that by inference he is the
symbol of forces that initiated and carried out the anti-intellectual
purge, with its undertones of a witch hunt, in 1968. At the same
time, Andrzejewski generates compassion for this man whose illness
is largely a consequence of his harrowing and degrading experiences,
accumulated in a lifetime, experiences resulting from Poland's
national predicament. *Appeal* is an extreme book that creates a national atmosphere in which almost anything is possible, while symbolically evoking the most depressing year in recent Polish history.

CZECHOSLOVAKIAN FICTION

In Czechoslovakia as well, the war was a collective experience,
exceedingly hard to forget. Czech and Slovak literature in the first
few years after the war was deliberately overstating the share of
these two nations in the struggle against the Germans, although most
observers realized that "disregarding the Slovak National Rising,
Czechoslovakia did nothing significant to further her own liberation,
except for the political campaigns undertaken in exile; her active
share in the defeat of Nazism was the minimum." [13] Overstatement,
then, was a form of compensation: the Prague uprising that lasted
only a few days and could not be meaningfully compared with the

[12] *Ibid.*, 70.
[13] Ladislav Mňačko, *The Seventh Night* (London, 1969), 29.

holocaust of Warsaw was immortalized in Jan Drda's *The Silent Barricade* and given maximum publicity at a time when no truthful account could yet be published about the Warsaw Uprising. As for the Slovak national uprising of 1944, it served as a great face-saving device for Slovak authors who loathed to admit the deep involvement of the Slovak puppet state in Hitler's aggressive war and his New European Order.

During the same period, Czech and Slovak fiction produced naïvely romantic or excessively heroic positive characters and uniformly wicked negative ones. It took years before the Germans could be spoken of not as a species but as a group of individuals (some cruel, others stupid, still others only obedient) who were forced into a senseless and terrible adventure; it also took years before the Russians could be depicted without overidealization (the latter tendency often being only camouflage for a badly suppressed feeling of guilt). In this, incidentally, lay one of Škvorecky's cardinal sins; in *The Cowards*, the soldiers of the Red Army, arriving in Kostelec, appear to Danny as "dusty, sweating, wild and barbarous Scythians," very alien and yet rather attractive in their strangeness. Though Škvorecky wrote his novel in 1948–1949 and published it only nine years later, the "irreverent" picture of the liberation, the alleged defamation of such terms as "fatherland" and "revolution," still made him a target of violent attacks in 1959.

Since then *The Cowards* has seen several successive editions totalling 100,000 copies. This enormous success was partly due to the extraordinary publicity which the book received as a result of its public exorcism by irate officials of the Czechoslovak Writers' Association. On the other hand, Škvorecky's book was probably the first to describe the last days of the German occupation and the first muddled days of liberation in deliberately nonheroic or "realistic" terms that appealed to the public. His first and foremost sin against socialist literary convention was the lack of a "positive" hero as the central character of the book: Danny, the young jazz musician, is nothing more than a nice boy with the usual dreams and ambitions of adolescence. He wants, of course, freedom but resents the false theatricality that surrounds the birth of freedom. Danny has very little use for those respectable citizens of Kostelec who had been on quite good terms with the occupation authorities until the twenty-fourth hour, when they reappeared posing as unflinching patriots. He prefers the English to the Russians and does not feel guilty about it (after all he does come from a middle-class family and speaks tolerable English), but he accepts the Russians as long as they let him play his saxophone. His main preoccupations are girls and jazz, but this does not make him unpatriotic; to the contrary, he is the only one who, with a friend, actually does something noteworthy in the mock-uprising of this little Czech town. Škvorecky's slangy, deliberately sloppy, amusing, and somewhat melancholy style reflects Danny's world, and the structure of Danny's inner monologues follows the musical structure of the blues. The young jazz musician in his thoughts and casual conversations with colleagues and townspeople, punctuated by mild curses and jokes, ignored Socialist Realist norms and upset critics to the point of calling the author "decadent" and "a literary teddy-boy." Only a few years later *The Cowards* was hailed as the first novel of a new de-heroizing trend not devoid of relevant social criticism: the respectable citizens of Kostelec, whom Danny dislikes, are representing, after all, the secret disease of the old and the new republic—opportunism.

A similar kind of "positive de-heroization" also took place in Hrabal's *A Close Watch on the Trains* (1965). Hrabal's hero, the young railway apprentice Miloš Hrma, is not a highly motivated man, at least not in terms of patriotic rhetorics. Whereas Danny's thoughts revolve around good jazz and the most effective way to impress his teenage ideal, Hrabal's young man is miserable because of his failure in love (in medical terms *ejaculatio praecox*), which he regards as a kind of terrible disease. Luckily, a female Resistance worker helps young Hrma in proving that he is a man, after all. This gives a tremendous boost to the lad's self-confidence and makes him blow up a German ammunition train. There is a deep psychological parallel between the two achievements: both acts are expressions of virility. Again, Hrabal simply ignores the conventional positive heroes of Soviet and postwar Czech literature; the microcosm of Czech society at the little railway station of *A Close Watch on the Trains* is part of an unlikely fairy-tale; it is fantastic and commonplace, idyllic and grotesque at the same time. His gallery of characters includes a pigeon-breeding station-master and an eccentric dispatcher whose protest against the boredom of life is manifested in stamping the bare buttocks of the lady-telegraphist with all available stamps at the station. This, as we are reminded by the one and only pro-Nazi Czech official in the novel, is tantamount to desecration of German, the state language. Though hardly an act of sabotage, it is enough to frustrate the pro-Nazi official who exclaims in despair: "Czechs! You know what they are? Grinning beasts!" [14]

In Hrabal's book the tragedy of the war and the occupation, even the devastating Allied air raid against Dresden, are only a background against which Miloš Hrma is trying to become a man. This does not mean that Hrabal is not concerned with the war: the little railway station is full of trains coming and going to the front, and young Hrma comes into contact with all sorts of Germans. His reactions to them are psychologically sound, though hardly typical. At one point when two SS men come very close to killing him, he is stunned by their extraordinary good looks; later, when he encounters some dazed civilian refugees from Dresden, he cannot feel pity for them—they should not have started the war. Yet by the end of the story when a mortally wounded Miloš is lying in a ditch with an equally badly wounded German soldier, he feels sorry for him and shortens his sufferings. These few examples might indicate what an impressively wide range of feelings is displayed on the pages of this short but well-written and oddly touching novel.

Both Škvorecky and Hrabal are typically Czech authors; what makes them part and parcel of Czech tradition is their fundamental humanity and quiet, wry sense of humor. Both relish human weaknesses and are fascinated by the eccentric and the bizarre. All this is very different from the Polish and also from the Slovak tradition. Slovak literature after the war was at least as much addicted to facile heroics as its Czech counterpart; this was especially explicit in the first novels about the National Uprising and the partisan movement. The serious re-examination of wartime experiences in Slovak literature began only in the mid-fifties. Alfonz Bednár was the first to use a different, more psychological approach, showing in his collection of stories, *Hours and Minutes* (*Hodiny a minúty*) (1960), the complexity of heroism and man's basic loneliness in "existential" situations. He was followed by others, namely by Vladimir Mináč, Dominik Tatarka, and Ladislav Mňačko, whose work between 1958 and 1961 introduced a note of skepticism and a tendency toward de-heroization into Slovak prose.[15]

Mňačko's *Death Is Called Engelchen* (*Smrť sa volá Engelchen*) (1961) was perhaps the most important single novel of this "new wave." Probing into the problem of treason and guilt, Mňačko man-

[14] Bohumil Hrabal, *A Close Watch on the Trains* (London, 1968), 57.
[15] Milan Pišút (ed.), *Dejiny Slovenskej Literatury* (Bratislava, 1962), 719.

aged to create a gripping account of the wartime activities of a partisan unit in Moravia near the Slovak border. This unit carries out sabotage tasks and keeps harassing the Germans until the tables are turned and Skorzeny's special troops launch a big manhunt in the mountains. Most people in Volodia's group (he is the narrator of the story) survive even this ordeal, but only at the horrible price of leaving their mountain village base Ploština defenseless. The Germans, tipped off by traitors, surprise and exterminate the entire male population of Ploština and burn the village. Volodia will not disown the responsibility for the fate of Ploština: "Each of us would carry the burden of guilt from this day on. Forever." [16] At one point the burden seems to be too much, and the seriously wounded Volodia momentarily loses his will to live. All those people had to die for one tactical mistake committed by the partisans! Volodia recovers from his wound, but in a sense he will never recover from his *crise de conscience:* he will remain an emotional cripple of the war.

Another such victim is Martha, Volodia's lover who, while pretending to work for the Gestapo, in fact works for the partisans. She is Jewish, and the complex and dangerous nature of her work drives her daily to the limits of psychological endurance. She survives the war but something is broken inside her; she cannot face new life in Czechoslovakia and eventually commits suicide. Martha is the victim of a double guilt complex: she cannot forgive herself for surviving both Auschwitz and the massacre of Ploština.

Mňačko feels an even more violent revulsion for the typical turncoat who had collaborated with the Germans and now comes forward to embrace the Russians than does Škvorecky. Suddenly Czechoslovakia is full of fake partisans and unlikely "heroes" of the Resistance. Mňačko's Kroupa is one of them; he even tries to worm his way into the Communist party. The narrator of *Death Is Called Engelchen* fears the spineless careerism of such characters and with good reason. He also resents the sight of Czech army officers on the streets who, after the liberation, can be seen everywhere in well-preserved prewar uniforms. Where had they been during the occupation and the fighting?

It is worthwhile to have a look at Mňačko's Germans. Again, much of the original postwar prototype has changed. One of the most dramatic conflicts of the novel takes place in Volodia's mind

---

[16] Ladislav Mňačko, *Death Is Called Engelchen* (Prague, 1961), 256.

when he has to execute a German captain whom the partisans had captured in the woods. The German is a quiet, intelligent type who is just reading *The Forsyte Saga;* nonetheless, he has to be shot. Mňačko confesses: "In the final analysis it was a horrible thing to kill—even Germans." [17] Later on, when two German deserters join Volodia's unit, it is interesting to see how they win, in spite of a great deal of initial suspicion, the respect and sympathy of the unit, including that of the Yugoslav Peter, the most feared and passionate German-killer of them all. [18]

As in Poland, the second theme that involved a rethinking of values and a critical examination of the national character was the human price of Czechoslovakia's "socialist transformation," meaning, of course, the Stalinist period. While in Poland the year 1956 meant a moment of truth for the regime, followed by a reshuffle in the party and state apparatus, in Czechoslovakia (notwithstanding a few critical speeches at the 1956 Writers' Congress) everything remained the same. Was this the result of a historical inertia of the Czech nation, a late consequence of the Munich sell-out, or else of "Schweikism" that allegedly became a second nature to Czechs? It was only in the early sixties that the relaxation of political controls over literature led to the slow emergence of the modern Czech novel, the demands of Socialist Realism being conveniently forgotten. The Slovaks freed themselves from this ideological straight-jacket a few years earlier than their Czech colleagues, but after 1963 it was the Czechs' turn. Criticism of Czechoslovakia's postwar development could take a variety of forms. Taking an interest in the eccentric and the socially marginal, Hrabal revealed in his prose an indirect rejection of Zhdanovist literary norms; the same holds true of describing everyday experiences and frustrations in terms of the fantastic or of the grotesque, as found in the writings of Karel Michal and Ivan Vyskočil. In other cases the criticism was more direct, though it was usually couched in a form which stressed the irrational, humorless, and self-righteously narrow-minded nature of the bureaucratic regime. Such were the lines on which many writers of the younger generation, including Václav Havel and Ivan Klíma,

[17] *Ibid.,* 213.

[18] One of the most attractive figures of *Engelchen* is Nikolai, a Russian officer, parachuted to organize the partisan unit. However, Mňačko's latest book, *The Seventh Night*, shows that after the Soviet occupation of Czechoslovakia in 1968, his unconditional pro-Russian sentiments have been subject to serious reconsideration.

attacked the aberrations of the system, but this approach also characterized the later works of such writers of the middle generation as Škvorecky, Ludvík Vaculík, and Milán Kundera.

Škvorecky's short story "Song of Forgotten Years" is a case in point. As he did in *The Cowards*, here again Škvorecky measures the freedom-content of a regime by its attitude toward jazz. The narrator remembers how he and his comrades playing in an army ensemble got into trouble for "doing a swing arrangement of the well-known Army song 'Marshal Buddony.'" [19] This happened in 1951 when jazz was once again forced underground as the music of "spiritual decadence." Škvorecky's hero would have forgotten the whole amusing episode had he not met Venus, a girl singer from the Prague Conservatoire who used to sing with his army ensemble. Venus is now married, has children, and though she has not given up singing, the twist-fans find her old-fashioned. She could have been a hit in the fifties; now she is just another aging singer, hardly appreciated by the young. "If you ask me," she confides to her old friend, "we got born a little before our time." [20] Behind Škvorecky's nostalgia lies a resentment: he resents that neither he nor his generation was allowed to live in such a way as to make the most of their lives. This is not a "bourgeois" resentment, for it is not the end of the world or the destruction of prewar norms which saddens Škvorecky, but the unnecessary stupidity and philistinism of the new regime.

The millenarian fanaticism of the fifties is attacked in a similar vein but more vindictively and with a gloomier, more savage irony by Milán Kundera. His novel *The Joke* [21] is the story of Ludvik Jahn who was expelled from the party and from the university for sending a funny and deliberately silly postcard bearing a mock political slogan to a girlfriend. Fifteen years later Jahn tries to revenge himself on the party hack responsible for his expulsion and political degradation by seducing his wife. The revenge backfires, as the party hack, now a reformed and "enlightened" functionary, left his wife years ago; at the same time a problem occurs when the deserted wife falls in love with Jahn, her seducer. At this point Jahn realizes the futility of revenge and the grotesque nature of the situation into

[19] George Theiner (ed.), *New Writing in Czechoslovakia* (London, 1969), 72.
[20] *Ibid.*, 79.
[21] The English translation of *The Joke* was mutilated and the text rearranged by the translators or the publisher, Macdonald, an incomprehensible practice which provoked an energetic protest from Kundera in the *Times Literary Supplement*.

which he maneuvered himself: "Then I realized how feeble it was to annul my own joke when throughout my life I was involved in a joke which was all-embracing, unfathomable and utterly irrevocable." [22] The worst joke of history is a revolution betrayed, a movement of liberation turning into its exact opposite.

According to Ernst Fischer, humor for Czechs is the antidote for the horrible. *The Joke*, with one exception, has no purely tragic characters: their muddled lives and irrational reactions to outside events, including Helena's suicide attempt, are on the whole tragicomic. Kundera's heroes are all deformed in one way or another, the only difference being that some of them chose their particular form of deformation whereas others did not. For all its comic episodes Kundera's book is a sad inventory of the failures of a generation and of a system that had promised to make human life more precious, more worth living. Though Kundera is more interested in situations than in social types or milieus, perhaps one is justified in calling *The Joke* the *Lost Illusions* of Czech communism.

If in Kundera's novel blame is apportioned between individuals and the system, in Mňačko's last novel, which was still published in Czechoslovakia, the spotlight is firmly trained upon a single man. This man, however, happens to be the former head of the government. The framework of this novel, *The Taste of Power* (1967), is the description of the dead statesman's funeral and the sequence of thoughts which this event recalls in the mind of a former friend, a photographer. "What is remarkable in this story," writes Max Hayward in his foreword, "is not the gradual corruption of an idealist by the fruits of office—this is universal—, but the sickening fear which gradually makes the 'statesman' into a craven figure almost devoid of tragic quality." [23] The photographer's memory recalls the moral decline and disintegration of this strong-willed man step by step, in sharp close-ups and quick, naturalistic flashbacks. Mňačko's technique, his directness and almost pamphleteering sharpness in this book, grew out of the common frustration of Slovak intellectuals ruled and terrorized by such unscrupulous political bosses as Viliam Široký, Karol Bacilek, Václav Kopecký, and Pavol David; compared to these, Novotny was almost a gentleman. But the main problem of *The Taste of Power* is not the bad character of this or that political leader, but their shared incompetence, their collective inability to govern in a human way: "We weren't prepared for it," comments

---

[22] Milán Kundera, *The Joke* (London, 1969), 271.
[23] Ladislav Mňačko, *The Taste of Power* (London, 1967), 8.

Mňačko on power, "we didn't know how to handle it and we still don't." [24] Since August 1968 Mňačko has been living outside Czechoslovakia, but his judgment has not been refuted by facts. On the other hand, Czech and Slovak writers are forced back into the same political conditions which had made them rebel against the Soviet-installed Novotny regime. In the meantime, the problem of "how to use power" remains unanswered.

HUNGARIAN FICTION

Postwar Hungarian prose reminds us of a boa constrictor which swallowed a large chunk of meat and is trying very hard to digest it. In other words, its main problem is the sheer size and poor digestibility of its heterogeneous prey of themes: the war, the radical social changes that followed liberation, culminating in a local but particularly tough version of Communist dictatorship, the revolution of 1956, and the period of repression that led up to the consolidation of the Kádár regime. All this has proved to be too much for a literature traditionally less strong in prose than in poetry. Consequently, it should not strike us as unusual that the interwar period still provides the majority of themes for Hungarian prose writers. Sharply critical, or half-epic, half-lyrical treatments of prewar society still constitute the most popular vehicle in recent Hungarian fiction, as the enormous success of such writers as Magda Szabó and Endre Fejes has shown. The fifties witnessed ambitious attempts to draw a comprehensive picture of prewar reality from the point of view of the working class, as exemplified by Tibor Déry, and of the poor peasantry, as seen in Péter Veres and Pál Szabó. After 1956 writers like Magda Szabó and László Németh came to the fore with novels concentrating on psychological conflicts of small-town, middle-class heroes, and Endre Fejes wrote *The Scrap-yard* (*Rozsdatemető*) (1962), the anti-saga of a half-proletarian, half-peasant family from a Budapest suburb. Though Németh and Szabó are writers of greater stature than Fejes, the author of *The Scrap-yard* managed to define a specific Hungarian problem by means of an up-to-date literary technique. This is the problem of the "little man" muddling through life and history, never being able to understand the causes and results of wars, dictatorships, social stagnation or transformation. Indifference to politics, lack of civic courage, naïve providentialism

[24] *Ibid.*, 144.

coupled with extreme parochialism are the chief characteristics of the Hábetlers, the family-nucleus of the novel. It is not surprising that social progress was throttled in Hungary for so long, implies Fejes; there were far too many Hábetlers.

Fejes's short novel with its cool, matter-of-fact style and dramatic flashes of emotion, together with an equally short novel by Tibor Cseres, *Cold Days* (*Hideg napok*), started a new trend in Hungarian literature when it came out in 1964. *Cold Days* was probably the first prose work in Hungary since the war which exposed the problem of guilt and responsibility in clear-cut, nonpropagandistic terms. Here a few words should be said about Hungary's wartime role. Hungary was Hitler's reluctant ally until 1944 when German troops occupied the country in an attempt to foil Horthy's plan for a separate peace treaty. It was liberated by the Red Army, but the social and political significance of the liberation was obscured in the eyes of most Hungarians by Russian atrocities in 1945 and even more so by the continued stationing of Russian troops on Hungarian soil. For instance, before August 1968 there had been no Russian troops in Czechoslovakia. As to the war itself, Communist historiography blamed the Hungarian upper classes for everything; the man in the street, on the other hand, could see only treason. He saw Hungary's involvement in the war as an unsuccessful attempt to rectify the injustices of the Versailles-Trianon peace treaty, which had assigned two-thirds of historical Hungary to the neighboring states and blamed the Germans as well as the Russians for the war crimes and Hungary's postwar difficulties.

The popular judgment that blamed foreign powers for most of Hungary's troubles was at least partly correct; nonetheless, there was much for which Hungarians themselves were responsible. The worst was the Novi Sad affair. In 1942 the Hungarian army and gendarmerie in a round-up claimed to be an "anti-partisan operation" massacred thousands of defenseless civilians in the mixed Serbian-Jewish-Hungarian town of Ujvidék. This episode forms the background to Cseres's story in which four Hungarian soldiers, of whom only one took part in the actual executions, are held responsible for the terrible atrocities. The four men are awaiting trial in a prison cell after the war and through their inner monologues and occasional conversations the story of the crime unfolds. They are neither Fascists nor brutes, yet they are all guilty, and responsible.

Cseres himself, commenting on his book, said: "only by the free confession and discussion of each painful truth can the peoples co-existing in Central Europe hope to abate their nationalist passion and pride." [25] *Cold Days* was a step forward toward the ideal of such a Danubian coexistence. Although he caused a nationwide controversy by exposing Hungary's greatest wartime crime, Cseres destroyed a popular myth, "We are less guilty than others"; but at the same time, he established a moral right to condemn any excesses committed against Hungarians in other countries in the name of rival nationalisms.[26] Also, the book may have promoted a redefinition of patriotism in the minds of the young—Cseres showed them that unthinking nationalism leads to inhuman reactions which by their very nature are counterproductive and self-defeating.

Cold Days, though unusual in its theme, was typical of the Hungarian novel of the sixties which one critic defined as "problem-seeking." [27] In contrast to the novel of the fifties in which the individual was submerged in the tide of a great social movement and subordinated himself to the collective aims of the day, the new novel of such writers as Déry, Cseres, Ferenc Sánta, and others was either trying to define the meaning of "the human essence" of the individual, or it was probing into the unexplored depths of recent history. Ferenc Sánta, the most promising writer of the younger generation which emerged around 1954–1955, combined both tendencies, setting his novel *The Fifth Seal* (*Az ötödik pecsét*) (1963) in 1944 when, after Horthy's unsuccessful attempt to end the war, Fascist gangs of the Arrow Cross [28] took over in Hungary. Sánta's protagonists are simple, average people, and, on the whole, apolitical citizens; but in these extraordinary times even they have to make a decision, even they have to stand up and be counted. Like Cseres, Sánta places his people in extreme situations where they are forced to reveal their essential selves. Nearly all of these meek and insignificant little people grow into heroes in the hour of trial; only one, a watchmaker, breaks down and commits a symbolic act of treason which saves his life. We know that the watchmaker is sheltering

[25] *New Hungarian Quarterly* 9, no. 32: 11.

[26] There are sizable Hungarian minorities in all neighboring countries. After the war anti-Hungarian outbreaks or campaigns took place in nearly all of them.

[27] Dezső Tóth (ed.), *Élő irodalom* (Budapest, 1969), 394.

[28] The Arrow Cross was a Hungarian Fascist movement at one point suppressed by Horthy but supported by the Germans; it came to power for a brief spell after Horthy's arrest by the Germans in October 1944. The Arrow Cross was responsible for atrocities against Jews and people active in the resistance.

Jewish children in his home and his death would probably mean theirs as well. This certainly extenuates the watchmaker's sin, though it does not absolve him; all one can say is that his choice was tragic by definition. Sánta's message is, nevertheless, different from that of the existentialists. For him the split between individual goodness and society's evil, between freedom and power, is almost absolute. Man is crippled in his freedom and severely limited in his choices by the vast mechanism of external, inhuman powers.

It is by no means accidental that individual responsibility became a central theme, almost a catchword of the Hungarian prose of the sixties. This was only to be expected after the undigested experience of a disastrous war and the social trauma of the brutal, arbitrary, and slogan-happy Communist dictatorship of the postwar years, now usually referred to as the Rákosi era.[29] The 1956 uprising, and its aftermath, also left behind considerable bitterness and apprehension. In consequence of all these events, the more ambitious Hungarian writers came to accept a paradox: totalitarian forces can destroy the individual without reason or justification, but the individual is responsible, at least for his own actions. He is condemned to choose. In the last analysis he cannot avoid a personal commitment. The validity of this paradox is demonstrated in Ferenc Sánta's career with amazing consistency. For after *The Fifth Seal*, where historical background still played a crucial part in the exposition of the final conflict, he wrote *The Traitor*, a pseudo-historical novel concerned entirely with the problem of the individual's responsibility for himself and for social progress.

If *The Fifth Seal* idealized to a certain extent the decency and the inner reserves of the common man, *The Traitor* (*Az áruló*) moved toward psychological realism and could be described as a successful attempt in de-heroization. Its framework is entirely contemplative and intellectual: the writer "invites" four characters from another age, the time of the Hussite wars, for a night of argument. His guests are Eusebius, a hedonist priest; Václav, a Hussite warrior; Jan Zitomir, the emperor's soldier; and a peasant who buries both Václav and Zitomir after their last, fatal struggle. Which of them is the traitor? The answer, recalling Kurosawa's brilliant *Rashomon*, is that all are traitors to some extent, for each of them is guilty either of the sin of indifference or violence. Indifference and violence are

---

[29] Mátyás Rákosi was Hungarian party leader until 1956. He died in the USSR in 1970.

the two qualities which Sánta detests most.[30] Consequently in *The Traitor* the cynical hedonism of Eusebius equals total indifference to society and gets the least sympathetic treatment. Zitomir—though Sánta gives a hearing to his appeals to reason and moderation—is on the side of reaction and is also judged severely. Václav may be objectively right, but his fanaticism makes the author's nerves bristle. Sánta would prefer to side with the peasant, everyone's underdog, but he cannot, for the peasant is passive and fearful of change, and if it were up to him, the world would not move an inch forward. In the final analysis, Sánta's judgment is certainly ambiguous. He is for the historical process of liberation; he is for the revolution but with serious qualifications. When the revolution violates elementary moral laws and tramples down human dignity, Sánta withdraws his support. This potentiality is implied in his act of conscious choice.

As in Poland and in Czechoslovakia, so in Hungary the critical re-examination of the recent past brought interesting literary results. The Hungarian peculiarity of this trend, however, is its dramatic lack of continuity in the years 1957–1961. After the 1956 eruption of social criticism, the Kádár regime first suppressed this trend, encouraging only the Berkesi-type fiction about the tribulations of Communists imprisoned by Rákosi; it was only in the early sixties that writers of such different backgrounds and allegiances as Déry, Erzsébet Galgóczi, Sánta, and György Moldova could return to this half-abandoned theme. In 1956 Tibor Déry was the most prominent of the critics. His short stories—"Love," "Behind the Brick Wall," "Encounter"—and his short novel *Niki* showed his grave concern for the crimes of the Rákosi regime and his deep dissatisfaction with the state of Hungarian socialism. *Niki*'s main characters are a Communist mining engineer and his dog; whatever happens to her master affects Niki. Both the engineer and the dog are manipulated by mysterious outside forces, the logic of which they are in no position to understand. The engineer is arrested and jailed by the Communist authorities for no good reason; the dog loses her master for no reason. At the end of the story Niki quietly dies, perhaps—as the engineer's wife thinks—"for want of liberty." Her life and death are symbolic; creative freedom cannot flourish in a society which is manipulated in such a manner. In the tears the engineer sheds for Niki when he is released from jail and returns as a sad and

[30] See Sánta's statement in *Látogatóban, Kortárs magyar irók vallomásai* (Budapest, 1968), 389.

a broken man, he mourns his wasted years as well as his wasted opportunities.

Between 1956 and 1963 no book of Tibor Déry was published in Hungary. He himself was jailed by the Kádár regime and released only in 1960. Déry recalls episodes from this period in his loosely composed, richly autobiographical narrative *No Verdict* (1969), one of the most important books of recent years. In parts of *No Verdict* Déry gave a subjective justification of his role in the reform movement of 1956 which preceded the anti-Stalinist movement and, by extension, anti-Soviet revolution. "I felt myself responsible...for the whole past period (the Rákosi era) and what made me happy was that I could begin to pay back my debt." [31] Many "revisionists" in Poland and Czechoslovakia had similar feelings; but in 1969 Hungary was the only one of the three countries where a former revisionist and ex-prisoner could make such a statement in print.

The objective justification for 1956 (not for the lunatic fringe but for the driving force of the revolution) was left to someone other than Déry—to Ferenc Sánta. His *Twenty Hours* (*Húsz óra*) (1964) is in some respects the most significant Hungarian novel of the decade. It is a synthesis of views on the central event of recent Hungarian history, the 1956 revolution in the Hungarian countryside.

In *Twenty Hours* Sánta's premises are not those of intellectual morality as they are in his other two novels. Here he follows the convention of "the literature of facts." He spends twenty hours in a Hungarian village on something like a fact-finding mission, tirelessly talking to people, interviewing them about the events of 1956 which they see through the prism of their personal involvement. As people put forward their very different views, the conflict unfolds in its totality. *Totality* is a key word here, for Sánta feels that everyone should be given a hearing, even the most blindly dogmatic or the most reactionary participant of this conflict. This method results in a new kind of realism, a multilateral realism which will, as in *The Traitor*, eventually reveal its strongest truth, not by ignoring, but rather by superseding other, more particular, less relevant truths.

Twenty Hours is a definite break with the schematic, simplified interpretation of right and wrong in the history of the Hungarian political novel. Sánta is looking for an answer to the question: what

---

[31] Tibor Déry, *Itélet nincs* (Budapest, 1969), 540.

made the popular uprising of 1956 possible? The life of old Balogh, formerly a landless peasant, is a case in point. As were most poor peasants in the village, he was a Communist, but only until 1952, when he returned his party card as a protest against official policy which put unbearable burdens on the backs of the peasantry. This policy was repudiated during Imre Nagy's first premiership in 1953, but Nagy was soon removed from his position and the wounds inflicted in the Stalinist period remained. In 1956 Balogh and many other peasants wanted to settle accounts with those functionaries who had humiliated and insulted them in the name of higher interests, in the name of the Communist party.

Director-Joe, Balogh's old friend, is also a Communist. When he is almost killed by a bullet fired by old Balogh, he experiences a deep crisis. It is not the former count, the class enemy, who wants his blood, but his own folk. He understands that the Communists lost the confidence of the village poor, in the old days their most determined supporters. The recognition of this truth causes Joe to renounce revenge, but he cannot prevent the vengeful return to the village of former party secretary Varga after a successful Russian intervention and the arbitrary murder of another peasant. All he can do is protect Balogh and the rest of the village from Varga and his ilk, and work as before, only more patiently, for the peasants, hoping for a better government policy.

Both Balogh and Joe are characters close to Sánta's heart. For him the tragedy of 1956 is that these two people have to face each other in an almost deadly conflict. Although the objective scale is slightly tipped in Joe's favor (after all he stands for all the social reforms of the Socialist regime, for "people's power"), subjectively Sánta accepts Balogh's arguments. He knows as well as old Balogh that the original Communist platform after the war had not mentioned forced collectivization, a system of compulsory deliveries, the impoverishment of the few individual peasants who resisted the collectivization drive, and he is not afraid to put these arguments into Balogh's mind during his post-1956 confrontation with Joe: "Why is he talking about factories, schools, new towns when one's honor, one's integrity, one's pride was trampled into the mud? ... The lords were plundering in their own country, but here we were told that the power belonged to us and yet a man's honor was treated like dirt!" [32]

A man's honor—perhaps we are not mistaken when we call this

----

[32] Ferenc Sánta, *Húsz óra* (Budapest, 1964), 237.

concept crucial in the context of Hungarian socialism. Sánta's "honor" has nothing in common with the exaggerated and anachronistic concept of honor cultivated by the prewar Hungarian or Polish gentleman; it is simply one's self-respect and the respect paid by others to decent men. Sánta is pleading here for "socialism with a human face," for a social order which, though striving for equality, has enough respect and good will toward the individual to allow him to live his own life, to develop his creative faculties in his own way. For all its strong critical accents, Sánta's novel nurtures the hope of a different kind of human relations, of a different, more human kind of socialism.

CONCLUSION

Throughout this study we have been concentrating on the two main themes of contemporary East European literatures: the Second World War and the social and political problems of the postwar period. This was done at the price of some simplification. Although we tried to discuss war fiction in detail, particular themes such as the persecution and tragedy of the Jews had to be by-passed or cursorily treated. Again, it should be stressed that neither the pseudo-historical novel nor the self-critical and socio-critical fiction describing Stalinist terror in Eastern Europe could give a complete picture of the societies concerned, or indicate the directions in which they are now moving. As a general tendency, we could point out here the emergence of a trend of semidocumentary, semifictitious prose with a sociological or individually psychological bias, a prose almost devoid of ideological or moralistic interpretation. Such literature, it seems, is closer to the style of life of the young people and, indeed, the problems of this new trend are often related to the "conflict of generations" or to the feeling of nonbelonging in Socialist society, the society of grown-ups—a common enough phenomenon amongst the long-haired, guitar-strumming descendants of partisans, functionaries, and ex-revolutionaries.

Coming back to the main differences between the contemporary prose of Poland, Czechoslovakia, and Hungary, it is clear that the war and the imminent postwar period as a literary theme is still most in evidence in Poland. Inasmuch as postwar Polish fiction stresses the themes of frustration and disillusionment, it returns to this period regarding it, perhaps subconsciously, as the root of all evil. Another trait of this prose is its inability to grasp life in all its relations, its never-ceasing struggle with grievances, complexes, and nightmares. On the other hand, its marked fragmentariness and anti-realism make contemporary Polish prose the most Western of the three literatures discussed.

Czech, Slovak, and Hungarian writers are also engaged in a struggle with the ghost of the past, but they recall and stress different things. There is a basic guilt complex underlying postwar Czech fiction. The feeling of guilt for the post-Munich capitulation and the minimal role that Czechoslovakia played in its own liberation, coupled with the guilt felt by Communists for Stalinism, all make modern Czech prose extremely introspective. What extenuates the severity of self-judgment is a peculiar Czech sense of humor. It is a melancholy sort of irony—*melankolické anekdoty* was the subtitle of an earlier book by Kundera—which makes Czech fiction the most human and, in a positive sense, most old-fashioned of these literatures.

Finally, contemporary Hungarian prose is distinguished less by its sophistication than by its sincerity and willingness to come to terms with Hungary's difficult past. Hungarian writers went farthest in their criticism of national attitudes and stereotypes, stating with the greatest force the law of individual responsibility which does not know classes, religious differences, or state boundaries. Yet it is difficult to measure the real impact of writers like Déry, Németh, Sánta, and Cseres on the nonintellectual reading public. It may be argued that this impact is only skin-deep and that the dramatic seriousness of Hungarian prose in exploring new themes and redefining moral imperatives has so far been ineffective against native "Hábetlerism" which wants only to exploit, never understand, history.

BIBLIOGRAPHY

GENERAL WORKS IN ENGLISH, ANTHOLOGIES

Contemporary Polish Short Stories, selected by Andrzej Kijowski. Warsaw: Polonia, 1960.

Gömöri, George, and Charles Newman (eds.). *New Writing of East Europe.* Chicago: Quadrangle Books, 1968. Poetry, prose, and essays are mixed in this anthology concentrating on Polish, Czechoslovak, Hungarian, and Yugoslav authors. It prints stories and prose excerpts by Bocheński, Déry, Gombrowicz, Hłasko, and Hrabal. See also George Gömöri's introduction, "Literature Deprophetized," 13–24.

Kuncewicz, Maria (ed.). *The Modern Polish Mind: An Anthology of*

Stories and Essays. Boston: Little, 1962. Also in American paperback. Kuncewicz's broad and, on the whole, representative selection includes fiction by Szczepański, Zawieyski, Rudnicki, Dąbrowska, Różewicz, Woroszylski, and others.

Miłosz, Czesław. *The History of Polish Literature.* New York: Macmillan, 1969. Of special relevance are pp. 488–510 devoted to postwar Polish prose.

Theiner, George (ed.). *New Writing in Czechoslovakia.* London: Penguin, 1969. The editor wrote a short but informative introduction to this volume, which made available for the first time stories by Škvorecký, Blažková, Pecka, Michal, Kundera, Kliment, Výskočil, and others in English.

Wieniewska, Celina (ed.). *Polish Writing of Today.* London: Penguin, 1967. A paperback in the "Writing Today" series, this anthology prints mainly texts of the younger generation, including prose pieces by Bocheński, Kabatc, Grynberg, Stanuch, and Nowakowski.

WORKS RELATED TO PARTICULAR COUNTRIES

Poland

Andrzejewski, George. *Ashes and Diamonds,* trans. D. F. Welsh. London: Weidenfeld and Nicholson, 1962. Also in Penguin paperback.

——. *The Gates of Paradise,* trans. James Kirkup. London: Weidenfeld and Nicholson, 1963. Also in Panther paperback.

——. *The Inquisitors,* trans. Konrad Syrop. New York: Knopf, 1960.

Andrzejewski, Jerzy. *Apelacja.* Paris: Instytut Literacki, 1968.

Borowski, Tadeusz. *Wybór opowiadań.* Warsaw: PIW, 1967.

Brandys, Kazimierz. *Sons and Comrades,* trans. D. J. Welsh. New York: Grove, 1961.

Bratny, Roman. *Kolumbowie rocznik 20.* 3 vols. Warsaw: PIW, 1957.

Brycht, Andrzej. *Dancing w kwaterze Hitlera.* Warsaw: PAX, 1966.

Hłasko, Marek. *The Graveyard,* trans. Norbert Gutterman. New York: Dutton, 1966.

——. *Next Stop—Paradise,* trans. Norbert Gutterman. New York: Dutton, 1960.

——. *Piękni, dwudziestoletni.* Paris: Instytut Literacki, 1960.

Kijowski, Andrzej. *Arcydzieło nieznane.* Cracow: Wydawnictwo Literackie, 1964.

Nowakowski, Todeusz. *Aleja dobrych znajomych.* London: Polish Cultural Foundation, 1968.

Sandauer, Artur. *Dla każdego coś przykrego.* Cracow: Wydawnictwo Literackie, 1966.

Stawiński, Jerzy Stefan. *Kanał—Ucieczka.* Warsaw: Czytelnik, 1966.

Szczepański, Jan Józef. *Za przełęczą.* Warsaw: Czytelnik, 1967.

Czechoslovakia

Bednár, Alfonz. *Hodiny a minúty.* Bratislava: Slovenský spisovatel, 1960.

Buriánek, František. *Současná česká literatura.* Prague: Orbis, Praha, 1960.

Dejiny slovenskej literatury, ed. Milan Pišút. Bratislava: Vydavatel'stvo Osveta, 1962.

Hrabal, Bohumil. *A Close Watch on the Trains,* trans. Edith Pargeter. London: Cape, 1968.

———. *Ostře sledované vlaky.* Brno: Československý spisovatel, 1965.

Karfík, Vladimir. "Recent Czech Prose," *Books Abroad* 43, no. 3 (1969), 326–33.

Kundera, Milán. *The Joke,* trans. David Hamblyn and Oliver Stallybrass. London: Macdonald, 1969. This English edition contains unauthorized cuts and changes.

———. *Žert.* Brno: Československý spisovatel, 1967.

Mňačko, Ladislav. *Death Is Called Engelchen,* trans. George Theiner. Prague: Artis, 1961.

———. *The Taste of Power,* trans. Paul Stevenson, with a preface by Max Hayward. London: Weidenfeld and Nicolson, 1967.

Škvorecký, Josef. *Zbalbělci.* Vimperk: Československý spisovatel, 1958.

Hungary

A magyar irodalom története, Vol. VI. A magyar irodalom története 1919-től napjainkig. Szerkesztette Szabolcsi Miklós. Budapest: Akadémiai Kiadó, 1966. Only pp. 1047–58 written by Dezső Tóth are relevant.

Cseres, Tibor. *Hideg napok.* Budapest: Magvető, 1964.

Déry, Tibor. *Ítélet nincs.* Budapest: Szépirodalmi, 1969.

———. *Niki, the Story of a Dog,* trans. Edward Hyams. London: Secker and Warburg, 1958. Also in Penguin paperback.

———. *Szerelem és más elbeszélések.* Budapest: Szépirodalmi, 1963.

Fehér, Ferenc. "There is a Verdict," *New Hungarian Quarterly* 36, 126–36.

Fejes, Endre. *Rozsdatemető.* Budapest: Szépirodalmi, 1962.

Sánta, Ferec. *Az áruló.* Budapest: Magvető, 1966.

———. *Az ötödik pecsét.* Budapest: Szépirodalmi, 1963.

———. *Húsz óra.* Budapest: Magvető, 1964.

Sükösd, Mihály. "Hungarian Prose Literature Today," *Mosaic* 1, no. 3 (1968), 110–19.

Tóth, Dezső (ed.). *Élő irodalom. Tanulmányok a felszabadulás utáni magyar irodalom köréből.* Budapest: Akadémiai, 1969. One of the best chapters, directly relevant to our study, is the chapter written by Miklós Béládi, pp. 381–446.

The Soviet Dream: Nationalism
in Soviet Prose Fiction

E. J. CZERWINSKI

I

Nationalism in Soviet literature has always existed. It is the term
"Soviet literature" that is open to question: that phenomenon
has never been clearly defined nor its boundaries circumscribed.
Anything controversial or deviating from Soviet ideology is often
considered non-Soviet. Even E. J. Brown in his history of Soviet
literature narrowed his field of vision and concerned himself "not
so much with the propagandist and Party-oriented literature, which
the term 'Soviet' suggests to the Western mind, nor with the volumi-
nous literature written in the many languages of the non-Russian
republics, but primarily with that Russian literature which has inherited the great tradition of Tolstoy and Dostoevsky." [1]
    If we were to follow Brown's dictum in analyzing the theme of
nationalism in Soviet prose fiction, we would be faced with the possibility of discussing the works of a mere handful of writers—Boris
Pasternak, Aleksandr Solzhenitsyn, Andrei Sinyavsky, Yuli Daniel,
Anatol Kuznetsov, and perhaps Yury Kazakov and Yury Nagibin.
Unfortunately, the profile that would emerge from the works of
these writers would be quite incomplete and incomprehensible to
the reader unfamiliar with the vagaries of Soviet literature. For this
reason, before discussing the theme of nationalism, it is necessary
that we place certain limits on our subject and explain the state of
literature in the Soviet Union.
    It would not be inaccurate to state that the writers mentioned

[1] *Russian Literature Since the Revolution* (New York, 1963), 21.

above never display any predilection toward nationalism, that is, the standard Soviet type. On the contrary, there exists in the prose fiction of these writers a type of nostalgia for the past which in many instances echoes the sentiments of Dostoevsky, especially those contained in his Pushkin speech, in which the nineteenth-century novelist advocated a type of pan-humanism, Pan-Slavism. But one hesitates to simply limit a discussion of nationalism to these writers who stand outside the barriers set up by the strictures of Socialist Realism. Something must be said about the thousands of novels and short stories created by those other engineers of the human spirit.

To better understand these works it may prove helpful to give a brief account of the vicissitudes of the theme of nationalism during the past fifty years of Soviet literature, that is, works written since 1917. Every literary period was prefaced by a political upheaval. There is some truth to the statement that the early years of the Soviet Republic, roughly up to 1932, was a comparatively idyllic period, at least for the writer. These were the years during which the people and their writer-spokesmen had hopes of building a dream. The spirit of nationalism during this period was real. Even when writers seemed ambiguous in their works (e.g., Aleksandr Blok's *The Twelve*) concerning the direction and the means of achieving the ideal, nevertheless, the dream was pursued with an uncompromising intensity by the majority of people and writers. Vladimir Mayakovsky, the declared spokesman of the revolutionary writers, rarely raised doubts in his poetry and plays about the ultimate good of the Soviet Dream. Only his suicide on the eve of the ideological change in literature (1930) opened the doors to speculation and "gossip," which he himself hoped to avoid.[2]

But after 1932 and Andrei Zhdanov's proclamation of Socialist Realism as the future artistic idiom in the Soviet Union (at the First Congress of Soviet Writers in 1934), the Soviet Dream ceased its natural development and an imposed ideology superseded it. From that date even mediocre literature and art failed to appear in the Soviet Union. This fact is not surprising, given the narrow scope and arbitrariness of Socialist Realism. The inner emigrés (like Pasternak and Solzhenitsyn), the inner renegades (like Daniel and Sinyavsky), and the outsiders (like Kuznetsov) have tried to amend

[2] See L. Kassil', *Mayakovsky sam* (Moscow, 1960), 146. Also a photographic reproduction of Mayakovsky's suicide note in *Literaturnoye nasledstvo* 65 (Moscow, 1958), 199.

or defy the ideology and have produced honest (if not always meritorious) works of art. But their histories are tragic and stand apart from the Soviet Dream.

To better understand the role of nationalism in achieving the Soviet Dream, let us briefly review the important periods which have in the past affected literary and artistic policies in the Soviet Union. Each cataclysmic action brought with it an inevitable cataclysmic reaction. The October Revolution, the internecine struggles, the New Economic Policy, the Five-Year plans, the Second World War, the Stalinist purges—each altered the contours of a country and its people. These violent vicissitudes also left their imprint on literary theory.

One must also keep in mind when speaking of literary theory in the Soviet Union that never has there really been unanimity of opinion regarding the exact application of the theory of "dialectic materialism" in literature. Western observers are often misled by the unnatural and artificial conformity induced during the Stalinist period. Suffice it to say that a great gap exists between the theories of G. V. Plexanov (1857–1918), whose theory of literary criticism was founded on the Marxist analysis of social and economic determinants; V. G. Pereverzev (b. 1882), whose theory of strict economic determinism in literary criticism carried Plexanov's ideas to an extreme; and Andrei Zhdanov (1896–1948), the father of Socialist Realism, whose theories included an obscure program espousing "party spirit," "revolutionary romanticism," "the positive hero," and a general insistence on sweetness and light. Since 1932 Socialist Realism has been the reigning doctrine in Soviet art and literature.

With this in mind, we can better evaluate the fluctuations regarding the spirit of nationalism which have occurred in Soviet prose fiction during the past fifty years. Only during those periods when Mother Russia seemed in danger of attack from outside powers have the writers rallied around the revolution and written unashamedly patriotic works. The list of excellent works in which the spirit of patriotism and nationalism played an important role include the following: Boris Pilnyak-Vogau's *The Naked Year* (1922), Leonid M. Leonov's *Road to the Ocean* (1935), Mikhail Sholokhov's *The Silent Don* (completed in 1940), and Aleksey N. Tolstoy's *The Road to Calvary* (1941). But it is an irony reserved for Soviet writers that even patriotism and nationalism are suspect. Even these works were criticized during the country's many periods of literary upheaval for deviating in one way or another from the strict precepts of Socialist Realism.

"Artistic freedom in the Soviet Union has been reduced to the 'freedom' to praise the Soviet system and the Communist Party and to urge people to fight for Communism," according to A. Anatol (formerly the nonwriter of a nonliterature, Anatol Kuznetsov). Furthermore, the nonwriter's "job is to receive slogans and orders from the party and make propaganda out of them." [3] If Anatol's comments are correct, then nationalism in Soviet fiction is not only a party demand but the ultimate goal, the Soviet Dream.

The role forced upon the Soviet Union's thousands of nonwriters (who, through no fault of their own and certainly not because of a lack of talent and genius, continue to produce nonpoetry, nonfiction, nondrama, nonart) was firmly outlined by Lenin himself in an article he wrote in 1909, "The Party Organization and Party Literature." The document has been enshrined as something of a papal bull by officials in the government and by conservative members of the Union of Writers. As a result of its rigidity, the policy has managed to destroy creativity and has produced a nation of nonartists.

It would be impossible to explore the complexity of the subject within the narrow limits of this essay; but because of its impact on its own country and others, nationalism as the Soviet Dream must be reckoned with and understood. To put it simply, the creative energy of a great nation has been channeled to achieve that dream. Thousands have died as a direct result of refusing or not being able in good conscience to implement Lenin's highly simplistic policy. Sixty years after the appearance of Lenin's article, it is doubtful whether the battle to achieve the dream has been won. What is more doubtful is whether the battle was worth the losses. Today the artists of the Soviet Union are proud of their heritage, love their country, and fear their rulers and officials that manipulate the system that has desecrated the memory of Mother Russia. Whether that fear could have been replaced by love and respect had another artistic policy been employed is open to debate. What is no longer a point of contention is that the system has lost the respect of its artistic community, whose voices today have been almost completely silenced.

Having made these statements, one readily admits that the opinions are those of a critic who stands outside the fortress. Because fear of

[3] *Time* 84 (8 Aug. 1969), 30.

the outsider is also part of the system (not necessarily of Lenin's policy), the critic must rely on "leaks," smuggled manuscripts (usually translated into Polish and published in the Paris journal *Kultura*), "official" interviews, or in rare cases the confessions of an Anatol or Svetlana Alliluyeva. To study the theme of nationalism the critic must first of all consider whether the theme is handled artistically or as blatant propaganda. In this case the critic is an insider since art has little respect for political boundaries, and the evidence can be examined first-hand. It is the work itself that a critic judges, "trying to penetrate into the unknown," as Anatol suggests, hoping to extract from it that rare moment of truth. Here the critic is on safer ground and can determine whether the censor has "ruthlessly cut everything out of it," or whether or not the work is "just one more 'ideological' potboiler." [4]

Critics of Soviet literature have long been aware of the struggle of conscience that each Soviet writer has had to wage. Anatol Kuznetsov's indictment of Soviet dictatorial policy merely verifies suspicion. The problem of nationalism, of necessity, is closely tied up with the problem of freedom of expression. Recently, for example, when Aleksandr Dementjev published an article in *Novij Mir* which attacked excessive nationalism in Soviet literature, he was brutally criticized by his more conservative colleagues and was soon relieved of his position on the board of editors of that journal. Since that time the entire editorial board and its editor, Aleksandr Tvardovsky,* have been replaced. These incidents merely indicate the relationship between writer and party: blind devotion is demanded and given, or one suffers the consequences.

These events are highly significant, perhaps even more so than the trials of Sinyavsky and Daniel, or the combined painful experiences of Boris Pasternak, Anna Akhmatova, and Aleksandr Solzhenitsyn. What lies behind these attacks on Dementjev and the recent removal of Aleksandr Tvardovsky as editor of *Novij Mir* is not merely an attack on liberals. It is a new subtle policy which has been introduced to destroy feelings of nationalism among non-Russian minority groups: the new policy seems to be a return to Pan-Slavism, but this time with Lenin and the Soviet Union as a symbol of the Third Rome.

To those familiar with Russian and East European history this

---

[4] *Ibid.*, 30.
* *Editor's note:* A. Tvardovsky died in December 1971.

new policy seems more like a return to sixteenth-century Russian attempts to become the Third Rome than a twentieth-century concept of improving one's national image. In reality the modern idea of Pan-Slavism is simply accepting the Soviet Dream in the old guise of Mother Russia. Today's adherents of Pan-Slavism have learned their lesson from Dostoevsky: they play on the emotions of the Russian people by emphasizing the religious (Orthodoxy), humanitarian (socialism and communism), and cultural (Mother Russia) heritage of the Soviet nation.

Various theories have been presented regarding the emergence of Pan-Slavism in the Soviet Union. Some see in it a means of keeping restless writers (e.g., Solzhenitsyn, Sinyavsky, and the liberals who once composed the editorial board of *Novij Mir*) occupied with an ideology that does not quite run counter to the principles of communism. Others see in the new awakening the hand of the KGB (Soviet Secret Police) and Soviet officials, who hope to use this patriotic fervency for their own ends. The leading spokesman for the new group is Victor Chalmayev, a literary critic whose idols, according to Paul Wohl, include "Ivan the Terrible, Peter the Great, and, implicitly, Stalin." [5] That a man like Chalmayev should be the most articulate spokesman for the group suggests that the government, too, would like to become beneficiary of some of the spoils.

There is little doubt that the time is right for a return to these nineteenth-century ideals in the Soviet Union. But the policy seems to be directed more in keeping the minority groups (Baltic countries and the Ukraine in particular) and the other Slavic countries (Poland, Czechoslovakia, etc.) in line than with bringing all peoples together. It is no secret, for example, that the spirit of nationalism in East Europe has created a problem for the Russians (Great Russia), who today find themselves just another minority group (although the largest) among the other minority groups in the Soviet Union. At one time the majority group in their country, today the Great Russians comprise less than 50 percent of the population. Although exact figures are withheld, this new development certainly is cause for concern among Soviet officials. Perhaps the new turn of events toward Pan-Slavism can be directly tied in with official attempts to halt the feelings of nationalism among its minority groups

---

[5] "Pan-Slavism Spreads in Soviet Union," *Christian Science Monitor* (17 Feb. 1970), 9.

and satellites and to instill life into the old image of the Soviet Dream —nationalism, Russian style.

But 1970–1971 has introduced another facet into the Soviet Union's pursuit of the dream. This year marks the centenary of Lenin's birth. As early as 1967 the Soviet Union launched its campaign to celebrate the great day with all sorts of memorials—in art, in literature, and in the press. These novels, plays, poems, and essays explore every aspect of Lenin's life and heap praise on a personality that undoubtedly will become the new saint to world Communists, even greater than Stalin during his golden years. Always venerated, Lenin now seems destined for godhood. His elevation may be exactly what the Soviet Union needs to recover the prestige lost when Stalin was toppled from his pedestal by Khrushchev in his speech to the Twentieth Congress of the Communist party in February 1956. The Soviet Union has been in need of a new inspirational force to regain its position of leadership within the Communist movement. It did not have to go far to find it.

However, judging by recent shifts of party *apparatchiki* within the government apparatus, one hesitates to evaluate the present literary and political situation in euphoric terms. In the past year, for example, Vladimir I. Stepakov has been dismissed as chief of the party Central Committee's Department of Propaganda and Agitation. In addition to Stepakov, the chairmen of the State Committee on the Press, Cinematography, and Radio and Television have been removed from their positions of eminence. These changes certainly indicate a concern at the top about ideological affairs. There is no doubt, however, about the importance and future eminence of Lenin as the leading light and impetus behind the Soviet Dream. These recent shifts in the apparatus merely indicate a concern about procedural matters, that is, how to implement the making of a new pope and messiah. The dissatisfaction lies not with the goal itself, but with the bureaucratic tedium that has overshadowed the dream.

The underground press—Samizdat or self-publishers—has reacted most violently to the bureaucratic tedium. The works circulating in Samizdat have changed radically during the past five years, from purely artistic to highly political. The intellectuals in the Soviet Union today are in step with their counterparts in East and West Europe. Literature today, especially drama and poetry, is a matter of politics. Since censorship is especially tight in the Soviet theater, the intellectuals have formed their own kind of theater, a type of pocket drama which if performed would perhaps rank with the best drama produced anywhere, if for no other reason than because of its subject matter.

These underground artists and intellectuals are the Soviet Union's real patriots, with their goals fixed on a better future and a more humane form of government, Dubček's "socialism with a human face." Last year's issues of the "Chronicle of Human Rights Year in the Soviet Union (1968–1969)," is a good example of the group's activity.

But the "group" is not merely a handful of "reactionaries and psychopaths," but a solid block of dissenters who include Baltic minorities resisting Russification, Ukrainian Nationalists, persecuted Jews, and millions of former victims of oppression. This situation presents a problem for the critic attempting to evaluate the role of nationalism in Soviet prose fiction. Should he include the underground Samizdat publications (few of which are available either in East Europe or the West), or should he merely record the dullness which passes for (perhaps sincere) patriotism and nationalism in the official Soviet press?

I have chosen to comment on the most representative works from all these categories: the inner emigrés, the inner renegades, and the inner circle. From among the inner emigrés Boris Pasternak's *Doctor Zhivago*, published in 1958 but completed probably before 1954, and Aleksandr Solzhenitsyn's *The Cancer Ward* (1967) will be discussed. The inner renegades will be represented by Andrei Sinyavsky (pseud. Abram Tertz) and his novel *The Trial Begins* (1960); and by Yuli Daniel (pseud. Nikolaj Arzhak) and his novel *This Is Moscow Speaking* (1962). Mikhail Sholokhov and his novelette *Fate of a Man* (1957) will speak for the inner circle.

II

Literary hacks have been busily at work during the past few years turning out short stories and novels whose themes are reminiscent not only of the superpatriotism of the war years but of the blatant cult of personality of the Stalinist period. The most notorious examples of propaganda in the guise of fiction are *In the Name of the Father and the Son* (1969) and *Love and Hate* (1970) by Ivan Shevtsov and *What Exactly Do You Want?* (1969) by Vsevolod Kochetov. These works have become so popular in the past year that one would think that "camp" literature has become acceptable to citizens of the Soviet Union. But in fact the novel has become popular among the hard-core conservatives. Significantly it has acquired "camp" status among the intellectual elite and, according to Charlotte Saikowski (staff correspondent of the *Christian Science Monitor*), a parody of Kochetov's novel has already appeared in the Samizdat or underground press.

So long as Soviet intellectuals ridicule such pieces that pass for literature in the Soviet press, the intellectual climate will remain the same and the stark years of the Stalinist era will not return. But it is true that not everyone shares the same opinion. There is little doubt that "some Russians probably sympathize with [the novels'] appeal for chauvinistic patriotism, anti-Western vigilance, and puritan morals." [6]

Criticism, however, has not been kind to either work. Even *Literaturnaya Gazeta* and *Komsomolskaya Pravda*, often the champions of conservative causes, were appalled by the hardly veiled caricatures of poets like Andrei Voznesensky and Bella Akhmadulina (in Shevtsov's novel—Artur Vozdvizhensky and Novella Kaparulina), described as "the scum on the mighty ocean of Soviet society." [7] They could hardly have been impressed by the following outburst, made by an old Bolshevik sculptor: "I am convinced that true Communists fight for the art of Socialist Realism because that is the art of the working people, because it expresses the bright ideals of mankind." [8] At one time or another in the novel Shevtsov manages to comment on every theme dear to the hearts of the conservatives: Zionism, translations of foreign works, denunciation of the United States, justification of the Soviet Union's past, and a whitewash of Stalin's reputation.

Kochetov's novel, although less offensive, is, nevertheless, an innocuous work that seems better suited to be ranked with the potboilers written during Stalin's heyday. As the Soviet critic Andreyev points out, the most important problems which the novel discusses is that of father and sons; in fact "the very title of the novel—the problem [*What Exactly Do You Want?*]—is directed at the young hero." [9] In the final analysis, according to Andreyev, although Kochetov explores "a number of serious questions concerning con-

[6] " 'Camp' Rations for Soviet Readers," *Christian Science Monitor* (21 April 1940), 2.

[7] *Ibid.*, 2.

[8] *Ibid.*, 2.

[9] Yu Andreyev, "About Vsevolod Kochetov's Novel, *What Exactly Do You Want?*" *Literaturnaya Gazeta* (11 Feb. 1970), 4.

temporary ideological debate," his novel "should be evaluated on the whole as a work which does not give a true picture of reality." [10]

This is not to imply that these novels have been dismissed as literary failures and are not read by the public. On the contrary, these two works have become the most popular novels of the year. Given the fact, however, that very little of value has appeared recently, one should not be be surprised at this phenomenon—for phenomenon it is. One can only explain the current craze in the Soviet Union for this type of literature as a recognition of their writers' poor tastes. Such works, reminiscent of the thirties and late forties, with the emphasis on black and white characters, "conflictlessness," and pursuit of the Soviet Dream, can only provoke laughter from a public that knows better. It very well may be that "camp" has come to the Soviet Union.

In this respect, it is prophetic that Yuli Daniel mentioned Vsevolod Kochetov in his novel *This Is Moscow Speaking* as early as 1960, long before Kochetov's novel *What Exactly Do You Want?* was conceived. But even then there was no doubt that Daniel's feelings toward the neo-Stalinist were far from ambivalent. He has one of his characters remark in the novel: "Kochetov hired thugs from the Moscow suburbs to act as a bodyguard [on Public Murder Day]." [11] Ten years later, after the appearance of his latest novel, it would seem that Kochetov has a real need of such bodyguards.

But lest it be assumed that all the works of the inner emigrés and inner renegades are attacks on the system itself, it may be opportune at this point to comment on the areas of conflict and dispute. In the novels of the inner emigrés (and renegades) there is never a direct attack on the government or communism. Stalin is Solzhenitsyn's favorite target, and the bureaucrats who served under the notorious leader are objects of his scorn and satire. But there is a love of country, of heritage, of the people that rescues Solzhenitsyn's works from diatribe. His humanity rises above his hatred of institutions and their leaders. Injustice is merely shown up for what it is.

Pasternak's novel differs considerably from Solzhenitsyn's work. Love of country, culture, and the people is also present, but these are woven into the fabric of a work that is less a novel and more an epic. One is struck by the thematic and structural similarities between the two works. There is about it a nostalgia for a lost moment,

---

[10] *Ibid.*, 4.
[11] Yuli Daniel (Nikolai Arzhak), *This Is Moscow Speaking and Other Stories*, ed. Max Hayward (London, 1968), 62.

a lost heritage, and the realization that the glorious past will never return. The narrator, Zhivago-Pasternak, is much like the bard of old, except for the fact that the individual, the lyrical "I," takes the place of the objective singer of past glories.

Above all, however, *Doctor Zhivago* is a paean to Russia. For Zhivago-Pasternak hope lies in Russia and the Revolution. In an exalted moment, Zhivago confides to Larisa his feelings about the past, present, and future:

> "Just think what's going on around us! And that you and I should be living at such a time. Such a thing happens only once in an eternity. Just think of it, the whole of Russia has had its roof torn off, and you and I and everyone else are out in the open! And there's nobody to spy on us. Freedom! Real freedom, not just talk about it, freedom, dropped out of the sky, freedom beyond our expectations, freedom by accident, through a misunderstanding. . . . You might say that everyone has been through two revolutions—his own personal revolution as well as the general one. It seems to me that socialism is the sea, and all these separate streams, these private, individual revolutions, are flowing into it—the sea of life, the sea of spontaneity. . . . These days I have such a longing to live honestly, to be productive. I so much want to be a part of all this awakening." [12]

It is significant that nowhere in the novel is there a positive statement made about the government aparatus or about hope for the future after the Revolution has succeeded. Zhivago is caught in the spirit of the Revolution and at first believes in the dream. He is willing to bear the sacrifice, but somehow, with his poet's intuition, he senses that what will emerge from the chaos of the present is a terrible void. In his drunken speech to his friends he tries more to convince himself of the soundness of pursuing the dream than to impress them:

> "I too think that Russia is destined to become the first socialist state since the beginning of the world. When this comes to pass, the event will stun us for a long time, and after awakening we shall have lost half our memories forever. We'll have forgotten what came first and what followed, and we won't look for causes. The new order of things will be all around us and as familiar to us as the woods on the horizon or the clouds over our heads. There will be nothing else left." [13]

In the end, as he embarks on his trip to his refuge, Varykino, Zhivago finally realizes that there is "nothing else left." He confides in Samdeviatov that he is going to Varykino to recapture the lost Eden

---

[12] Boris Pasternak, *Doctor Zhivago* (New York, 1958), 146–47.
[13] *Ibid.*, 182.

—Mother Russia—that was destroyed by the Revolution. When Samdeviatov accuses him of being naïve and idyllic, Zhivago answers his charge: "You are a Bolshevik, and yet you yourself don't deny that what's going on isn't life—it's madness, an absurd nightmare." [14] The nightmare continues until there is no hope left, and Zhivago decides to meet death on his own terms:

> "Death is really knocking at our door. Our days are really numbered. So at least let us take advantage of them in our own way. Let us use them up saying goodbye to life, being together for the last time before we are parted. We'll say goodbye to everything we hold dear, to the way we look at things, to the way we've dreamed of living and to what our conscience has taught us, and to our hopes and to each other." [15]

Lara and Zhivago escape to their Eden, attempting to recapture moments from the past, recounting old stories, reading the Russian classics that somehow now seem part of a different world. Varykino is the end of their dream and as such is the end of their lives.

For Zhivago (and we can assume for Pasternak) achieving the dream was worth any sacrifice. It would bring new glory to Mother Russia. But when the Soviet Dream turns out to be neither as glorious as Old Russia nor as promising as imagined during the painful years of the Revolution, faith gives way to pessimism. Tania, the alleged daughter of Lara and Zhivago who appears in the closing pages of the novel, is a symbol of the fruits of the Revolution. Pasternak has Gordon pass judgment on the dream: "It has often happened in history that a lofty ideal has degenerated into crude materialism." [16] The remark is a *cri de coeur*. As a poet writing a novel, Pasternak could not help but assemble an autobiography, a diary that literally subtly fills in the ellipses of life.

With Aleksandr Solzhenitsyn,* on the other hand, we are dealing with a different type of writer, a chronicler much like Pepys or Boswell, a declared novelist who is, perhaps, a far better short-story writer. There is little of the poet in Solzhenitsyn; there is much of the educator and enlightener, a hound of truth, who can truly be called the Nemesis of the Kremlin.

[14] *Ibid.*, 260.
[15] *Ibid.*, 426.
[16] *Ibid.*, 518.
* *Editor's note:* After this essay was written, Solzhenitsyn was awarded the Nobel Prize for literature in 1970, an honor that was earlier bestowed on Pasternak, thus creating one more point of comparison between these two Soviet writers.

Cancer Ward no doubt contains autobiographical elements, but unlike *Doctor Zhivago*, it is more an account of a painful period (Stalin's rule) than a writer's philosophic or poetic journey through memory. His description of suffering and torment is real and effective, but his characters are like all other men, not like one special man. Zhivago was a poet, an artist, a humanitarian. Kostoglotov is like Gorky's Makar Chudra and Chelkash, who embody the indomitable spirit of tramps, or like Sholokhov's Andrei Sokolov (*Fate of a Man*), or even like Tolstoy's Platon Karatayev, the idealized peasant in *War and Peace*. Zhivago was like Pasternak.

It would be difficult to do justice to Solzhenitsyn's work in the space alloted here. For this reason perhaps it would be best to cite those aspects of the novel that touch upon the theme of nationalism. Again, comparing *Cancer Ward* and *Doctor Zhivago*, we can see that love of country (in the case of Pasternak—Mother Russia) is central in both works. Kostoglotov dislikes party *apparatchiki* like Rusanov and leaders like Stalin, but he has an all-encompassing love for the Soviet Union and communism. Although his brand of patriotism and nationalism is based on his peasant love of the land and institutions like the church and family, these are all tied in with his understanding of government and political leaders. Kostoglotov is a tragic figure and his apparent death at the end of the novel ("The train went on and Kostoglotov's boots dangled toes down over the corridor like a dead man's)" [17] emphasizes the emptiness of one man's life. Having spent most of his life either in far-off places in the Soviet Union or in a cancer ward, Kostoglotov was a victim of circumstances—like Solzhenitsyn himself who spent most of his adult life in prison camps or in a cancer ward. The description of Kostoglotov's pathetic wanderings in the city (the last two chapters of the novel) is Solzhenitsyn's finest writing. In the suffering of this "little man" the reader is brought face to face with all of humanity: it is a feat accomplished by few writers.

"It should be stressed," as Vladimir Petrov writes, "that in his struggle Solzhenitsyn remained a loyal and patriotic Soviet citizen, notwithstanding the attacks on him by Party hacks. His protests were directed against the bureaucracy's excesses and abuses, not against Soviet authority and the communist society. His aim was to improve and perfect the Soviet system, not to destroy it." [18]

[17] Alexander Solzhenitsyn, *Cancer Ward*, trans. Nicholas Bethell and David Burg (New York, 1969), 532.
[18] *Ibid.*, 536.

The same can be said of Daniel and Sinyavsky. Both writers possess a passion for their country that borders on chauvinism. The comments made by the young poet Alexander Ginsburg actually give voice to the sentiments of all the writers—inner emigrés, inner renegades, and those within the inner circle. They deserve to be quoted here so that this aspect of the question is made perfectly clear: "I love my country and I do not wish to see two more writers [Daniel and Sinyavsky] sent off, under guard, to fell trees." [19] Ginsburg's remarks were made in the form of a letter to Kosygin, shortly after the arrest of Daniel and Sinyavsky. In 1968 Ginsburg was sentenced to five years in prison for compiling a White Book on the trial. [20]

It is significant also that during his trial Andrei Sinyavsky insisted that he was in no way an enemy of the Soviet Union: "I did not regard my works as anti-Soviet and therefore there was nothing to own up to." [21] Daniel, too, adamantly resisted the prosecutor's attempts to make of him a traitor: "I am convinced that there is nothing anti-Soviet in my works." [22] At one point he accurately sums up the areas of sensitivity on which he differed from party hacks: "I've always thought and I continue to think that my books were not anti-Soviet and that I put no anti-Soviet meaning into them, since I did not criticize or make fun of the basic principles of our life. I do not equate individuals with the social system as such, or the government with the state, or a certain period with the Soviet epoch as a whole. The state may exist for centuries but as a government is often short-lived and frequently inglorious." [23]

In the final section of his novel which deals with the establishment of a Public Murder Day by government decree, Daniel has his hero-narrator express views that could only have been uttered by someone who loves his country passionately:

> I walk along the street, along the quiet, cosy avenue, feeling for the notebook in my pocket, and thinking of what I have written. I believe that it might equally well have been written by anyone else of my generation and my destiny, who loves this damned, this beautiful country as much as I do. I have judged it and its people and

---

[19] Daniel, 8.

[20] See *On Trial: The Soviet State Versus Abram Tertz and Nikolai Arzhak*, trans. Max Hayward (New York, 1966).

[21] *Ibid.*, 138.

[22] *Ibid.*, 76.

[23] *Ibid.*, 80.

myself both more and less severely than I should. But who will blame me?

I walk along and tell myself: "This is your world, your life, you are a cell, a particle of the whole. You must not allow yourself to be intimidated. You must answer for yourself, and you are thereby answerable for others." And the endless houses sailing like a convoy of ships to an unknown destination, hum softly in unconscious agreement and astonished approval.

This is Moscow speaking. [24]

Daniel's nationalism is not different from that of Kochetov except for the fact that he distrusts the easy way: "You must not allow yourself to be intimidated," not even to compose novels filled with government-solicited expressions of patriotism. During his defense, Daniel explained that he loved to write and felt the urge common to all writers, that is, to see his works in print. Since he knew they could not be published in the Soviet Union, he sent his works abroad. Perhaps the real difference between Daniel and other Soviet writers is not that he loves to write but that he is incapable of prostituting that love.

Although the feelings toward their country and their art may be similar, Daniel and Sinyavsky are writers with different temperaments. Sinyavsky selects subjects which are far more controversial than those chosen by Daniel. *The Trial Begins* is reminiscent of some of the novels written during the early years of the Revolution, especially those with an emphasis on sex, negative types, and corruption. The novel which is set against the background of the doctors' plot, the famous witch-trial which took place in the last year of Stalin's life, deals with the experiences of a handful of people— young and old—caught on the periphery of that event.

The writer-narrator merely relates the story but his tragedy, too, is hinted at, especially in the final moments of the novel when he, Seryozha, and Rabinovich (one of the doctors accused of plotting to kill government officials) take up their "spades as one man" in the prison camp where they have been banished. [25]

The main character in the novel is Marina's husband, Globov, who seems unaware of his wife's affair with Karlinsky. He has a penchant for platitudinizing: "A man who surrounds himself with children is bound to be a good citizen." [26] As an *apparatchik par excellence*, Globov is the object of Sinyavsky's scorn. Proud of his treachery,

---

[24] Daniel, 66.
[25] Abram Tertz, *The Trial Begins*, trans. Max Hayward (London, 1960), 128.
[26] *Ibid.*, 31.

Globov muses: "For who was it, after all, who had uncovered Rabinovich's plot and launched this whole series of trials?—He, Prosecutor Globov! Who had taken the place of judge and jury at a moment of crisis?—Globov!" [27] Globov considers himself the nemesis of all enemies of the state—real and imagined—and pursues his victims like a Greek fury: "We shall not allow our enemies to destroy us, it is we who will destroy them." [28]

Sinyavsky condemns that which must be condemned and praises that which deserves praise. The following dialogue between the old grandmother and Globov's son, Seryozha, is perhaps the most touching excuse for suffering and sacrifice that anyone in the Soviet Union has written:

> "But are we going to get on together, Granny? I shan't give up my principles."
> "Principles indeed! You think I'm old and I haven't got my eyes in my head. Well, I dare say I see more things wrong than you do. But don't you understand, Seryozha, you must have faith, you simply must believe.... The whole of our life is devoted to this. It's —our aim...."
> Seryozha lay on his back and opened his eyes.
> "You know, Granny," he said happily, his voice still raw with tears, "I've come to a conclusion: there's only one thing that can help us now—a world revolution. What d'you think—will there be a world revolution?"
> "Well, of course there will be! How can you doubt such a thing?...Let me warm up something for you to eat," said Granny.[29]

Seryozha and Katya, the young lovers in *The Trial Begins*, like Sinyavsky, are not against communism. Their new "Society," they both insist, must not be taken advantage of by capitalists and imperialists. They both envision "a new world, Communist and radiant," where "money, torture and thievery would be abolished" and "perfect liberty would dawn." [30] Their idyll ends when Seryozha is arrested and Katya is accidentally killed.

Youth in the Soviet Union, Sinyavsky suggests, are the tragic ones because they still believe in a new world and true communism. But in the real world, where the "aim justifies any sacrifice," [31] there is no place for anyone who believes that "a noble end ought to be

[27] *Ibid.*, 57.
[28] *Ibid.*, 57.
[29] *Ibid.*, 47–48.
[30] *Ibid.*, 62.
[31] *Ibid.*, 83.

served by noble means." [32] In Globov's drunken outburst the villain
is finally exposed: "Our goal is reached. We have conquered. Master,
hear me! We have conquered! Do you hear me?" [33] The answer is
given by Sinyavsky: "The Master was dead." [34]

Sinyavsky explores the tragedy of the Soviet Dream. He does not
villify it. He simply cannot understand the ramifications of a system
whose leaders deem it necessary to sacrifice human lives: "Victims
are unavoidable. But then—it's for the Aim." [35] Even capitalized and
given dubious dignity, the word remains ominous. During his trial
Sinyavsky insisted that he had no quarrel with the Soviet Dream nor
with its founder. His enemy was one man that destroyed the natural
growth of that dream: "Stalin was possessed. People with a petty-
bourgeois mentality cannot rise to the level of Lenin." [36]

Sinyavsky, Daniel, Solzhenitsyn, and Pasternak were unable to accept the precept that "any means" justifies the Aim. Mikhail Sholokhov seems never to have had any difficulty with his conscience and
has always sided with the government in regard to this issue. A friend
of Stalin's, a man of considerable talent, author of *The Quiet Don*,
one of the finest Soviet novels, Sholokhov seemed always willing to
serve the state as novelist-in-perpetual-residence. His output after
the war was small, a few short stories, an embarrassing potboiler—
They Fought For Their Country—, and an excellent novellette, *Fate
of a Man*. The latter adheres to all the strictures of Socialist Realism
and yet somehow manages to overcome the handicaps that such a
narrow artistic policy forces upon a work of art.

The hero of the story is Andrei Sokolov who adopts an orphan
after returning from the war and finding his wife and children dead.
Sentimental and obvious, the story nonetheless is moving. As in most
Soviet fiction, the cruelty of the Germans is played up: "Don't fall
down, for God's sake! Keep going, as long as you've got any strength
left, or they'll kill you." [37] Sokolov perserveres and joins his fellow
sufferers. But he has no qualms about killing a Russian who is about
to inform on a platoon commander ("I know you're a Commu-

[32] *Ibid.*, 86.
[33] *Ibid.*, 114.
[34] *Ibid.*, 115.
[35] *Ibid.*, 121.
[36] *On Trial*, 118.
[37] Mikhail Sholokhov, *Sud'ba cheloveka* (Moscow, 1960), 28. Translation is
mine.

nist") [38] because killing him meant "one traitor less." [39] Although it could be argued that the situation called for the killing, it nevertheless brings up a moral question that cannot be answered simply with the words—"It's for the Aim."

Nowhere in the work is there a note of pessimism, of doubt, or even of simple questioning. The government is the country, the country is the dream. The listener-narrator emphasizes this message: "What did the future hold for them? I wanted to believe that this Russian, this man of unbreakable will, would stick it out, and the boy would grow at his father's side into a man who could endure anything, overcome any obstacle—if he was called upon to do so by his country." [40] In this last sentence we hear echoes of nationalism, patriotism, Jack London, Hemingway, and the Soviet censor—but strangely, we also manage to hear Sholokhov himself. Retaining fixedly his place in the inner circle, he seems at times attached to that same invisible chain that binds all his fellow writers outside the circle. Perhaps, in honest pursuit of a dream, a man can express his love of country and humanity, even from within the forbidding walls of his psychic prison.

BIBLIOGRAPHY

Andreyev, Yu. "About Vsevolod Kochetov's Novel, *What Exactly Do You Want?*" *Literaturnaya Gazeta*, 11 Feb. 1970, 4.
Brown, Edward J. *Russian Literature Since the Revolution*. New York: Collier Books, 1963.
Daniel, Yuli (Nikolai Arzhak). *This Is Moscow Speaking and Other Stories*, ed. Max Hayward. London: Collins and Harvill, 1968.
Gibian, George. *Interval of Freedom: Soviet Literature during the Thaw, 1954–1957*. Minneapolis: University of Minnesota Press, 1960.
Kassil', L. *Mayakovsky sam (Mayakovsky)*. Moscow, 1960.
Kochetov, Vsevolod. *Chevo zhe ty hochesh'? (What Exactly Do You Want?)* Serialized in *Oktyabr'* (Sept. through Dec. 1969).
Literaturnoye nasledstvo (Literary Heritage) 65. Moscow, 1958.
Lukács, Georg. *Solschenizyn*. Neuwied, Germany: Hermann Luchterhand Verlag, 1970.
Mathewson, Rufus W. *The Positive Hero in Russian Literature*. New York: Columbia University Press, 1958.

[38] *Ibid.*, 31.
[39] *Ibid.*, 32.
[40] *Ibid.*, 58.

On Trial: The Soviet State Versus Abram Tertz and Nikolai Arzhak, trans. Max Hayward. New York: Harper, 1966.

Pasternak, Boris. *Doctor Zhivago.* New York: Pantheon, 1958.

Rühle, Jürgen. *Literatur und Revolution.* Köln, Germany: Kiepenheuer & Witsch, 1960.

Saikowski, Charlotte. "'Camp' Rations for Soviet Readers." *Christian Science Monitor,* 21 April 1970, 2.

Sholokhov, Mikhail. *Sud'ba cheloveka (Fate of a Man).* Moscow: Children's Publishing House (Detgiz), 1960.

Solzhenitsyn, Alexander. *Cancer Ward,* trans. Nicholas Bethell and David Burg. New York: Bantam Books, 1969.

Struve, Gleb. *Soviet Russian Literature, 1917–50.* Norman: University of Oklahoma Press, 1951.

Swayze, Harold. *Political Control of Literature in the USSR, 1946–1959.* Cambridge, Mass.: Harvard University Press, 1962.

Tertz, Abram. *On Socialist Realism.* New York: Pantheon, 1960.

——. *The Trial Begins,* trans. Max Hayward. London: Collins and Harvill Press, 1960.

Trotsky, Leon. *Literature and Revolution.* New York: Russell and Russell, 1957.

Vickery, Walter N. *The Cult of Optimism.* Bloomington: Indiana University Press, 1963.

Yarmolinsky, Avrahm. *Literature under Communism.* Bloomington: Indiana University Russian and East European Institute, 1960.

Cultural Nationalism
in Modern Italian Fiction

SARAH D'ALBERTI

Before dealing with the specific theme of the present study, a theme which *grosso modo* is bound up with the years following the Second World War, it will be necessary to dwell briefly upon the events that ensued in Italy in the wake of the military defeat and the fall of fascism, as well as upon the current trends in the peninsula.

Whereas normally a military defeat is accompanied by the desire for revenge and, in consequence, by an exploitation of the cultural and social aspects of life linked to the idea of nation or fatherland, as was the case in France after 1870 or in Germany after 1918, a reverse phenomenon transpired in Italy. Italians clung to the themes of antifascism, for fascism was identified as the real enemy; fearing a revival of nationalism which had been the matrix of fascism, they banished everything which in some way or other smacked of the very idea of nationhood. Thus Italian culture was oriented in two different directions, toward cosmopolitanism, on the one hand, and toward the Marxist social theme, on the other.

The theme of cosmopolitanism, of which Giuseppe Antonio Borgese had made himself the bearer, rapidly died of inanition either because the idea of nationhood, although it was not set in bold relief, remained alive in the innermost recesses of every Italian's being, or, if we want to put it more crudely, because the individualism of the Italians, like that of other European peoples, stood firm.

On the other hand, the Marxist social theme, artistically revived by Ignazio Silone immediately following the re-establishment of freedom, found it possible to develop and identify universally with a kind of conformism that hitched almost all Italian writers to the wagon of communism.

Now, if there is anything to which the Italian mind is impervious it is Marxism, Marxism be it understood, as a political philosophy and, hence, as a cultural matrix. For this reason it could never effect a marriage with Italian culture. And the writers who from time to time became its interpreters, from Alberto Moravia to Pier Paolo Pasolini—to cite the two most noted Italian novelists of recent years —are substantially alien to the national culture.

When Vittorio Emanuele Orlando, immediately after the war, scathingly stigmatized the "cupidity for servility" of Italians, his words fell on deaf ears because the generations chronologically nearest to his time had been stunned by defeat in the Second World War and exhibited utter indifference to every exhortation to national dignity, while their younger contemporaries tended toward disintegration and skepticism with regard to any and all ideals.

Nor can it be said that the younger generations, let alone the youngest, assumed a different tone. The most recent writers, those who are now riding the crest of the wave, seem to be lost in an empty estheticism and they feel no desire whatsoever to draw from the wellspring of the national culture in their creative work. Today Vincenzo Gioberti's *The Moral and Cultural Primacy of the Italian People (Il primato morale e civile degli italiani)* (1843), on which so many cultured minds of the Risorgimento were reared, would be an object of derision or commiseration.

Hence the possibility of developing the theme ought to be denied just as we are setting out to explore it. But a conclusion imposed by rigorous logic is not acceptable on the cultural plane. Accordingly our study must be conducted and understood as a contribution to a knowledge of those Italian writers who were influenced by the national consciousness at closer quarters, even if its elaboration is bound to be of general character.

Moreover, culture is a vital process and, as such, its facets are infinite; it is nourished on the past and lives in the present. Therefore, we shall try to link the present to the past in an attempt to illuminate the most valid aspects and revelatory moments of a national culture which, though repudiated or denied, always remains at the base of every form of the nation's spiritual life.

In Italy the novel, as a literary genre, from its inception has been characterized as one of the artistic factors linked to the theme of the reawakening of the national consciousness. For this reason, in the romantic generation of the early nineteenth century, it was one of the ways of giving substance to the notion of fatherland, to the idea of Italian tradition, to the reflected feeling of the nation. The novel accompanied or fostered the movement of national reawakening known as the Risorgimento. It suffices to consider the popular-national theme that was the object of the historical novel to convince ourselves that the success of the genre would not have achieved sizable culture dimensions had the political objectives of the Risorgimento advocated by the patriots not been presented to the reader in a singularly effective emotional manner.

From this point of view the following novels must be considered as creations which in content and inspiration were chiefly of a national character: *Ettore Fieramosca* as well as *Niccolò de Lapi* by Massimo D'Azeglio; *The Battle of Benevento* (*La battaglia di Benevento*) and *The Siege of Florence* (*L'assedio di Firenze*) by Francesco Domenico Guerrazzi; *La Margherita Pusterla* by Cesare Cantù; and *Marco Visconti* by Tommaso Grossi. We must quickly add, however, that none of these novels attained great distinction as works of literature compared to Alessandro Manzoni's *The Betrothed* (*I Promessi sposi*), which served several of them as a model.

In Manzoni's novel the national theme is certainly one of the author's original motifs, and it is also reflected in singular and recurrent emphases which he assigns to events and to the characters of his masterpiece. In the novel's economy, however, the national motif is neither solitary nor preeminent. Indeed, it is grounded in a larger and more comprehensive view of spiritual life in which meditation on the nature of man, on Providence, and on the dialectic of moral life stands at the center of the artist's poetic imagination. It is precisely for this reason that we cannot consider the Manzonian masterpiece as a typical national novel, even if it is true that all practitioners of the genre in Italy, and in particular those who harbored intentions of developing patriotic themes, always looked toward the lesson of *The Betrothed* as an authoritative model.

It is a fact, therefore, that although the initial period of the contemporary Italian novel flourished in the name of an idea of the fatherland, it often shifted to other historical periods. But the idea of the fatherland was always considered as a real stimulus for the passions of a people. Only rarely did it happen that some writer ventured to deal with contemporary national themes. But even in such cases the stress fell on the expectation of Italy's independence and resurrection. This holds true for Giovanni Ruffini's novels, *Doc-*

tor Antonio (*Il dottor Antonio*) and *Lorenzo Benoni*, and it still held true in the following generation in the work of Ippolito Nievo, *The Castle of Fratta* (*Le confessioni di un ottuagenario*) and in *One Hundred Years* (*Cento anni*) by Giuseppe Rovani. Indeed under a certain aspect, precisely in a work of the post-unification generation, *The Gale* (*La bufera*) by Edoardo Calandra, we have the most perfected example of national historical content in the Italian novel. But the proclamation of the kingdom of Italy which finally came to pass and the emergence of new tastes and of new artistic influences soon modified the theme of the Italian novel.

To a certain extent the novel ceased to claim the function of mirroring a society and its diverse institutions. Preference was expressed for the novel in the manner of Stendahl, Balzac, or Flaubert—that is to say, the novel in which an event that touches on few characters is narrated with a closeness of psychological observation and human sincerity, locating the heroes in a temporal, social, and cultural dimension alien to any precise ethnic differentiation, alien to any specific national physiognomy.

Everyone knows, in fact, that Julien Sorel, or Fabrizio del Dongo, or Emma Bovary, the protagonists of the three novels, *Rouge et Noir, La Chartreuse de Parme*, and *Madame Bovary*, have only a symbolic nationality, not intrinsically affecting the artistic validity of the personages and the work of which they form a part. In Italy, however, a cosmopolitan literary trend of such a nature in practice enjoyed only doubtful or intermittent success.

If we consider, for example, the social novel which was the genre most popular with the Italian realistic school, we will find that the images of the province, which Italian writers wanted to give us, were always set within a nationalistic framework. Let us recall young Malavoglia who in the novel of the same name by Giovanni Verga dies in the naval battle of Lissa, in the War for Italian Independence. Or let us consider the acute intuition of De Roberto who in *The Viceroys* (*I Vicerè*) describes the decadence of the aristocracy, but who describes it within the setting of the Italian national revolution. Or Antonio Fogazzaro, whose subjective themes, impregnated with mysticism, successfully unfolding his skill as a narrator at a tranquil pace, harmoniously spinning out the thread of the tale especially when he recounts the vicissitudes of the Maironi family in *The Little World of the Past* (*Piccolo mondo antico*), similarly relates his material very closely to the Italian national theme.

The heart of contemporary fiction in Italy is to be sought in the irreversible literary trend which induced writers to withdraw from the objectivity of the story in order to find refuge in complete subjectivity. Here we can cite Luigi Pirandello.

In fact, the Sicilian writer was a novelist before he turned to writing short stories and plays. As a novelist he tested his talents in diverse types of fiction—ranging from the social-psychological, as in *The Excluded One* (*L'Esclusa*) to the social irony of *The Late Mattia Pascal* (*Il fu Mattia Pascal*), up to the characteristic Pirandellian problem-complex found in *One, No One, One Hundred Thousand* (*Uno, nessuno, centomila*). Among Pirandello's novels, however, there is one that many critics consider the greatest test of his aptitude as a writer of fiction in which the theme of nationhood occupies the foreground of the story. We are referring, of course, to *The Old and the Young* (*I vecchi e i giovani*), which is a vigorous representation of a critical moment in Italian society poised on the border between the fading ideals of the Risorgimento and the nascent demands for social justice and economic well-being.

We can say that on the eve of the First World War (*The Old and the Young* was published in 1913) a real divorce had already been effected between the novel and ordinary life, between the novel and the sentiments of the nation and, perhaps more generically, between literature and real life. How else can we explain, on the one hand, the recurrent crises of Italian men of letters in the years astride the first world conflict and, on the other, their resumption, increasingly uncontested, of themes rooted in psychological situations inspired by the inner disorientation of the individual rather than by a real, comprehensive view of the nation?

It is a fact, for example, that the literature linked to the war of 1914–1918 at that time did not produce a single novel that took the theme of the nation as the artistic core of the work. In the best novels, diaries, memoirs, essays, and short stories dealing with the war, which are often examples of very fine writing (who does not remember Paolo Monelli's *To Turn One's Toes Up to Die* [*Le scarpe al sole*]?), we find men contending with human, all-too-human, problems and desires; we move within dimensions of individuals or of groups by way of individual or group solutions, but Italy is in no way present.

Nor is Italy present in the literary problem-complex of the first postwar period. To be sure, the first aftermath was a felicitous literary season. It saw the gradual reawakening of the vein of a poetic realism (humanistic, naturalistic, social) in authors such as Federigo

Tozzi and Grazia Deledda, while the interior analyses of the subject in its shadows and contradictions were deepened in Italo Svevo's most singular novel *Confessions of Zeno* (*La Coscienza di Zeno*).

But national events remained constantly alien to the inspiration of many writers. Two facets of the self-same problem can be explained: on the one hand, we can attest to the decadent dissociation between the social state of man and his concrete existential situation; on the other, we end up by confirming the implicit contempt which the authoritarian governments and the Fascist hierarchies reserved for those creations defined by them as the futile tittle-tattle of men of letters, sterile efforts, and childish byzantinisms substantially alien to the profound march of history and to the impetuous initiatives in which the great movements of the people participate.

This, we believe, lies at the heart of our present study. The theme of nationhood which appeared rhetorical and false to the anti-Fascist or, at least, non-Fascist bourgeoisie did not succeed in even nourishing a nonexistent, antidecadent literature, as illustrative of the imperial ideology of Fascist youth.

What was the Italian novel in the years when fascism was in power and there was talk of Socialist leagues and Fascist street-squads, of strikes and royal guards, of nationalistic youth, or, say, of the Ethiopian expedition? Astride the advent of fascism a novel by G. A. Borgese, *Rubè*, published in 1921, enjoyed a certain success. Its protagonist meets death in Bologna during a volley fired by the forces of order on the occasion of serious riots, and the most singular and Pirandellian epilogue to the event is that both Fascists and Socialists wrangle over the body of the hero, Filippo Rubè, whom each of the contending factions view as a martyr fallen for their cause.

But who, in fact, was Filippo Rubè? He was an individual caught up in the conflict of ideology and faith, a man crushed by ambiguities and disenchantments, *un uomo finito*, a failure, like the one described about a year before by Giovanni Papini. But unlike the latter, he was unable to seek the answers to his own doubts in religious faith and dogma.

Consequently, national life, barely perceptible against the obscure background in *Rubè*, became almost the symbol of something absurd and incomprehensible. Further, it has no connections with the internal life of the protagonist and with the anxieties that torment his existence day in and day out. We can understand the persistent interest of the critics in Borgese, which has also manifested itself recently. But their interest addresses itself to the structure of the novel and not at all to its nationalistic content.

> 1921 was the year of publication of the novel *Rubè*, that is to say when the post-war crisis reached its peak, when a world, a society, a scale of values had fallen in the monstrous conflict. Borgese was among the first to perceive that the economic, social and political crisis was before all else a spiritual crisis. And that crisis, transposed onto the literary plane, allowed the discovery of a new type of character and the elaboration of a new style, a new prose.[1]

In short, not even Borgese succeeded in catching a glimpse of the nation beyond the intellectual concepts.

Now we shall analytically consider the most noted Italian writers of the Fascist era (1922–1944) in order to document our study and arrive at conclusions that go beyond generalities even if, in examining individual authors and individual works, true nationalistic themes appear only rarely.

The most authoritative writers in Italian fiction in the ascendant phase of fascism (1922–1935) have been formed by a concept of the fatherland and of tradition that was clearly stamped by the Risorgimento. But because of a kind of political modesty, as it were, they made no effort to deal with nationalistic trends or concepts. Consider, for example, the case of Alfredo Panzini. There is nothing in the fiction produced by this author that goes beyond a highly colored moralism or an amused hedonism. In his essays, on the other hand, the theme of nationhood is dominant, as can be seen from the following works: *1859: From Plombières to Villafranca* (*Il 1859: da Plombières a Villafranca*); *The War Novel in 1914* (*Il romanzo della guerra nell'anno 1914*); *The True History of the Tricolor* (*La vera storia dei tre colori*); and *The Count of Cavour* (*Il Conte di Cavour*). This proves, in our opinion, a certain inhibitory complex on the part of Panzini, who felt that the theme of nationhood was too solemn and sacred to entrust to the fictional world of the novel.

In *I'm the Boss* (*Il padrone sono me*), the only case in which the content of a novel seems to refer to a concrete contemporary social condition, or the so-called Socialist subversive activities in the province of Romagna, Panzini is concerned with resolving in esthetic terms of elements of a concrete experience that weighs upon him beyond all words.[2]

---

[1] Sarah D'Alberti, *Giuseppe Antonio Borgese* (Palermo, 1971), 119.
[2] Arnaldo Bocelli, "Alfredo Panzini," in *Orientamenti culturali: Letteratura Italiana* (Milan, 1969), 1:27 ff.

To be sure, if we look beyond the written page, we can perceive in many writers of that time the stirring of Italian nationality, if not in its political expressions, at least in its ethnological and cultural characteristics. It is, to cite one case, what Cecchi observes in connection with the stories of Enrico Pea, literary spokesman of those seafaring people who were the sailors and emigrants of Lucca. Cecchi writes:

> Whoever delves into the less remote history of this population of sailors and these workers in marble quarries will find in it interminable and bloody strikes ever since the siege of Famagosta. He will read there of revolts, volleys of stones, barricades, and of mass emigrations such as those to Brazil at the time of Crispi. The Carbonara tradition of Romagna descends the Apennines and flowing down from these mountains along the swampy coast of Grosseto and Corneta it ends up in the alleys of Trastevere. In Versilia the black flag, the red flag; but in Lucchesia, the Holy Face.[3]

But the model of literature suggested by Cecchi is vitiated by *a priorism* and arbitrariness. The image of a people's Italy, of the society that he presupposes and considers reflected in Pea's prose, is posed *a priori*. And the assumption of a particular content as a symbol of a permanent situation, as the common parlance of the nation, is arbitrary.[4]

To find the Italian nation in contemporary fiction is no easy task. There is a novel, to cite but one example, by Piero Jahier entitled *Results Regarding the Life and Character of Gino Bianchi* (*Resultanze in merito alla vita e al carattere di Gino Bianchi*), a novel which simultaneously discloses and conceals the civil intent, the national pedagogical purpose. The satire of the bureaucracy, the polemic against formalistic conduct, against the ethic of mere conformity to custom certainly constitute the book's merits, which are by no means negligible, but they do not warrant its classification as a national novel. It is, perhaps, only the unbosoming of a disappointed love for a fatherland fashioned of Mazzinian dreams, more mature and conscious than later experience, in fact, was to show.[5]

---

[3] Emilio Cecchi, "Prosatori e narratori" in *Storia della Letteratura Italiana* under the direction of Emilio Cecchi and Natalino Sapegno, *Il Novecento* (Milan, 1969), 9:570.

[4] A less participatory and more objective attempt at analysis in Pietro Pancrazi, *Ragguagli di Parnaso: dal Carducci agli scrittori d'oggi*, 3 vols. (Milan, 1968).

[5] Paolo Gonnelli, "Piero Jahier," in *Orientamenti culturali: Letteratura Italiana*, 1:531 ff., and particularly 536 f., for Gino Bianchi.

No one ignores how much of the refinement of taste and how much of the mature wisdom that characterizes the man of the province Vincenzo Cardarelli has bequeathed to Italian prose writing. But the content of his prose unfailingly has the tranquil tone of the fable, the harmonious accent of the classic myth. In short, it is an attitude that deliberately ignores the political passions of the present, the choices and ideals of the man and the citizen. Even the pieces collected in the volume *Let's Talk About Italy* (*Parliamo dell'Italia*) (1931) preserve a provincial character. The profound national theme is not present because its absence is in keeping with the author's wish.[6]

Cardarelli, and he is not the only one, can serve as an example of willed inattentiveness, an acquired forgetfulness, and a precise ostracism of the national theme from the customary literary productions.[7] Nor should we let ourselves be deceived by appearances. *My Carso Front* (*Il mio Carso*) by Scipio Slataper, for example, is not a book inspired by a positive, cohesive, historical sense of the nation or of the First World War. Rather, its inspiration lies in a taste for decadent, subjective, lyrical impressions recorded by a participant of open and sensitive mind.[8]

Thus Italian men of letters seemed to close themselves within the frame of a protective fantasy, as a shield against the adulterated nation that was being presented precisely in those years by the propaganda of the regime and its driving center, the Ministry of Popular Culture.

Anyone today rereading the fine prose of Antonio Baldini[9] or the writings of Massimo Bontempelli[10] might register surprise at the insistence that these authors attest and repeat: a formalistic, escapist model aspiring to rigmaroles rather than open to a grasp of the real problems of the time. True, it is the contention of some critics that in *Italy of Bonincontro* (*Italia di Bonincontro*), or, even more, in *Rugantino*, Baldini ended up by offering his own domestic version of a polite and pacifist Italy which he found congenial. But, in all

---

[6] Giuseppe Ravegnani, "Vincenzo Cardarelli," in *Orientamenti culturali: Letteratura Italiana*, 2:118 ff.

[7] Enrico Falqui, *La Letteratura del ventennio nero* (Rome, 1948).

[8] Enrico Falqui, "Come è nato 'Il mio Carso,' " *Letteratura* (1935), 9–12.

[9] Eurialo De Michelis et al., "Omaggio ad Antonio Baldini," *Nuova Antologia*, Jan. 1963.

[10] Carlo Bo, *Bontempelli* (Padua, 1943).

events, Baldini's theme was literature and not the nation, the charm of the cultured turn of a phrase and certainly not the bulky concreteness of the nation.

A similar argument can be made for the books of Massimo Bontempelli, which seemed to express the glorious officialism of the literature of the Fascist regime until the day in which, in November 1938, the writer was coerced into silence.

Committed or uncommitted, attentive or inattentive to the level of the country's civic maturity, when Baldini and Bontempelli bent over their pages what they particularly had in mind was the pleasure of writing good prose, a taste for the beauties of literature. Yet they were men who at a certain moment in their lives had assumed a precise position in the affairs of the nation. Toward the end of 1947 Baldini, in fact, had been requested to act as linguistic consultant to the framers of the text of the Republican constitution by the president of the Constituent Assembly. And Bontempelli had actively participated in the parliamentary labors of the first Senate of the Republic to which he was elected as an independent in the ranks of the Popular Front.

Therefore, we are warranted to assert, although with the risk of overgeneralizing, that only rarely did Italian writers of the Fascist era exhibit the courage, during or immediately after the regime's twenty-year rule, to tell us what they had really felt and suffered with respect to the events of their own time.

We shall now broaden the field of our investigation and test another case. The autobiography of Giuseppe Raimondi, *Giuseppe in Italy* (*Giuseppe in Italia*), a novel published in 1947, is emblematic. This writer has lived alone, or at least it would seem so from the remembrance that he has committed to writing. This is not to say that society did not exist around the protagonist Giuseppe: the Bologna of artisans and of the petty bourgeoisie at the time of the first worker organizations and of the first strikes is the setting in which life competed and contended with the young author's literary project. But it was only the inwardness of the remembrance and the emergence of some artistic and ethical values that interested the writer, not the surrounding society.[11]

---

[11] Renato Bertacchini, "Giuseppe Raimondi," in *Orientamenti culturali: Letteratura Italiana*, 3:299 ff. For the particular attitude toward national life, see the review of the novel by G. Corsini, *Società* (1950), 107 ff.

An argument of a different character is suggested for the book *My Seasons* (*Le mie stagioni*) by Giovanni Comisso. It is not a novel but a book of memoirs centered on the author's reactions to the contemporaneous national scene and its events, but, he is, above all, interested in describing such events in an artistic and vivid manner.[12]

Comisso, a legionnaire in D'Annunzio's expedition to Fiume, evokes *a posteriori* the state of mind of the moment.[13] And he does this with an honest objectivity. Indeed we must say that he tried to make himself the narrator of the Italian nation in relation to all the great occasions of our century. In *War Days* (*Giorni di guerra*) published in 1930, he evoked the attitudes of the populace and the emotions of the combatants of the First World War. But the book enjoyed no success because it seemed to the Fascist regime that the author showed scant inclination to involve himself in patriotic hagiography. In *Youth That Dies* (*Gioventù che muore*) published in 1949, he treated of the partisan war and, as in his other books, he tried to understand what substratum of feelings was operative in the depth of the human mind in support of the enthusiasms of the moment. Hence the following observations by Cecchi strike us as pertinent: "Some day or other the history of Italy from the beginning of the first war, which marked the fatal turn, simply will have to be written. And there will also be someone who will not feel inclined to limit himself to dividing the pros and cons, the black and the white abstractly ... he will want to re-evoke the attempt to understand the spirit of that tumultuous era, and bring it back to life in its unadorned reality."[14]

Could we say, therefore, that the nationalistic theme which could not manage to enter the Italian novel through the door of plot somehow enters into fiction through the window of the memory of the protagonists? This, of course, would be an exaggeration. On the other hand, it is true that we are at a turning point of Italian culture, which is beginning to commit itself to social themes. The upshot of its new concern, however, is that it lets itself be carried away, as we have said, by a current of ideas that are imported and that have not ripened in the matrix of national traditions. The sudden discovery of the American novel of commitment in the manner of Erskine Cald-

[12] Arnaldo Bocelli, "Comisso adriatico," *Il Mondo*, 17 Nov. 1953.
[13] The novel dedicated to the Fiume expedition is entitled *Il porto dell'amore*, published in 1925.
[14] Cecchi, 673.

well and the advent in Italy of Jean-Paul Sartre's literary production are part of this current.

Some reference to the *nation* theme can be found in certain pages from the novels of Corrado Alvaro. In the novel *Man in the Labyrinth (L'uomo nel labirinto)* Alvaro, for example, proposed to deal with the drama of the impossible integration of a southern ex-serviceman into the postwar civilian world. In *Twenty Years (Venti anni)* he evoked the tragic period of the war in a disenchanted portrayal of disappointed aspirations and dashed hopes; in *Man Is Strong (L'uomo è forte)* we note that the protagonist is placed in the anguished atmosphere of the Fascist dictatorship. It is an atmosphere, however, which is no longer conveyed in provincial terms (as in the first book) or in national terms (as in the second) but wholly in European and international terms, almost, indeed, with the sense of imminent catastrophe which the most acute minds perceived on the eve of the Second World War.[15]

In Vitaliano Brancati we can also find, in some degree, an eagerness to commit oneself to the life of the people. This statement is not based on a desire to overvalue the satiric treatment of the philandering and impotent Fascist *gerarca* in *Il Bell'Antonio,* but on the content of *The Old Man With the Boots (Il vecchio con gli stivali)*, a work committed to the creation of a moral and political portrait of the most opaque phase of the Fascist regime. A sincere portrayal of the problems of a certain stratum of the white-collar petty bourgeoisie is given in the story of Aldo Piscitello, the employee destroyed by the machine of his time. Here, in fact, the political subject offered Brancati the means of bringing to fruition a sincere work of clarification.[16]

It is in the fictional works of Riccardo Bacchelli that the national theme appears as most central to his concern. A writer of fluid prose with great underlying subtlety, Bacchelli has given literary expression to the popular passions of a particular period, as in *Nostalgia for Africa (Mal d'Africa)*. In *The Devil At Pontelungo (Il diavolo al*

---

[15] Armando Balduino, *Corrado Alvaro* (Milan, 1965); on reflections of his native Calabria in Alvaro's works, cf. Antonio Palermo, *Corrado Alvaro* (Naples, 1967).

[16] Brancati's novel *Paolo il caldo* was published posthumously in 1955. It is the author's most mature work; its theme is Sicily, which breaks up and is decomposed to the point of a confession of an atavistic sorrow akin to the most profound aspect of the theme of immobile Sicily of the *Gattopardo*. See Giacinto Spagnoletti, *Romanzieri italiani del nostro secolo* (Turin, 1957).

Pontelungo) he evoked with curiosity and ardor the anarchist plot of 1874, ingenuously devised in Italy by the Russian exile Michael Bakunin. And in *The Mill on the Po* (*Il mulino del Po*), he sketched in broad lines an historical-social portrait of the Italian bourgeoisie in the epic of the Scacerni family.[17]

At this point the following consideration is opportune. As is known, Bacchelli passed from the group around the literary journal *Ronda* and from writings marked by formal literary interests to writings attentive to a national political and social content. Well, at the very moment of this transition he succeeded in disengaging himself from the stifling friendships of cenacles and in arousing the interest of a broad public. In fact, *The Devil at Pontelungo*, published in 1927, was the first occasion in which Bacchelli succeeded in addressing a larger reading public. The success was due to the fact that the national novel presents a battery of emotional elements that are more immediately perceptible and of a much larger impact. Bacchelli has showed that he has understood this, so much so indeed that he has continued to embark on the path of the novel interwoven with elements of a national and social character.

In his pages the vicissitudes of the individual (the veteran of the Napoleonic campaign in Russia, the soldier of the First World War) succeed in assuming the dignity of events of collective interest: it is precisely for this reason that, among the writers of the Fascist era, Bacchelli appears to us as the one most linked to a view of the continuity of national life which he successfully projects onto the plots of his novels. Obviously such a projection, precisely because it was based on a very long period of time, required a cycle of novels rather than just one. Indeed, Bacchelli was, and remains, a master of cyclic fiction.

To the better-known novels of Bacchelli we must add the book published by him in 1932 entitled *Today, Tomorrow and Never* (*Oggi domani e mai*), a grandiose fresco of the Milanese bourgeoisie in the aftermath of the First World War. In this novel we find the Italy of Bacchelli's young adulthood, contemporary Italy grappling with her economic and social problems, the silk industry and the deflation, the drop in production and exports, the reflection of a determined policy in the attitudes of the characters of the novel. In some way this already represented a return to the concrete theme

---

[17] For Bachelli's openness to new human and social ideas, see Antonio Gramsci, *Letteratura e vita nazionale* (Turin, 1966).

of the nation and a sign of the imminent abandonment of the poetics of escape into formalism.[18]

It can be said, therefore, that the puritan vocation of the artist who detaches himself from the social world in which he lives began to decline around 1930 or a short time later, and a return to direct contact between the world of the artist and the world of man took place. This seems to be confirmed in many books that came into being in the era of declining fascism, even if in some cases they were published only many years later. We are referring to the novel by Carlo Emilio Gadda, *That Awful Mess in Via Merulana* (*Quer pasticciaccio brutto de via Merulana*), a psychological study of a contemporary news item, in which nevertheless one notes the distinct tone of the Fascist era, the mores of the middle bourgeoisie, the mentality of the ruling class which constitute the background of the story.

To be sure, the literary case of Gadda is richer and more complex than we can indicate here. In the *Pasticciaccio*, for example, we feel the true reality of the Italian nation in the incomparable variety of subplots and sundry dialects, in the extraordinary animation of the novel's characters who are thieves, prostitutes, and shady middlemen. Gadda observes them with the eyes of a professional, that is of the commissar Ingravallo, who has been assigned the investigation of the baffling murder of the young Liliana Balducci, which will remain insoluble.[19]

All this, however, does not mean "nation" in the commonly accepted sense. But the truth is that the national theme in the patriotic sense is not present in the representatives of the generation that was formed under fascism just in time to take up arms, in the Resistance, against the Nazis and against the funereal epigones of fascism. Such a consideration is dictated, for example, by Cesare Pavese in whom the theme of existentialism was illustrated by its most extreme consequence, that of suicide.

Pavese's fiction focuses on peasants, middlemen, and women and workers of the Langhe region and of the Piedmontese valleys. In those personages, however, Pavese sees men but certainly not Italians, either in their expressions or in their characteristics. To be sure,

[18] See Gianfranco Contini, *La letteratura dell'Italia unita (1861–1968)* (Florence, 1968).

[19] The presence of the distant fatherland is most alive in the *Giornale di guerra e di prigionia*, published in 1959. See Alfredo Gargiulo, "C. E. Gadda," in *Letteratura italiana del Novecento* (Florence, 1958), 567 ff.

society and inequality, injustice and sorrows are the object of Pavese's fiction. But he gives them a cosmic dimension and views them within a cosmopolitan framework outside the specific reference to the Italian nation and people.[20]

It is certainly not easy to pinpoint the moment in which Italian fiction succeeded in making the leap from the extrinsic to the intrinsic, from the ornamental to the essential, from the sterile baroque to the sincere rediscovery of the world of man, either as an existential problem of the individual, or as the social problem of the community. The nation in some way is a community which, by virtue of our formation and romantic tradition, we are better able to understand and in which we are better able to participate. It is opportune, therefore, to fix 1935 roughly as the date of the spiritual turning point effected in the cultured circles of Italian national society.

Whoever meditates, with the requisite detachment, on the sociocultural phenomena of those years will not take long to discover in the published essays and fiction a reborn moral commitment and a rejection of the hedonistic stance. A commitment and a rejection that obviously constituted the proof of an inner renewal, and palingenesis: it was perhaps an empirical mode, but certainly new and salutary so that one could move along the paths leading to a rediscovery of the positive quality of the real man. To be sure, if we look carefully, there was the risk that the writer might assume an ambivalent attitude toward reality (which, after all, was fascism) and might let himself be guided exclusively by the desire for a better reality which some saw in a rebirth of liberal democracy, others in a turn toward Socialist democracy.

Some have compared the cultural earthquake which took place in Italy in the thirties to the other which had occurred twenty-five years earlier, through the action of the avant-garde operating in the Florentine reviews *La Voce* and *Lacerba* of which Giuseppe Prezzolini and Giovanni Papini respectively were the leading spirits. But the parallel is only an apparent one. Twenty-five years earlier nobody contested the hypothesis, and the fact, of the existence of a bourgeois cultural unity. Therefore, the ferment of the young expressed only the desire for new experiences, the demand that new paths be opened up, the longing for the new, an affinity for literary complexity. At that time there was a desire to escape from the province in order to learn from Europe the language of decadence

[20] Franco Mollia, *Cesare Pavese* (Padua, 1960).

and of symbolism, a language which invited a fragmentation in expression, and stimulated literary experiences debouching into lyricism, and channeled the protests and the turn toward ideology of an individualist, anarchistic, aristocratic and, in short, an essentially reactionary character.

Twenty-five years later, the turn was conceived in an opposite sense: certainly not to break up an archaic cultural unity, but in order to construct a new one. In 1935 one started out from social and cultural fragmentation in order to move toward a search for a synthesis or, in other words, for an organic society.

In this sense there is a marvelous exactness in the expression adopted by an acute Italian writer, Geno Pampaloni. He has spoken of a constituent literature,[21] that is, of a literature that postulates or, at least, seeks the new foundation of a positive ethical-social life. Whereas, for this reason, a deliberately fragmentary lyrical impetus had issued forth from the innovative efforts of 1910, from the new efforts there gradually emerged a new vocation of the novel, as extended narration, as myth of an ardently longed-for reconciliation between literature and life. This had to be said because even the most inattentive reader notes that the tone and the secret hopes of writers changed during fascism and changed in a direction capable of giving a more adequate and concrete expression to the idea and to the feeling of the fatherland.

In fact the odyssey of the nation was rediscovered through the sufferings of the war and the most acute tensions of the social struggle. The rhetorical aura that had enveloped the theme of nationhood and of the fatherland in the generations preceding fascism fell away and fell away forever. It fell away to yield its place to a concrete approach, to a nation, that is to say, made up of human beings, workers, fathers, mothers, sons, soldiers, unemployed, families of professionals, peasants, real and alive personages. We consider that from this point of view the first name that must be cited is that of Secondo Tranquilli, better known under the pseudonym of Ignazio Silone, and in particular the novels first published abroad, *Fontamara* and *Bread and Wine (Pane e vino)*.[22]

It is not our intention here to overvalue the artistic validity of

[21] Geno Pampaloni, "La nuova letteratura," in *Storia della Letteratura Italiana*, 9:751 ff.

[22] *Fontamara* was published in Zurich in 1930 but the first Italian edition did not appear until 1947; *Pane e vino (Bread and Wine)* was also published in Zurich in 1937 and in Italy in 1955.

Silone's novels, even if we ourselves are not at all convinced by some of the critical judgments of his work which are overly restrictive.[23] In all events the fact remains that Silone was the first to suggest a new way of looking at people, villagers, and the *cafoni* or peasants.

The task of placing Silone's fictional work, however, does not appear either easy or free of controversy. It is a fact, for example, that to read Silone after reading Antonio Baldini or Riccardo Bacchelli can engender a certain disappointment. The critic Luti trenchantly expressed the reasons for such an impression when he wrote that Silone "starting out from the most valid tradition of Italian realism oriented his research toward the great examples of European fiction between the nineteenth and twentieth centuries thereby remaining in an eccentric position *vis-à-vis* the more advanced experiments of the contemporary novel which had already positively influenced the most vigorous personalities of our literature." [24]

This helps us to understand the scant success that Silone has met with readers and critics in Italy. Moreover, the Italian public was able to read Silone only much later, when the other writers had suggested to readers a more realistic way of looking at the society in which we live. True, in some cases, it was a question of a polemical realism, a willed iconoclastic desacralization, a radical contempt which did not arrive at any affirmation at all. But it was already a stimulating suggestion. This is the case of Curzio Suckert, known as Curzio Malaparte, a writer of the most acute brilliance, but cynically commited to develop the themes of contemporary culture and society to the point of paradox. Consider, for example, *The Skin* (*La pelle*), a book that appeared four years after the end of the war but which was enormously effective in its portrayal of a certain segment of Italian society.

Panders, rogues, liars, turncoats swarm in the pages of *The Skin*, a book which Malaparte considered the most spirited defense of the Italian people. From a certain aspect this is true because certainly the Fascist image of Italians, those fighters in Africa marching along the roads of the ancient imperial legionnaires, was false and absurd. It was more genuine to consider the image of the Italians of the mandolin and of spaghetti. But Malaparte linked to the Naples of *O sole mio* a dramatic saraband of theft, acts of violence, indecencies

---

[23] See, for example, Giorgio Pullini, *Il romanzo italiano del dopoguerra (1940–60)* (Padua, 1965), 203.

[24] Giorgio Luti, *Narratori italiana contemporanei* (Florence, 1967), 147.

which certainly did not constitute the real image of Italian society.[25] Nevertheless it only serves here to point out and underline how much that was positive lay in that new interest in the people, in the new way of looking at the streets and squares of Italy.

In an inquiry on the historical novel in Italy, aroused by the unexpected success of *The Leopard* (*Il Gattopardo*) by Tomasi di Lampedusa, the critic Wladimiro Cajoli asserted: "As regards the national sense of the future historical novel, we may expect that will spring forth from the achieved sense of nationhood. . . . The accusations and polemics are useless: we are a nation of recent vintage and we would not be able to have a historical novel which would not reflect this historical truth." [26] We have cited Cajoli's opinion here because we too are convinced that the nation is not a fact, it is not an immutable datum. Rather, it is a spiritual value *in fieri*, something in the making that is accomplished by way of the tribulations and the sorrows of generations.

Accordingly, let us see how the tribulations and grievous sorrows that struck the generation of Italians living at the time of the Second World War and of the Resistance have found expression in the Italian novel.

We can begin with the novels of Mario Tobino, in particular *The Desert of Lybia* (*Il deserto della Libia*).[27] In this book, Tobino, a neurologist, relates his experiences as a soldier curious about the customs of other peoples and alert to the most unexpected happenings. Between the diary and the tale, Mussolini's colonial war becomes for the protagonist, who is a medical officer, an opportunity for the unexpected discovery of the world, of Arab women, of the emotional excitement of bombings, of the sense of insecurity and adventure that dominates in the heart of one immersed in the war.

Giuseppe Berto's *War in Blackshirt* (*Guerra in camicia nera*), published in 1955, is a most singular book in which the destiny of the nation is reflected in the personal crisis of a volunteer combat soldier. In the beginning the author avows his acceptance of the Fascist justification of the war, but then, while relating the evolution of his feelings, he involuntarily betrays a pacifist vocation.[28] Another book

---

[25] See Giampaolo Martelli, *Curzio Malaparte* (Turin, 1968).

[26] Walter Mauro, *Inchiesta sul romanzo italiano* (Rome, 1960), 80.

[27] *Il deserto della Libia* was published in 1952. Among Tobino's subsequent writings the theme of nationhood is resumed in *Due italiani a Parigi*, published in 1954, and particularly in *Passione per l'Italia*, published in 1958.

[28] For a close analysis of the novel see Pullini, 155 ff.

of exceptional interest is that by Giose Rimanelli, *Day of the Lion* (*Tiro al piccione*), which is the testimony of a soldier of the Fascist armed forces of the republican government established by Mussolini at Salò in the months of the partisan struggle. The inner dilaceration expressed by Rimanelli also strikes at the fatherland, explicitly accused of having willed the ruin of its own sons.

It can be said that Italian fiction concerning the second world conflict discovered the sense of peace through the sufferings of the war and that it can be generally inscribed in a curve that moves from adventure and, by way of the cognition of sorrow, arrives at a more serious discovery of nationhood. This itinerary is not only typical of the writers just mentioned, but also of the books by Renzo Biasion and by Ugo Pirro.

Here we shall recall Biasion's *Sagapò*,[29] a demythologized representation of the expedition to Greece, and Pirro's *The Camp-Followers* (*Le Soldatesse*) and *Jovanka and the Others* (*Jovanka e le altre*).[30] Pirro's war is a war between males and females, between Greek whores looking for a loaf of Italian bread and Italian soldiers looking for erotic release. In substance these books, which a certain sector of moderate Italian public opinion has tried to reject as dangerous and antinational, end up by suggesting an image of an Italy of civilization and peace that is much more convincing than the flashing forest of bayonets invoked with ardent oratory by il Duce. The same can be said for the very beautifully written book by Mario Rigoni Stern. *The Sergeant of the Snow* (*Il sergente della neve*),[31] a view of the sufferings and of the frank humanity of the Italian army sent to the Russian front.

The partisan war, in addition to the aforementioned work by Rimanelli, which is the book of a chaotic youth in crisis, is also reflected in the novel by Vigano: *Agnese Goes to Die* (*L'Agnese va a morire*),[32] in *The Path of the Spider's Webs* (*Il sentiero dei nidi di ragno*)[33] by Italo Calvino, in *The Twenty-three Days of the City of Alba* (*I ventitrè giorni della città di Alba*)[34] by Beppo Fenoglio, in *A Night in the Year '43* (*Una notte del '43*)[35] by Giorgio Bassani,

[29] Turin, 1953.
[30] Milan, 1956 and 1959.
[31] For a detailed interpretation of this novel, see Franco Antonicelli, "Un sergente in Russia," *La Stampa*, 21 April 1962.
[32] Turin, 1949.
[33] Turin, 1947.
[34] Turin, 1952.
[35] Published in *Cinque storie ferraresi* (Turin, 1956).

in *Overcast Sky* (*Cielo chiuso*) by Gino Montesanto.[36] There is a vigorous and virgin quality in the feelings that dominate these works, almost a sense of the rebirth of the nation whose people perceive the solidarity between classes, individuals, and groups in the name of an ideal of humanity and brotherhood, which constitutes the real base of the new-found peace.

Among the most recent novels inspired by the theme of nationhood we must recall the work of Luigi Preti, *Giovinezza, Giovinezza* ....[37] It recounts the odyssey of a generation educated by fascism, shaken by a dramatic experience, and committed finally in a vigorous effort aiming at the rediscovery and liberation of its own civic and national dignity. It is an ambitious novel, even if questionable as regards the solidity of the narrative structure and the rhythm of the exposition. In it is described the progressive acquisition of a national and civil consciousness on the part of a group of university students. The story is articulated in three phases: triumphant fascism, the war unleashed by the Axis powers, and the partisan struggle. The author's moral commitment is evident, indeed bared all too much, and the work seems to be inspired by a concern and a fear that the new crop of young people born in an affluent society may forget and abandon the values for which the generation of their fathers had suffered and fought for so long.

At this point we can ask ourselves: when actually did the new literary generation appear on the scene of Italian culture?

We could point to Alberto Moravia's first novel *The Time of Indifference* (*Gli indifferenti*) (1929) which is, so to speak, the forerunner of a new breed of writers. But the subsequent stages of development in Moravia's work, although gradually making him more sensitive to the themes of the internal contradictions of the personality, have by no means driven him to consider the social structures along the lines of nationhood and the idea of fatherland. From this point of view, Vasco Pratolini, who was alert to the popular vein of Italian life at the beginning of the twentieth century, deserves to be remembered more than Moravia. We could focus on his trilogy of Italian social history, begun with *Metello*, continued with *Extravaganza* (*Lo Scialo*), and concluded with *Allegory and Derision* (*Allegoria e derisione*).[38] But it seems to us to be even more opportune

---

[36] Milan, 1956.
[37] Milan, 1966.
[38] See Gian Franco Vene, *La letteratura della violenza e altri saggi* (Milan, 1961) (in particular on *Lo Scialo*).

here to refer to the Syracusan, Elio Vittorini, whose discovery of
man, in the dimension of his psychological and cultural components,
proceeded from *Conversation in Sicily* (*Conversazione in Sicilia*),
Men and Nothing (*Uomini e no*), up to *Women of Messina* (*Le
donne di Messina.*)[39]

The importance of the role played by Vittorini in contemporary
Italian culture has not yet been sufficiently stressed. But whoever had
the occasion, years back, to read the issues of the review *Politecnico* is
quite aware that the commitment to renewal proposed by Vittorini
was not only a formula or an abstract desire but a concrete rhythmic
progression and a serious attempt to formulate new cultural values.

Many readers found *Conversation in Sicily* a difficult book, almost
cryptographic and hermetic. But once we understand the key, we
can appreciate the extremely poetic recital of a return to the island
by Silvestro, the young protagonist who is possessed by abstract
rages, that is, by the anti-Fascist political passion.

But Vittorini, unable to express himself under the Fascist dictatorship, was no better off in the ranks of his Communist comrades who
imposed upon him a certain dogma based on the truths of Moscow
and a certain cult of the personality of Stalin to which the free writer
would not bow, preferring a new silence.

A significant core feature of contemporary Italian fiction is to be
seen in that vein of essay-writing, so to speak, the greatest expression
of which certainly was Carlo Levi's *Christ Stopped at Eboli* (*Cristo
si è fermato ad Eboli*).[40] The critic Contini has defined that book as
"a brilliant report on the extremely archaic life of Lucania" and has
declared that in it we find "the grace of the encounter between a
peasant world of primitive culture and an unprejudiced spirit of
observation." [41] Everybody is familiar with its subject matter: the
South seen by a native of Piedmont, banished to Lucania by the
Fascist regime. The South of Carlo Levi is a world without time, a
setting without a dynamic, a society without ferment.

By this we do not mean to say that Levi intuitively grasps the
historical and economic core of the Southern question. Rather, the
eye of the painter-writer succeeds in locating the people of Lucania,
as later those of Sicily in *Words Are Stones* (*Le parole sono pietre*),
in a national context that asks for patriotic solidarity in order to
raise to the level of the modern world an underlying population

---

[39] Giacinto Spagnoletti, *Romanzieri italiani del nostro secolo.*
[40] R. Crovi, "Meridione e letteratura," *Il Menabò* 3 (1960).
[41] See Contini, 569.

whom adverse circumstances and institutions have forced into a state of social stagnation.

Wherever the new interest in the concrete problems of Italian society swoops down with a greater vigor of expression into a choral drama, into an episode that constitutes a kind of cross-section of the life of the nation and of the life of the people—there we have the fruition of the new Italian fiction at its best.

This is the case with novels of Francesco Jovine, *Mrs. Ava* (*La Signora Ava*), *The Empire in the Province* (*L'Impero in provincia*), *The Lands of Sacramento* (*Le terre del Sacramento*). *Mrs. Ava*, which appeared in 1942, draws its inspiration from an ancient popular song of the South placed as an epigraph to the book, almost as if to symbolize an atavistic and immutable condition. We find in it the reconstruction, at once realistic and loftily poetic, of the historical setting of the Milisan province at the time of Garibaldi's Expedition of the Thousand and of the annexation of the Kingdom of Italy. The same theme recurs in *The Empire in the Province*, published in 1945, which presupposes the failure of the bourgeoisie in the unification attending the Risorgimento.

An extremely severe and deep artistic representation slowly matured along this theme, introducing personages whose chief traits are a bitter consciousness of the external world and disenchanted irony. This had its greatest expression in *The Lands of Sacramento*, which appeared posthumously in 1950. The novel is linked to the searing peasant experience of the South, to the hunger for land, to the abuses of power practiced by the landowners, and to police repression—themes that were very much alive and diffused in the Italy of yesterday and, in part, also in the Italy of today.[42]

As the years flowed by and the second postwar period began to draw to a close, new constructive attitudes also matured on the literary scene. Among others, attention should be drawn to the attitudes of those who tended to relate the novel more and more to sociology and less and less to the imagination. We note the attitude of those who transcribe literary problems in terms of semantics or semiology and no longer in terms of styles and of genres; the attitude of those who advocate the passage "from a poetry straining toward essential experience in the dominion of the word and of the inner life, to one straining toward essential experiences in the dominion of reality and of the world of relation." [43]

[42] See Piero De Tommaso, "Francesco Jovine," *Belfagor* 3 (March 1960).
[43] A. Romano, *Officina* (1955), 118.

But before the signs of such a new mode of understanding were perceptible in practice, there appeared, in 1959, a novel which brought everything up for discussion again: *The Leopard* by Giuseppe Tomasi di Lampedusa. The author was a Sicilian nobleman who had died the year before, an aristocratic and disdainful spirit, skeptical and embittered. Poised between elegy and history, *The Leopard* relates an event that is at once familial and social with passionate intensity and peaks of sheer lyricism.

In Sicily, between 1860 and 1910, against the background of the Expedition of the Thousand and the end of the Bourbon monarchy, the protagonist, Prince Fabrizio Corberi di Salina, lives in an age of transition. He is a living witness to the twilight of the baronetage and to the advent of a plebeian and mercantile society. Don Fabrizio is aware of the progressive eclipse of that prestige which had permitted members of his family to achieve power and distinction in the past. But he is just as convinced that nothing really new will happen despite the revolutionary events transpiring on the political scene.

His nephew Tancredi shares the illusion of young people who believe that times are ripe for renewal, but the old man's skeptical wisdom is there to belie him and to disenchant him. And, in fact, in the end, the Garibaldino Tancredi does not marry the "leopardess" Cencetta, but Angelica Sedara, a beauteous and comely girl with newly acquired bourgeois money. It is an emblematic marriage, linking the ambitions of the new rich with the bloodless traditions of the ancient nobles, in order to perpetuate a hierarchic and fundamental social condition thanks to a compromise that is perpetually renewed: "If we want everything to remain as it is, it is necessary that everything change."

The success of *The Leopard* has been the climactic point in the most recent history of Italian literature. The novel, as one critic writes, develops the theme "of the mutual indifference between history and individual fates that find their forlorn truth in the procession toward death." [44] Herein lies the surprising modernity of the novel, in whose pages we discern a tone derived from Proust, James, and Pirandello.

In Italy, however, the book was primarily effective in involving and orienting the reader's interest toward historical-social themes, leading in practice toward a return to the poetry of Italian nationhood as a laborious construction of human beings and generations. [45]

[44] Pampaloni, 857.
[45] See Gaetano Stammati, "Gattopardeschi o no," *Belfagor* 3 (March 1960).

The polemics that ensued in the wake of *The Leopard* found an impressive response not only among novelists but also among critics. And, in fact, the present condition of Italian fiction gives the impression of participating in an alert experimentalism that keeps all roads open as possible itineraries without precluding any *a priori*.

It will suffice to consider a few of those names which we come upon most frequently in the literary news. Giuseppe Dessì, a Sardinian, has resumed with a new zest the theme of the cultural and social depression of his fellow islanders. In consequence, he has pondered over the theme of nationhood as a choral experience of people who progress toward a confused goal of material well-being and civil maturity.[46]

Giovanni Arpino, above all with *A Crime of Honor* (*Un delitto d'onore*),[47] has revealed himself as a novelist alert to reality, clearly oriented toward the social-cultural and psychological interpretation of facts, and skillful in narration, because he possesses that rare Ariosto-like gift of letting the story flow along so spontaneously.

Goffredo Parise, whom many appreciate for his detached and cynical *The Handsome Priest* (*Prete bello*),[48] has perhaps given the best of himself in the youthful *The Dead Child and the Comets* (*Il ragazzo morto e le comete*)[49] where the recent war, the bombings, Americans, and the girls who marry Americans constitute the elements of a plot set in a community in which the whole life of the nation pulsates.

In conclusion, we can assert, first of all, that any prescriptive criteria regarding the content of the novel are to be rejected. The general plan of our argument has an ideal and not a material validity in the sense that we are seeking, to use Luigi Russo's phrase, the transcendental nation, and certainly not the objective expression of the Italian state and of the ideologies around the fatherland expressed by the political tendencies of either the government majority or the opposition.

Let us add that to express the national conscience is rarely, in the man of letters, a precise aim. Rather, it is the shadow or the projection of a mode of feeling things, one's own self, and society. Therefore, nationalism in the contemporary Italian novel is colored by a

---

[46] On Giuseppe Dessì, cf. Michele Tondo, "Giuseppe Dessì," in *Orientamenti culturali: Letteratura Italiana*, 3:559–86.

[47] Florence, 1961.

[48] Milan, 1954.

[49] Vicenza, 1951.

subjective feeling of sincere human solidarity when the author's eye falls on the present iniquities, on unjust privileges. On the other hand, this concept of nationalism is colored with more-or-less explicit reservations when the author is inspired by existential anxieties and by the tribulations of the individual rather than by the collective evils of society.

This is the critical and sociological core of this study. It is not true that a Socialist novel, because it is internationalist, cannot give voice and expression to the national theme. Neither is the reverse true, namely, that only an avowedly patriotic writer can sing poetically of national fortunes or tragic disasters. Ideology and a political stance have nothing at all to do with it. The nation surfaces, or does not surface, as an image and state of mind, only if the writer has felt—or has not felt—his destiny as man, not indeed as that of an absurd fragment hurled into the infinitude of time and space, but, rather, as that of a citizen, son of a father, or father of a son, linked to someone who like himself has rights and duties, linked to someone who, like himself, fears and hopes within the frame of a certain time and upon a certain part of the earth and awaits that the future be better than the past in order to allow, at last, the fulfillment of the hopes of the people.

BIBLIOGRAPHY

Alvaro, Corrado. *L'uomo è forte*. Milan: Garzanti, 1966.
———. *Vent'anni*. Milan: Bompiani, 1964.
Antonicelli, Franco. "Un sergente in Russia." *La Stampa*, 21 April 1962.
Arpino, Giovanni. *Un delitto d'onore*. Milan: Mondadori, 1966.
Bacchelli, Riccardo. *Il diavolo al Pontelungo*. Milan: Mondadori, 1962.
———. *Il mulino del Po*. Milan: Mursia, 1969.
———. *Mal d'Africa. Complete Works 6*. Milan: Mondadori, 1962.
———. *Oggi domani e mai*. Milan: Garzanti, 1940.
Baldini, Antonio. *Italia di Bonincontro*. Florence: Sansoni, 1940.
Balduino, Armando. *Corrado Alvaro*. Milan: Mursia, 1965.
Bassani, Giorgio. *Cinque storie ferraresi*. Milan: Club degli Editori, 1969.
Bertacchini, Renato. "Giuseppe Raimondi." *Orientamenti culturali: Letteratura Italiana 3*. Milan: Marzorati, 1969.
Berto, Giuseppe. *Guerra in camicia nera*. Milan: Garzanti, 1967.
Biasion, Renzo. *Sagapò*. Turin: Einaudi, 1954.
Bo, Carlo. *Bontempelli*. Padua: Cedam, 1943.
Bocelli, Arnaldo. "Alfredo Panzini." *Orientamenti culturali: Letteratura Italiana 1*. Milan: Marzorati, 1969.

———. "Comisso adriatico." *Il mondo,* 17 Nov. 1953.

Borgese, Giuseppe Antonio. *Rubè.* Milan: Treves, 1921.

Brancati, Vitaliano. *Il bell'Antonio.* Milan: Bompiani, 1969.

———. *Il vecchio con gli stivali e altri racconti.* Milan: Bompiani, 1958.

———. *Paolo il caldo.* Milan: Bompiani, 1969.

Calandra, Edoardo. *La bufera.* Milan: Garzanti, 1964.

Calvino, Italo. *Il sentiero dei nidi di ragno.* Turin: Einaudi, 1967.

Cardarelli, Vincenzo. *Opere complete.* Milan: Mondadori, 1962.

Cassola, Carlo. *Fausto e Anna.* Turin: Einaudi, 1967.

———. *La ragazza di Bube.* Turin: Einaudi, 1967.

Cecchi, Emilio. "Prosatori e narratori." *Storia della Letteratura Italiana: Il Novecento* 9 Milan: Garzanti, 1969.

Comisso, Giovanni. *Giorni di guerra.* Milan: Longanesi, 1965.

———. *Il porto dell'amore.* Milan: Longanesi, 1960.

Comisso, Giovanni. *Le mie Stagioni.* Milan: Longanesi, 1963.

Contini, Gianfranco. *La letteratura dell'Italia unita (1861–1968).* Florence: Sansoni, 1968.

Crovi, R. "Meridione e letteratura." *Il Menabò* 3 (1960).

D'Alberti, Sarah. *Giuseppe Antonio Borgese.* Palermo: Flaccovio, 1971.

De Michelis, Eurialo, et al. "Omaggio ad Antonio Baldini." *Nuova Antologia* (Jan. 1963).

Dessì, Giuseppe. *I passeri.* Milan: Mondadori, 1965.

De Tommaso, Piero. "Francesco Jovine." *Belfagor* 3 (March 1960).

Falqui, Enrico. "Come è nato 'Il mio Carso.'" *Letteratura* 9–12 (1935).

———. *La letteratura del ventennio nero.* Rome: La Bussola, 1948.

Fenoglio, Beppe. *I ventitrè giorni della città di Alba.* Turin: Einaudi, 1966.

Gadda, Carlo Emilio. *Quer pasticciaccio brutto de via Merulana.* Milan: Garzanti, 1965.

Gargiulo, Alfredo. "C. E. Gadda." *Letteratura italiana del Novecento.* Florence: Le Monnier, 1958.

Gonnelli, Paolo. "Piero Jahier." *Orientamenti culturali: Letteratura Italiana.* Milan: Marzorati, 1969.

Gramsci, Antonio. *Letteratura e vita nazionale.* Turin: Einaudi, 1966.

Jahier, Piero. *Resultanze in merito alla vita e al carattere di Gino Bianchi.* Florence: Vallecchi, 1967.

Jovine, Francesco. *L'impero in provincia.* Turin: Einaudi, 1967.

———. *Signora Ava.* Turin: Einaudi, 1967.

———. *Le terre del Sacramento.* Turin: Einaudi, 1962.

Levi, Carlo. *Cristo si è fermato a Eboli.* Milan: Mursia, 1968.

Malaparte, Curzio. *La pelle.* Florence: Vallecchi, 1969.

Mariani, Mario. "Ignazio Silone." *Orientamenti Culturali: Letteratura italiana. I contemporanei* 1 (Milan: Marzorati, 1969).

Martelli, Giampaolo. *Curzio Malaparte.* Turin: Borla, 1968.

Mauro, Walter. *Inchiesta sul romanzo italiano.* Rome: Opere nuove, 1960.

Mollia, Franco. *Cesare Pavese.* Padua: Cedam, 1960.

Monelli, Paolo. *Le scarpe al sole.* Milan: Mondadori, 1955.

Montesanto, Gino. *Cielo Chiuso.* Milan: Mondadori, 1967.

Moravia, Alberto. *Gli indifferenti.* Milan: Bompiani, 1968.

Palermo, Antonio. *Corrado Alvaro.* Naples: Liquori, 1967.

Pullini, Giorgio. *Il romanzo italiano del dopoguerra (1940-60).* Padua: Marsilio, 1965.

Pampaloni, Geno. "La nuova letteratura." *Storia della Letteratura Italiana* 9 (Milan: Garzanti, 1969).

Pancrazi, Pietro. *Ragguagli di Parnaso: dal Carducci agli scrittori d'oggi.* 3 vols. Milan: Ricciardi, 1968.

Panzini, Alfredo. *Il padrone sone me!* Milan: Mondadori, 1967.

Parise, Goffredo. *Il prete bello.* Milan: Garzanti, 1966.

Pirandello, Luigi, *Tutti i romanzi.* Milan: Mondadori, 1966.

Pirro, Ugo. *Jovanka e le altre.* Milan: Bompiani, 1960.

———. *Le soldatesse.* Milan: Bompiani, 1965.

Pratolini, Vasco. *Una storia italiana (Metello—Lo scialo—Allegoria e derisione).* 4 vols. Milan: Mondadori, 1968.

Preti, Luigi. *Giovinezza, Giovinezza....* Milan: Mursia, 1967.

Ravegnani, Giuseppe. "Vincenzo Cardarelli." *Orientamenti culturali: Letteratura Italiana* 2 Milan: Marzorati, 1969.

Rigoni Stern, Mario. *Il sergente nella neve.* Turin: Einaudi, 1967.

Rimanelli, Giose. *Tiro al piccione.* Rome: Trevi, 1969.

Silone, Ignazio. *L'avventura di un povero cristiano.* Milan: Mondadori, 1969.

———. *Una manciata di more.* Milan: Mondadori, 1964.

———. *Il segreto di Luca.* Milan: Mondadori, 1965.

———. *Vino e pane.* Milan: Mondadori, 1963.

Slataper, Scipio. *Il mio Carso.* Florence: La Nuova Italia, 1967.

Spagnoletti, Giacinto. *Romanzieri italiani del nostro secolo.* Turin: Eri, 1957.

Stammati, Gaetano. "Gattopardeschi o no." *Belfagor* 3 (March 1960).

Svevo, Italo. *Romanzi.* Milan: Oglio Publishers, 1969.

Tobino, Mario. *Il deserto della Libia.* Turin: Einaudi, 1966.

———. *Due italiani a Parigi.* Florence: Vallecchi, 1954.

———. *Passione per l'Italia.* Turin: Einaudi, 1958.

Tomasi di Lampedusa, Giuseppe. *Il Gattopardo.* Milan: Feltrinelli, 1969.

Tondo, Michele. *Narratori italiani contemporanei.* Rome: La Bussola, 1965.

Vene, Gian Franco. *La letteratura della violenza e altri saggi.* Milan: Sugar Ed., 1961.

Viganò, Renata. *L'Agnese va a morire.* Turin: Einaudi, 1954.

Vittorini, Elio. *Conversazioni in Sicilia.* Turin: Einaudi, 1968.

———. *Le donne di Messina.* Milan: Bompiani, 1964.

———. *Uomini e no.* Milan: Mondadori, 1966.

The Crises of French Nationalism
in the Twentieth Century

RIMA DRELL RECK

The shock waves of historical change have divided France many times in the twentieth century. Every political and social upheaval has been in some sense a crisis of nationalism, with each side proclaiming that it alone was truly French. The polarities which characterize the rhythm of French history, those intense and painful alternations between anarchy and absolutism, have all borne the banner of nationalism.

The French national identity is based on a persistent belief in a unique and superior culture. When the French refer to something as "truly French" they mean that it has its roots in a continuous and consistent culture going back at least to the seventeenth century. This sense of a culture has persisted through two world wars, several revolutions and civil wars, and a number of foreign invasions. The French national consciousness is in large measure formed by the knowledge imparted to every schoolboy that the nation which produced Racine, Molière, and the palace of Versailles has once and for all time reached the acme of cultural development; it need only continue to respect its past in order to retain its superiority. The "truly French" is grounded in the literature, language, and art of the French nation.

Any study of French cultural nationalism in this century must take account of the diversity of causes nationalism has been called on to justify and defend. At this moment in history and for the purposes of the present volume, it has seemed to me pertinent above all to examine French cultural nationalism in terms of the cultural or artistic traditions on whose behalf it has been invoked. To limit the study of French cultural nationalism to political camps would merely demonstrate more specifically what we already know in a general way, that the primary divisions are leftist and rightist, with the centrist camp generally too dull and unconvincing in its style of protest to attract any long-term attention. Another limitation of the purely political approach to cultural nationalism in France is that ultimately it is totally uninformative. French nationalism in this century is generally associated with rightist movements such as the Action Française and with men such as Maurice Barrès and Charles Maurras. This association is not incorrect; however, it is seriously incomplete. The French Socialists and Communists have also at various times carried the banner of nationalism. Indeed, they have done so as often and as loudly as their opponents.

The rightists and the leftists have claimed themselves the sole heritors of the French tradition and called their opponents traitors. To feel that one's cause is just, when one is French, is also to feel that one is a true son or daughter of France. The relationship between cultural nationalism and the creative artist in a nation which has a long-established sense of self-identity is shaped by a variety of factors. Particular interpretations of the literary tradition, questions of Parisian versus provincial culture, judgments on the relationship of France to the whole of Europe, personal vengeance and public morality—all of these questions have contributed to the phenomenon we call cultural nationalism in France. An examination of the views of several outstanding French prose writers of this century can lead us to understand better the peculiar nature of French cultural nationalism.

Charles Péguy (1873–1914), a poet and essayist born in Orléans, represents a recurrent form of French cultural nationalism, less striking than the nationalism of Maurice Barrès, but as characteristically French and as enduring. For Péguy, the self-conscious provincial who came to Paris and never felt at home there, the true spirit of France was embodied in historical figures such as Joan of Arc. Péguy believed that the roots of French culture lay not in classicism but in the Middle Ages. His nationalism was totally unintellectual, its appeal above all emotional and religious. Péguy sought a renewal of the French national spirit through symbols, through historic myths. His long poem on Joan of Arc, published in 1909, made him famous. He had already become well known in select circles as the founder in 1900 of the literary review *Les Cahiers de la Quinzaine.* In his magazine and in his poetry and essays, Péguy expressed his stunningly simple but powerful vision. The creative renewal of France was to be based on French history, architecture, and common speech. The language and idioms of the people were the means by which Péguy hoped to bring his nation to a new era of glory, truth, and faith.

Péguy was a self-styled nationalist prophet; he also considered himself a republican and a Socialist. H. Stuart Hughes points out that Péguy shared with Georges Sorel (1847–1922), the French sociologist and political theorist, a genuine sympathy for the people, an inflexible moralism, and an impatience with intellectual rhetoric. Péguy hated France's political and academic elite as much as did Sorel.[1] However, the peculiar bundle of beliefs which animated Péguy isolated him from the conventional categories of French politics. He found some points of agreement with Sorel, others with Maurras and Barrès. He hated intellectuals, but when in the heat of the Dreyfus Affair some nationalist students attempted to attack the classroom where Émile Durkheim was lecturing, Péguy struggled physically to defend him. Ultimately, Péguy managed to cut himself off from both the Left and the Right.

Militant republicanism and militant Catholicism were for Péguy the two great systems of belief which gave France its uniqueness. To others these beliefs may have seemed mutually exclusive. Not to Péguy. They were, as he said, *mystiques* and not *politiques*; they could coexist and together revive "spiritual France" and save the nation. Péguy's visionary oddities led him to quarrel at one time or another with everyone he knew. He began to become disillusioned with the possibility of seeing within his lifetime the spiritual renewal of France he sought. He went off to fight in the First World War and died on the eve of the Battle of the Marne in 1914. Péguy's death made him a symbol of French unity, a unity he had never been able to foster while still alive. In the years since his death Right and Left alike have invoked Péguy's name and quoted his poetry and essays in defense of their conflicting nationalisms.

The master figure of twentieth-century French cultural nationalism was Maurice Barrès (1862–1923). As novelist and polemicist he shaped the minds of several generations. In his evolution from *le culte du moi* ("the cult of oneself") to *le culte de la terre et des morts* ("the cult of the land and the dead") Barrès swept along with him most of the writers who were to become the leading nationalists

---

[1] H. Stuart Hughes, *Consciousness and Society* (New York, 1958), 346.

of the post-World War One years and after. Men little younger than himself, such as Maurras, looked upon him as a kind of spiritual and intellectual father. Pierre Drieu la Rochelle, Robert Brasillach, Louis Aragon, and Jean-Paul Sartre, to name just a few, have confessed to the formative influence of Barrès.

The Uprooted (Les Déracinés), a novel Barrès published in 1897, depicted the alienation of a generation separated from its spiritual roots. With this novel Barrès became the prince of conservative provincial nationalism, what came to be called integral nationalism. The literary historian Pierre de Boisdeffre ranks The Uprooted with the teachings of Henri Bergson as the most crucial intellectual influences in France during the early years of the twentieth century.[2] Like Péguy, Barrès resented the Paris establishment and the concentration of cultural and intellectual activities in the capital. He felt that the true moral and spiritual force of France was to be found instead in the provinces, in those provinces from which most of the writers living in Paris had originally come. In his search for the basis of his own identity Barrès gave concise expression to currents of thought and feeling common to many of his contemporaries. Most of the intellectuals considered themselves patriotic; for them love of country was an axiom. Barrès phrased cogently the malaise of his generation: France was in a state of moral decay; national energy was being sapped by the phenomenon of decadence.

The Symbolist movement had left its imprint on France; lethargy and a sense of the unreality of things often dulled or paralyzed creative activity. Barrès identified these problems as symptoms of uprootedness. He went on to propose that the self could best survive by attaching itself to concrete and permanent realities outside of itself—*la terre et les morts* ("the native soil and the dead.") He defined psychic rootedness in terms of the nation and personal salvation in terms of political activism.

The parochialism of Barrès's cultural nationalism was to have far-reaching effects after his death. In order to perpetuate and to reinforce the innate genius of the French nation, Barrès believed it was necessary to minimize and even eliminate "foreign" influences. During the Dreyfus Affair, when it had become apparent that the evidence against Dreyfus was collapsing, Barrès still found it possible to condemn Dreyfus—for having divided the country as he did:

---

[2] Pierre de Boisdeffre, *Métamorphose de la littérature. De Barrès à Malraux,* 2nd ed. (Paris, 1950), 49–50. In this essay, all translations from the French are mine.

"He should perforce be ashamed at having aroused such sympathies."
For Barrés the cohesiveness of the community was more important
than the innocence or guilt of the individual. Barrès had a great
many hatreds. He mistrusted Jews; he intensely feared and detested
the Germans. (His animosity toward the Germans is easily understood—Barrès was from Lorraine.) Barrès's Jews and Germans and
other "foreigners" all bore a striking resemblance. They were cardboard figures without minds or souls. Barrès's nationalistic cast of
mind led him to simplify "others" most effectively. In his polemics
(*Scènes et doctrines du nationalisme*, 1902) and in his novels (*Colette
Baudoche*, 1909) Barrès portrayed the outsider, the non-Frenchman,
as a kind of natural enemy in a Darwinian vision of racial as well as
cultural struggle.

The ultimate doctrine of Barrèsian nationalism was the cult of
energy, the desire for *un homme nationale* ("a national figure"), *un
homme drapeau* ("a flag bearer") to embody the national consciousness. In *The Uprooted* Barrès had described the ideal leader as one
who would be "nourished by thousands and thousands of roots,"
who would be "the living sum of countless souls striving for the
same goal." [3] Napoleon had been such a "professor of energy"; so
had Bismarck. France needed strong leaders. True democracy, that
is democracy which truly expresses the will of the people, is authoritarian. The liberal slogans politicians mouth for their own personal
benefit have nothing to do with true freedom. According to Barrès,
true freedom springs only from a mystical psychic bond between
the leader and the people. The hero of *The Uprooted* says that the
republican system, the modern ideal of the French bourgeoisie,
is inimical to the great personality and to "that liberty which is truly
great." Barrès himself remarked, "I love the Republic, but armed,
glorious, organized." [4]

In the two trilogies of novels, *The Cult of the Self* (*Le Culte du
moi*) (1888–1891) and *The Novel of National Force* (*Le Roman
de l'énergie nationale*) (1897–1902), Barrès gave fictional form to
his ideas. He shaped the thought of countless French writers who
came after him. Garine, the adventurer-hero of André Malraux's
The Conquerors (*Les Conquérants*), is a reincarnation of Barrèsian

[3] For an excellent discussion of Barrès's conception of the externalized self,
see Robert Soucy, "Barrès and Fascism," *French Historical Studies* (Spring,
1967), 75–76.
[4] Maurice Barrès, quoted in Pierre de Boisdeffre, *Barrès parmi nous* (Paris,
1952), 99.

political activism. Pierre Drieu la Rochelle's fictional heroes all suffer from the spiritual malady Barrès had identified at the end of the nineteenth century, that malady for which he had prescribed *le culte du moi.* Louis Aragon admits that his youthful restlessness, even his surrealistic polemics, were inspired by the spiritual master who shaped him and most of his contemporaries, Maurice Barrès.

Barrès's influence was pervasive even on writers whose moral convictions evolved far beyond the simplistic formulas of individualism and energy. Jean-Paul Sartre envied Barrès his ability to ignore the moral ambiguities inherent in action. Barrès did not face the dilemmas of the modern intellectual. In an essay on the revolutionary changes painfully taking place in China, Sartre reflects on the ease with which Barrès celebrated bloodshed, misery, and death: "Happy Barrès. He died when his time came, carrying with him into his grave the secret of a good conscience." [5] Sartre's remark underlines what was perhaps Barrès's greatest appeal, his fundamental single-mindedness and anti-intellectualism. For the writer who suffers from an excess of awareness, who knows that any moral choice is tainted by hidden realities which will perhaps be revealed too late, Barrès's conviction that direct contact with life's ugly realities can harden and perfect a man has an almost fatal charm. So too does his simple view of political realities—the end justifies the means; any action in the ultimate service of integral nationalism is justified. What succeeds is right. Force is virtue.

The obvious romanticism of Barrès's self-styled "realism" is also part of its appeal. Barrèsian nationalism satisfied a deep-seated need for a simplified world, one in which values are clear, where by willing something a man can accomplish it, a world in which France represents what is most admirable and most noble. In such a world, all a Frenchman has to do is truly be French to stand at the summit of the natural order.

Charles Maurras (1868–1952) was the leading rightist of the early part of this century in France. Along with Jacques Bainville and Léon Daudet he published the daily newspaper *Action Française* from 1908 to 1944. *Action Française* has become synonymous with the political movement inspired by Barrès's integral nationalism. This movement contributed to the fall of the Third and Fourth republics and has been held accountable for a number of crimes in French history in this century. No balanced assessment of the Ac-

[5] Jean-Paul Sartre, *Situations V* (Paris, 1947), 16.

tion Française movement, examining its constructive as well as negative contributions to French thought in the first half of the century,
has yet been undertaken. There are a number of historical studies
which once again condemn Maurras, as he was condemned after the
Liberation, for having paved the way for and abetted the German
Occupation of France.[6] None of these gives just weight to Maurras's
consistently anti-German prejudices or to those elements of his
theories which reflect long-standing French traditions.

Maurras represented a quintessentially traditional form of French
nationalism. He advocated a return to the characteristic institutions
of the Ancien Régime: monarchy, a fixed social hierarchy, decen-
tralization, and Catholicism as the organizing element in the total
order. His "integral nationalism," as Roy Pierce has aptly pointed
out, assumed that nationalist sentiments could only be fully expressed within the framework of those traditional institutions he
sought to restore. The nation, however, was the prior condition of
every social and individual good. National unity was therefore the
very condition of justice.[7] Any threat to French society was to be
detected, rooted out, and destroyed. Pierce speculates convincingly
that Maurras's hatreds (for the Jews, the Protestants, the Masons)
may have preceded his doctrines, rather than been a result of them.
In any case, the negative, oppositional flavor of the Action Française made it ultimately distasteful even to those authorities its beliefs seemed to favor.

Maurras envisaged a return to a monarchy which in many ways
was more benign that the one overthrown by the French Revolution. He dreamed of a decentralized France where there would be a
purely voluntary acceptance of the national community. This acceptance would spring from the provinces in a kind of instinctive
spiritual communion. And, of course, Catholicism would be the
pillar of a proper political system. By the mid-1930s the hate-filled
polemics of the Action Française group and many of its activities

---

[6] See Michael Curtis, *Three against the Third Republic: Sorel, Barrès, and
Maurras* (Princeton, 1959); Samuel M. Osgood, *French Royalism under the
Third and Fourth Republics* (The Hague, 1960); Edward R. Tannenbaum,
The Action Française: Die-Hard Reactionaries in Twentieth-Century France,
(New York, 1962); and Eugen Weber, *Action Française, Royalism and Re-
action in Twentieth-Century France* (Palo Alto, Cal., 1962). For a questionable
interpretation of Péguy as a precursor of French fascism, see Hans A. Schmitt,
Charles Péguy, The Decline of an Idealist (Baton Rouge, La., 1967).

[7] Roy Pierce, *Contemporary French Political Thought* (London and New
York, 1966), 12–13.

had completely alienated the world Catholic community. The Action Française was formally condemned by Pope Pius XI in 1927. Among the youthful adherents of the Action Française was the novelist Georges Bernanos, who was imprisoned briefly after a clash with the police in Paris. Bernanos never relinquished his fundamental royalism or his belief in the need for firmer spiritual values to counteract France's moral decline. However, he parted company with the Action Française group when he began to glimpse the rising Nazi menace and the specter of another world war. Unlike Maurras, Bernanos became identified with the Resistance by the time of the Liberation.

The Action Française was an outgrowth of the Dreyfus Affair. As René Rémond has pointed out, royalism was almost totally dead until the Action Française revived it by fusing it arbitrarily with the wave of nationalist feeling which had been aroused during the Dreyfus case. In fact, the French Right acquired its deliberately reactionary philosophy almost intact when it became mobilized around the Action Française.[8] During the thirties in France national values came to be associated with the Right. The Right managed to endow their leftist political adversaries with the reputation of being bad citizens; the rightists alone were good citizens. In the repressive measures taken by the French government against the Left during the thirties we see the influence of rightist propaganda. Nevertheless, the movement which centered on Charles Maurras and his followers was always unstable, prone to sudden surges forward and equally sudden abdications. The successes of the Maurras group were determined less by external events than by the mysterious waxing and waning of the often contradictory passions which animated it. Maurras combined activism with a kind of reverential mysticism. As Pierce has noted, "Maurrassian doctrine amounted in the final analysis to an evasion of the problems of politics. By insisting dogmatically on a whole package of historically-oriented preferences, the doctrine could not cope with a situation in which a choice had to be made among other competing claims." [9]

In 1942 the only answer Maurras offered to the choice he faced between resistance and collaboration was to deny both. "La seule France" ("France alone") were his only words. His allegiance was to an ideal France which existed only in his mind. As a result, he was totally out of touch with the contemporary reality of the occu-

---

[8] René Rémond, *La Droite en France de 1815 à nos jours* (Paris, 1954), 184.
[9] *Contemporary French Political Thought,* 16.

pied nation. He continued to edit his newspaper and to address himself to an audience which no longer existed. His detachment was no defense against the charge of collaboration made against him after the Liberation. He was condemned to life in prison, where he spent his remaining years.

The tide of patriotic nationalism aroused by the First World War receded gradually when that war ended. Except for ardent rightists such as Barrès and Maurras, only a few literary figures continued to protest against the excessive importance of Paris in French national life. In the early 1920s the Surrealists declared that nationalism and the emotions it aroused were inimical to the spirit of poetry. Karl Epting has characterized the "middle generation," young men who read Nietzsche in French translation and fought in World War One, as a group whose pessimism was far deeper than that of Barrès.[10] These young men no longer believed that contact with the "hard realities of life" would toughen them or that an energetic cultivation of provincial values could provide a remedy for the deepening moral decline of France. The new Marxist state in Russia loomed ever larger on the European horizon.

As French intellectuals began to choose sides with respect to Russia they also took positions regarding French nationalism. Those who rallied to the vision of a Socialist utopia espoused the spirit of internationalism. They sought answers to national dilemmas in movements outside of France. During the decade preceding the outbreak of the Second World War the rightists alone remained staunchly nationalistic. Their activities did little to foster national unity. Ultimately they further divided a country already splintered by intense factionalism, leaving France unprepared to meet the foreign invasion which was to take place in 1940. The decade of the thirties is one of the most complex in recent French history, a time of constant political crisis and of intense self-examination for French writers.

Novelist and essayist Pierre Drieu la Rochelle (1893–1945) may well be the most representative French writer of the first half of the twentieth century. Every significant literary and political venture of his time left its mark on him. A young poet when he went off to fight in the First World War, Drieu became a brilliant polemicist and an outstanding writer of fiction in the twenties and thirties. During the last years of his life, he edited the *Nouvelle Revue Française* under the German Occupation. At last, having met disil-

---

[10] Karl Epting, *Frankreich im Widerspruch* (Hamburg, 1943), 86.

lusionment in every intellectual adventure of his life, Drieu committed suicide in Paris in 1945. Barrèsian romanticism, the Surrealist
adventure, Marxism and European internationalism, the rise of fascism, the fall of France, the Collaboration are all vividly mirrored in
Drieu's work. With prophetic vision he foresaw every major movement of his era; by the time each one of these movements became
widespread and fashionable, Drieu had already tired of it and gone
on to some other uncharted adventure. As René Girard has observed, Drieu's work is "more complete and more authentic than the
wholly heroic or wholly sordid work in which this century abounds.
Drieu shows us the other side of Malraux, and the other side of
Céline, or even Beckett." [11]

Drieu was a nationalist for only part of his life. His break with
nationalism and his subsequent critique of it reveal many of its weaknesses and illustrate why French cultural nationalism has had such
discontinuous fortunes in this century.

Like Péguy, the young Drieu left to fight in World War One
hoping to find in the experience of battle a transcendent vision.
Drieu's first collection of poems, *Interrogations*, was published in
1917. In "Paroles au départ" we find echoed the Barrèsian reverence
for action and heroism:

> Et le rêve et l'action...
> La totale puissance de l'homme il me la faut...
> Je ne puis me situer parmi les faibles. Je dois mesurer
> ma force....[12]

> (I claim, in dream and deed...
> The total strength of man...
> I shall not take my place among the weak.
> I then must take stock of
> my own strength....)

Drieu calls war "une révolution du sang" which will cleanse and re-
build the house of France. For Drieu the barbarism of battle and the
naïve patriotism of his fellow soldiers are encouraging; they signal
an emergence from the decadence which had paralyzed France in
peacetime. In "A vous, allemands," he states the central theme of the
volume:

> ... J'exalte la guerre
> parce qu'elle est liée à la grandeur.
> ......

[11] René Girard, review of Frederick Grover, *Drieu la Rochelle* (Paris, 1962),
in *Modern Language Notes*, May 1964, 336.
[12] Pierre Drieu la Rochelle, *Interrogations* (Paris, 1917), 9.

...La guerre tue les peuples moribonds.[13]

(...I sing of war
because it's bound to grandeur....

...War kills the dying nations.)

Several years later, in *Mesure de la France* (1922), Drieu assessed what he had sought on the battlefields of Europe. "I believed in the strength of our enemies. I dreamed more of offering up my own death than of victory for my country.... This was the last funereal stage of my adolescence." And with a tone of resigned disappointment he adds, "The war began, went on for a while, and ended." [14] France had been too weak to win alone; the French did not savor the joy of an untainted victory. The "measure of France" had been taken: a country with a great soul, but a weak and bloodless body.

In 1922 Drieu still believed in the doctrines of nationalism. However, in the light of his experiences in the war he was beginning to foresee that a nation such as France could only survive by fusing her spiritual gifts with the strength of more elemental nations such as Germany. He wrote, "The role of nations is not yet over. The nation will for a long time still, perhaps forever, be the constant classic form which action naturally takes. Its measure is a point of equilibrium. . . . But if the era of Nations is not ended, the era of Alliances has nonetheless begun." [15] In a collection of poems which appeared in 1924, Drieu foresaw the death agonies of nationalism:

L'ancien temps des patries s'en va de la mémoire
Les empires furieux vont ravager l'histoire
Les poteaux sans verdeur se sont tous renversés
Sous la fatale roue des dernières années.[16]

(The ancient time of nations fades away
And other empires appear to ravage history
And the leafless stakes of our past
Have been cut down by the grinding wheel of our era.)

By 1927, when he published *The Young European* (*Le jeune européen*), Drieu had decided that nationalism was above all a continuation of the cult of individualism. Young men who read Bergson, Claudel, Gide, and Barrès, "those sensual *fakirs*," tossed restlessly in their beds at night, impatient to find adventure and

---

[13] *Ibid.,* 67.
[14] Pierre Drieu la Rochelle, *Mesure de la France* (Paris, 1922), 2–3.
[15] *Ibid.,* 64.
[16] Pierre Drieu la Rochelle, *Plainte contre inconnue* (Paris, 1924), n.p.

exaltation.[17] But the death agony of individualism had begun on the battlefields of World War One. In *Geneva or Moscow* (*Genève ou Moscou*) (1928) Drieu at last delivered the funeral oration for Barrèsian nationalism: "Our most pressing task is to create Europe. We must create Europe just as one must breathe in order to live. We must create a united Europe . . . or we shall let a huge pyre accumulate on which, in less than twenty years, all civilization, all hope, all human honor will go up in flames." [18]

Drieu foresaw another world war, one which would be caused by two doctrines inherited from the nineteenth century, socialism and nationalism. Drieu heaped his scorn on the second-rate thinkers who kept these doctrines alive. "A great man leaves his disciples only a bone to gnaw on . . . . What timid and pitiful formulas Barrès and Maurras made of the powerful ideas of Comte and of Taine!" [19]

In *Geneva or Moscow* Drieu explains the relationship between French nationalism and literature in the early years of the twentieth century.

> After that great movement of foreign trade in the nineteenth century, that industrious coming and going across all our intellectual frontiers, those rich imports of Oriental color, of German philosophy, of English poetry, of Russian and Scandinavian tragedy, after the unfolding of romanticism—and at the very moment when all of that was still fermenting in the great experimental and transformational workshop of Symbolism—a movement of withdrawal, of undisturbed meditation was absolutely necessary.
>
> From that need sprang the effort to go back to our own roots, to arm ourselves once again with our most efficacious disciplines, an effort accomplished by men as diverse as Barrès, Maurras, Péguy, Claudel, and Gide.[20]

As a spiritual doctrine nationalism needed no other justification in the days of its prime. For Drieu, *The Free Man* (*L'Homme libre*) by Barrès was the masterpiece of literary nationalism. It was the link with the nineteenth century, "a secret poem, a magic spell." But rereading it, he found in it "all the limitations of a conservative mind." [21] Barrès had nothing more to say to the Frenchman of 1928. If France was to survive the threat of Russia and to triumph over it, it had once and for all time to be cured of its romantic malady. It

---

[17] Pierre Drieu la Rochelle, *La jeune européen* (Paris, 1927), 13.
[18] Pierre Drieu la Rochelle, *Genève ou Moscou* (Paris, 1928), 109.
[19] *Ibid.*, 51.
[20] *Ibid.*, 60.
[21] *Ibid.*, 62.

had to become realistic and practical, to think in terms of Europe as a unified whole.

Drieu decided in the thirties to become active in politics, to break free of paralyzing self-analysis and find renewal in action. Power and action appeared to him antidotes to the decadence which was subtly devastating France. In 1933 he joined the Parti Populaire Français (PPF), an extremist group with Fascist principles. Drieu rejected Barrès's cult of individualism and nationalism because he at last knew that they were fundamentally romantic and self-defeating. Political engagement was to replace the paralysis of individualism, to regenerate the self in new externalized forms of combat. Drieu chose what Paul Sérant has aptly called "fascist romanticism." [22] Under the Occupation, he found himself standing side by side with the nationalistic French rightists he had once rejected. And the political party he chose for its "realism," the PPF, was based on doctrines which, except for its pro-German stance, resembled turn of the century Barrèsian nationalism in almost all respects.

Ultimately, Drieu la Rochelle was a victim of that romantic individualism from which he had tried to escape. His career illustrates both the pervasive influence of Barrèsian thought and the peculiar nature of cultural nationalism in twentieth-century France. In new or emerging nations nationalistic doctrines can serve to unite a people by expressing their new-found sense of identity. However, in nations with a long history and a rich cultural tradition, nationalism can easily become a form of protest, a means of challenging the status quo. Movements of cultural nationalism in France in this century have had above all a disruptive effect.

French Marxists of the thirties were beginning to look to Russia and to advocate internationalism. The rightists initiated doctrines modeled after the new movements in Italy and Germany and proclaimed themselves nationalists of a special and superior kind. Jacques Doriot, head of the PPF, claimed in *The Reshaping of France* (*Refaire la France*) that France was in dire need of a new kind of nationalism, one which could restore the unity of purpose and produce the unintellectualized strength that were such prominent features of Italian and German nationalism. Doriot wrote, "A truly national government would long ago have closed its frontiers to that army of intellectuals which is invading France from the outside." [23] He went on to deplore the "intellectual unemployment" which made France's

---

[22] Paul Sérant, *Le Romantisme fasciste* (Paris, 1959).
[23] Jacques Doriot, *Refaire la France* (Paris, 1938), 33.

best educated young men unfit to hold the country together. "To save our country from decadence, we must end this incoherence, we must restore to France unity of command and unity of action.... *We must see a rebirth of sacred national egoism.*" [24] An active collaborationist under the Germans, Doriot considered himself a revolutionary of a new breed. "As a revolutionary, I am driving France into the path of national and social revolution, the only way I can restore its unity," he remarked in 1942.[25]

René Rémond has chronicled the history of French rightist movements since 1815. Rémond describes the salient features of European Fascist movements as follows: "All fascist experiments combine the same ingredients. Against a background of irritated or wounded patriotism and with a 'former soldier of one's country' mentality, the following patterns flourish and become dominant: an anti-parliamentarianism which is at once ideological and practical; devotion to the State; a passion for order; the admiration of power; the cult of the strong leader; party dictatorship and official corporatism." [26] On the basis of this definition of Fascism Rémond concludes that although France has produced many vocal rightist movements in this century, some of them quite active, there has never been an indigenous French Fascism. His reasoning is based on the last segment of his definition, "party dictatorship and official corporatism," which one must admit has never been achieved by any of the French rightist movements. However, several movements have existed which evinced all the other characteristics of Fascism Rémond lists; these movements were certainly Fascist in their objectives and their methods. It is true that their doctrines were frequently inconsistent; their "parties" coalesced and dissolved with unsettling suddenness. These rightist coalitions were all ultimately unsuccessful. But if we judge recent French history by Rémond's criteria of consistency and success, France has probably never had an indigenous republican system either. The salient characteristic of French political and social movements has been their discontinuity and instability.

The central difficulty in assessing nationalism in France in this century lies in the difference between the spirit of cultural nationalism and its practical application. The spirit has been present throughout the last forty years in a variety of forms. However, the practice has been historically discontinuous and theoretically inconsistent.

[24] *Ibid.*, 94–95; italics Doriot's.
[25] Jacques Doriot, *Réalités* (Paris, 1942), 106.
[26] *La Droite en France*, 204.

When you are a Frenchman to be French means to be better. Thus any artist or ideologist who wants to challenge a reigning literary or political fashion is likely to claim that he and his followers speak for "spiritual France." The fashion he opposes is of course undermining the true spirit of France and is therefore justifiably challenged.

Vast fluctuations in political and social structures have been characteristic of modern French history. France's political nationalism has fluctuated widely, ushered in by one wave of cultural nationalism and undermined by the next. French cultural nationalism may have contributed to the characteristic instability of the French political system. Nevertheless, above all political differences and beyond the life spans of particular forms of nationalism, France as a cultural ideal has endured. In recent years the fluctuations have been more frequent, precipitated by the Second World War and by the smaller wars fought during the gradual decline of French colonial power.

The intense conflicts which French nationalism has aroused are strikingly illustrated by the Occupation, the Liberation, and the immediate postwar period. Conflicting nationalisms of the Right and the Left had paved the way for France's fall to the Germans. Torn by internal political dissension, France was totally unprepared for the unified and well-trained German troops who walked into France in 1940. In 1943 Alphonse de Chateaubriand, an apologist for the Collaboration, described in *The Psychology and the Struggle of Today* (*La Psychologie et le drame des temps présents*) what he called the drama of self-image. Without this self-image and the vision it inspires, a nation cannot survive. "Because Germany recovered this vision, the only such vision in the modern world strong enough to have any influence, I have urged that France recreate her own vision by allying herself with her German neighbor." [27] Chateaubriand's viewpoint is typical of many Collaborationists. They believed that cooperation with Germany would restore to France, by a kind of spiritual transfusion, some of the vigor and unity of purpose they attributed to Germany. An outspoken advocate of collaboration, Chateaubriand was arrested after the Liberation. Another collaborationist, Lucien Rebatet, provides us with an insider's view of the state of mind of French rightists in the prewar years. *Ruins* (*Les Décombres*) (Paris, 1942) is the spiritual and intellectual autobi-

[27] Alphonse de Chateaubriand, *La Psychologie et le drame des temps présents* (Sceaux, 1943), 12.

ography of a young man who saw with striking clarity the course
which lay before the fiercely anti-Communist groups of which he
was a part. Rebatet diagnoses clearly the moral malady which was
to reveal its severest symptoms after the Liberation. The factions
Rebatet observed were only temporarily absorbed into the Collaboration or the Resistance. They surfaced again after 1944 and continued to devastate France by their conflicts for ten years more.
Rebatet survived the *épuration* ("purge") and has once again resumed his career as a journalist. He is one of the few collaborationists to re-establish the semblance of a normal existence in France.

The war provided a temporary and unstable respite from the
crises of nationalism of the prewar years. From his exile in England
Charles de Gaulle spoke to his occupied French countrymen in
June 1940. His voice and his words inspired a resurgence of nationalism as much cultural as it was political. De Gaulle's appeal to
the French consciousness invoked the sense of national heroism,
that heroism exemplified by Joan of Arc and by de Gaulle himself.
La France spirituelle of Péguy, the appeal to provincial rootedness
of Barrès, the mistrust of Germany of Maurras all found their echoes
in de Gaulle's words. As Paul Sérant has said, "From that moment
General de Gaulle knew his mission. He incarnated true France, that
true France which was at war with official France." [28] De Gaulle
called for true Frenchmen to resist the Germans. The nationalism
which identified itself with the historic traditions of French cultural
and moral superiority was thus placed in direct confrontation with
the defeatist nationalism of the collaborationists. However, as R.-L.
Bruckberger points out, "De Gaulle did not create the Resistance.
The Resistance was a spontaneous reaction to the dishonor of the
armistice. De Gaulle gave a voice, authority, a tangible and sustained
majesty to this reaction by the French sense of honor." [29] There
seemed to exist during the war a genuine possibility of ultimate reconciliation between those factions which had fought so bitterly
before 1940.

The Liberation did not bring about the hoped-for reconciliation.
Instead, the old conflicts of nationalism reappeared under new guises.
Bruckberger wrote in 1948, "This is an era of false antitheses. France
is being torn apart by the internal contradiction first introduced by
integral nationalism: the conflict between country and honor. I
hoped ... that the Resistance could accomplish a great blessing for

[28] Paul Sérant, *Les Vaincus de la Libération* (Paris, 1964), 172.
[29] Raymond-Léopold Bruckberger, *Nous n'irons plus au bois* (Paris, 1948), 29.

France, that it could reunite these two elements." [30] Bruckberger saw clearly the central moral issue which underlay the excesses of the postwar purge. Some Frenchmen were wreaking a dishonorable and illegal vengeance on others in the name of France and of patriotism. A small number of intellectuals protested the *épuration*. In 1947 Maurice Bardèche wrote to François Mauriac, "Everything which is being written in France at this moment is based on the following intangible postulate: that whoever was not a *résistant* ["Resistance fighter"] was a disloyal Frenchman." [31]

The French Communists, who at first had refused to participate in the struggle against Germany, had joined the Resistance in large numbers in 1941. By the war's end they constituted a large segment of France's moral leadership. Their underground activities had endowed them with the aura of patriotic nationalism. The Comité Nationale des Écrivains de la Résistance (CNE), formed under the Occupation, included Communists and existentialists as well as writers who belonged to neither of these two groups. At the first full meeting of the CNE after the Liberation its ranks were swelled by a great many newcomers, most of them Communists. Albert Camus and R.-L. Bruckberger resigned. François Mauriac wanted to resign, but seemed afraid to do so. Despite its internal difficulties, the CNE retained the prestige it had acquired from those members who had organized it under the Occupation. When it published its famous blacklist naming writers and intellectuals who had differed from the principles of the CNE during the Occupation and began to prosecute them in the name of France, the literary *épuration* began.

The history of the *épuration* is just beginning to be written. Works by Robert Aron and Paul Sérant, among others, are bringing to light the scope and long-range effects of legal procedures which often resembled a reign of terror. Collaborators were shot in the streets or imprisoned. Of those imprisoned, many were condemned to be executed. Among those executed in Paris in 1945 was Robert Brasillach, one of the most gifted writers of his generation. Maurice Bardèche was imprisoned several years later, primarily for the doubts he expressed in *Nuremberg or the Promised Land* (*Nuremberg, ou la terre promise*) about the legality of the war crimes trials. Bardèche was ultimately released, but his personal possessions had been confiscated, his home destroyed, his career ruined. He is still

---

[30] *Ibid.*, 30.
[31] Maurice Bardèche, "Lettre à François Mauriac," reprinted in *La Pensée Libre* (Paris, 1947), 14.

alive today in Paris, living in obscurity. The *épuration* often imposed severer penalties on writers for their printed statements than on military men who had shot hostages and sent many of their countrymen to concentration camps during the Occupation.

French nationalism was the chief justification for many of the postwar excesses. Writing in *Les Lettres Françaises* in July 1946, Communist poet and novelist Louis Aragon, secretary of the CNE, invoked the symbol of France: "There is above us a common reality, a force which carries us along and which we must not deny—that is the history of France, that is France." In an open letter to the members of the CNE Jean Paulhan criticized the vague principles which had determined the choice of names on the blacklist: "irreparable crime, irreversible harm done to the nation." Paulhan pointed out that *la patrie* ("the fatherland") was the key term in most of the condemnations, that atrocities were justified in the name of *la patrie*. He questioned the logic and legality of these principles and pointed out in a striking series of textual citations that many of the present members of the CNE would be condemned by their own organization if judged by statements they had made in earlier years. Among the writers Paulhan cited were Romain Rolland, Julien Benda, Paul Eluard, and Louis Aragon.[32] Paulhan's second and last open letter to the CNE addressed itself to the central issue of the *épuration*, the schism between country and honor. He examined the reasoning of Julien Benda, who was instrumental in a great many literary reprisals: "Julien Benda tells us that he would have considered the Collaboration a gift from the gods 'if Germany had brought us a better regime than the one we had.' What then is your reproach to those Collaborators whose massacre you demand, Benda? That they betrayed their country? No, not if you were yourself ready to betray her. Their crime is to have belonged to a party which was not yours. You are not, whatever you say, a patriot. You are a partisan . . . ."[33] Paulhan's own definition of patriotism was clear enough —to no longer divide the French nation by a destructive appeal to spiritual France. In other words, Paulhan laid the blame for the postwar atrocities directly at the feet of the tradition of cultural nationalism inherited from Barrès.

Ultimately the post-Liberation convulsions died down. While

---

[32] Jean Paulhan, "Lettre aux membres du C.N.E.," facsimile reprinted in *La Pensée Libre* (Paris, 1947).

[33] Jean Paulhan, "Dernière lettres aux membres du C.N.E.," facsimile reprinted in *La Pensée Libre* (Paris, 1947).

today many older Frenchmen still divide the world between *résistants* and *collabos* ("collaborationists"), the younger generation has begun to read the works of the condemned collaborationist writers in an entirely different light. To the French university students of the sixties and seventies Drieu la Rochelle and Brasillach appear to be fellow outsiders who had the courage to oppose the "establishment" and the bad luck to come out on the losing side. The irony of this reversal is apparent. Most significant is the fact that nationalism seems no longer to be the strong and destructive force it was for over half a century in France. The New Right of the 1950s did indeed have, as Pol Vandromme has noted, a Barrèsian cast. When Charles de Gaulle was returned to power in 1958, "the sensibility if not the nationalist ideology of Barrés returned with him."[34] André Malraux's Ministry of Culture under de Gaulle was above all inspired by an exalted vision of *la France spirituelle*, France as the genius of civilization and disseminator of culture to other, less gifted nations. De Gaulle's essential appeal, even in the severest moments of May 1968, was to *la grandeur française* and to his own role as continuer of the tradition which began with Joan of Arc.

De Gaulle was at last removed from power. And now he is dead. France seems to be somewhat less proud and a great deal more practical at this moment. She is beginning to willingly become part of Europe. It is too soon to predict that the intense nationalism which both illuminated and undermined France for almost eighty years is finally dead. In many ways it would be a great loss. Perhaps instead French cultural nationalism has passed into a new more tempered phase, one in which love of country will no longer create an unending spirit of crisis.

BIBLIOGRAPHY

Albérès, R.-M. *Bilan littéraire du XXe siècle.* Paris, 1956.
Aron, Raymond. *L'Opium des intellectuels.* Paris, 1955.
Aron, Robert. *Histoire de la libération de la France.* Paris, 1959.
———. *Histoire de Vichy.* Paris, 1954.
Bainville, Jacques. *Histoire de deux peuples continuée jusqu'à Hitler.* Paris, 1935.
Barrès, Maurice. *Scènes et doctrines du nationalisme.* Paris, 1925.
Barrès, Philippe. *Sous la vague hitlérienne.* Paris, 1933. A study from the

---

[34] Pierre Aubéry, "L'Intelligence des Juifs chez Maurice Barrès," *Romanic Review*, Oct. 1960, 193.

inside of the fever of National Socialism as it gripped Germany by a frequent and sympathetic visitor.

Bernanos, Georges. *La France contre les robots.* Paris, 1947.
———. *La grande peur des bien-pensants.* Paris, 1931.
———. *Les grands cimetières sous la lune.* Paris, 1937.
———. *La liberté, pourquoi faire?* Paris, 1953.
———. *Nous autres Français.* Paris, 1939.
Bonneville, Georges. *Prophètes et témoins de l'Europe, Essai sur l'idée d'Europe dans la littérature française de 1914 à nos jours.* Leyde, 1961.
Bosquet, Alain. *Verbe et vertige.* Paris, 1961.
Brasillach, Robert. *Une Génération dans l'orage.* Paris, 1968.
———. *Lettres écrites en prison.* Paris, 1952.
———. *Notre avant-guerre.* Paris, 1941.
Camus, Albert. *L'Homme révolté.* Paris, 1951.
———. *Lettre à un ami allemand.* Paris, 1945.
Carré, Jean-Marie. *Les Écrivains français et le mirage allemand.* Paris, 1947.
Cristiani, Chanoine Léon. *La Fin d'un régime, Tableau de la vie politique française de 1919 à 1939.* Lyon, 1946.
Dami, Aldo. *Dilemmes des maurassiens.* Milan, 1958.
Drabovitch, Wladimir. *Les Intellectuels français et le Bolchévisme.* Paris, 1937.
Duhamel, Georges. "Lettre à Lucien Descaves." *Les Nouvelles Épitres,* 23 Feb. 1946.
Frank, Bernard. *La Panoplie littéraire.* Paris, 1958.
Germain, André. *Les Croisés modernes (De Bloy à Bernanos).* Paris, 1958.
Gide, André. *Journal 1940–1942.* Paris, 1946.
———. *Journal 1942–1949.* Paris, 1950.
Lang, Renée. *André Gide et la pensée allemande.* Paris, 1949.
Mann, Klaus. *André Gide and the Crisis of Modern Thought.* New York, 1943.
Marcel, Gabriel. *Les Hommes contre l'humain.* Paris, 1950.
Massis, Henri. *Maurras et son temps.* Paris, 1951.
Maulnier, Thierry. *Au-delà du nationalisme.* Paris, 1938.
Maurras, Charles. *De la colère à la justice.* Geneva, 1942.
———. *Lettres de prison, 8 septembre 1944–16 novembre 1952.* Paris, 1958.
———. *Mes Idées politiques.* Paris, 1937.
———. *Le Patriotisme ne doit pas tuer la patrie.* Paris, 1946.
Paulhan, Jean. *De la paille et du grain.* Paris, 1948.
Peyre, Henri. *Les Générations littéraires.* Paris, 1948.
Ploncard, d'Assac, Jacques. *Doctrines du nationalisme.* Paris, 1958.
Politzer, Georges. *Révolution et contre-révolution au XXe siècle.* Paris, 1947.
Rambaud, Henri, and Pierre Varillon. "Enquête sur les maîtres de la jeune littérature." *Revue Hebdomadaire,* 4 Nov. 1922.
Sieburg, Friedrich. *Défense du nationalisme allemand.* Paris, 1933.
Spenlé, Jean-Edouard. *Nietzsche et le problème européen.* Paris, 1943.
Sperber, Manès. *Le Talon d'Archille.* Paris, 1957.
Tison-Braun, Micheline. *La crise de l'humanisme, tome 1, 1890–1914.* Paris, 1958.

Cultural Nationalism and Internationalism in Postwar German Literature

REINHOLD GRIMM AND H. G. HÜTTICH

The destruction of the German nation in 1945 brought with it the destruction of the culture which was part and parcel of the historical events leading to that final resolution. However, this situation of *tabula rasa*, this "point zero," which had until recently been widely accepted in cultural criticism, lasted only for an instant. The Germans had to be re-educated and a culture re-established to create a temperate zone in the rapid chilling process which made the hot war into a cold one.

Both the direction which this process would take and the basis from which it would develop were dramatically evident in the opening issue of *Die Wandlung*, one of the first cultural harbingers of the "new" society. The basis was defined by Karl Jaspers in the introduction: "We have lost almost everything: the state, the economy, and the basic necessities of our physical existence, and worse than that: the normative unifying values, the moral dignity, the unifying self-identity as a people." [1] The direction of the new culture became explicit with the printing of "East Coker," one of T. S. Eliot's *Four Quartets*, toward the end of this issue. From nothingness on page one, Germany was well on her way to an integration with the prevailing cultural flow by page thirty-four.

If our objective is to deal with this development in the realm of

[1] "Wir haben fast alles verloren: Staat, Wirtschaft, die gesicherten Bedingungen unseres physischen Daseins, und schlimmer noch als das: die giltigen uns alle verbindenden Normen, die moralische Würde, das einigende Selbstbewusstsein als Volk." Karl Jaspers, "Geleitwort," *Die Wandlung* 1, no. 1 (1945), 3.

literature, we must examine critically both the famous point zero of 1945 and the concept of *tabula rasa*. This concept, which goes hand-in-hand with Wolfgang Weyrauch's *The Felling of the Trees* (*Kahlschlag*) and Heinrich Böll's *The Literature of Fragmentation* (*Trümmerliteratur*), has lost its validity now that we are somewhat removed from that time of misery and yet hope, of growling stomachs but flashing eyes,[2] and have gained the necessary historical perspective. Hans Mayer states flatly that the year zero did not exist, not even in the history of literature.[3] Similarly, the young critic Frank Trommler refutes this concept in an in-depth study of the phenomenon,[4] and Günter Grass states, taking issue with the new generation of today: "I refuse to take politics or history unconditionally . . . . That is unhistorical and can only lead to catastrophe. Basically they're making the same mistake as their fathers, who in 1945 thought 'Now it's all over, now we can start again at zero.' But there was no zero. There was only an unconditional surrender, but that was the consequence of something." [5] Seen in this way, such literary documents as Hans Egon Holthusen's poem "Tabula rasa" (also in the first issue of *Die Wandlung*)[6] and Wolfgang Borchert's neo-expressionistic play *Outside in Front of the Door* (*Draussen vor der Tür*) are not representations of any point zero, but reflect the necessary consequences of a common experience which is inherently connected with the history and predicament of the German people. Perhaps it is this inherent contradiction, not apparent in the atmosphere of crisis at that time, which led Jaspers to say, "We have lost *almost* everything," and not "we have lost everything." For now, in retrospect, we can see that there was still a common bond, a unity of suffering, of hunger and fear, and a slight touch of self-pity.[7]

[2] Die Mägen knurrten, aber die Augen blitzten." A formulation by the writer Erich Kästner in Munich, 1947.

[3] Hans Mayer, *Deutsche Literatur seit Thomas Mann* (Reinbek bei Hamburg, 1968), 53.

[4] Frank Trommler, "Der 'Nullpunkt 1945' und seine Verbindlichkeit für die Literaturgeschichte," *Basis* 1 (1970).

[5] "Two Interviews," *Encounter* 35, no. 3 (1970), 28.

[6] "To make an end. To set a beginning / new and unheard of, which frightens and weakens us. / The human race wants one more time / to wet this earth with blood and tears." In: *Die Wandlung*, 1, no. 1, p. 65.

[7] Bertolt Brecht, for instance, noted after his return from exile: " 'Isn't it true that the three world-sustaining impulses were developed and formulated in our nation: reformation, fascism, and Marxism?' This I was told by a white-faced never-wrong youth one day, and his eyes shone proudly and fanatically." Both the quotation and Brecht's comment refer to his "Gespräche mit jungen Intellektuellen." In *Schriften zur Politik und Gesellschaft* (Frankfurt, 1968), 313.

But even critics learn, so let us not discard the concept entirely. Let us instead remodel it. For viewed under the aspect of cultural nationalism, point zero does indeed retain its effectiveness. Only it was not 1945, but rather 1949. The aftermath of the German Reich persisted in reality as a common experience until 1949, as did the state itself, if only theoretically. In this new perspective, point zero becomes psychological and tenuous, but more historically relevant than it was in its previous application. With the creation in 1949 of two political entities, Bundesrepublik Deutschland and the Deutsche Demokratische Republik, any common experience, any vestige of "the German people," was dramatically devastated. This was something the bombs had not achieved directly. Not only did this cause national schizophrenia by creating two new identities to cope with, but it also removed—formally, even if only symbolically—the point of reference common to each part, the cancerous rubble of the Reich. With this concrete point zero of national cultural identification finally at hand, German cultural nationalism, in any recognizable form, ceased to exist.

But there are other forms. In East Germany, heavily influenced both politically and ideologically by Russia, there was the immediate remodeling of the culture according to the nature of the animal. The result was the formation of a new socialistic national culture, and it soon became sweet and honorable to write and sing for the fatherland again. In 1949, the basic task of life and art was prescribed by the official program of the Sozialistische Einheitspartei Deutschlands (SED) as "the intellectual evolution of the human being in the socialistic society and the development of the socialistic national culture."[8] What this amounted to, in short, was the formation of a new cultural nationalism. This attitude prevailed through the formative years of the Democratic Republic of Germany and was again lucidly restated at the Second Bitterfeld Conference in 1964.[9] It is thus, by definition of that East German society, that its cultural ac-

---

[8] "Die geistige Formung des Menschen der sozialistischen Gesellschaft, und die Entwicklung der sozialistischen Nationalkultur." Reprinted in Marianne Lange, *Kulturrevolution und Nation* (Berlin, 1966), 22.

[9] "In the current period of the all-encompassing build-up of socialism—now that the socialistic modes of production have taken over the entire economy—it is true that the further development of our socialistic national culture, as a true peoples culture, is in close and manifold alliance with the mastering of the technical revolution by the working class, and the effective realization of our new economic system of the planned management of the national economy." Reprinted in Lange, 40.

tivity—except in times such as the quick thaw and even quicker refreeze which literally put the revisionists on ice—partakes of a rigorously imposed and enforced cultural nationalism.

To recapitulate, the year 1945 is far less important than the year 1949. Since then, we have two Germanies which exist side-by-side. Consequently, the question whether there is any such thing as cultural nationalism in postwar Germany is a dual one. In the case of East Germany, we cannot but admit the existence of this phenomenon, justified by a characteristic mixture of Marxist and nationalistic thinking. Even such people as Ernst Moritz Arndt, the author of a *Catechism for German Soldiers (Katechismus für deutsche Soldaten)*, and the famous Prussian generals Scharnhorst and Gneisenau, have been re-established as national heroes.[10] One is indeed reminded of the situation in 1813, when the eastern part of Germany, that is Prussia, was united with Russia against the western parts of Germany and France under Napoleon. The ideological justification of this pronounced cultural nationalism stems from the Marxist concept of a great cultural heritage which only a Socialist society—the proletariat—is able, and entitled, to continue.

In West Germany, the situation is quite different. There, especially in the realm of literature, an almost outspoken internationalism has prevailed since 1945–1949.[11] It was highly significant that T. S. Eliot's objective correlative was loosed upon the German lyricists in 1945, so to speak. Since three distinct Western cultures were a part of daily existence, in the form of occupying forces as well as through cultural propaganda and re-education, it follows almost logically that one should postulate a development toward universality, or at least away from the traditional direction.[12] And there is no doubt

[10] The importance of Gneisenau and Scharnhorst as sources of nationalistic pride cannot be underestimated. Gneisenau (1760–1831) was the chief of staff of Blücher's army and was mainly instrumental in attaining German and allied victories at the Battle of Leipzig in 1813, and at Waterloo in 1815, these proving to be the decisive blows in the final downfall of Napoleon. Scharnhorst (1755–1813), who died of wounds suffered in action, preceded Gneisenau as chief of staff and was the director of the war department since 1807. In this role he proved to be the organizational mainstay of the German (Prussian) forces.

[11] The same holds true for the other arts. Compare, for instance, Fritz Kortner's statement in his autobiography, *Aller Tage Abend* (Munich, 1959), 414: "Musically, West Germany has become denazified, yes even international." Kortner, a famous Jewish actor who was forced into exile by the Nazis, can certainly be considered an unprejudiced witness.

[12] Franz Schonauer provides a concise summation: "In 1945 the victors occupied Germany and implemented their program of 're-education.' Books and periodicals, printed on bad paper, already appeared in the first months of the

that this development did take place. If we try to differentiate, we find several phases, dominated by both a pronounced cultural internationalism and the rejection of any kind of cultural nationalism.

The first phase, ending by the mid-fifties, is the period of lyric poetry.[13] It is important to realize that this poetry, mostly nature poetry, does not represent a new beginning. Rather, it continues the tradition of such inner emigrants as Wilhelm Lehmann and Oskar Loerke. The poetry of this first period was dissociated from concrete reality, and generally rarefied. It can be characterized as rejecting any national consciousness in line with the prevailing total suspicion of any ideology. The realm of nature, pastoral scenes, mythological images, and a metaphysical preoccupation with death were dominant. However, a theoretical wrinkle developed, as the controversial poet Gottfried Benn reappeared. It was Benn who gave this already purified lyricism a programmatic theoretical basis and provided it with fascinating examples. The idea which he propounded was primarily one of esthetic rationalism or rational estheticism. At any rate, Benn, continuing the great tradition of French symbolism, proclaimed the doctrine of art for art's sake. Benn's concept of poetry admits of no social implications whatsoever, let alone any political commitment. The word and the lyric self are the sole determining factors. Structure and form predominate in an esthetic vacuum which admits only two things as valid in the making of poetry: the void and the voice of the poet.[14] It must be noted, however, that in *Art and the Third Reich (Kunst und Drittes Reich)*, an essay written during the Third Reich, Benn had already expressed the hope for a future period of all-European intellectual activity.[15] Clearly, with his poetic theory and his world view, he fol-

occupation. The confrontation with the literature of the West—even if at first it was obligatory as a primer for the first-graders of democracy—was nothing less than a shock. The reaction which followed was a complete and unqualified acceptance of the new, and for most German readers, the unknown. There were the Americans Hemingway, Faulkner, Dos Passos, Steinbeck, and Thomas Wolfe; the French existentialists; and the greats of European literature, Valéry, Gide, James Joyce, and Eliot ...." *Bestandsaufnahme*, ed. Hans Werner Richter (Munich, 1962), 480.

[13] The drama can be neglected. Besides *Draussen vor der Tür, Des Teufels General*, and *Die Illegalen*, mostly foreign plays dominate. One of the most popular and most frequently played pieces was Thornton Wilder's *The Skin of Our Teeth*. The German title of Wilder's play, *Wir sind noch einmal davongekommen*, reflects the trend to overcome, to eliminate the past.

[14] "Es gibt nur zwei Dinge: die Leere / Und das gezeichnete Ich." Gottfried Benn, *Gedichte* (Wiesbaden, 1960), 342.

[15] His criticism of unilateral nationalistic art of the Third Reich concludes with the expression of his belief: "This essay then submits the belief that one

lows the tradition of pessimism, nihilism, and *l'art pour l'art* of the French poets Baudelaire, Rimbaud, and Mallarmé.

These esthetic phenomena, identified with Benn, were not only found in poetical production but had a corresponding application in a new criticism, which reflected the artistic interest in form and texture. For example, Hugo Friedrich's *The Structure of Modern Lyric Poetry* (*Die Struktur der modernen Lyrik*) (1956) far transcends any national boundaries in its analysis. It shows the development of modern poetry as an international movement originating with the French symbolists. In doing this, Friedrich uses almost no German examples. Wolfgang Kayser's *The Literary Work of Art* (*Das sprachliche Kunstwerk*) (1948) testifies to a similar international approach. On another level, *European Literature and the Latin Middle Ages* (*Europäische Literatur und lateinisches Mittelalter*), by Ernst Robert Curtius, a friend of Benn, and Heinrich Lausberg's *Handbook of Literary Rhetoric* (*Handbuch der literarischen Rhetorik*), reflect the rise of comparative literary criticism in a historical sense. Published in 1948 and 1960 respectively, these works testify to the continuity of this broad critical approach. It is interesting to note here that both Curtius and Lausberg, as well as Friedrich, have their background in romance literature, and not in *Germanistik*.[16]

Summing up this first period, we have to conclude that since then, German literary history has been recognized as an integral part of world literature. Every poet worked with this concept in mind. He worked, manufactured, constructed rationally as a *poeta faber*, in the proper sense of the term. Since it was considered as impossible to seek an esthetic orientation in the national past dominated by romantic concepts, the orientation process constantly aimed at integration into the larger tradition of international models, by emphasizing the universal esthetic principles of art. Esthetic formalism appears as a companion to the method of textual criticism. One looks at the artistically manufactured microcosm so that the concrete his-

---

day there will be an all-European tradition of the intellect of which Germany will partake, from which she will learn, and to which, after learning, she will contribute." *Essays, Reden, Vorträge* (Wiesbaden, 1959), 322.

[16] The critical reassessment within the ranks of *Germanistics* came rather belatedly. Cf. *Nationalismus in Germanistik und Dichtung*, ed. B. von Wiese and Rudolf Henss (Berlin, 1967); *Germanistik—eine deutsche Wissenschaft*, contributions by E. Lämmert, W. Killy, K. O. Conrady, and P. V. Polenz (Frankfurt, 1967); and *Ansichten einer künftigen Germanistik*, ed. J. Kolbe (Munich, 1969).

torical relationships can be ignored. This enables the poet to drift into an unhistorical, unpolitical vacuum on a cloud of generalities. In fact, it is Benn-like poetry without the agony of the Benn point of view, without the "torn self." On a lower level, in everyday life, the same attitude is perfectly reflected in the essential *ohne mich* ("cop-out"), the motto of the unpolitical fifties.

The second phase in the literary and cultural development of West Germany emerges around the turn of the decade, in the late fifties and early sixties. This is the period of the great critical novels by writers such as Günter Grass, Martin Walser, Heinrich Böll, and Uwe Johnson—all of whom attained a remarkable degree of world-wide recognition. To a great extent their critical approach was prompted by the so-called *Wirtschaftswunder*: [17] the economy was in high gear; the Germans ate well, lived well, dressed well, and traveled widely; and there was a prevalent mood of self-satisfaction. A restorative tendency had become evident: "Look at us now! Not only did we just get away by the skin of our teeth, but we have attained a new position as an economic and political force." [18] This was somewhat nurtured by rearmament and a defensive foreign policy toward the East. *Abendland* [19] was spelled with a capital A, the Iron Curtain had been lowered, and the myth of the Free West was flourishing. In short, West Germany had been completely integrated into the social, political, and cultural system of Western Europe and North America. There is no doubt that it was this self-satisfied attitude which motivated the critics we mentioned.

With *Marriages in Philippsburg* (*Ehen in Philippsburg*) in 1957 and *Halftime* (*Halbzeit*) in 1959 Martin Walser satirized the media-oriented culture of consumerism and exposed the growing reactionary tendencies.[20] In 1959 *The Tin Drum* (*Die Blechtrommel*) by Günter Grass became a worldwide success. Grass categorized postwar German culture from a historical perspective, and through this, achieved an international view. Also appearing in 1959—which we now realize was a very good year—Heinrich Böll's *Billiards at Half Past Nine* (*Billard um halbzehn*) showed its author actively engaged

---

[17] A term used to describe the fabulous economic recovery after the total destruction and collapse of the Third Reich.

[18] See R. Hinton Thomas and Wilfried van der Will, *The German Novel and the Affluent Society* (Toronto, 1968).

[19] This term refers to the Spenglerian concept of the Western world and implies a cyclic decay of its civilization.

[20] For criticism from a conservative point of view, compare Gerd Gaiser's novel *Schlussball*, published in 1958.

in opposition to national consciousness as he ruthlessly examined the reactionary tendencies of church, state, and bureaucracy.

These works demonstrate a new "engagement," a growing sense of responsibility in the face of social problems, and a decisive orientation toward political and historical issues. In the case of Grass and Walser, it was perhaps their age which permitted this new view. They had just started their careers as writers and had never before— except in their childhood—experienced an ideological identification with the past. Thus, they readily could assume a critical pose. In the case of Böll, this pose centered around a strong personal motivation, an antipathy toward any national culture or consciousness. Any such nationalism, according to Böll's view, leads to the inhumanities of power politics. Therefore he consciously strove for the devaluation of these concepts.

In the novels of Böll, Grass, Walser, and Johnson, regionalism plays an important role. It is a regionalism, however, which does not result in isolationism, but, quite the contrary, serves as a basis for an international view.[21] The authors present a concrete microcosm to which they can relate their universal perspective. Walser presents us with an array of Swabians, Grass starts with the petty bourgeoisie of Danzig, and Böll deals with the Catholics of Cologne, and the Rhineland in general. Walter Jens aptly characterized this process: "In any case, we notice that the writer of our day approaches German reality from the periphery, without class attachments and without a patriotic mandate. He does this (for the sake of orientation) by setting up tiny models, Cologne, and Danzig, which may serve to make the strange and foreboding qualities of our situation understandable in a familiar framework." [22] By the same token, the situation in Germany, although seen from the perspective of a narrowly delimited locality, permits a historical view in reference to the contemporary social and political conditions of Europe and the world.[23] All reactionary tendencies are unmasked by this technique, and the favored international cultural heritage is inserted.

---

[21] There has been another type of regionalism, represented by *Vertriebenen-literatur* (refugees' literature), which does contain nationalistic overtones in a highly localized sense. A close investigation of this unduly neglected phenomenon might prove to be revealing.

[22] Walter Jens, *Literatur und Politik* (Pfullingen, 1963), 14.

[23] Johannes Bobrowski's 1964 novel, *Levins Mühle*, dealing with individual, religious, and national disputes of the 1870s along the Polish-German border (with a view to the twentieth century) is another example of the micro-macro technique. This novel, as Bobrowski stated, is told for our sake.

A closer look at certain facets of Böll's and Grass's work will substantiate this contention and identify some direct non-German influences. Böll's early novel, *And Said Not One Word* (*Und sagte kein einziges Wort*), published in 1953, already shows the influence of Hemingway and Joyce in the tight diction and economy of language, and in its narrative technique. Similarly, the symbolism in *Billiards at Half Past Nine* aims at universal archetypes. The sacrament of the lamb represents the international Christian tradition, whereas, conversely, the sacrament of the buffalo stands for the reactionary power players, oriented toward a restorative nationalism. The symbolic assassination of the latter by the former, which ends the novel, is pictured as a necessary action resulting from the fear that the world could again be threatened by the stampeding totalitarian buffalos. The most explicit antinationalistic situation in the novel concerns the fate of the monastery St. Anton. Built by the grandfather, it had become a monument of German culture. The demolition expert, his son, destroyed it at the end of the war. He had the alternative of not carrying out the order, since the military collapse was at hand. Nevertheless, he did destroy it, because of his pacifistic and antinationalistic convictions. In the narrative present of the book, the monastery is in the process of being restored by the grandson. When he realizes that it was his father who destroyed it, he surmises the reasons behind the demolition and refuses to continue the restoration. From this story of the futile labors of three generations, we can also surmise Böll's perspective: it is better that nationalistic culture remain destroyed, because such cultural manifestations are always political and psychological tools of those who partake of the sacrament of the buffalo.

In *The Tin Drum*, Grass presents a historical perspective of war, great international events, and troop movements, all concentrated at Danzig. We again delight in the defrocking of national monuments. In addition, the novel is a stylistic tour de force and a great intellectual game in various styles of world literature. A direct Faulkner influence can be traced through the convoluted disorientations and reorientations of the narrative perspective, and actual as opposed to narrative time. An application of Faulkner's sense of all time being present is evident here as well as in Grass's next novel, *Dog Years* (*Hundejahre*) (1963). Furthermore, the figure of Oskar as the drummer of truth, physically three years old, reminds us more than slightly of Benjy, always mentally three years old, who functions as the yardstick of truth in *The Sound and the Fury*. Benjy is strangely attached to an old shoe, not a drum, but he does have a psychologically important and sustaining relationship with the family's old black cook. Perhaps this could shed some little light on that enigmatic figure of *The Tin Drum.*

From *l'art pour l'art* and the secluded estheticism of the first period, literary production turned to an outward expansion toward social criticism and historical analysis in the prose which characterizes the second phase. This process resulted in a new *littérature engagée.* The third phase, which lasted until recently, was the heyday of postwar German drama. Granted, Bertolt Brecht had been active previously, working passionately with his "Ensemble" in East Berlin; but it was not until several years after he died that his plays finally succeeded in overcoming the various boycotts that were launched against them in West Germany. The last of these, naturally, was caused by the building of the Berlin Wall.[24]

In the fifties, the situation on the German stage was entirely international. Plays from abroad, mainly from France and the United States, dominated the scene. Even the Swiss, Max Frisch and Friedrich Dürrenmatt, participated in this movement. Samuel Beckett, Jean-Paul Sartre, Jean Anouilh, and Albert Camus, but especially Eugène Ionesco, exerted a great and lasting influence.[25] The Americans were also well represented, with their favorite topics of family relationships, individual psychology, and especially of the problem of noncommunication. Eugene O'Neill, Tennessee Williams, Elmer Rice, and William Saroyan enjoyed an enormous success, and Arthur Miller's *Death of a Salesman* was unbelievably successful. In short,

---

[24] After the Brecht phenomenon became untracked from the surrounding political contingencies of the Cold War, its impact cannot be underestimated. Brecht's influence was not only, as one would expect, imitative. Brecht's theory and techniques became the great new standards. But two most important aspects: his extreme rationalism was irrationalized (by Weiss, in *Marat / Sade,* with the influence of Artaud), and his abstracted parable structures were oriented to specific historical realities (*Die Ermittlung, Joel Brandt*) by the movement toward documentation and political immediacy. Another facet of the phenomenon is that Brecht indeed accepted the *Nationalkultur* concept of East Germany. In "Thesen zur Faust Diskussion," referring to Hanns Eisler's opera text which had been criticized for lacking national consciousness, he defends Eisler in terms of national cultural heritage. In a short statement, "Kosmopolitismus," he lauds the completely new type of national consciousness of the proletariat, in complete correspondence with the *SED Programm* (see *Schriften zur Literatur und Kunst* [Frankfurt, 1967], 3:199-205, 194-95).

[25] This is reflected even in Walser's *Halbzeit,* where Anouilh is the favorite topic of cocktail party conversation in the sense of Françoise Sagan's *Aimez-vous Brahms?*

the German stage was full of translations during those unpolitical fifties. Only Grass and Wolfgang Hildesheimer tried their hands at a theater of the grotesque or absurd but never succeeded in dominating the stage. As late as 1959 we have the world premiere, in Germany, of Ionesco's *The Rhinoceros* (*Le Rhinocéros*) in Darmstadt, and in 1960, Edward Albee's *The Zoo Story*, in Berlin.

But then, in the sixties, Bertolt Brecht attracted an ever-increasing number of followers. Before that, his direct influence had been limited chiefly to his East German disciples, Peter Hacks and Helmut Baierl, and in the West, to such questionable attempts as Walser's *Oak and Angora* (*Eiche und Angora*) and *The Black Swan* (*Der schwarze Schwan*). The year 1963, however, initiated a quick succession of plays which suddenly re-established the reputation of German drama. In 1963, Rolf Hochhuth contributed *The Deputy* (*Der Stellvertreter*). The year 1964 saw Peter Weiss's *Marat/Sade* and Heinar Kipphardt's *In the Matter of J. Robert Oppenheimer* (*In der Sache J. Robert Oppenheimer*). Weiss followed with *Die Ermittlung* in 1965; Grass, with *The Plebeians Rehearse the Uprising* (*Die Plebejer proben den Aufstand*) in 1966; and Hochhuth again, with *The Generals* (*Die Soldaten*) in 1967. This was also the year of Weiss's obesely titled *Viet Nam Discourse* (*Viet Nam Diskurs*), which was preceded by his *Song of the Lusitanian Boogey* (*Gesang vom lusitanischen Popanz*) (1966). The themes presented here are the universals of political history. Many of these plays reveal an international tendency toward documentation in literature. It is most interesting that non-German topics predominate throughout. *Marat/ Sade* is an international revolutionary drama, as is Weiss's latest play, *Trotsky in Exile* (*Trotzki im Exil*) (1970). Kipphardt's *Oppenheimer* deals with the Cold War security risk problems of the United States and Russia. *The Generals* is historical in reference to England, Poland, and Russia in the Second World War. Finally, Weiss introduces the concept of the third world with *Viet Nam Discourse* and *Song of the Lusitanian Boogey.*

Even if the situations in such plays happen to be German, still the perspective from which they are seen is that of world history. Examples are *The Deputy, Die Ermittlung,* and Kipphardt's *Joel Brandt.* There is no doubt that at least one of these works, namely *Marat/Sade,* represents a major artistic achievement in the contemporary theater and must simply be classified as *Weltliteratur.*

In generalizing about this third phase, one has to conclude that it is again characterized by rationalism as well as internationalism. In that, it differs only slightly from the second phase. More and more, however, the development now drifts toward a concrete political commitment. The social criticism of the late fifties is being replaced by the political activism of the late sixties. The new battle cry is "art as a weapon." This holds true not only for the drama, but for the other genres as well, especially for political poetry.

Meanwhile, German literature has entered a fourth phase. Again we are confronted by an internationalism which is even more outspoken than before. Yet, there seems to be one great difference. This last phase is no longer permeated with rationalism, but with irrationalism. The current literary scene in Germany is in the grasp of the pop-rock culture, or rather anticulture, a completely international movement which originated in the United States and England. The principle of the new movement, apart from an unlimited consumerism, lies essentially in the destruction of art as such. A dramatic illustration is provided by Peter Handtke's volume *German Poems* (*Deutsche Gedichte*) (1970). These "poems," which are anything but, are contained in a "book" which must literally be "consumed"— actually to be torn apart and destroyed, in order to be read. Similar attempts, both in literature and on stage, have come from other young people, the most violent practitioners being Otto Mühl, Bazon Brock, Wolf Vostell, Hubert Fichte, Rolf Dieter Brinkmann, Peter O. Chotjewitz, and Renate Rasp.[26] Even Martin Walser, with a booklet called *Fiction* (1969), tried to join the movement. However, this consumer-oriented art, or anti-art, shows a somewhat confused perspective, especially if one considers that quite a number of its followers would like to give themselves cloaks of leftist ideology. This is either hypocrisy or a grotesque misunderstanding; for in making their attack by affirming the consumerism of the established society, they support, in fact, the conservative economic principle they profess to demolish. The only thing which they actually destroy is the traditional concept of culture. Therefore, their attack on the art of Weiss, Grass, Böll, and others who are certainly cosmopolitan and leftist in scope, must be denounced as essentially rightist.

This connects the current avant-gardists in a curious manner with a voice they would certainly not like to be identified or connected with: Kurt Ziesel. The Austrian Ziesel, an ultraconservative critic, sees himself as the representative mouthpiece of West Germany's "silent majority." He started softly, almost timidly, but his harangue

[26] See Jost Hermand, "Pop oder die These vom Ende der Kunst," *Basis* 1 (1970).

became louder, shriller, and more vociferously conservative as the restoration of West Germany progressed. In his boisterous polemic *The Literary Factory (Die Literaturfabrik)*,[27] for example, Ziesel launches his attack from a would-be Christian, national, and moral basis. To use Böll's metaphor, he has certainly partaken of the sacrament of the buffalo. His rhetoric is abundant with such terms as "decadent," or "sick" art, "decay of national pride," and "destruction of decency and morality." In short, this coincides with the thinking and diction of the Nazi version of literary criticism.

But giving credit where credit is due, we must admit, albeit reluctantly, that Ziesel does have some degree of critical insight. He sees the domination of the media, and its real, dangerous aspect, the molding of public opinion. Instead of formulating a constructive criticism, however, he uses these insights to call for the destruction of the cultural internationalism established in West Germany since 1945. He attacks the literary tradition which we have discussed not only as worthless, but as downright evil.

Ziesel, then, has as his final goal the same objective as the makers of anti-art, except that he operates from and with "morality," and he advocates a new nationalism. Of course it will be much to the chagrin of many poppers and rockers when they finally realize this. Ziesel's attack is from the bottom up. He claims to represent the people, the common man on the street, the consumer of literature. The pop movement is also concerned with the people, as it tries to filter down from above and wants to appeal to everyone; it also demands consumers. Thus, these two forces have in common not only their rightist attitude, but also their desire for "popularity," their vicious attack against what they call "elitist" culture.

One final formulation of our perspective in terms of East and West Germany would perhaps be a fitting conclusion. It is evident that in East Germany, culture and nationalism are synonymous. Their common denominator is socialism. For West Germany, a dialectical proposition comes to mind. With regard to Ziesel and his followers, we may say that where there is nationalism, there is no culture, and where there is culture, there is no nationalism. The absence of nationalism, however, by no means automatically guarantees culture. This is made painfully clear by what is currently dominant on the literary scene in West Germany.

[27] Kurt Ziesel, *Die Literaturfabrik. Eine polemische Auseinandersetzung mit dem Literaturbetrieb im Deutschland von heute* (Vienna, 1962).

BIBLIOGRAPHY

Bracher, Karl Dietrich (ed.), *Nach 25 Jahren. Eine Deutschland-Bilanz.* Munich, 1970.

Cwojdrak, Günther. *Eine Prise Polemik. Sieben Essays zur westdeutschen Literatur.* Halle, 1968.

Grass, Günter. "Two Interviews," *Encounter* 35, no. 3 (1970).

Hermand, Jost. "Pop oder die These vom Ende der Kunst," *Basis* 1 (1970).

Jens, Walter. *Literatur und Politik.* Pfullingen, 1963.

Lange, Marianne. *Kulturrevolution und Nation.* Berlin, 1966.

Mayer, Hans. *Deutsche Literatur seit Thomas Mann.* Reinbeck bei Hamburg, 1968.

Moras, Joachim, and Hans Paeschke (eds.). *Deutscher Geist zwischen gestern und morgen. Bilanz der kulturellen Entwicklung seit 1945.* Stuttgart, 1954.

Richter, Hans Werner (ed.). *Bestandsaufnahme.* Munich, 1963.

Schallück, Paul (ed.). *Deutschland. Kulturelle Entwicklungen seit 1945.* Munich, 1969.

Schröter, Klaus. *Literatur und Zeitgeschichte. Fünf Aufsätze zur deutschen Literatur im 20. Jahrhundert.* Mainz, 1970.

Trommler, Frank. "Der 'Nullpunkt 1945' und seine Verbindlichkeit für die Literaturgeschichte," *Basis* 1 (1970).

von Wiese, Benno, and Rudolf Henss (eds.). *Nationalismus in Germanistik und Dichtung: Dokumentation des Germanistentages in München vom 17.–22. Oktober 1966.* Berlin, 1967.

Ziesel, Kurt. *Die Literaturfabrik: Eine polemische Auseinandersetzung mit dem Literaturbetrieb im Deutschland von heute.* Vienna, 1962.

National and European Culture in the Contemporary Spanish Novel

KESSEL SCHWARTZ

From the Middle Ages on, as Erasmian and Krausist [1] conflicts with the establishment testify, Spain has both accepted and rejected foreign cultural elements in conflict with its own traditional ones. Spaniards have had to struggle against the limitations of their intellectual life since the Counter Reformation isolated them from the mainstream of European thought. Spain has almost always suffered a cultural lag in accepting literary movements, often trying them briefly first, rejecting them in reactionary fashion, and finally accepting them after they have almost run their course elsewhere. In the early twentieth century Manuel Bartolomé Cossío fostered the esthetic and spiritual revaluation of the artist, and Joaquín Costa, the "Apostle of Europeanization," encouraged Spaniards to copy European culture and economics. The "Generation of 1898," [2] profoundly influenced by Nietzsche, among others, searched for new values to

---

[1] Christian F. Krause (1781–1832) was a Kantian who taught philosophy at Heidelberg. Sanz del Río, who held a scholarship at this university, returned to his native Spain imbued with Krause's ideas and began what was later termed the "Krausista" movement in Spain. This actually turned more into a humanistic and harmonious style of life than a philosophy, but it became an active element in the endless struggle between liberals and conservatives. Krause himself remains virtually unknown in philosophical circles, but his influence on Spanish thought shows once again how completely Spain was isolated from the European mainstream and how strongly the Spanish intellectual reacts when brought into contact with the outside world.

[2] The most important members were Unamuno, Baroja, Azorín, Valle Inclán, A. Machado, and Maeztú. Later Ortega y Gasset and Pérez de Ayala would constitute a sort of Second Generation of '98.

replace traditional ones. At the same time the Modernists emphasized, in a continuing Apollonian-Dionysian conflict, the exotic cosmopolitan and universal concerns along with a dedication to the remote past. In the first three decades of the twentieth century, Miguel de Unamuno created novelistic "agonists" who searched for immortality, Pío Baroja lamented the irrational and illogical universe of delusive moral values, and Pérez de Ayala documented the relationships between life and art, tempering his metaphysical yearnings by an intellectual approach to life.

Unamuno, hoping to "Hispanicize" Europe, rejected European science and culture and anathematized those who wanted to bring the Western industrial world to Spain. Yet he knew German, French, Italian, and Danish and was keenly aware of European philosophical and literary currents. Ortega y Gasset, on the other hand, through the *Revista de Occidente*, promoted from 1923 on, as he had been doing in essays since 1910, the thought that "Regeneration is inseparable from Europeanization. . . . Truly from the beginning it was quite clear that Spain was the problem and Europe the solution." [3]

Ortega believed that the novel was a kind of hermetic exercise which should stress form and refinements of techniques. He seemed to define the novel as something dehumanized, cold, and objective. Pío Baroja, whose vision of the world was as chaotic as life itself, held that the novel is an instrument of communication and representative of life and that form and technique are relatively unimportant. In the prologue to *Ship of Madness* (*La nave de los locos*) (1925) he describes the novel as multiformed and states that every novel has its own type of skeletal structure, although some, biologically, appear to be more invertebrate than vertebrate.

Ortega encouraged Benjamín Jarnés, Gómez de la Serna, and Francisco Ayala in their adherence to European avant-garde movements. The first two novelists mentioned followed the French surrealists and wrote esthetic, somewhat mannered, and intellectual novels, copying from foreign rather than from national models. Ayala experimented with first- and second-person narrative, although he did not immediately succumb to vanguard attitudes. In general, formal renovation and the search for new forms along with a determination to follow European art, poetry, and fiction seemed to control novelists of the day. [4]

[3] José Ortega y Gasset, *Obras completas* (Madrid, 1957), 1:543.
[4] Guillermo de Torre, "Hacia un más allá del realismo novelesco," *Revista de Occidente* 4 (July 1963), 106–14.

Juan Luis Alborg, in *The Present-day Spanish Novel* (*Hora actual de la novela española*) (1958), suggests that post–Civil War Spanish novelists broke with the Generation of 1898 and with all predominant Western cultural currents. Although the novelists of the 1940s and early 1950s wanted to escape their heritage, few really understood the technical innovations of the modern novel, even those which had been in use for more than a quarter of a century. Spaniards traditionally reject extreme manifestations of literary movements and, as Ricardo Gullón points out, have "customarily taken from foreign currents that part which is best attuned to their intrinsic nature and to their particular modes of expression...." [5]

In a polemic with Julián Marías, Robert G. Mead, Jr., excepting the "Generation of the Emigrés," referred to the geographic and spiritual isolation from liberal currents of European thought suffered by Spaniards. Marías insisted, a message he has kept repeating to the present, that "Spain is in Europe." [6] José Mariá Gironella, on the other hand, contended that "our novel has enclosed itself within an hermetic world, ignoring the great universal problems with a certain self-satisfied provincialism." [7] He believed that obsessive interest in localism, exaggerated sentimentalism, and superficial characterization were typical of the Spanish novel.

Writers born between 1922 and 1936, according to José Mariá Castellet, belong to what he calls the "Mid-Century Generation." He distinguishes these writers from earlier ones like Camilo José Cela and Miguel Delibes because of their social compromise, collective heroes, subjective experience of misery to convey reality, and especially their "profound sense... of the dynamics of history." [8] Also called a "wounded generation" and "innocent generation" (because of their lack of direct involvement in the Spanish Civil War), these novelists witnessed and denounced Spanish social injustice, an attitude which became so fixed that it became petrified and in itself provincial in the early 1960s after a decade of such writing. Although they were largely not European-oriented, they used European techniques at times to carry out their tasks.

[5] "The Modern Spanish Novel," *Texas Quarterly* 4 (1961), 83.

[6] See Robert G. Mead, Jr., "Dictatorship and Literature in the Spanish World," *Books Abroad* 25 (1951), 223–26; also see Julián Mariás, *Books Abroad* 26 (1952), 232–36, and *Meditaciones sobre la sociedad española* (Madrid, 1966), 36.

[7] "Por qué el mundo desconoce la novela española," *Estudios Americanos* 10, no. 47 (1955), 139–66.

[8] *Sur* 284 (Sept.–Oct. 1963), 51; and "Juan Goytisolo y la novela española actual," *La Torre* 9, no. 33 (1961), 132.

Contemporary Spanish novelists discuss most frequently the influences of the Italian neo-realists, French existentialists, and the *nouveau roman*. They learned from Italian neo-realists to confront reality while avoiding unidimensional and emotive involvement in their concentration on the poor and the proletariat. The Italians believed that the novelist might modify society, but they avoided stereotyped realities of a single truth. In the 1950s young French writers stressed uncommitted description in their *nouveau roman*, believing that the novel was a sufficient statement of its own reality which the reader had to interpret. The objectivists borrowed from the movies and radio in attempting to create a pure novel whose reality was neither absurd nor significant. Other European novelists combined essay, painting, music, literary criticism, and biography in new ways. Existentialist anguish continued, but some novelists seemed more concerned with technique than meaning and employed strange symbols to appeal to multilevel perceptions of readers. They superimposed simultaneous structural levels involving circular time, the multiple view, and various esthetic devices which served more to hide than to convey. Style became disjunctive as though metaphor no longer sufficed to carry the burden of guilt of the modern world. Man, a finite being, lived more and more in the present in the face of the knowledge of his certain death and the absurdity of the world.

Around 1965 a younger Spanish generation, born in the 1940s, moved away from more traditional literary values and from objectivism and the *nouveau roman*. Some members of the innocent generation also became more discriminating in their mastery of European culture. Rejecting old traditions which seemed to be irrelevant in a computerized world, these novelists despairingly search for meaning in a disintegrating society whose chaos they convey through the destruction of normal chronology. Spanish novelists continue to express varieties of Sartrean existentialism and have produced lyrical and sexual experience together with an esthetic exercise in twisted time and ruptured novelistic structures to avoid old dimensions and to modify the novel's structure to fit their own reality. As Guillermo de Torre states: "Today nothing is foreign to fiction: not metaphysics, nor the political-social, nor the latest introspective intimacies, nor the most concrete brutal deeds. No territory is forbidden to it; no shadow of ancient taboos survives. Everything may be included within its incredibly elastic limits." [9]

[9] *El espejo y el camino* (Madrid, 1968), 12.

It must be remembered that Spanish novelists were isolated for fifteen or twenty years from European intellectual sources, and only recently have they begun to overcome the tragic heritage of the Spanish Civil War and its political consequences. As Francisco Ayala says: "In Spain many writers who have lived segregated from the rest of the world are now discovering Europe.... I believe that in the last ten years this confinement has ceased ... and that Spanish literature is beginning to lose its provincial character." [10] The Civil War destroyed even the lines of communication previously established by the *Revista de Occidente* in the 1920s, and for many years readers were all but limited to expensive and scarce Argentine editions. Even in the 1960s, as one of the young writers states, novels by Cesare Pavese, Vasco Pratolini, or Henry Miller were prohibitively priced and "among young Spaniards interested in literature, how many have read Proust, Henry James, D. H. Lawrence, or Virginia Woolf?" [11] At the same time the novelists were deprived of the stylistic and literary progress made by their own countrymen, since most of the good novelists were living in exile. Deprived of European cross-fertilization for so long, once channels of communication were opened, Spanish novelists eagerly examined the heterogeneous mixtures of almost half a century of European fictional experimentation, which accounts for the strange jumble of influences from several distinct generations (all new for these writers). Among them are Marcel Proust, Franz Kafka, James Joyce, Alberto Moravia, Aldous Huxley, André Gide, Virginia Woolf, Jean-Paul Sartre, Thomas Mann, William Faulkner, and Alain Robbe-Grillet and his contemporaries. Many give lip service to even later antinovelistic novels, but few understand them.

In 1956 the suspension of the Congress of University Writers triggered attempts to use new techniques to describe the Civil War, childhood memories, rural and city life, and social and political events. Because of censorship novelists had to convey their ideas indirectly, especially in the 1950s, in order to escape charges of doctrinal deviation, and they encouraged the reader to penetrate their surface view of reality and draw conclusions which they could not more openly endorse. The European Community of Writers, founded in 1960 by G. B. Angioletti to promote contact among all European writers, had about one hundred Spanish members. In 1959,

[10] María Embeita, "Francisco Ayala y la novela," *Insula* 22 (March 1967), 6.
[11] Andrés Amorós, "Novelas y novelistas," *Revista de Occidente* 5, no. 47 (1967), 240–46.

1960, and 1961 a number of internationally known novelists like Michel Butor and Alberto Moravia participated in the colloquia on the novel held in Formentor, Majorca. Spanish novelists, among them Cela and Goytisolo, participated in the discussions and debates on technique, form, and fictional realism. Butor had been translated previously into Spanish, but he was known only to a few intellectuals. The Formentor experience helped bring him, Max Frisch, Marguerite Duras, and others to the attention of Spanish novelists. In the 1963 Madrid colloquium on the new novel, essentially a debate between social realists and objectivists, the Spaniards, for the most part, defended social realism.

Almost all the European novelists began to be translated with some regularity into Spanish in the 1960s. *Insula* published reviews of European works in their column, "The Foreign Novel in Spain," with commentary by Domingo Pérez Minik and news from European centers by J. Corrales Egea and others, in order to keep readers abreast of cultural movements. The *Revista de Occidente*, *Papeles de Son Armadans*, and other journals also followed European cultural activity. A cursory glance at a few issues of *Insula* reveals, among novels translated and commented upon, those of Leonardo Sciascia, Julian Mitchell, Alain Robbe-Grillet, Claude Simon, Marguerite Duras, Yuri Kazakov, Yuri Nagibin, Elizabeth Bowen, Ivy Compton-Burnett, Graham Greene, Jean Cau, Friederich Dürenmatt, Elio Vittorini, Italo Calvino, Cesare Pavese, Vasco Pratolini, Edmunde Charles-Roux, Christiane Rochefort, José Cabanis, Lawrence Durrell, Nathalie Sarraute, Iris Murdoch, Angus Wilson, Günther Grass, Heinrich Böll, and Witold Gombrowicz. For the most part, however, these novels were known only to critics and not read by Spanish novelists. Critics also knew the Marxist theories of Lucien Goldmann and George Lukács, but few novelists read their works, and fewer yet, having read them, had digested their theories or applied them. Even among critics only a limited number knew about the new European novel: "There are so few of us Spanish critics who preoccupy ourselves with the contemporary non-Spanish novel." [12]

Spanish novels were also published in many foreign languages. Juan García Hortelano's works have been translated into a dozen languages. Ignacio Aldecoa has appeared in German, Italian, Swedish, and Polish. Ana María Matute is also much translated and Juan

[12] Andrés Amorós, *Insula* 24 (Jan. 1969), 6.

Goytisolo's novels have sometimes been published in French before they appear in Spanish. Yet, until about 1965, the Spanish novel was largely provincial, reflecting the legacy of Pío Baroja, Valle-Inclán, and even Pérez Galdós, basically a nineteenth-century realist.

The Spanish Civil War has never fully lost its impact as a unique event involving human values and sacrifice and impelling many writers, through their own brand of social realism, to attempt to rejuvenate and transform their society in the hope of future spiritual unity. The Spanish novelists wanted to define their reality and at the same time to serve their society. They could not easily divorce themselves from content and from their moral miseries, and they lacked the freedom of other European countries to represent their true feelings. In the post–Civil War period French youth had a free choice between moral suicide as defined by Albert Camus and a new system of values based on their war experience, occupation, and concentration camps. Frenchmen had their country and their enemy. Spaniards, on the contrary, lacked ideas in common, facing, not a foreign enemy, but their own blood relatives.[13]

Themes of the exploited peasant, underpaid worker, and slum-dweller[14] took precedence over European theoretical and formal advances. Some of the novelists, in their descriptive expositions of social reality without exegesis, analysis, or explanation, ignored formalistic and esthetic preoccupation almost completely, which confined them to the excessively narrow limits of the present, "naturally extraordinarily ephemeral,"[15] and explains their recent relative silence. As the members of the "innocent" generation examined man's isolation, his anguish, and his inability to communicate along with social factors, they often combined their satirical view of society and the metaphysical role of man in the world within a traditional framework; and with the rarest of exceptions only those novels concerned with social man and contemporary Spanish reality had much success.

As we have seen, the *nouveau roman* was known in Spain, but the Spanish novelists could not avoid social commitments or accept the individual's loss of self-determination and lack of emotional association. Objective accounts of ordinary people were common in the 1950s, but Spanish novelists rejected efforts to replace words by image to reflect reality. They could not completely abandon plot and character development in the name of structure and style nor

---

[13] Manuel Lamana, *Literatura de posguerra* (Buenos Aires, 1961), 36.
[14] Pablo Gil Casado, *La novela social española, 1942–1968* (Barcelona, 1968).
[15] J. Corrales Egea, "Crisis de la nueva literatura," *Insula* 20 (June 1965), 10.

could they understand the often contradictory explanations emanating from French novelists about objectivity, subjectivity, and infra-realism.[16] Although Spaniards accepted visual description and respected Michel Butor's desire to force the reader to make interpretations (the anonymous narrator enabled them to penetrate the reality of appearance in their hypocritical country), they were more influenced by Italian neo-realists like Pratolini.

It must be remembered that members of former generations continue to publish in the current decade. Ramón Sender (1902–), possibly the greatest living Spanish novelist (almost unknown to contemporary Spanish writers until about 1965), had given a direct view of Spanish reality in *Magnet* (*Imán*) (1930) which was unmatched by later social novelists. Together with Arturo Barea and Max Aub he created the only outstanding fiction about the Spanish Civil War. In most of his novels Sender shows a compassionate love for human beings as he combines the metaphysical, mystical, lyrical, and sensual with an existential search for self. One finds Kafka's sense of nightmare and Joyce's subconscious flow, but even more in his works one senses the presence of Ramón de Valle-Inclán. In his idealistic and humanitarian concerns Sender seems to be the direct heir of Pérez Galdós; and his realistic literature, "of a social and testificatory nature," foreshadows the newer generations' literary interest.[17]

Among his latest novels are *Chronicle of the Dawn* (*Crónica del alba*) (1967), whose definitive version he elaborated for a quarter of a century and which examines the awakening consciousness and moral formation involved in becoming a man; *Morose Chronicles* (*Las criaturas saturnianas*) (1967), a historical novel about Cagliostro and a Russian princess, which combines epic, farcical, and literary historical elements; *A Look into the Life of Ignacio Morel* (*En la vida de Ignacio Morel*) (1969), winner of the Planeta Prize; and *Nocturne for the 14* (*Nocturno de los 14*) (1969), which deals with suicide, reality, fantasy, and literature. Sender is a unique and intuitive writer not easily classified. Some of his novels deliberately defy a level of logical association in the surrealistic tradition. Others, almost parables or allegories, stress man's place in the universe and his need for self-knowledge. In his examination of the interrelationships of

---

[16] Infra-realism: the novel is its own reality, and the imaginary therein becomes more real than exterior reality and thus goes beyond it.

[17] José R. Marra López, "Ramón J. Sender, novelista español," *Insula* 19 (April 1964), 5.

the real world and creative imagination, in his search for harmonic visions of human brotherhood, and in his existential search for immortality, he represents the best traditions of the Spanish novel. Although his primary preoccupation is with freedom and responsibility for one's fellow man, the Spanish problem has never been far removed from his work.

Camilo José Cela (1916–), himself influenced by Pío Baroja and Valle-Inclán, owes more to them than to European literature, although he anticipates current novelists in his emphasis on language and structure. He was among the earliest Spanish novelists to experiment with Bertolt Brecht's *Verfremdungs-effekte*, a distancing which made the familiar remote. Uncommitted to any specific form, Cela through the years has contended that it is impossible to define what a novel is. *The Family of Pascual Duarte* (*La familia de Pascual Duarte*) (1942) probably encouraged "authors and titles . . . that promise to make Spain, if not a leader in the European novel, at least part of European trends"; [18] but as Robert Kirsner shows, preoccupation with Spain and the cruelty which is an inherent part of Spanish life constitute the predominant themes of his novels.[19] *The Beehive* (*La colmena*) (1951), a complex documentary reflecting the counterpoint of Aldous Huxley, opens the formal aspects of style and esthetic treatment of social preoccupations, and *Mrs. Caldwell Talks to Her Son* (*Mrs. Caldwell habla con su hijo*) (1953) resembles the *nouveau roman*. His latest novels are *Hungry Ride* (*Tobogán de hambrientos*) (1962), which contains cinematographic views concerning the relationships of one hundred people, and *A Hero's Family* (*La familia del héroe*) (1965), a burlesque monologue on Spanish pride which seems inspired by the European novel. Cela, then, has been influenced by European culture but not to the extent of betraying his Spanish ancestry. He exposes the smells, sounds, and cruelty of Spain, and in his portrayal of people trapped by life, death, and violence, as victims of sexuality, existential anguish, and despair, he is traditionally Spanish.

Miguel Delibes (1920–), in his glorification of rural life, seems to reflect Ortega y Gasset's gloomy prediction that the modern novelist will resemble a talented woodcutter in the Sahara desert, refraining

[18] David Foster, *Forms of the Novel in the Works of Camilo José Cela* (Columbia, Mo., 1967), 158–59.
[19] *The Novels and Travels of Camilo José Cela* (Chapel Hill, N. C., 1963), 182.

from great plots because "a bit of tension and movement suffices."[20] Delibes, in his themes of alienation, preoccupation with youth, and his gray world of ordinary people, reveals his relationship to the "mid-century generation." He believes that the novelist must be true to his time and avoid forms which do not answer urgent artistic needs. In the prologue to his *Complete Works* (*Obras completas*) (1966) he admits that he started as an unconscious or intuitive rather than intellectual writer, stressing simplicity of style and attempting to escape the unpleasant contemporary world through the evocation of childhood. In the prologue to the third volume (1968) he notes that there is more intellectual content and existentialism in his works than he had realized, although childhood, death, and nature are continuing themes. He rejects the social novel, but he agrees that Spanish society urgently needs revision. Above all he stresses the need for what he calls "the sentiment of one's fellow man," a concern for the human situation. One critic states that a definite change of style from the traditional to a more introspective analysis occurs in Delibes's works from about 1950 on, as the author places the reader in contact with *el pueblo* ("the common people"), an apparent objectivity which disguises what in reality is a clearly subjective portrayal.[21] In *Five Hours With Mario* (*Cinco horas con Mario*) (1967) Delibes's psychological penetration is substantiated through the long monologue of the woman before her husband's corpse, but the novel reflects equally clearly an external reality fashioned by stupidity, injustice, and ignorance.

Ignacio Aldecoa (1925–1969), probably Spain's best contemporary short-story writer, rejects esthetics, although he admires Malraux. Among his Spanish literary ancestors he acknowledges Valle-Inclán and Gómez de la Serna, both aloof and "aristocratic," but his protagonists are humble folk, truck drivers, gypsies, transient farmers, and fishermen, little people fenced in by life but striving for human dignity. In their solitude as victims of fate they typify the Spanish *pueblo* and what Aldecoa himself once called "immutable Spain." He stated that "what moves me above all is the conviction that there is a Spanish reality, crude and tender at the same time, which is almost unpublished in our novel."[22] His two latest novels are *Big Sun* (*Gran sol*) (1957), about fishing boats, life on board, and the monotony

---

[20] José Ortega y Gasset, *Obras completas* (Madrid, 1957), 3:416.
[21] Ramón Buckley, *Problemas formales de la novela española contemporánea* (Barcelona, 1968), 85–136.
[22] Juan Luis Alborg, *Hora actual de la novela española* (Madrid, 1958), 263.

and fatalistic resignation of the fishermen, and *A Partial History* (*Parte de una historia*) (1967), about the effect of foreign tourists on a fishing village.

Ana María Matute (1926–) concentrates on alienation, violence, love, hate, pain, cruelty, death, the passage of time, solitude, and nature, which often reflect her pessimistic view of mankind. Largely lyrical and subjective, she differs from the pseudo-objectivists of her generation through her special talent "in extracting the invisible reality of the external world... and 'eternal Spain.' " [23] At times, with a childlike view of magic and mystery, she recalls the Mansilla region of her youth, but she cannot escape the contemporary world of fear, suspicion, cruelty, and tormented children in need of love. Her pessimism, revealed also through her Cain-Abel confrontations, undoubtedly a reflection of the tragic fratricidal Spanish struggle which she cannot forget, is only occasionally relieved by a religious awareness of the need for redemption. She refuses to exclude herself from the sorrow of Spain, believing that in addition to portraying national reality the novel should wound the conscience of readers.

She uses a diversity of stylistic techniques, "lush and poetic... harsh and realistically detailed... grotesque and fantastic... tentative stabs at literary experimentation... in fact, an intentional effort to fuse the manner of expression with the development of the material." [24] She also shows a predilection for oneiric symbols, interior monologue, flashback, and temporal experimentation. When asked in 1960 about European contacts Matute stated that "as a novelist my critical freedom is limited to society and its vital forms and not to literature written because of the same critical function of other creators," [25] but she admits that her European favorites are Sartre, Camus, Pratolini, Vittorini, and Pavese. Her trilogy *The Merchants* (*Los mercaderes*), set in Mallorca, is at times a bitter allegory. *First Memory* (*Primera memoria*) (1960), the first volume, records the passage from childhood to adolescence. *The Soldiers Cry at Night* (*Los soldados lloran de noche*) (1964), the second volume, shows man as a victim of his world, and *The Trap* (*La trampa*) (1968), a tender and poetic novel, reveals a continuing existential preoccupation with loneliness, the meaning of human freedom, and man's in-

[23] George Wythe, "The World of Ana María Matute," *Books Abroad* 40 (1966), 19.

[24] Margaret Jones, "Antipathetic Fallacy: The Hostile World of Ana María Matute's Novels," *Kentucky Foreign Language Quarterly* 13 (1967), 6.

[25] *Insula* 15 (March 1960) 4.

ability to adapt to the real world in which he himself has perverted the Christian message.

The objectivist pattern in Spain was shaken in 1962 with the publication of *A Time of Silence* (*Tiempo de silencio*) by Luis Martín-Santos (1924–1964). Martín-Santos wanted the reader to assume "mentally the situations described through a new procedure: it is no longer a question of submerging directly—as all forms of recent realism have done—into an objectivity which is offered in a direct way, but of capturing and introducing him to it by the magic of the verbal form." [26] The novel's antirhetorical language, interior monologues, and linguistic subjectivity reveal the author's indebtedness to European novelists like Mann, Proust, and his favorite, Joyce. But unlike Joyce he attempts to interpret his reality and use his mythology in a social framework. He stated that "the new French novel seems sterile and precious to me. Italian realism is breathing its last. I believe that one may rely on a German renovation of a romantic, intellectual nature, one might say Kafkaean...." [27] Martín-Santos evinced great interest in the existentialist philosophy of Sartre and read Martin Heidegger, Wilhelm Dilthey, and Oswald Spengler.

In his novel Martín-Santos, through the failure of his young doctor protagonist, shows us alienated man in a cruel and tragic Spain, the social sores, and the shortcomings of the Catholic church in his country, where one can live only in "the time of silence" because society rejects and frustrates the individual who criticizes the status quo. Yet man will continue to struggle with his inability to communicate, ensuing loneliness and anguish, and with a variety of other spiritual problems.

Juan Goytisolo (1931–) combines the traditional picaresque novel with interior monologue, reportorial, temporal, or cinematographic techniques to treat the fate of the postwar generations. Extracting incidents from his own experience and contrasting the indifference and cynicism resulting from the death and destruction caused by the Spanish Civil War with an innocent world of make-believe, of fairy tales and fables, he finds in the actions of children, torn apart by adult emotions of love and hate in a poverty-stricken world of violence and hunger, a microcosm of adult life.

Goytisolo's favorite novelists are the Americans: John Dos Passos,

[26] José Antonio Gómez Marín, "Literatura y política. Del tremendismo a la nueva narrativa," *Cuadernos Hispanoamericanos* 45, no. 193 (1966), 112–13.

[27] Janet Winecoff, "Luis Martín-Santos and the Contemporary Spanish Novel," *Hispania* 51 (May 1968), 230–38.

Carson McCullers, Truman Capote, William Styron, and William Faulkner; but he was also impressed by French writers like André Malraux, Proust, and especially Gide, and by the Italians Pavese and Vittorini.[28] At first he seemed almost a disciple of Robbe-Grillet, but since 1959 he has rejected the latter's excessive objectivity, stressing his lack of lyrical and esthetic intent, unity of form and content, and uncertain value system. Goytisolo cannot accept Robbe-Grillet's contention that literature may not serve a political cause,[29] nor can he escape his role in attempting to further justice.

Goytisolo held Ortega y Gasset as primarily responsible for having created a situation in which Spanish readers found more in foreign novels than in national ones to satisfy their sentimental and moral needs, unfulfilled by the stylized efforts of Ortega's aristocratic followers. In spite of Goytisolo's own insistence on a national novel he has borrowed extensively from European sources, experimenting with narrative rhythms, abrupt transitions from past to future, and impressionistic portrayals of groups of people whom he joins and abandons and whose lives intersect briefly in parallel and contrapuntal plots. Some of his characters seem devoid of real humanity, but all have relevance to the total structural complexities he creates. He later came to believe that in molding the material of his novel to a specific form and by using cinematic techniques he had indulged in an intellectual exercise because in his search for a structured originality he had deformed authenticity of situation and character.

Sleight of Hand (*Juegos de Manos*) (1954), a beautiful description of adolescent hate, love, and rebellion, bears a definite relationship to Gide's *Les faux-monnayeurs*; *Mourning in Paradise* (*Duelo en el Paraíso*) (1955) resembles both William Golding's *Lord of the Flies* (1954) and *Les Enfants Terribles* by Jean Cocteau, showing us the tragedy which ensues when children act out adult roles. In these tales of defeated and disillusioned victims of society Goytisolo, along with his characters, indulges in an idealistic search for a viable future.

In *The Undertow* (*La resaca*) (1958), more clearly a reportorial novel about religious and political factors in Spain, he uses focus shifts and objective description. *The Island* (*La isla*) (1961) continues his indictment of society, emphasizing Spanish sexuality in a grotesque and self-righteous country dedicated to self-destructive

---

[28] Letter to Maurice Coindreau, 29 June 1955 in *Jeux de Mains* (Paris, 1956), xx.

[29] Juan Goytisolo, "Formalismo e compromismo literario," *Casa de las Américas* 4, no. 26 (1964), 149.

hedonism and alienated from the world of the spirit. The reader of these novels can only conclude that the wicked world will always frustrate the noble and good.

In Search of Identity (Señas de identidad) (1966), his masterpiece, is his most outspoken attack on the Franco police state. Goytisolo describes Spain as a "dark river bed of suffering, an immense sea where no ray of light has touched or ever would: a barefoot, empty-handed and broken life of millions and millions of countrymen, frustrated in their personal essence, relegated, humiliated, sold, a suffering mass of beings entering the world without apparent logic. . . . " [30] Imposed intellectual conformity is so strong that soon a secret police will no longer be necessary for the thirty million Spaniards who welcome millions of European and American tourists to enjoy the local sun. Alvaro Mendiola, the protagonist, searches for himself through documents and memory recall, exploring historical, geographical, temporal, and spatial relationships in a search for Spain's signs and their meaning.

Goytisolo's mature novels intensify the faithful transcription of Spanish society, but his detailed documentation does not detract from his identification with his creations in a world where normal passions and the quality of being human are frustrated. Goytisolo projects reality through strange symbols and structures which appeal to a reader's multilevel perceptions. He extracts esthetic possibilities from ordinary life to achieve a combination with his ethical preoccupations. Always keenly aware of European literary movements and the infinite possibilities of artistic creation, he has not functioned absolutely within the esthetic limitations imposed by any movement.

Goytisolo's generation, in attacking Ortega y Gasset and Unamuno, wanted not to destroy but to modify their literary inheritance in conformity with their new culture. In 1965, when France had ceased for almost thirty years to concentrate on Gide or Valéry, Spanish critics still operated around the writers of the Generation of Ninety-Eight. Goytisolo himself feels more at home with university positivism, Marxist criticism as exemplified by Lucien Goldmann, existentialist theories, structural criticism of Lévi-Strauss, or formalist criticism by Robbe-Grillet than do most of his fellow novelists. He firmly believes that Spaniards, in keeping with new findings in anthropology, sociology, and psychology, should no longer limit

---

[30] Juan Goytisolo, *Señas de identidad* (Mexico, 1966), 376–77.

themselves to a single monolithic and dogmatic level. Tradition is an unmoving force and culture cannot be exclusively inherited; it must be forged by each new generation.

In spite of the apparent immobility of its political superstructure, Spain, in accepting the modern industrial world, is undergoing concomitant moral and cultural changes. The nobility and loyalty which supposedly characterized Spaniards have disappeared, along with "the sentimental and moral reasons for our adhesion to the *pueblo*, so brave during the Civil War but responsible, because of its passivity, for the present government." [31] Europeans in their esthetic admiration of "backward Spain" help support its old structures and to petrify its history, although tourists have opened Spanish eyes to the possibility of a new monetary religion. In copying the superficial aspects of foreign models without having had the requisite social education and training, Spaniards have created the caricature of a Western society. Before Spain can recreate itself it must be willing to face its reality, uncover the hypocrisy and egotism beneath its masks of pride, and reinforce the cause of human aspiration in its populace which has deteriorated into the "shadow of a people."

As one examines other well-known contemporary Spanish novelists one finds that some are traditional, some reveal older European influences, some relate new techniques to traditional matter, and a very few experiment with a universal thematic and structural matrix. Antonio Ferres (1925–) subordinates technique to ideology and a direct transcription of unpleasant reality in *The Pickaxe* (*La piqueta*) (1959) and other novels. He likes Pavese, Pratolini, and Moravia and is familiar with Butor's works, but he believes that foreign models will have to be greatly modified before they can influence Spanish contemporaries interested in reflecting their own time and culture.[32] Antonio Martínez-Menchén (1930–) follows Proust, Joyce, and Kafka. His *Five Variations* (*Cinco variaciones*) (1963) is a sociological exposé combining themes of alienation and sexual frustration. Daniel Sueiro (1931–), in *The Sieve* (*La criba*) (1961), also shows the influences of Kafka, and reveals the sordid life of journalists in Madrid. In *The Hottest Night* (*La noche más caliente*) (1965) he details the brutal sexual and alcoholic obsessions of contemporary Spain. *A Cut of the Bark* (*Corte de corteza*) (1969), a realistic science-fiction novel about a near future world, deals with an in-

[31] Juan Goytisolo, *El furgón de cola* (Paris, 1967), 4.
[32] *Insula* 22 (March 1967), 6.

creasing awareness of universal problems and man's alienation in an industrialized and technical society. The author explores the moral and ethical problems involved in brain transplants as the protagonist, given a new body, cannot accept the joys of love or beauty in an otherwise cynical and hypocritical world.

Some readers profess to find in the contemporary Spanish novel "a radical liquidation of tradition... their effort transcended the limits of previous renovations, giving them an amplitude, a universality which has only rarely been seen in their literature." [33] More reasonably, Edmund Stephen Urbanski believes that the "cultural environment of Spain of today gives witness to certain intellectual phenomena which seem to indicate a change in the evaluation of its culture and in the revision of its orthodox thought toward the foreign." [34] The younger novelists are abandoning social realism as they become more and more absorbed by the world around them, intensifying and magnifying reality through shaping its infinite possibilities rather than its mere reproduction. A few have been educated in European cultural centers or have been in close contact with European authors. Jesús Torbado (1942–), who has traveled all over Europe as a kind of vagabond, tells of corrupting factors in modern life, sings of the corruptibility of one's faith in God, man, and self, and follows Sartre, Joyce, and Hermann Hesse in *Corrupting Influences (Las corrupciones)* (1966); but his protagonist, José Antonio Fernández, seems straight out of a novel by Pío Baroja. *The Structure of Hatred (La construcción del odio)* (1968), inspired by Kafka, protests against the establishment and man's lack of freedom. His latest novel, *A History of Love (Historia de amor)* (1969), has a timeless setting. Torbado continues to expose man's hypocrisy and deceit and the self-deception in which he lives. He believes that solitude, which usually invites despair or stoicism, may imply hope and become the key to modern man's existence. José María Guelbenzú (1944–) in *Mercury (El mercurio)*, in which he himself is a character, relies on the technique of stream-of-consciousness, creating a mosaic of illogical and absurd situations, strange obsessions, word tricks, and literary allusions, especially to his favorite, James Joyce. Germán Sánchez Espeso, a young Jesuit professor of theology, breaks completely with Spanish tradition in *An Experiment in Cre-*

[33] Juan Carlos Curutchet, *Introducción a la novela española de posguerra* (Montevideo, 1966), 10–11.

[34] "El revisionismo en la valoración de las letras y cultura contemporánea de España," *Hispania* 48 (1965), 816.

ation (Experimento en Génesis) (1967), a detailed and stylized intellectual description filled with cinematographic imagery, geometric forms, and interior monologue. His protagonist, an alienated writer who has been abandoned by a girl and a young criminal he has protected, serves as a point of departure for an allegorical elaboration of biblical themes. Juan Benet Goitia (1927–), fond of Melville, Faulkner, and Henry James, in *You'll Return Home (Volverás a Región)* (1967) uses a ninety-page first chapter to introduce the historical and geographical background and two alternating monologues to convey a pessimistic vision of contemporary life. Región serves as a focal center for a symbolic re-creation of tragic Civil War events. *A Meditation (Una meditación)* (1969), also set in an imaginary country, is a long discourse, the living memory of a man, his motivations and sentiments, which he himself analyzes, reinforcing the author's view that existence is an enigma in an unknown universe.

Allegorical, lyrical, introspective, and existentialist novels exist in contemporary Spain, but one still encounters more commonly autobiographical and cathartic novels about the restrictive and gray Spanish world. After 1965 Spanish novelists at times show a more sophisticated involvement with European trends, but essentially themes are traditionally Spanish. Other countries have economic and cultural environments largely foreign to the Spanish way of life, and European culture has had much more effect on Spanish critics than on its novelists. Some novelists, as we have seen, rejected the traditional modes but without ending their alienation from Europe which has no validity for their private search for authenticity. Others have created artificial but unoriginal visions of the world. As life becomes more industrialized and the economic level rises, the feeling of alienation, entrapment, and discontent grows, but Spanish fiction has not been fundamentally altered. The novel continues to fulfill its political, social, and journalistic function because today one is still severely limited by censorship in Spain. In the novelist's continuing concern with his society and commitment to social change he employs new forms but reflects, in the given moments of the contemporary scene, old philosophies. Few Spaniards can convey or utilize a three-dimensional experience to communicate in an ever-shifting and changing world. Realism, fantasy, and the quest for authentic values in a society without them have created a confused jumble in the novelist's mind. Whereas in other parts of Europe novelists express their own visions and obsessions, their own reality, Spanish novelists still, by and large, continue to describe a country where old myths survive, even though they have lost their functional powers in a nation which has stopped being truly Spanish without ever having become European.

BIBLIOGRAPHY

Alborg, Juan Luis. *Hora actual de la novela española*. Madrid, 1958.
Amorós, Andrés. *Introducción a la novela contemporánea*. Salamanca, 1966.
Buckley, Ramón. *Problemas formales de la novela española contemporánea*. Barcelona, 1968.
Casado, Pablo Gil. *La novela social española, 1942–1968*. Barcelona, 1968.
Castellet, José María. *Sur* 284 (Sept.–Oct. 1963).
Curutchet, Juan Carlos. *Introducción a la novela española de posguerra*. Montevideo, 1966.
E. D. "Entrevista con Ana María Matute," *Insula* 15 (March 1960), 4.
Egea, J. Corrales. "Crisis de la nueva literatura." *Insula* 20 (June 1965), 3–10.
Embeita, María. "Francisco Ayala y la novela." *Insula* 22 (March 1967), 4–6.
Foster, David. *Forms of the Novel in the Works of Camilo José Cela*. Columbia, Mo., 1967.
García-Viñó, Manuel. *Novela española actual*. Madrid, 1967.
———. *La nueva novela europea*. Madrid, 1969.
Gil Casado, Pablo. *La novela social española, 1942–1968*. Barcelona, 1968.
Gironella, José María. "Por qué el mundo desconoce la novela española." *Estudios Americanos* 10, no. 47 (1955).
Goytisolo, Juan. *El furgón de cola*. Paris, 1967.
Gullón, Ricardo. "The Modern Spanish Novel." *Texas Quarterly* 4 (1961).
Jones, Margaret, "Antipathetic Fallacy: The Hostile World of Ana María Matute's Novels." *Kentucky Foreign Language Quarterly* 13 (1967).
Kirsner, Robert. *The Novels and Travels of Camilo José Cela*. Chapel Hill, N. C., 1963.
Lamana, Manuel. *Literatura de posguerra*. Buenos Aires, 1961.
López, José R. Marra. "Ramón J. Sender, novelista español." *Insula* 19 (April 1964).
Mead, Robert G., Jr. "Dictatorship and Literature in the Spanish World." *Books Abroad* 25 (1951).
Nora, Eugenio de. *La novela española contemporánea*. Madrid, 1958–1962.
Ortega y Gasset, José. *Obras completas*. Madrid, 1957.
Torre, Guillermo de. *El espejo y el camino*. Madrid, 1968.
Wythe, George. "The World of Ana María Matute." *Books Abroad* 40 (1966).

North America
THE BESIEGED MINORITY CULTURE

II

Contributors to Part II

LEWIS P. SIMPSON is William A. Read Professor of English Literature and coeditor of the *Southern Review*, Louisiana State University, Baton Rouge. He has published one book, *The Federalist Literary Mind*, and several essays bearing on regionalism, nationalism, and cosmopolitanism in American literary culture. He is a member of the Board of Editors of *American Literature* and general editor of the Library of Southern Civilization, Louisiana State University Press.

O. B. EMERSON was born in Tennessee and holds an M.A. and Ph.D. degree from Vanderbilt University. He has been a member of the English department at the University of Alabama since 1946 and was honored there as the Outstanding Professor in 1966. He has edited *Short Fiction Criticism* as well as *Alabama Prize Stories* and contributed to the Festschrift *Reality and Myth: Essays in American Literature in Memory of Richard Croom Beatty*. His articles have appeared in half a dozen journals and deal largely with aspects of Southern writing, concentrating on William Faulkner. He is presently finishing a book on Faulkner as well as on William March. His interest in black studies led him to pioneer the teaching of Afro-American literature in the deep South.

ALLEN GUTTMANN did his doctoral work at the University of Minnesota, concentrating on American Studies. Since 1959 he has been associated with Amherst College where he teaches American literature and is chairman of American Studies. He has written *The Wound in the Heart: America and the Spanish Civil War* and *The Conservative Tradition in America* and has been a prominent contributor to the Problems of American Civilization Series. He is presently engaged in a comprehensive study of cultural nationalism and assimilation of American Jews as seen in their literature. His "The Conversion of the Jews," which originally appeared in *Contemporary Literature,* has been revised for this collection of essays on cultural nationalism. The original essay was also the germ of a much longer study, *The Jewish Writer in America: Assimilation and the Crisis of Identity.*

JACQUES COTNAM was born in Quebec City and did his graduate work at Laval University, after which he went to live in the "other" Canada where he is presently teaching French literature at York University in Toronto. Although French is his mother tongue, his subsequent interaction with Anglo-Saxon society created a social confrontation that led him to look at Québécois culture and language in a contrastive manner. He has dedicated much time to the study of André Gide and is bringing out a scholarly work on the French novelist, *The Anglo-Saxon Sources in André Gide,* but he clearly shows his deep interest in the cultural and literary problems of Quebec in such books as *The Poet of Quebec (Poètes du Québec), Panorama of the Quebec Novel (Panorama du Roman Québécois),* and *Do We Have to Invent a New Canada? (Faut-il inventer un nouveau Canada?).* His essay on French-Canadian nationalism has been translated from the original French in a most competent version by Professor Noël Corbett of York University.

Southern Spiritual Nationalism:
Notes on the
Background of Modern Southern Fiction

LEWIS P. SIMPSON

The Civil War, Richard M. Weaver says in his essay entitled "The South and the American Union," confirmed in the South "the feeling that it was in spirit and needs a separate nation." Weaver continues:

> It [the South] might be viewed as an American Ireland, Poland, or Armenia, not indeed unified by a different religious allegiance from its invader, but different in its way of life, different in the values it ascribed to things by reason of its world outlook. . . . The South has in a way made a religion of its history, or its suffering, and any sign of waning faith . . . may be met with a reminder of . . . its saints and saviors. . . . Being a Southerner is definitely a spiritual condition, like being a Catholic or a Jew; and members of the group can recognize one another by signs which are eloquent to them, though too small to be noticed by an outsider.[1]

Weaver is speaking of the Southerner in a general way; but if, as we can assume, he speaks primarily out of his own experience of being a member of an intensely self-conscious intellectual and literary community of Southerners, we may recognize in his comment an unusually frank confession of a modern Southern writer's sense of identity. His statement may strike one familiar with the history of the literary vocation in the South as being something like the revelation of a hidden motive; for he associates his role as a writer not in the conventional way with the concept of a Southern regionalism

---

[1] Louis D. Rubin, Jr., and James Jackson Kilpatrick (eds.), *The Lasting South* (Chicago, 1957), 63–64.

but, more nearly, with the concept of the South as a spiritual nation; he implies, or almost does, that the South is a special redemptive community fulfilling a divinely appointed role in the drama of history. In so doing, Weaver, I think, recognizes that the true form of Southern nationalism (I mean basically literary or cultural nationalism but I also mean political nationalism) is not to be found in an image of the South as a region, or even as a section. The image of the South that lies at the heart of the modern Southern writer's imagination of the South is more integral. Even though it may be an image that so repels him in its blatant self-consciousness, in its aspect of Southern chauvinism, that he denies it, it is nonetheless fundamental to his imagination of himself as a writer and to his relation to his subject, the condition of human existence in the South. The Southern writer has tended to be a kind of priest and prophet of a metaphysical nation, compelled in his literary construction of human existence in the South—whether he is historian, philosopher, critic, poet, or novelist—to represent it as a quest for a revelation of man's moral community in history. The revelation may be ironic, tragic, humorous; it may be all three at once, but it is salvational. The quest for it is an underlying motive in the major imaginative works of the brilliant renaissance in Southern letters during the past forty years, a flowering that can hardly be said to have ended yet. And it is notably present as a motive in the most prolific and extensive accomplishment of the renaissance, the large body of remarkable fiction it has generated.

I am going to set down some notes and to make some comments on the image of the South as a spiritual nation in Southern literature with particular reference to the bearing this subject has on Southern fiction. My remarks, no doubt more impressionistic than analytical, will fall into two general divisions: the emergence of the idea of the South as a spiritual nation; important aspects of the development of this idea in the one hundred years or so from the 1820s down to the 1920s and 1930s, when it reached fulfillment as a controlling image in modern Southern fiction.

I

It is probably impossible to determine when a Southern literary imagination began to develop or when it began to move toward the idea of the South as a redemptive community, but I doubt that we can place either moment with any precision earlier than the age of the American Revolution. Now by this time, it is important to note, the image of New England as a spiritual nation had reached an advanced stage of development. Since the effort to define the connection between the South as a spiritual nation and Southern fiction may be considerably illuminated by looking at the relationship between New England as a spiritual nation and New England fiction, let us for a moment consider the situation in New England, particularly in the case of Nathaniel Hawthorne.

The rise of New England as a spiritual nation was integral in the origins of New England, which was established as the result of an exodus of a chosen people from an old England, a world in which they had become spiritual aliens. To purify and to fulfill their personal and corporate relationship to God, they set out on an "errand into the wilderness," explicitly identifying their errand with that of the Israelites. In the primitive wilderness, according to one of the metaphors they used to describe their achievement, they set up a city on a hill. According to another metaphor, they made a garden and enclosed it in a wall. This garden became their place, and New Englanders developed a deep sense of locality. By the time the New England garden was made, or before, it was threatened by many evil forces. Among these the most powerful and insidious were not from the outside but from the inside of the garden. Some of these forces were long familiar—including the love of money—but they assumed their meaning as a part of the massive secularization of the mind that had begun to occur in Western civilization by the seventeenth century. The New Englanders could not wall out this process from their own minds. By the time of the second generation of the Puritans, the unity of their errand had been broken. Declamations against apostasy and nostalgic laments for an irrecoverable time of wholeness and purpose became common. "But O! Alas! Our great and dangerous declensions!" Thomas Prince cries in 1730, longing for that first generation of his people who, in contrast to the present one, "made a heaven upon earth." In other words, history soon began to happen to the people of New England. What happens to a chosen people when they begin to realize that their vision of redemptive community exists in the context of the disorder of history and that this disorder has invaded, often brutally, often subtly, the very sanctuary of their vision, and that the vision so invaded resists purification? They look for another revelation which must surely come. In a way the American Revolution provided this second revelation for New England, and from this time on New England identified its oldest sense of being a redeeming community with the rise of the Union as a redemptive nation. There were members of the New England community who became separatists, arch-Federalists who began the secessionist movement that finally came to a dead end in the compromising of the secessionist issue in the Hartford Convention of 1814. The Hartford secessionists like Timothy Pickering told their fellow Yankees "again and again that they were the earth's chosen people, that the Constitution was weighted against them, and that the annexation of Louisiana absolved them from all obligation to remain in the Union." [2] But the New England effort to embody in political form the surviving pure spirit of the New England mission was not accomplished. By this time the mission of New England had become identified with the idea of the destiny of the new Republic in such a way that New England would from now on represent the ethos and mystique of the Union. In this mystique the United States was identified with the providential growth of modern scientific and capitalistic materialism, the eschatology of progress.

And yet the distinctive New England of the mind and spirit scarcely lost its being. As New England became more cosmopolitan in its literary education, it was the old intense sense of New Englandness that provided for the self-conscious community of writers I have elsewhere called the New England "clerisy"—and for the very substance of the New England renaissance.[3] The myth of New England came to possess the imaginations of its poets and storytellers. They were conscious not only of the New England past but of their own existence in the drama Emerson referred to as the "interior and spiritual history of New England." [4] They lived in the myth, and the myth lived in them. Some of them expressed it in a version of action in their times. This we can see in the history of the Abolitionist movement.

But Hawthorne began to live the myth in an ever deepening meditation on the history of the human spirit of New England. This

[2] Samuel Eliot Morison and Henry Steele Commager, *The Growth of the American Republic* (New York, 1942), 1:427. An important recent book for the student of New England nationalism is *The Wall and the Garden: Selected Massachusetts Election Sermons, 1670–1775*, ed. A. W. Plumstead (Minneapolis, 1968). Thomas Prince's "The People of New England," from which I have quoted a sentence, may be found on pp. 183–220.

[3] "Joseph Stevens Buckminster and the New England Clerisy," in *Essays in Honor of Esmond Linworth Marilla*, ed. Thomas A. Kirby and John Olive (Baton Rouge, La., 1970), 259–82.

[4] *Selections from Ralph Waldo Emerson*, ed. Stephen E. Whicher (Boston, 1960), 3.

became the center of his literary achievement. In his mind the myth of New England as a spiritual nation reached the stage of consciousness in which it existed at once both in the past and in the present, both in piety and irony. Out of Hawthorne's meditation came a series of stories, climaxed by *The Scarlet Letter,* which is not only one of the indisputably great romances in nineteenth-century literature, but also a synthesis of the inner life of New England.

There were various reasons why Hawthorne chose to introduce *The Scarlet Letter* with a long essay called "The Custom House." One undoubtedly was to get back at some people in Salem who had, he believed, caused him to be fired from his political job as the surveyor in the Salem Custom House. But there is, I think, a deeper reason. Hawthorne realized himself that his story is a realization of the whole myth of New England as a redemptive community. He felt the need to make this clear, although it meant fabricating a tale— in a playful way with no intention of literally fooling anyone—about finding documentary evidence for the story of Hester and Dimmesdale in the ancient custom house. This was a way of bringing the past into the present and showing, to use the words William Faulkner gives to Gavin Stevens in *Requiem for a Nun,* that "the past is never dead; it is not even past." Into the midst of his concern about his job and about the fate of artist in the materialistic society which he mocks and condemns in "The Custom House" (a symbol of the death of the spirit from "the daily materiality of life"), Hawthorne introduces the discovery of old Surveyor Pue's papers and "a certain affair of red cloth, much worn and faded." Hawthorne centers his story on the fall of the hero of the New England myth, a charismatic minister, the Reverend Mr. Dimmesdale. Further, he centers the last great scene of the story on Election Day, an annual occasion in each New England colony of a sermon before the legislature and the public. Election Day was a day when the minister, the chief figure in the redemptive community of New England, gave what amounted to an official revaluation of the state of the chosen people. His sermon, prepared with the utmost care and art, was usually in part a record of apostasies from the original sense of the errand into the wilderness, to some degree an expression of nostalgia for an irrecoverable past, and a forecast, often ominous, of the future. Immediately before Dimmesdale reveals to the chosen people his own awful corruption of their mission, he has spoken to them with an eloquence and authority such as they have never heard before on the subject of "the relation between the Deity and the communities of mankind, with a special reference to the New England which they were planting in the wilderness." It has been suggested that in his final sermon Dimmesdale makes the greatest of all conversions: he converts himself. When he does so he is led inevitably to reveal on the scaffold the sin he has committed and the emblem of it upon his breast, "his own red stigmata . . . the type of what has seared his inmost heart." "As one who, in the crisis of acutest pain, has won a victory," the hero of the chosen people, who has been worshiped to the point of apotheosis, sinks down upon the scaffold and dies "his death of triumphant ignominy before the people" of New England.[5] With consummate irony and piety Hawthorne tells the inner and spiritual history of New England, making the scarlet letter the symbol of a chosen people—the redemptive community of New England, in all of its complex, tortuous, ironic historical dimensions.

These dimensions, we must observe, were those of a relatively latitudinarian world. After the second generation of Puritans, New England had become, not an open, but at least a half-way open society. Both heresy and reaction were logical and coherent, the attack on and the defense of a well-developed metaphysic. The New England mind was at no time given to excesses of nostalgia for the past. Past and present were a continuum, both for the conservatives and liberals. This was true down through the age of Emily Dickinson, even down to the time of Henry Adams. Not until Adams knelt before the Virgin in the Cathedral of Chartres at the end of the last century was all the coherence lost, the image of New England as a redemptive community shattered.

But at the end of the nineteenth century the image of the South as a spiritual nation had only begun to reach the stage of coherence in the Southern literary imagination.

II

Although, like the myth of New England, it has been basically an assertion against the materialistic way of life, the myth of the South as a spiritual nation is considerably more complicated than the myth of New England. This is for several reasons. I mention some of the leading ones.

---

[5] Passages from Hawthorne's novel are quoted from the edition in the New World Writers Series edited by Terence Martin (Cleveland, 1967). Martin makes the suggestion concerning Dimmesdale's self-conversion (p. 237 n).

To put it in a negative way, the Southern myth is more complex because it did not originate in a systematic Protestant theology expounded by a class of learned clerics, who were the prophets of an inspired biblical exodus from the Old World. The revelation that they were a special people came to Southerners only after the Republic had been launched, and then it did not come with any clear illumination. One general reason for its lack of focus and intensity is that by the time of the founding of the United States the secularization of the Western mind—at the intellectual class level—had been consolidated in the American Enlightenment. At the literary and intellectual level the Southern myth originated in eighteenth-century rationalism and humanism—in the concepts of nature, human nature, and the new concept of history. The Southern literary imagination, no matter how much the mass of nonliterary Southerners subscribed to a Protestantism motivated by the Christian sensibility of a millennial apocalypse, was not compelled by a vision of the South's fulfilling a millennial destiny. The Southern literary imagination was not to be heavily influenced by Christian historical determinism until later.

I think we can approach an understanding of the origins of the myth of the South as a spiritual nation by referring to Thomas Jefferson's *Notes on the State of Virginia* (1787). The most famous passage in this widely read book is Jefferson's description of Virginia as an agrarian or pastoral civilization made up of self-subsistent yeoman farmers. It comes in the nineteenth query, one dealing with the question of manufacturing.

> Those who labour in the earth are the chosen people of God, if ever he had a chosen people, whose breasts he has made his peculiar deposit for substantial and genuine virtue.... Corruption of morals in the mass of cultivators is a phaenomenon of which no age nor nation has furnished an example. It is the mark set on those, who not looking up to heaven, to their own soil and industry, as does the husbandman, for their subsistence, depend for it on the casualties and caprice of customers... While we have land to labour then, let us never wish to see our citizens occupied at a work-bench or twirling a distaff...let our work-shops remain in Europe. It is better to carry provisions and materials to workmen there.... The loss by the transportation of commodities across the Atlantic will be made up in happiness and permanence of government.[6]

---

[6] *Notes on the State of Virginia*, ed. William Peden (Chapel Hill, N. C., 1955), 164–65. I am indebted in some of my remarks to the brilliant interpretation of the nineteenth query by Leo Marx in *The Machine and the Garden: Technology and the Pastoral Ideal in America* (New York, 1964), 116–44. I

Although Jefferson ostensibly is making an economic argument in this celebration of a self-subsistent, yeoman farming world, he is in truth projecting a vision—setting forth the revelation of Virginia as the pastoral repudiation of the Old World dominated by cities, factories, customers, mobs, and wars. Virginia is to be the purification of civilization, the reassertion of man's timeless relation to the mothering earth, which is the source of all virtue. Both Hebraic and classical in inspiration, this passage primarily represents the pastoral (and essentially non-Christian) humanism which was first fully articulated by Virgil and which has been a constant shaping force on the Western literary imagination in its search to transcend the confines of history and society.

We usually think of Jefferson's revelation of the redemptive economy of pastoral—the community of yeoman farmers—as having reference to Virginia generalized as America and the new nation. And it no doubt is. At the time Virginia was, we recall, the largest and the most populous of the states formed out of the old colonies. Jefferson envisions a free, Anglo-Saxon moral American community —the moral result of natural liberty regained in the Revolution—a community freed from avarice and power, existing in peace and permanence of government. Essentially in Query XIX Jefferson envisions a people not chosen to fulfill history but a people freed from history, living in a mortal but indeterminate dimension of time we might call "Arcadian time," a dimension of pastoral permanence.

But we seem always to overlook the fact that the context of this beautiful poem is a vexed treatment of the problem of slavery—the peculiar problem of the plantation world of Virginia and the South, in which Jefferson, the master of that perfection of plantations, Monticello, lived and died as the owner of around ten thousand acres and two hundred chattels. Indeed it is against the background of the plantation world of masters and slaves, and in startling contrast to it, that Jefferson projects his vision of the redemptive yeoman community. I refer to the discussion immediately preceding the one celebrating the yeoman, the eighteenth query, in which Jefferson is concerned with "an unhappy influence on the manners of our

---

am, as will be apparent, generally indebted to William R. Taylor's *Cavalier and Yankee: The Old South and American National Character* (New York, 1961). I should also like to acknowledge the aid of William C. Havard, "The Self-Interpretation of the South through Reform, Rebellion and Reconstruction," in *The Spirit of a Free Society: Essays in Honor of James William Fulbright* (Heidelburg, 1962), 75–103.

people produced by the existence of slavery among us," asserting that "the whole commerce between master and slave is a perpetual exercise of the most boisterous passions, the most unremitting despotism on the one part, and degrading submissions on the other." Jefferson says that slavery destroys the manners, morals, and industry of a people. His revelation of the horror of slavery comes to a climax in a vision of an apocalyptic judgment made on his world in the form of a slave insurrection: "Indeed I tremble for my country when I reflect that God is just: That considering numbers, nature and natural means only, a revolution of the wheel of fortune, an exchange of situations, is among possible events: that it may become probable by supernatural interference!" The eighteenth query concludes with the hope that a "total emancipation" of the slaves may come about before the "extirpation" of the masters.[7]

The language of this inquiry into manners is no more sociological than that of the nineteenth query is economic. The eighteenth query is a heightened, dramatic projection of feelings originating, it may be, no less in Jefferson's intimate experience of slavery than in his Enlightenment conviction of the universal nature of man in freedom. The conception of slavery in the eighteenth query must be read, however, in the context of Jefferson's belief in the inferiority of the Negro by reason of color and faculty. In the Great Chain of Being the Negro race belongs in a place below the white race—Jefferson remained convinced of this as an absolute principle of natural history. Taken out of the context of this conviction, the eighteenth query seems more socially revolutionary than it is. When Jefferson speaks of emancipation, he means *only* emancipation by foreign colonization of the freed slaves. "Among the Romans emancipation required but one effort," Jefferson states in Query XIV of the *Notes on Virginia* (on laws). "The slave, when made free, might mix with, without staining the blood of his master. But with us a second is necessary, unknown to history. When freed, he is to be removed beyond the reach of mixture." [8]

Emancipation by colonization—Jefferson knew Americans must accomplish this to avoid a conflict between natural and racial history and Jefferson also knew such an unprecedented action in the history

---

[7] *Notes on Virginia*, 161, 162–63. On Jefferson and slavery see in particular Winthrop D. Jordan, *White Over Black: American Attitudes Toward the Negro, 1550–1812* (Baltimore, 1969), 429–81; William Cohen, "Thomas Jefferson and the Problem of Slavery," *Journal of American History* 56 (Dec. 1969), 503–26.

[8] *Notes on Virginia*, 143.

of slavery was probably beyond historical possibility. The eighteenth query in *Notes on Virginia*, although it ends on a note of some hope, is close to being an apocalyptic vision of a doom of history to be visited on the South. Against the background of this vision, the vision that follows of the redemptive community of yeomen laboring in the earth represents a kind of counter-apocalypse. It is a golden apocalypse of freedom in a society emancipated from the historical necessity of being what it is, an uneasy and insecure society dominated by the relationship of white masters and black chattels.

Looking at Jefferson's hymn to the chosen people against the background of his fearful contrary vision of the fate of the slaveholding world, we conclude that in the nineteenth query Jefferson is struggling to awaken from the nightmare of the history in which he was intimately involved as a Virginian and a slave master. History, we may say, had happened to Thomas Jefferson; or, we may say, history had chosen his fate, and his image of a yeoman people chosen of God is an effort to resign from it. At any rate, in the *Notes on Virginia* we are in the province of a distinctly Southern sensibility. We are within the realm of the sensibility of what John Alden has called "the First South." By the age of the Revolution the South had indeed been chosen to have a special role in the spiritual and moral history of America, but the terms of the choice were ambiguous. It was not clear whether the South had been chosen to be a redemptive agrarian civilization or a doomed slavocracy.

In the years before the Missouri question came up around 1820, there is some indication that if slavery could somehow have been allowed to lie passive in the mind, the Southern imagination might have created a coherent vision of a nonmaterialistic, redemptive, agrarian South. We glimpse such a vision here and there in Jefferson's writings, still more in the works of John Taylor of Caroline. Taking his stand against the "paper aristocracy" of the North, Taylor became a strongly self-conscious Southerner. Convinced that America must choose between agrarianism and capitalism, he at times generated a vision of the South that suggests an agrarian metaphysic with a Christian coloration.[9]

But significantly about this time there began to appear in the Southern imagination an image of the South as a dispossessed world. Consider the mind of John Randolph of Roanoke. Thoroughly versed in the imaginative literature of the classical ages and the

[9] See especially Number 59 of Taylor's *Arator*. This is reprinted in *Literature of the Early Republic*, ed. Edwin H. Cady (New York, 1950), 262–65.

eighteenth century, a neurotic genius, the poet as orator, Randolph foreshadows a resistance of the Southern literary mind to the formulation of any actualistic image of the South's role in history. Randolph, to be sure, was the first "last gentleman" of the South. "The old gentry have disappeared," he declared with finality. Their world was gone. "I made a late visit to my birthplace," Randolph says in a letter in 1814. "At the end of a journey through a wilderness, I found desolation and stillness as if of death—the fires of hospitality long since quenched—the hearth cold—& the parish church tumbling to pieces, not more from natural decay than sacrilegious violence. This is a faithful picture of this state from the falls of the great river to the sea-board." [10]

Meanwhile, the self-consciousness of the South increased. If we follow Jefferson on the Missouri question, we begin to feel how remorseless the operation of history began to seem to a *philosophe* who had once believed that in America man might choose his condition—how caught up in historical necessity the Jeffersonian dream of freedom and permanence in a nonmaterialistic agrarian civilization became. In 1821, Jefferson wrote to John Adams: "The real question as seen in the States afflicted with this unfortunate population [slaves], is, are our slaves to be presented with freedom and a dagger? For if Congress has the power to regulate the conditions of the inhabitants of the States, within the States, it will be but another exercise of that power, to declare that all shall be free. Are we then to see again Athenian and Lacedaemonian confederacies? To wage another Peloponnesian war to settle the ascendancy between them?" [11]

III

It was under pressure of the knowledge of the fatal separation of the Union by slavery that the South's full awareness of its existence as a historical entity developed; and it was under this pressure that the South began to seek a redeeming identity as a people. The South to Southerners obviously represented more than the dissolution of the Union. Did not the South represent the truth of the American Republic? This question is an implied theme in the crisis of self-

[10] The passages from John Randolph are quoted in Jay B. Hubbell, *The South In American Literature, 1607-1900* (Durham, N. C., 1954), 223-29.

[11] *The Writings of Thomas Jefferson*, ed. Andrew S. Lipscomb and others (Washington, D. C., 1905), 15:308-309.

consciousness that rose in—indeed, that created—"the mind of the South." I refer to the mind of the pre-Civil War or Old South, and in a sense to all the minds of all of the Souths envisioned by Southerners down to the present day. One way, and not the only way but one way, to describe the history of Southern fiction as it begins to develop from the 1820s on is in terms of the effort of Southern story-tellers to focus the idea of the South as the truth of the Republic in a coherent image. In doing this they altered—shall we say "fictionalized"?—the "interior and spiritual history" of the South as this had been developing in the historical first South and helped to create that illusory South which would after the Civil War become known as the Old South.

Let us regard for a moment the situation in antebellum Southern fiction.

Antebellum Southern novelists were given the drama which emerges from the *Notes on Virginia* and, generally, from the letters and papers of Jefferson and other Southern intellectuals from the 1780s on. The implied plot of this drama concerns the permanence of liberty in opposition to historical necessity. The leading figures in it are the *philosophe* (the eighteenth-century rationalist), the master of the plantation, the yeoman farmer, and the African slave. (In the *Notes on Virginia* we can see that the first three are all guises of Jefferson.) The last figure, although he is interpreted as a distinctly inferior human being, is yet an alien and threatening presence. He is a threat to the rational man who in his rationality regards the slave as a lesser human form in the Great Chain of Being and the potential destroyer of its beautiful harmony; he is a threat to the yeoman whose self-subsistent relation to nature will be destroyed if he acquires slaves; he is a threat to the master whose soul he corrupts by fascinating him with the love of power and of money and by alienating him from the restoring source of virtue, labor in the earth. Whether the pastoral garden of the South is thought of as a farm or a plantation, the slave is an evil in it.

Obviously if Southern novelists could have realized the potential of the drama of the inner history of the South as this may be seen in Jefferson and Randolph, a Faulkner might have been Hawthorne's contemporary. From the first South the Southern novelists inherited a divided vision: the South as world of sturdy and independent yeomen and the South as possibly doomed plantation society of masters and slaves. The conflict in a society trying to subscribe to such antithetical images of itself would seem to be rich matter for the literary imagination. How much so, as a matter of fact, is suggested to a degree in such a novel as George Tucker's *The Valley of Shenandoah*, in which something is made of the struggle between the Southern yeomanry and an insecure plantation aristocracy, often unhappily aware of the evil of buying and selling slaves: as of course something is made of this in a number of antebellum Southern novels. But after Tucker's novel, published in the mid-1820s, whatever may be made of the yeoman world in Southern fiction, it is dominated by the image of the plantation. The informing rationale of the antebellum Southern novel was dictated by the need—accentuated after 1830 by the nullification controversy and antislavery agitation—to establish the image of the South as a redemptive plantation order. Logically, the Southern novel, under the compulsion to defend slavery, must seek to define the Southern plantation as the static image of a community of chosen people existing in a pastoral dispensation which it is America's destiny to fulfill. The logic of definition further demanded that the planter be made into a pastoral patriarch (not, it must emphasized, a feudal lord) and that somehow the slave be conceived as a pastoral figure. The Southern plantation would then emerge as a version of pastoral unique in literary history but continuous with the tradition of Western pastoral as a celebration of the nonmaterialistic realm of existence.

　　Some such version of the plantation South as the pastoral redemption of America was created by the antebellum Southern novelists. All of them were influenced by the literary strategy John Pendleton Kennedy employs fully in the prototypical plantation romance *Swallow Barn*. This resembles the strategy of Arcadian time Jefferson used in the nineteenth query of *Notes on Virginia*. Kennedy aims to foster the illusion that in contrast to the disorder of the present (to innovating materialism justified by a spurious faith in "progress") Swallow Barn represents a life of pastoral permanence. But to idealize the plantation in the pastoral mode, opposing the image of the plantation to the historical present, was difficult. Indeed it proved to be impossible. One notes from the beginning of the literary plantation that it exists not in an indeterminate or ideal time but in an indeterminate past time, in nostalgic time, in the dimension, like Swallow Barn plantation, of "old-fashioned" time; and it is filled with old-fashioned persons, notably the two figures whose relationship comes to be central and critical in the plantation novel, the old-fashioned planter-master and the old-fashioned slave.

　　They had to be creatures of nostalgia because the literary imagination could not reconcile the distance between their historical existence and the sense of pastoral time. To do so would be to conceive of them in a natural relationship transcending slavery, when their actual relationship to the source of all virtue, the earth, was a bondage that confounded them both.

If virtue is rural, if it stems from labor in the earth, then the slave should be as virtuous as the master—acting in some sense as the peasant was imagined to act in the capacity of an intermediary between the virtue conferred by direct contact with the soil and the lord's supervision of his labor and his life. But the slave was a chattel, in brutal economic terms a thing. He did not even (as Allen Tate has pointed out) belong to the land like the peasant; he was a barrier between the master and his connection with the earth, connecting the master logically with the marketplace, where the product of the slave's labor was sold and where he himself might be sold. The slave, moreover, was as much a cog in the industrial machine as he was a laborer in the earth, the product of his labor being the raw material of the mills of New England and Europe. Also, it might be observed in a kind of lame afterthought, the European pastoral tradition did not include Africans among the herdsmen and swains who sing in the pastoral gardens of literary imagining, even though a slave might be named Theocritus or Virgil.

In sum, the image of the South as a redemptive community in the ideal of the plantation portrayed in the antebellum novels was not convincing. Southern story-tellers were not able to dramatize a vital mythic opposition between a redemptive plantation life and the materialistic drive in society. And there was no way out of the dilemma they were placed in by historical necessity. They were compelled by the ideology of slavery, centering in an absolutist defense of the peculiar institution as an agrarian institution (when in fact the context of slavery was the industrial revolution, not an agrarian restoration), to make the plantation the central image of the South.

Nonetheless, as the Southern novel sought to reveal a moral and spiritual South in the community symbolized by the literary plantation, it amounts to a good deal more than a mere rationalization of the slavery system. From George Tucker's *The Valley of Shenandoah* through the works of William A. Carruthers and John Esten Cooke, Southern novels are a part of a yearning, and of a struggle, in the Southern literary imagination to discover in the life of the plantation South an image of the South transcending historical existence. Such an image would emerge after the evolving myth of the South was liberated from the static worldview demanded by the defense of slavery, and the South as a spiritual nation became subject both to the nostalgic and apocalyptic modes of perception in the literary mind. I mean after the Southern literary imagination experienced the most intense form of historical consciousness known in the modern age, when nationalism has been the chief form of existence in history. This is the consciousness of the spiritual condition of the invaded, defeated, and occupied nation.

IV

I cannot explore this consciousness in any detail here. Let me merely suggest that after the Civil War—the war the South called the "War for Southern Independence"—the defeated nation, the Confederate States of America, began to emerge out of the older image of the South as a sacramental nation. Purified by the war, the South in defeat more than ever symbolized to its citizens the truth of the Republic to which it had been forcibly returned, and to them the South would continue in an America reunited and yet divided to represent this truth. What the South now stood for, as a matter of fact, was more expansive and transcendent than before the war. The cause of political and economic Southern nationhood was lost but not the cause of Southern civilization: redemption from the ever-increasing power of modern materialism. In his highly influential history of the Civil War from the Southern point of view (1866) Edwin A. Pollard, editor of the Richmond *Examiner* during the war years, warns against the South's concentrating upon "recovering the mere *material* prosperity" and admonishes Southerners to assert their well-known superiority in civilization. If the South has lost its political autonomy, it has not lost its "peculiar civilization" nor its "schools of literature and scholarship" nor its "forms of . . . thoughts" nor its "style of . . . manners." [12] Moved by this conviction the Southern imagination began to establish a mystique of Southern identity based on a poetic attitude toward victory-in-defeat. "But once the War was over," Robert Penn Warren has observed, "the Confederacy became a City of the Soul, beyond the haggling of con-

[12] *The Lost Cause: A New Southern History of the War of the Confederates* (New York, 1866), 751.

stitutional lawyers, the ambitions of politicians, and the jealousy of localisms." [13]

But the impulse to divinize Southern civilization did not proceed alone from military defeat; it proceeded more powerfully from the reaction to the massive effort of the conquering power to impose "reconstruction" upon the aborted nation. The martyrdom of the South became more nearly Reconstruction than military catastrophe, and the metaphor of the destiny of Southern civilization became the Christian Resurrection. Thomas Nelson Page in his once-famous address "The Old South" proclaimed in the late 1880s:

> Two-and-twenty years ago there fell upon the South a blow for which there is no metaphor among the casualties which may befall a man. It was not simply paralysis; it was death. It was destruction under the euphemism of reconstruction. She was crucified; bound hand and foot; wrapped in the cerements of the grave; laid away in the sepulchre of the departed; the mouth of the sepulchre was stopped, was sealed with the seal of government, and a watch was set. The South was dead, and buried, and yet she rose again. The voice of God called her forth; she came clad in her grave-clothes, but living, and with her face uplifted to the heavens from which had sounded the call of her resurrection.[14]

In such an imagining of the Southern destiny the image of the redemptive South is obviously transformed from the Arcadian image into one primarily derived from Christian eschatology. The South represents a truth of man and society God will not allow to remain dead but summons back to fulfill its divine mission in history.

Page creates the impression that the whole of the Civil War and Reconstruction constitutes an apostasy not only from the true principles of the Union but from the true principles of Christian civilization. Both sets of principles are based on the conservation of moral qualities as opposed to materialistic desires; the South stood, Page says, on the overall principle of "the reduction of everything to principles." And Page offers the hope that the South can yet save the American Union "from the materialistic tendencies" which still threaten its existence. At the same time in his address on "The Old South" Page is drawn toward creating the impression that the Old South represented a unique, doomed, and irrecoverable civilization, for which the present can only have the greatest nostalgia. But more

---

[13] Robert Penn Warren, *Legacy of the Civil War* (New York, 1961), 14–15.
[14] *The Old South: Essays Social and Political* (New York, 1892), 4.

significant than the tension between apostasy and nostalgia Page sets up is the reason he gives for the South's defeat in the war. It was lost because the Old South did not create a literature. And the Old South did not do so, paradoxically, because of her lack of interest in material wealth. Page has the idea that the South failed to set up a publishing industry and a literary marketplace because Southerners did not want to become this materialistic about letters. Southern writing consequently did not become a profession, and when the crisis came the South did not have the literary resources to solicit "the outside support" she needed. The North got this help. Page says: "Only study the course of the contest against the South and you cannot fail to see how she was conquered by the pen rather than by the sword; and how unavailing against the resources of the world, which the North had commanded through the sympathy it had enlisted, was the valiance of that heroic army, which, if courage could have availed, had withstood the universe." [15] But now the story of Southern civilization must be told—"the heroic story of the Old South ... must be sung through the ages." Not out of any simple motive of nostalgia. Southern writers, in Page's terms, become in effect the priests of a literary resurrection which will be the resurrection of the South.

I dwell on Thomas Nelson Page because it seems to me that he is the continuator of the literary plantation who is the direct prophet of the literary apocalypse that is modern Southern story-telling. In setting up an image of the South as a redemptive nation, he was motivated both by the conviction of an apostasy from the Southern moral order and by nostalgia for the Old South. In Page a combination of apostasy and nostalgia becomes the mythic perspective of the Southern story-teller. Most importantly, the South becomes a coherent revelation that occurs within the story-teller's imagination. And not only this, the revealing of the revelation becomes the imperative of his identity. In a hyperbolic paradox Page links the Southern writer to the doom of the South. It was a literary failure—the absence of the writer, the failure of his presence, which was in itself a result of the South's nonmaterialistic civilization—that caused the South to lose the War for Southern Independence. Now at last the writer is himself to become a redemptive figure in the fulfillment of the South as a redemptive community. Page discovers that the South-

[15] *Ibid.,* 150.

ern literary imagination is the medium through which the revelation of the meaning of the interior and spiritual history of the South is to be completed. This was potentially a momentous discovery.[16]

But Page made the discovery as a prophet, not as a story-teller. His most famous work of fiction, *In Ole Virginia*, is lacking in the dimension of the imagination that would bring about the full participation of the Southern story-teller in the ripening myth of the South. Page had, you might say, an excess of piety and a deficiency of irony. He lacked the sense of irony required if the modern writer is to control the myth of his people as a Hawthorne does.

V

It would take another generation and another great war, the First World War, before Southern writers would experience the revelation of the plantation South as a redemptive community with something approaching full artistic comprehension. The writers of the Southern renaissance—John Crowe Ransom, Allen Tate, Donald Davidson, Robert Penn Warren, William Faulkner, Eudora Welty, and others—experienced this, as I have tried to show elsewhere, when they became conscious of the coalescence of their sensibility as modern American writers and as modern Southern writers.[17] When, this is to say, they became sufficiently aware that the South is a part of the apocalypse of modern civilization: the revelation of the horror of a scientific-industrial-technological machine which is completely dependent on endless consumption, and is in fact consuming the world.

Of the Southern writers the one who most adequately realizes the apocalypse is William Faulkner. Like Hawthorne he became a lonely and withdrawn man and after making two or three more-or-less false starts in his writing, he had a revelation of the history of that little postage stamp of a world which was his own world, and that became Yoknapatawpha County—and not less than the whole South and, for that matter, the whole world. But Yoknapatawpha County remains the South, as Hawthorne's New England for all its univer-

[16] For lack of space I am isolating this discovery in Page. Other writers, notably Joel Chandler Harris and George Washington Cable, should be considered in relation to it, as indeed should Mark Twain, who, however, is a special case. But the sensibility of Page, now mostly unread, is central in the history of the Southern literary imagination.

[17] See Lewis P. Simpson, "The Southern Writer and the Great Literary Secession," *Georgia Review* 24 (Winter 1970), 393–412.

salism remains New England—a special place inhabited by a people who have perceived an image of themselves as a chosen and redeeming community. The story-tellers, the poets, of such a community are both shaped in this image and help to fashion it. Eventually in a late stage of this community the mind of one of the story-tellers, who is gifted with great literary genius, possesses—in piety and irony—the whole struggle of his people, in all their differences, to know their meaning. And the revelation is given culminating form. He writes down the inner truth of his people.

He writes it down, as Faulkner said, in agony and sweat; for the modern prophetic writer, Faulkner knew, as Hawthorne knew (and some modern writers have failed to see) is not an incarnation of God. I think of "The Bear" and one of the greatest scenes in Faulkner, that night in the McCaslin plantation commissary—the commissary as a symbol of Old South materialism may be one way to take the setting—when Isaac McCaslin tries to reveal to McCaslin Edmonds a revelation that he (Ike) has had in his heart: slavery has cursed the very earth of the South, and the only way he can atone for the curse is to dispossess himself of all title to the McCaslin land. Ike does not, like Dimmesdale, tear off his shirt and reveal a slave brand burning his flesh. But in a way he does preach an eloquent sermon. Ike talks about the revelation that has come to him in the light of biblical revelation. Cass reminds him what the Old Testament says about the sons of Ham. If the sons of Ham were not meant to be slaves, then the story-tellers in the Bible are liars. Isaac says, "Yes. Because they were human men. They were trying to write down the truth out of the heart's driving complexity, for all the complex and troubled hearts that would beat after them." [18] Ike is talking about the revelation of the community of human kind that comes from the complex and troubled heart of the biblical story-teller, seer, and prophet, who meditated deeply on the story of a chosen community's constant and doomed involvement in the struggle between freedom and necessity. He told to his people their story out of his own heart and art as God gave the story-teller the power to tell it.

It was this role that Faulkner himself assumed, once he found out it was the role that had been given to him. This is not to confuse Faulkner with Ike, still less to say that he was a scribe of God, but it is to say that he was a scribe of a people seeking a revelation of themselves as a redeeming community. Faulkner was a poet of the

[18] The quotations are from "The Bear" as it appears in *The Portable Faulkner*, ed. Malcolm Cowley (New York, 1964), 294–95.

complex and troubled heart, of the interior and spiritual history of the South. Focusing this history in the plantation legend, he embraced finally the wholeness of the diversity of Southern history, to become the writer who has made the most complete synthesis of the spiritual condition that was and still now is the American South. Faulkner's achievement is the measure of the revelation of the South that is the substance of modern Southern fiction.

BIBLIOGRAPHY

Brooks, Cleanth. *William Faulkner: The Yoknapatawpha Country*. New Haven, Conn.: Yale University Press, 1963. The symbolic meaning of Faulkner's world explored by a sensitive, complex critic, whose sensibility is thoroughly informed by the literary feeling for the South as a spiritual homeland.

Core, George (ed.). *Southern Fiction Today: Renascence and Beyond*. Athens: University of Georgia Press, 1968. Highly informed discussions of Southern literary regionalism and its context in modern literature by Walter Sullivan, C. Hugh Holman, Louis D. Rubin, and George Core.

Davenport, F. Garvin, Jr. *The Myth of Southern History: Historical Consciousness in Twentieth-Century Southern Literature*. Nashville: Vanderbilt University Press, 1970. Affords perceptive insights—limited by a singular emphasis on racial attitudes—into the dimension of the "past in the present" in the Southern mind.

Davidson, Donald. *The Attack on Leviathan: Regionalism and Nationalism in the United States*. Chapel Hill: University of North Carolina Press, 1938.

———. *Southern Writers in the Modern World*. Athens: University of Georgia Press, 1958. The Lamar Lectures delivered at Mercer University.

———. *Still Rebels, Still Yankees*. Baton Rouge: Louisiana State University Press, 1957. Drawing a distinction between "the great cities of the East" (especially New York) and "the hinterland" (especially the South), Davidson writes out of the sense of the South as "a traditional society" opposed to the scientific-industrial society of modernity. His writings constantly imply the spiritual nationhood of the South and must be consulted by anyone seeking to find the basis of the Southern sense of identity.

Donald, David. "The Proslavery Argument Reconsidered," *Journal of Southern History* 38 (Feb. 1971), 3–18. The proslavery argument considered as an aspect of a society's anxious search for permanence in a world of change.

Cowley, Malcolm (ed.). *The Portable Faulkner*. New York: Viking,

1945. An arrangement of selections from Faulkner that shows the scope and meaning of his mythical South.

Gaines, Francis P. *The Southern Plantation: A Study in the Development and Accuracy of a Tradition.* New York: Columbia University Press, 1925. The classic study of the plantation legend. Still indispensable.

Guttman, Allen. *The Conservative Tradition in America.* New York: Oxford University Press, 1967. See especially the comments on the Southern Agrarians, p. 148–57. Guttman sees true conservatism in modern America as based in literature rather than politics and suggests the context of the modern Southern literary mind in the tradition of American literature.

Havard, William C. "The New Mind of the South." *Southern Review* 4 n.s. (Autumn 1968), 865–83. Finds the "South's distinctiveness" in a cultural outlook related to the spiritual and the humanistic in the Southern mind.

———. "The Self-Interpretation of the South Through Reform, Rebellion and Reconstruction," in *The Spirit of a Free Society: Essays in Honor of Senator James William Fulbright.* Heidelburg: Quelle and Meyer, 1962. Pp. 75–103.

Hoffman, Frederick J. *The Art of Southern Fiction.* Carbondale: Southern Illinois University Press, 1967. "The pattern of the Southern imagination begins in a world desirable but not quite real . . ." (p. 12).

Hubbell, Jay B. "Literary Nationalism in the Old South," in *American Studies in Honor of William Kenneth Boyd,* ed. David Kelly Jackson. Durham, N. C.: Duke University Press, 1940. Pp. 175–220. Indispensable; the footnotes and other citations afford an important bibliography.

Jefferson, Thomas. *Notes on the State of Virginia,* ed. William Peden. Chapel Hill: University of North Carolina Press, 1955.

Jenkins, William Sumner. *Pro-Slavery Thought in the Old South.* Chapel Hill: University of North Carolina Press, 1935.

McDowell, Tremaine. "The Negro in the Southern Novel Prior to 1850." *Journal of English and Germanic Philology* 25 (1926), 455–73.

O'Donnell, George Marion. "Faulkner's Mythology," in *Faulkner: A Collection of Critical Essays,* ed. Robert Penn Warren. Englewood Cliffs, N. J.: Prentice-Hall, 1966. Pp. 23–33. An early assessment of Faulkner's sense of the Southern identity as growing out of a struggle between tradition and antitradition.

Osterweis, Rollin G. *Romanticism and Nationalism in the Old South.* New Haven, Conn.: Yale University Press, 1949. Interesting and informative but based on a very narrow thesis: the "Southern cult of chivalry . . . provided the very essence of Southern nationalism."

Page, Thomas Nelson. *The Old South: Essays Social and Political.* New York: Scribner's, 1892. See especially "The Old South," 3–54; "Authorship in the South before the War," 196–219; "The Want of a History of the Southern People," 253–73.

Rubin, Louis D. *The Faraway Country: Writers of the Modern South.* Seattle: University of Washington Press, 1963.

———, and Robert D. Jacobs. *South: Modern Southern Literature in Its*

Cultural Setting. Garden City, N. Y.: Doubleday, 1961. See especially
Louis D. Rubin, "Southern Literature: The Historical Image," 29–47;
Robert B. Heilman, "The Southern Temper," 48–59; Frederick J.
Hoffman, "The Sense of Place," 60–75.

———, and James Jackson Kilpatrick. *The Lasting South: Fourteen
Southerners Look at Their Home*. Chicago: Henry Regnery Co.,
1957.

Simms, William Gilmore. "Americanism in Literature," in *Views and
Reviews in American Literature, History and Fiction*. New York:
Wiley and Putnam, 1845. This volume has been reprinted with an ex-
cellent Introduction and commentary by C. Hugh Holman in the John
Harvard Library. Cambridge: Mass.: Belknap Press of Harvard Uni-
versity Press, 1962.

———. "Southern Literature, Its Conditions, Prospects, and History."
Magnolia 3 (Jan.-Feb. 1841), 1–6, 69–74.

Simpson, Lewis P. "O'Donnell's Wall." *Southern Review* 6 n.s. (Fall
1970), xviii–xxvii. The modern Southern literary mind and the "metaphysics of remembrance."

———. "The Southern Writer and the Great Literary Secession."
Georgia Review 24 (Winter 1970), 393–412. The South as a symbolic
homeland of the modern literary spirit.

Snyder, Henry N. "The Reconstruction of Southern Literary Thought."
South Atlantic Quarterly 1 (1902), 145–55. Reprinted in *Fifty Years of
the South Atlantic Quarterly*, ed. William B. Hamilton. Durham, N. C.:
Duke University Press, 1952. Pp. 28–52.

Taylor, William R. *Cavalier and Yankee: The Old South and American
National Character*. New York: Braziller, 1961. A significant study of
the "idea of Southern nationality, the popular supposition that Southerners and Northerners were distinct and different peoples" with considerable attention to fiction.

Smith, Henry Nash. *Virgin Land: The American West as Symbol and
Myth*. Cambridge, Mass.: Harvard University Press, 1950. Notably
Chapter XIII.

Tate, Allen. *Essays of Four Decades*. Chicago: Swallow, 1968. The most
important modern expression of the literary and spiritual nationhood
of the South will be found in the various essays in this volume. See
especially "The Profession of Letters in the South," "The New Provincialism," "What Is a Traditional Society?" "Religion and the Old
South," "A Southern Mode of the Imagination," "Narcissus as Narcissus" (Section IV, pp. 517–607).

Warren, Robert Penn. *Legacy of the Civil War*. New York: Random,
1961.

Woodward, C. Vann. *The Burden of Southern History*, rev. ed. Baton
Rouge: Louisiana State University Press, 1968.

Welty, Eudora. "Place in Fiction." *South Atlantic Quarterly* 55 (1956),
57–72.

Cultural Nationalism
in Afro-American Literature

O. B. EMERSON

I

Black literature in America has been shaped and informed by social, moral, and literary forces spanning three centuries and two continents.

The Civil War and Emancipation abruptly shifted the hopes and aspirations of American Negroes from a deepening pessimism of the 1850s to a new degree of optimism that at last they, too, were to be sharers of the American dream. During Reconstruction there was an increasing interest in Negro history and a move to "teach the Negro child more of himself and less of others, more of his elevation and less of his degradation ... to produce (in him) true pride of race, which begets mutual confidence." At times such emphasis on race pride and solidarity approached "a kind of nationalism." Prejudice and discrimination served to remind Negroes that they were a distinct ethnic group in American society. In its extreme form this nationalist sentiment led to a complete repudiation of American society and proposed emigrationist movements.[1]

In recent years black writers have turned to a cultural nationalism. Some writers and critics feel that blacks must determine their literary standards, develop their theater, and expose aspects of the black experience. In the past, blacks have not been encouraged and in some cases were not even permitted to use those themes and expressions which reflect their unique cultural background. Cultural nationalism

---

[1] August Meier, *Negro Thought in America, 1880–1915* (Ann Arbor, Mich., 1963; rpt. 1968), 53.

allows blacks to come to terms with the distinctive character of their lives and their experience in a way possible only for them.[2]

Yet prior to the Harlem Renaissance, a dominant white society that recognized only one culture and only one way of life prevented or discouraged blacks from developing their own cultural expression, causing black writers with the exception of James Weldon Johnson, Charles W. Chesnutt, and Paul Laurence Dunbar to ignore Negro folk culture until it almost disappeared from the literary scene; however, black culture experienced a rebirth when a group of gifted black writers drifted to Harlem in the 1920s and produced a steady stream of poems, short stories, plays, and novels celebrating the low life of the ghettoes.[3] This large body of work by a large group of talented black writers called the New Negro Movement, or more frequently referred to as the Harlem Renaissance, resulted from the social, political, and artistic awakening of blacks in the 1920s. Protest became more defiant, and racial bitterness became more prominent.

Black history and black folklore served the writers as a new source of inspiration and subject matter. Spirituals, blues, and jazz suggested themes and provided patterns of structure. Literary Garveyism issued forth from a fervent black nationalism. Marcus Garvey, leader of the United Negro Improvement Association, advocated a return to Africa, the lost homeland. The Garvey Movement glorified blackness, nurtured pride in Africa, agitated for freedom, and developed pride in a black culture in this country.

At the same time the rediscovery of African art and the disclosure of significant aspects of their racial past "spurred an upsurge of race pride among the Negro intelligentsia." This mounting interest in black culturalism was encouraged and enhanced by a more sympathetic interest of white writers in Negro life, a new awareness of white readers and publishers to Negro subject matter, a wide interest in Harlem, and the appearance of an exciting and talented group of black writers.[4] And many of the black authors reflected in their writing spiritual ties to Africa and fanned the dormant fires of African paganism in the Negro soul.

The importance of the Harlem Renaissance of 1923 to 1933 as a progressive movement in American Negro culture, both in a real

[2] Ronald Williams, "Black Studies: The Work to Come," *Negro Digest* 19 (Jan. 1970), 31.

[3] Edward Margolies, *Native Sons* (Philadelphia, 1968), 30.

[4] Hugh M. Gloster, *Negro Voices in American Fiction* (Chapel Hill, N. C., 1948; rpt. New York, 1965), 253.

sense and in a symbolic way, cannot be overemphasized. By 1925 Harlem was, as James Weldon Johnson phrased it, "the greatest Negro city in the world," and it quite understandably exercised a fascination and exerted an influence on a new breed of black writers.[5]

Along with the new black capital came a "New Negro," celebrated by Alain Locke in his introduction to *The New Negro*. The emergence of the New Negro and "Negro Writing" as a major movement resulted in part from a growing interest of American literary circles in the immediate and pressing social and economic problems of the Negro. Coincidental with this growing interest was the migration of Negroes from the South to the North and from rural areas to the larger cities; as a result the destiny of the Negro was placed more and more in his own hands, allowing him to develop responsibility and self-confidence.

The Harlem writers "turned to the folk for their major characters and a low-life milieu for their principal setting." Their distinctive culture began to be expressed in a distinctive language. Beginning with the Harlem Renaissance, Negro writers enriched the diction of the Negro novel by using the rhythms and inflections of Negro speech and especially by using jive, the colorful slang of the urban Negro.

The Negro writers associated with the Harlem Renaissance were even more interested in using and interpreting Negro culture in their writing than they were in advancing the case for racial justice. Affirming the existence of a distinctive Negro culture, they wrote avidly of Negro life. Although racial tension is present in these works, it occupies a secondary role. As Robert Bone has pointed out, Renaissance Harlem to them was a place of love and laughter, not one of struggle and oppression.[6]

In the last analysis it was a distinctive racial atmosphere and racial culture that gave the writings of the authors gathered in Harlem their revolutionary character and universal appeal. This quality was more than an exotic veneer, for it expressed a unique and partially non-Western way of life.[7] These writers were simply recalling and reworking their unique heritage and broad experiences.

They no doubt discovered that Negro folklore is one of the most

[5] David Littlejohn, *Black on White: A Critical Survey of Writing by American Negroes* (New York, 1966; rpt. 1969), 39–41.

[6] Robert Bone, *The Negro Novel in America* (New Haven, Conn., 1958; rev. ed., 1965), 65–66.

[7] *Ibid.*, 67.

prolific of all American folklore. In song, story, superstition, and rhyme the Negro has created a large store of traditional material, dominated for the most part by his social conditions and economic status under slavery. The folklore of the American Negro is characterized by work, worship, misery, superstition, and a sense of fun. "These forces caused him to develop a definite psychology—a fixed way of looking at life—as tragic or comic. The folksongs and superstitions are tragic for the most part, while the bulk of the rhymes and tales are comic in nature." [8]

According to Arna Bontemps, an authority on the subject, as varied and intriguing as the folktales are, they "give only a partial indication of the range and capacity of the folk who created them." Bontemps points out that "a less cozy, less contented side of folk life is recaptured by ballads like 'John Henry,' by work and prison songs, by the blues, and even by the spirituals. Still another mood of the folk may be detected in sermons, prayers and testimonials." To this list Bontemps adds the blues, which "provided a tap-root of tremendous vitality for season after season, vogue after vogue of popular music and became an American idiom in a broad sense." Bontemps said he would not overlook the artful style so importantly employed by the old-time Negro preacher to console and cajole, and even to lead.[9]

Jazz, according to Langston Hughes, is one of "the inherent expressions" of Negro life in America. It is, Hughes goes on to explain, "the eternal tom-tom beating in the Negro soul—the tom-tom of revolt against weariness in a white world, a world of subway trains and work, work, work, the tom-tom of joy and laughter, and pain swallowed in a smile." [10]

Bontemps quotes a "distinguished sociologist" who observed over thirty years ago that he

who would know something of the core and limitations of this life [Negro] should go to the blues. In them is the curious story of disillusionment without a saving philosophy and yet without defeat. They mark these narrow limits of life's satisfactions, to vast treacheries and ironies. Stark, full human passions crowd themselves into an uncomplex expression, so simple in their power that they startle. If they did not reveal a fundamental and universal emotion of the human heart, they would not be noticed now as the boisterous and

[8] J. Mason Brewer, "American Negro Folklore," in *Black Expression*, ed. Addison Gayle, Jr. (New York, 1969), 19–20.
[9] Arna Bontemps, "Introduction to *The Book of Negro Folklore*," *ibid.*, 29.
[10] Langston Hughes, "The Negro Artist and the Racial Mountain," *ibid.*, 262.

persistent intruders in the polite society of lyrics that they are. . . . Herein lies one of the richest gifts of the Negro to American life. . . .[11]

It is not surprising, under the circumstances, Bontemps concludes, that Negro writers, and "the many others who have used the Negro as a subject, should continue to dip into the richness of Negro folk life." He adds, it is seen, indeed it is conspicuous in black writing and not surprising that Negro writers such as Ralph Ellison, dip into the richness of Negro folk life, for they were born into a folk culture.[12] Besides Ellison, Bontemps points specifically to Jean Toomer, Richard Wright, and James Baldwin.[13] To Bontemps's list, I would add the names of later Negro novelists, John A. Williams and Ishmael Reed. These are the major writers that I shall consider in this study of cultural nationalism in Afro-American literature.

In the history and development of fiction by Negro writers, five authors and five works of fiction stand apart. In 1923 Jean Toomer's *Cane* reached unprecedented artistic heights. This work, more so than any other single work, helped to define and to dignify the Negro Renaissance. Robert Bone, who has made an intensive and comprehensive study of the American Negro novel, calls *Cane* an important American novel and "by far the most impressive product of the Negro Renaissance." He ranks it with Richard Wright's *Native Son* and Ralph Ellison's *Invisible Man* as "a measure of the Negro novelist's highest achievement." [14] Bone places Toomer in that "first rank of writers who use words almost as a plastic medium, shaping new meanings from an original and highly personal style" and says that the writing in *Cane* is "two decades in advance of the period." Toomer had "progressed beyond the naturalistic novel to 'the higher realism' of the emotions to symbol and to myth." [15]

Toomer attained a universal vision by coming to terms with his particular tradition and racial identity. Although he was born in Washington, D. C., and was educated in Wisconsin and New York City, Toomer made a pilgrimage to Georgia in a conscious attempt "to make contact with his hereditary roots" in the South. He wrote of Georgia that "there one finds soil in the sense that the Russians know it—the soil that every art and literature that is to live must be

[11] Bontemps, 35.
[12] *Ibid.*, 35–36.
[13] *Ibid.*, 36.
[14] Bone, 81.
[15] *Ibid.*

embedded in." This sense of the land is essential to an interpretation of *Cane* and to an understanding of Toomer's vision of life.[16]

The first section of *Cane* presents "the parting soul of slavery." The soul of slavery still persists in Toomer's terms in the " 'supper-getting ready' songs of the blackwomen who live on the Dixie Pike —a road which 'has grown from a goat path in Africa.' " It persists too in "the soft listless cadence of Georgia's South, in the hovering spirit of a comforting Jesus, and in the sudden violence of the Georgia moon." Above all it persists in the lives of all people, both black and white, who have been warped by their slave inheritance.[17]

This portion of *Cane* presents the portrait of six women, all primitives, in a kind of Dixie version of Anderson's *Winesburg, Ohio*. In this section Toomer deals with illegitimacy, prostitution, miscegenation, community guilt, infidelity, murder, sexual repression, and lynching.

Taking place not in Georgia, but in Washington, D. C., Part II of *Cane* is a contrast to the first part. Again Toomer presents an aspect of his primitivism in that the blacks represent a full life, whereas the whites are pictured as denying life. Negroes in Washington have "preserved their vitality" because their roots are in the rural South. Toomer's positive values are associated with the soil, the cane, and the harvest. Opposed to these symbols are those of burial or confinement such as houses, alleys, machines, theaters, nightclubs, and newspapers "which limit man's growth and act as barriers to his soul."

In "Box Seat," Bone thinks Toomer comes closest to expressing his central theme. This episode begins with a kind of invocation:

> Houses are shy girls whose eyes shine reticently upon the dusk body of the street. Upon the gleaming limbs and asphalt torso of a dreaming nigger. Shake your curled wood—blossoms, nigger. Open your liver-lips to the lean white spring. Stir the root-life of a withered people. Call them from their houses and teach them to dream.

The thought is expressed by a young man who plays a symbolic role. He says, "I was born in a canefield. The hands of Jesus touched me. I am come to a sick world to heal it." He also comes as a representative of "powerful underground races.... The next world savior is coming up that way. Coming up. A continent sinks down.

---

[16] *Ibid.*, 82.
[17] *Ibid.*

The new world Christ will need consummate skill to walk upon the waters where huge bubbles burst." This redemption theme is echoed in the young man's communion with an old slave and again in the case of the large Negro woman who sits beside him in the theater: "A soil-soaked fragrance comes from her. Through the cement floor her strong roots sink down and disappear in blood-lines that waver south." [18]

"Kabnis," the long episode which comprises the concluding section of *Cane*, is again set in rural Georgia. The protagonist, Ralph Kabnis, a Northern Negro, loses his job as a teacher in the South because to drown his fear of white Southerners he drinks excessively. Electing to stay in the South, he works as an apprentice in a blacksmith shop. He tries to find himself among his people in their ancestral home, but being morally weak, he finds only debauchery and impotence. According to Darwin Turner, Ralph Kabnis represents "the twentieth-century, educated, Northern Negro searching for his identity." Although he has made a pilgrimage to his ancestral home, he cannot identify himself with any Negroes who live there because they "discern his cultural dissimilarities." He despises his principal, an Uncle Tom, who abuses other Negroes "to compensate for the humiliation which he experiences in relationships with the white people." Kabnis is unable to imitate the principal who really rejects formal education because it fails to improve Negroes' lives and who derives pleasure and pride from working with his hands. Nor is he able to adopt the indifference of Layman, a self-appointed minister, who refuses to protest against the mental and physical indignities inflicted upon the Negro. Aware of the "impotence of the primitive religion he teaches, he offers its fervor as a drug to help Negroes forget the painful reality of existence." [19]

Intellectual and not physical, he is incapable of relating to Stella who "personifies the sensual Negro female, exploited by white men and black men alike." According to Turner, Kabnis can do no more than dream romantically of union with Carrie K., "the virgin-mother" of the work. He mates with Cora, "who is as flat mentally as she is physically."

Feeling betrayed by his faith in education and in religion, Kabnis awaits a message from Father John, "symbol of the Negro ancestor,

[18] *Ibid.*, 85–86.
[19] Darwin T. Turner, "Jean Toomer's *Cane*," *Negro Digest* 18 (Jan. 1969), 58–59.

the maker of spirituals, the voice of the past." But he is old and infirm and is only able to pronounce this judgment from the past that "the white people sinned when they made the Bible lie."

The story ends inconclusively and pessimistically. After a night of "debauchery and disappointment, Kabnis, carrying a bucket of dead coals, climbs the stairs to begin his labor as apprentice blacksmith" while in the cellar Father John "lies dying in the arms of Carrie K."

The only note of optimism in this "allegory of impotence and nonrealization" is provided by the character of Lewis, "a Christ-figure, who is what a stronger Kabnis might have been. Northern, educated, capable of acting according to emotional impulse or of controlling his emotion by will power, Lewis has come South for a month to observe and to communicate with his people. Compassionately, he wishes to assist them, but he is driven away when they swallow the anodynes of drink and sex." [20]

By the end of the First World War the Negro had become "defiant, bitter, and impatient." He began to put his feeling of hate and hurt in the literature that he produced. Thus the literature of the Harlem Renaissance was primarily the work of a race-conscious group.[21] Toomer's writing, for example, was "full of love and pride of race." In it he reveals the "inner yearnings as well as the joys and hurts of the New Negro." [22] In their poetry, plays, stories, and song, the writers of the Harlem Renaissance cried out against social and economic wrongs. Protest literature as we know it today was born. The Harlem writers protested against segregation and lynching. They pleaded for social equality and first-class citizenship.[23]

The depression of the 1930s brought an end to the Harlem Renaissance. It seems to have brought at the same time, however, a beginning of significant Negro fiction. The hard times of the depression hit the Negro hardest, and writers became concerned simply with the problems of survival rather than with cultural expression. The writing of this period did not center as much on freedom as on frustration of the Negro in the South and in the industrial North. Many of the black writers of this period have much in common with the naturalistic writers of the early part of the century. Like

---

[20] *Ibid.,* 59–60.

[21] John Hope Franklin, *From Slavery to Freedom: A History of Negro Americans* (New York, 1967), 499–500.

[22] *Ibid.,* 504.

[23] *Ibid.,* 500.

the naturalists they emphasized the control of man by his environment. Protest and race consciousness continued to find expression.

Protest, a recurring element in the writing of black American novelists, reflecting the social conditions under which they have been forced to live, found its most eloquent spokesman in the person of Richard Wright and its most powerful expression in his works. Wright is the first Negro to be recognized as an outstanding American novelist. *Native Son*, now a classic, is without doubt one of the important American novels of the period, and perhaps the most important black novel ever published.

Wright's first book, *Uncle Tom's Children*, published in 1936, consists of four horror stories about the plight of Negroes in the South. Of the eight Negro characters in that work, one is burned alive, four are shot, one is raped, and one is severely beaten.

One of the virtues of Negro art in America is its lack of sentimentality, "its insistence that life be peeled down to its real pains before it can be made livable." [24] When reviews of *Uncle Tom's Children* appeared, Richard Wright felt that he "had made an awfully naive mistake" in writing a book which "even banker's daughters could read and weep over and feel good." [25] He resolved not to be guilty of writing such fiction again. "I swore to myself that if ever I wrote another book, no one would weep over it, that it would be so hard and deep that they would have to face it without the consolation of tears," he later revealed.[26]

Published in 1940, *Native Son* turned the spotlight on Negro urban life in Chicago in the tragic story of Bigger Thomas in a tale of two sides of the city of Chicago, the ghetto South Side and the wealthy, fashionable North Side. *Native Son* is the ironically titled tale of twenty-year-old Bigger, like Wright a Mississippi-born resident of Chicago's South Side. Shut out from the American dream, which he sees in the movies, Bigger envies and hates the whites who can realize the dream. Unable to express his hatred in the way that he would like to, because he fears white people too much, Bigger takes out his frustrations on his fellow Negroes. In bullying other Negroes he tries to prove his manliness and courage. He fights a

[24] Jack Richardson, "The Black Arts," *The New York Review* 11 (Dec. 1968), 10.
[25] Richard Wright, "How 'Bigger' Was Born," *Saturday Review of Literature* 22 (1 June 1940), 19.
[26] *Ibid.*

Negro cohort to keep from robbing a white businessman. He is alienated from his friends, as well as from his own family. He argues with, deceives, and deserts his mother. According to Darwin Turner, Bigger "must maintain a distance between himself and them [his family] in order to prevent himself from becoming conscious of his impotence." [27]

Bigger becomes chauffeur for a wealthy white family who charge exorbitant rent to Negroes living in the slums of Chicago. Bigger accidentally kills his employer's daughter Mary Dalton. Forced by her drunken condition to carry her in his arms to her upstairs bedroom, he puts a pillow over her face to prevent her from telling her blind mother, who upon hearing a noise has come into the room to investigate. The mother, smelling the strong scent of alcohol, assumes that Mary has returned home drunk again and has passed out. When Mrs. Dalton has left the room, Bigger discovers that the girl is dead.

Ironic indeed is the fact that although the murder was accidental, Bigger hated all white people enough to murder them without provocation. He felt that he had been denied the good life, the American dream promised to all Americans that he frequently saw on the silver screen, and he blamed all white people for this unhappy condition.

The sensationalism and lack of sentimentality that Wright vowed to effect in his writing are seen in the action of this work: Bigger thrusts the body of the dead girl into the basement furnace feet first and, seeing that the dangling head cannot be forced in, he attempts to sever the head with his knife. Unable to cut through the bones with this small instrument, he completes the job with a hatchet.

In one of the most gruesome scenes in all of literature, Bigger, now a murderer hunted by the police, brutally rapes his mistress, Bessie, then bashes her head in with a brick, and throws her body down an airshaft. Ironically, Bessie dies neither from the beating nor the fall, but from pneumonia which develops while she lies freezing in the shaft. In analyzing the way that Bessie actually dies, Turner explains that it is as difficult for Bigger to destroy the symbol of his Negro personality as it is later for Ralph Ellison's protagonist to rid himself of a comparable symbol, the black sambo dancing doll of Tod Clifton's. Bigger is entirely free only after he has killed Bessie. First he destroyed the white force smothering him and now he has

[27] Darwin Turner, "*The Outsider:* Revision of an Idea," *CLA Journal,* 12 (June 1969), 312.

smashed the black chains that have bound him. Finally, at least spiritually, he has become free to think and to feel and to live.[28]

The power of *Native Son* lies not so much in characterization or in action, but in the ethical and sociological implications of that action. In the novel Wright shows that "social and economic barriers against race, lead to grave injustices toward racial minorities and that those injustices so distort character and personality growth" that criminals such as Bigger are produced.[29]

Wright supports this theory in the testimony presented in Bigger's murder trial. In the trial it is brought out that Mr. Dalton, the dead girl's father, has donated large sums of money to Negro charity and that he owns the South Side Real Estate Company in Chicago. The company is the landlord of Bigger who lives with his mother, brother, and sister. Upon being asked why he charges such exorbitant rents for such squalid quarters, Mr. Dalton replies that it would not be ethical for him to cut his competitors in such a way. Pressed further to answer the charge that rent for Negroes is higher than rent for whites, he replies that a housing shortage exists in the Negro neighborhood. Admitting that he owns property in other sections of the city where no shortage exists, he explains that he will not rent them to Negroes because Negroes are happier living together in one section. He admits also that he has never employed a single Negro whom he has helped to educate in any of his vast business operations.

Mr. Max, Bigger's attorney, charges Mr. Dalton with the murder of his own daughter, for it was he who helped create the conditions under which a Bigger Thomas could turn into a criminal. The attorney accuses the philanthropist of closing his eyes to the Negro's deeper longings for justice and equality and of salving his conscience by giving large sums to racial charities. Mr. Max points out that had Mr. Dalton provided clean and decent apartments for Negroes, as he had done for whites, had he established playgrounds for Negro children as he had done for white children, and had he provided employment equally to Negroes and whites, a murderer like Bigger might not have been created to take his daughter's life.[30]

In his analysis of *Native Son* and especially in his criticism of the last third of the book, which he finds "out of key with the first two-thirds," Edward Margolies says that

[28] *Ibid.*, 319.
[29] Nick Aaron Ford, "The Ordeal of Richard Wright," *College English*, 15 (Nov. 1953), 89.
[30] *Ibid.*, 89–90.

the chief philosophical weakness of *Native Son* is not that Bigger does not surrender his freedom to Max's determinism or that Bigger's Zarathustrian principles do not jibe with Max's socialist visions, it is that Wright himself does not seem to be able to make up his mind. The reader feels that Wright, although intellectually committed to Max's view, is more emotionally akin to Bigger's. And somehow Bigger's impassioned hatred comes across more vividly than Max's eloquent reasoning.

The very length of Max's address to the jury suggests that Wright is trying to convince himself.[31]

The publication of *Native Son* is the "high point in the history of the Negro novel." It is a work of art in its own right and has influenced more Negro novelists than any previous piece of fiction. Too, it is probably the most familiar novel by a black man, as well as the most powerful one, and its main character Bigger Thomas is the most memorable character in black literature. The novel was a success overnight and its popularity resulted in Wright's becoming "the first fully professional Negro novelist." [32] Indeed, before his death in 1960 at the age of fifty-two, Richard Wright was regarded as the world's leading Negro writer.

According to Ralph Ellison, perhaps the most distinguished and acclaimed of all black novelists, the folk culture into which Richard Wright was born influenced his early writings and "the specific folk-art form which helped shape the writer's attitude toward his life and which embodied the impulse that contributes much to the quality and tone" of his writing was the blues.[33]

What he says about Wright and the blues could well be applied to Ellison's *Invisible Man*. The attraction of the blues, Ellison insists, lies in the fact that they "at once express both the agony of life and the possibility of conquering it through sheer toughness of spirit." The blues, he feels, fall short of tragedy only in that they provide no solution, offer no scapegoat but the self. He feels Wright's *Black Boy*, with its refusal to offer solutions, is like the blues. He thinks, however, that in this work many Negroes for the first time will see their fate in print, and that "freed here of fear and the threat of violence, their lives have at last been organized, scaled down to possessable proportions." This, he sees, is Wright's most important contribution. Wright converted the Negro impulse "toward self-

[31] Margolies, 79–80.
[32] Bone, 142.
[33] Ralph Ellison, "Richard Wright's Blues," in *Black Expression*, 312.

annihilation and 'going-underground' into a will to confront the world, to evaluate his experience honestly and throw his findings unashamedly into the guilty conscience of America." [34] Ellison says that Richard Wright points out the obvious fact that Negro sensibility is socially and historically conditioned. Negro life is "a byproduct of Western civilization, and that in it, only one possesses the humanity and humility to see, are to be discovered all those impulses, tendencies, life and cultural forms to be found elsewhere in Western society." [35]

Ellison castigated Wright for cutting his ties to American Negroes and for being more concerned with world politics and with sociology than with literature. "People who want to write sociology," Ellison once wrote, "should not write a novel." [36] Characterizing Richard Wright as a man motivated by a passion for ideology and fascinated by power, Ralph Ellison rejected such a drive in favor of desire to write imaginative books, books that come out of the American Negro's culture and as works of art will become part of the culture of man. He has taken upon himself the task of identifying that culture and preserving it in literature.[37]

Rejecting both racial mysticism and significant kinship between American Negroes and Africans, Ellison turned down an offer in 1955 of a trip to Africa with the comment that he had no interest in such a trip and no special emotional attachment to the place. In the past Negroes, according to Ellison, "either repeated all the very negative clichés, or else laughed at Africa, or, in some cases, related to it as a homeland." As an example of the latter attitude he cited black nationalists like his character Ras the Exhorter in *Invisible Man*. Ellison points to pride among many American Negroes in Africa "now that things are finally moving" there. Conceding that some middle-class Negroes might share this pride to some extent, Ellison admitted that he did not know much about middle-class Negroes. As for Negro intellectuals he expressed contempt, especially for "fakery" in some of the new organizations springing up to exploit a new interest in Africa. He scorned a well-known Negro intellectual who "had taken to wearing African robes at Alabama State." [38] Although

---

[34] *Ibid.*, 324–25.
[35] *Ibid.*, 324.
[36] Harold R. Isaacs, *The New World of Negro Americans* (New York, 1963), 260–61.
[37] *Ibid.*
[38] *Ibid.*, 261.

he has an inordinate interest in African art, Ellison believes that the African origins had only a remote influence in the shaping of a distinctive American Negro culture.[39]

In 1952 Ralph Ellison's *Invisible Man* attained a new height of literary achievement for the Negro novel. In it Ellison, in expressing what he believes to be a distinctive American Negro culture, sees little or no African influence on this culture, past or present, or on himself. Remembering African princes, natives of Sierra Leone, and West Indians on the campus at Tuskegee when he was a student there, Ellison said he had no cultural identification with them. In *Invisible Man* the African theme appears only in the character of Ras the Exhorter, leader of the black nationalists in Harlem, patterned after successors to Marcus Garvey in the Harlem of the 1930s.[40] In the novel Ras, a West Indian black man, fights the Communists in the streets of Harlem. During one of these skirmishes caused by Ras's attempt to break up a Communist street meeting, Ras, with knife in hand, appeals to a black Communist:

> "You my brother, mahn. Brothers are the same color; how the hell you call these white men brother? Shit, mahn. That's shit! Brothers the same color. We sons of Mama Africa, you done forgot? You black, BLACK! You ——— Godahm, mahn!" he said, swinging the knife for emphasis. "You got bahd hair! You got thick *lips!* They say you *stink!* They hate you, mahn. You African. AFRICAN! Why you with them? Leave that shit, mahn. They sell you out. That shit is oldfashioned. They enslave us—you forget that? How can they mean a black mahn any good? How they going to be your *brother?*" [41]

In writing *Invisible Man* Ralph Ellison repudiated the naturalism of Richard Wright and turned to a kind of impressionism which he used most effectively in portraying the chaos of the modern world. Ellison, however, views this chaos through a particular cultural screen. It's Ellison's vision of the possibilities of Negro life, Robert Bone contends, that "has burst the bonds of the naturalistic novel." Ellison's style flows from his view of reality which in turn flows from his experience as a Negro. This unique experience, Ellison insists, requires "unique literary forms." These forms Ellison provides from the raw material of Negro culture. Ellison's work, Bone concludes, is a major contribution to the evolution of the Negro novel.

[39] *Ibid.*, 262.
[40] *Ibid.*, 265.
[41] Ralph Ellison, *Invisible Man* (New York, 1952), 321–22.

In *Invisible Man* Ellison's concern with Negro folklore and ritual brought him face-to-face with the Negro problem from an entirely different angle. He seemed less interested in racial injustice and more concerned with finding a new definition of Negro culture and with the problem of acceptance of a Negro folk identity. In his highly acclaimed novel Ellison draws on vast resources which Negro folk culture offers him. First there is the rhetorical skill of the Negro. The revival meeting, the funeral sermon, the graduation address, and the political speech are all used to great advantage in the novel. The dialogue is peppered with "sonorous biblical phrases," along with the spicier ingredients of jazz. To add vitality and freshness to "a jaded diction" Ellison employs a whole new vocabulary with terms "evocative of the numbers racket, of voodoo charms, of racing sheets, of spiritualist cure-alls, of the jazz world, the boxing ring, the ball park, the bar-room." [42]

Jazz and blues form an important part of Ellison's style. The very tone of the novel is early established in the novel by Louis Armstrong's wail, "What did I do to be so black and blue?" [43] This blue mood is enhanced and sustained by frequent refrains from the blues and by such passages as this: "I strode along, hearing the cartman's song become a lonesome, broad-toned whistle now that flowered at the end of each phrase into a tremulous, blue-toned chord. And in the flutter and swoop I heard the sound of a railroad train highballing it, lonely across the lonely night." [44]

Jazz forms also influenced the composition of the novel. "Something is always going on in the background of Ellison's prose— something not quite heard at first, but nevertheless insistent, which produces a feeling of depth and resonance when finally perceived." An example of this unusual technique can be seen in the "circling, diving, plummeting pigeons which hover in the background during the shooting of Tod Clifton." This passage is characteristic of Ellison's technique in which he writes a "melody or thematic line" and then "orchestrates" it. [45]

Invisible Man opens with a prologue in which the protagonist, in his underground sanctuary, informs the reader that he is about to chronicle the catastrophic events of his life. In the novel the protagonist in his journey from the South to Harlem, from innocence to

---

[42] Bone, 198–99.
[43] *Ibid.*, 200.
[44] Ellison, *Invisible Man*, 156.
[45] Bone, 200.

experience, assumes a number of poses and identities, most of which he thinks at the time reflect the role of the Negro in the eyes of the whites. In the end in his underground sanctuary or tomb, the narrator of the novel comes to the realization that he is invisible to the eyes of most beholders. At the same time he concludes that he must discover for himself his real identity and seek visibility.

In analyzing *Invisible Man* Edward Margolies says that Ellison's understanding of his early life corresponds to Negro jazz and that it is jazz and especially blues that shapes and informs his writing and is his "aesthetic mainspring." However tragic the message of Negro music may be, it is "an affirmation of life, a celebration of the indomitable human spirit, in that it imposes order and form on the chaos of experience." [46]

As has been indicated earlier in this essay, it was in the 1920s that black authors first dealt seriously with the folk materials in their culture. The black man in America in order to "sustain himself in the American environment . . . has had to fashion a culture that could preserve some semblance of his dignity and at the same time would not appear to threaten the paranoid white civilization." We are familiar today with the work songs, spirituals, folk tales, and legends that came from the South. But these form only "an integral portion of an underground culture of survival." Margolies states that one of the most characteristic expressions of Negro culture and a carry-over from the days of slavery is "the grinning minstrel mask." The Negro plays a role expected of him by the white man. But within that culture itself the situation is altogether different. Negro humor, songs and dances, stories and fables as well as movements, gestures, dress, speech, rhythms, verbal imagery are all a part of that culture which is distinct and apart from the white world. These aspects of that culture are passed on from generation to generation. [47] Margolies sees the novel as nothing more than a recapitulation of the pain the hero suffers in his twenty-year odyssey, "the telling of which is its own catharsis." He sees in the novel no social message, no system of beliefs, no intellectual conclusions. He does see in the comically absurd aspects of the protagonist's existence aspects of all existence. It is tragic at the same time it is comic, tragic in the sense that "it celebrates the hero's capacity to endure." [48]

Another critic, Jonathan Baumbach, sees gothic as well as comic

[46] Margolies, 130.
[47] *Ibid.*, 127–28.
[48] *Ibid.*, 131–32.

elements in the novel. Baumbach says that despite its obvious social implications, the novel is a modern gothic, "A Candide-like picaresque set in a dimly familiar nightmare landscape called the United States." He says that the novel for the most part takes place in an uncharted area "between the conscious and the unconscious, in the semilit darkness where nightmare verges on reality and the external world has all the aspects of a disturbing dream." Ellison's world, he sees, is "at once surreal and real, comic and tragic, grotesque and normal—our world viewed in its essentials rather than its externals." [49]

Ellison has described his view of life in terms of the blues. "The blues," he wrote in 1946, "is an impulse to keep the painful details and episodes of a brutal experience alive in one's aching consciousness, to finger its jagged grain, and to transcend it, not by the consolation of philosophy but by squeezing from it a near-tragic, near-comic lyricism. As a form, the blues is an autobiographical chronicle of personal catastrophe." [50] He also sees the blues serving another function, that of a ritual. "The blues," Ellison says, "speak to us simultaneously of the tragic and comic aspects of the human condition and they express a profound sense of life shared by many Negroes precisely because their lives have combined these modes." He goes on to say that this is a group experience "and any effective study of the blues would treat them first as poetry and ritual." [51]

Writing to *Time* sharply criticizing that periodical for including him among Negro writers living in exile because he had spent two years in Rome on a fellowship, Ellison remarked that for a writer the key question was where he could work best, adding that for Faulkner it was Mississippi, for James it was Europe, for Richard Wright it was Chicago and Brooklyn more so than Paris. He added, "Personally I am too vindictively American, too full of hate for the hateful aspects of this country, and too possessed by the things I love here to be too long away." [52]

In 1953 James Baldwin published his first novel. *Go Tell It on the Mountain*, the best of Baldwin's novels, ranks with Jean Toomer's *Cane*, Richard Wright's *Native Son*, and Ralph Ellison's *Invisible Man* as one of the finest products of Afro-American literature as

---

[49] Jonathan Baumbach, *The Landscape of Nightmare: Studies in the Contemporary American Novel* (New York, 1965), 68–69.
[50] Margolies, 132.
[51] *Ibid.*
[52] Isaacs, 262.

well as a major contribution to American literature. It is an ambitious book in which Baldwin attempts not only to interconnect all of the characters but also to relate these "to the Southern Negro experience and the consequent shock of urban slum living" [53] in which the church softens the impact somewhat and helps to make life endurable for many blacks.

As a matter of fact, his church is one of the few cultural institutions the Southern Negro transplanted in the North with some degree of success. In the beginning its primary function was to serve the spiritual needs of the community, but as time went on the church linked the newly arrived parishoners to their Southern past.[54] The mass migration of Negroes to the cities "constituted the most abrupt break in the Negro cultural experience since the days of the African slave trade." This change involved not merely the anxieties of the passage from a rural way of life to an urban one. The difficulty lay in the fact that "the racial mores, prejudices, and barriers of the North were ill-defined, vague, and elusive so that the Negro felt he stood on ever-shifting grounds whose pitfalls were at once invisible and treacherous." [55] The novel penetrates the walls and façade of the Harlem storefront church to the essence of Negro experience in America.[56]

Go Tell It on the Mountain is the story of the conversion of fourteen-year-old John Grimes. Essentially, however, it is the story of John's father Gabriel. Gabriel is the main character around whom every other person in the story revolves. In the novel Baldwin toys with many more elements than salvation. The novel is psychologically oriented, for we get flashbacks of all the major characters' lives before their journey north. All three guilt-ridden characters, Florence, Elizabeth, and Gabriel, lived in the South before going north. The fragmenting experience of ghetto living is a terrifying experience. So to preserve their identity, they all attempt to find solace in the church. It is obvious that Baldwin believes the Christian experience is a beginning. But he rejects the evangelical experience as the answer, the end whereby the black man will find freedom.

This church-oriented novel is divided into three parts. In the first part, "The Seventh Day," we learn the attitudes of John, his mother Elizabeth, and his Aunt Florence toward Gabriel. Collectively they

[53] Margolies, 109.
[54] Ibid., 102.
[55] Ibid., 103.
[56] Bone, 218.

all hate, fear, and distrust the stern authoritarian. Too, we get a deeper insight ino John's character. A boy of fourteen completely afraid to be himself, he desires desperately to break away; he wants to be a part of the world and to do the normal things a boy his age does—play ball, go to movies, cultivate an interest in girls. But John represses his worldly yearnings. Trapped in the ghetto, he is attracted to the white world around him. Yet, he must denounce any attraction he feels for it. At fourteen he must play the role of an unfeeling, stereotyped, good "nigger boy." And despite his longings that it were not so, John is hopelessly enslaved.

In the second part of the novel, "The Prayers of the Saints," Florence, Gabriel, and Elizabeth, the three other major characters are seen at their prayers. The seeds of John's fate are buried in the dark corners of their lives. At their prayers, each character wanders back and forth over memories of the past seeking to find the cause of their present miserable plight.

In Part Three, "The Threshing Floor," John experiences a religious conversion. Flinging himself frantically on the floor of the church, he remains there throughout the scene in the throes of forces beyond his control.

Robert Bone says that Baldwin sees the Negro as the bastard child of American civilization. The essence of Negro experience is rejection, the most deadly consequence of which is shame.[57] The Negro boy is made to feel that his skin is dirty and unclean, which Baldwin presents metaphorically as the dirt and grime that perpetually vexes the young boy:

> John hated sweeping this carpet, for dust rose, clogging his nose and sticking to his sweaty skin, and he felt that should he sweep it forever, the clouds of dust would not diminish, the rug would not be clean. It became in his imagination his impossible, lifelong task, his hard trial, like that of a man he had read about somewhere, whose curse it was to push a boulder up a steep hill, only to have the giant who guarded the hill roll the boulder down again—and so on, forever, throughout eternity.[58]

When the Negro preacher compares the plight of his people to that of the Israelites, he gives them "a series of metaphors corresponding to their deepest experience." In this way he offers his flock "a ritual enactment of their daily pain." [59]

[57] *Ibid.,* 223.
[58] James Baldwin, *Go Tell It on the Mountain* (New York, 1953), 25.
[59] Bone, 224–25.

At the depth of his despair, John hears a sound which eases his pain:

> Yes, he had heard it all his life, but it was only now that his ears were opened to this sound that came from darkness, that could only come from darkness, that yet bore such sure witness to the glory of the light. And now in his moaning, and so far from any help, he heard it in himself—it rose from his bleeding, his cracked-open heart. It was a sound of rage and weeping which filled the grave, rage and weeping from time set free, but bound now in eternity; rage that had no language, weeping with no voice—which yet spoke now to John's startled soul, of boundless melancholy, of the bitterest patience, and the longest night; of the deepest water, the strongest chains, the most cruel lash; of humility most wretched, the dungeon most absolute, of love's bed defiled, and birth dishonored, and most bloody, unspeakable, sudden death. Yes, the darkness hummed with murder: the body in the water, the body in the fire, the body on the tree. John looked down the line of these armies of darkness, army upon army, and his soul whispered: *Who are these? Who are they?* And wondered: *Where shall I go?* [60]

This is the sound of the blues. When Baldwin was writing the novel in Paris he was no longer ashamed to listen to such music. He listened, he tells us, to the records of Bessie Smith. And the sound that John hears is the sound of Bessie Smith. Bone says it is the sound of all Negro art and all Negro religion. "What Baldwin wants us to feel is the emotional pressure exerted on the Negro's cultural forms by his exposure to white oppression." [61]

A new Negro Renaissance seems to be occurring today. The New Negro writer is moving beyond anger and developing a new concern for the art of writing, its discipline and control, and seeking to be involved in the larger world of art and ideology. [62] The two writers who best epitomize this dedication and awareness are John A. Williams and Ishmael Reed.

It is true that there is plenty of anger in Williams's work; nevertheless one sees in his novel *The Man Who Cried I Am* a portrait of the black writer as artist. It is equally true that in reading the writings of both Williams and Reed one sees there just as one saw in the earlier writers "the many-faceted experience of the Negro in the turbulent American society." And these writers continue to view literature in general and their own in particular as a moral

---

[60] Baldwin, 272–73.
[61] Bone, 225.
[62] Addison Gayle, Jr., "Preface," in *Black Expression*, xiv.

force for change as well as an esthetic creation.[63] The Negro writer continues now and no doubt will continue in the future to produce a literature embodying the black experience.

Published in 1967, *The Man Who Cried I Am* has been regarded by many readers as the most powerful novel about blacks in America since *Invisible Man*. Reminiscent of *1984* in tone, it is a chilling chronicle of a diabolical plot which is only semifictional in the author's eyes.[64] The main character is an Afro-American "intellectual" from a lower-middle class background, Max Reddick. Max sees the woman he loves die after having an abortion, which she has chosen to have because he cannot afford to marry her. The "uptown" newspapers would not hire an Afro-American reporter. Max sees some light of hope when, after a blooming career, he is offered a position as a speech writer for the President of the United States. He finds that he was hired as a "show Negro." Max is never permitted to realize his capability as a writer and an Afro-American. His ability is accepted as a commodity, not art. Upon deciding whether or not to continue as a writer, Max says to himself:

> But already there were signs that nigger evil would become a real hot commodity (they were running out of everything else), right up there, by god, with the Jewish intellectuals combating the contemporary apikorsim. Yes, sir! Who ever thought the day would loom on the horizon when a Negro writer could say,
> GODDAMNIT! I AM ANGRY
> and get royalty on $4.45 per burst of anger, less advance and agent commission, for it? [65]

The main point of *The Man Who Cried I Am* and the novel's climactic revelation is a plan by the United States government (the white establishment) for the extermination of American blacks in the event of a full-blown race war. The dying vision of a black writer is the sum and substance of this explosive novel. The reader is first introduced to Max Reddick as he sits in a cafe in Holland waiting for his estranged Dutch wife. Dying of cancer, the pain of which is eased by frequent doses of morphine and even more frequent doses of alcohol which ease a different kind of pain, he thinks of the last twenty years of his life, back to the time when he decided to be a serious writer. As a young writer in the 1940s, Max Reddick

---

[63] *Ibid.*, xv.
[64] James A. Emanuel and Theodore L. Gross, *Dark Symphony: Negro Literature in America* (New York, 1968), 392.
[65] John A. Williams, *The Man Who Cried I Am* (New York, 1967), 224.

met and formed a close friendship with Harry Ames, who is a fictional counterpart of Richard Wright. In fact, Williams's characterization has been called "the most vivid portrayal of Richard Wright to date." [66] Reddick considered Ames not only his own mentor but the father of all black writers.

In a letter which falls into Reddick's hands after Ames's death, a letter written as it were from the grave, Ames reveals to Reddick the history of an international plot labeled the King Alfred Plan and informs his protégé how the document got into his hands. As Reddick begins to read, he is frozen by the opening remarks: "Knowing may kill you, just as knowing killed me and a few other people you'll meet in this letter." Ames goes on to explain that in the late 1950s, the African states threw a scare into their European masters when it appeared that they were headed toward forming a United States of Africa. Their white oppressors feared they were in danger of Africa's becoming another giant like China with even more hatred for the white race. The West was quick to respond to this threat. "Representatives from France, Great Britain, Belgium, Portugal, Australia, Spain, Brazil, South Africa and the United States of America, met along with White observers from most of the African countries that appeared on their way to independence." The meetings, called the Alliance Blanc, were held in complete secrecy and moved from country to country. The meetings in this country were held at Saranac Lake in New York. The letter goes on to point out that Europeans soon recovered from their panic when it became obvious that they could control Africa's destiny economically. But "America sitting on a bubbling black cauldron felt that it had to map its own contingency plan for handling 22 million black Americans in case they became unruly...." For this reason the King Alfred Plan was projected and was to be put into action immediately at the discretion of the President "in event of widespread continuing and co-ordinated racial disturbances in the United States." [67]

The federal agencies participating in the plan include the FBI, CIA, National Security Council, departments of Defense, Justice, and Interior. The document went on to say, "In case of emergency, minority members will be evacuated from the cities by federalized national guard units, local and state police and, if necessary, by units of the

[66] David Henderson, "*The Man Who Cried I Am*: A Critique," in *Black Expression*, 366.
[67] Williams, 299–307.

Regular Armed Forces, using public and military transportation, and detained in nearby military installations until a further course of action has been decided." The cities having the largest number of blacks are designated on a map. Leaders of all minority rights organizations are to be detained immediately. "Minority members of Congress will be unseated at once." [68]

The King Alfred Plan was given to Harry Ames by an African ambassador, named Jaja Enzkwu, who happened upon this plan while vacationing in Spain. The CIA and National Security Council tried to make a deal with Enzkwu when they learned that he had the report. According to Ames, Enzkwu promised to give up the paper and to keep silent if he were promised Nigeria. But he was killed— not before making sure that the papers were in the possession of Ames, however.

Ames's letter to Reddick revealed that he was fascinated by the material. He explained that he had spent so much of his life "writing about the evil machinations of Mr. Charlie without really knowing the truth, as this material made me know it. . . . I know now that the way black men live on this earth was no accident . . . if they killed me, I would know that this great evil did exist, indeed thrive." [69]

Reddick wanted to give America a vision of her existence and to inform black people of the ugly plot behind their existence. He wanted white people to know the blacks "would tear up the country" rather than swallow any more lies. He had spent his life trying to change the course of America. He advanced as high as any journalist could. He wrote for the most important weekly magazine and was an adviser to the President. He discovered, however, that he had no power, no say-so. His warnings went unheeded.

Harry Ames's death and his legacy give Reddick his last chance for redemption. Max calls up Minister Q in New York (Malcolm X) and reads the plan into Minister Q's tape recorder. Having passed on the truth to another, Reddick prepares to meet his fate. He loads his pistol and keeps it by his side as he drives back to Holland. He is in for a surprise, however, as death shows up in the form of two black CIA agents. He dies from a "pellet that has only to contact his skin to cause a heart eruption." Max Reddick has participated in the American establishment more than most black men get to. The symbol of this participation is the cancer that eats away at him. Harry Ames

---

[68] *Ibid.,* 307–10.
[69] *Ibid.,* 305–306.

thought he had found the truth in the plan of King Alfred. The truth killed him. Perhaps Williams is saying that the truth of the black man's existence in America is destined to be death.[70]

Max dies at the end of the novel, leaving Eugene Browning to come after him in *Sons of Darkness, Sons of Light*, published by Williams the following year, 1969. Both protagonists are involved in first the discovery of the white man's true nature and to what extent he will go to sustain and perpetuate the white power structure, and secondly, the shaping of a philosophy concerning how best to deal with it. The two men have much in common. Both are black, intellectual, and successful with women. Though both are basically non-heroic types, they engage in life-or-death battles with the white establishment. Though their personalities and life styles are similar, their professions represent different degrees of political involvement. Max is a writer who makes his living as a reporter. Eugene, a former political science teacher, works for the Institute for Racial Justice in New York.

Max learns that the white establishment isn't just out to "screw" him, hold him back or keep him down, but to kill him in order to achieve a political end. Max is killed by CIA agents—but not before he, in turn, has tipped off the black underground to the scheme. Max thus gains awareness. He has learned "to what extent they would go to keep black men niggers." It is then that Max adopts a philosophy of violence to counter violence.

Eugene is an extension of Max, taking up where Max leaves off. From the beginning of the novel, Eugene has no illusions. He has already reached the point at which he is fed up with trying to gain justice through legal channels. He finally commits himself to Max's philosophy of violence when he contracts to have a cop who has shot down an unarmed sixteen-year-old black youth assassinated. He then justifies the act to himself.

> They all went free or did their little bit of time, for that was the exchange rate still. *Maybe* a little time in exchange for a dead nigger; when the scales balanced things would be different, and white people appeared to have no intention of balancing any scale any time. Browning wanted people to know that if they were willing to take black lives the way they had been, then they also ought to know that they had to forfeit their own. Once everyone understood that, things would improve.

[70] Henderson, 366–70.

It would always be open season on blacks until blacks opened the season on whites. But how to begin again? [71]

One wonders if the author is not expressing his own philosophy through his protagonists when one reads his opinions concerning the racial situation, which he describes in *Beyond the Angry Black* (in "A Postscript Concerning the Times") as "rapidly becoming an insoluble problem." "It seems to me that reason has run out," he continues. "It appears that Negroes and whites alike, whites having hardly allowed reason to enter the picture at all, and Negroes finding that their use of it is mistaken repeatedly for weakness, are about to discard it altogether." Then he goes on to say, "One must dread the next stretch of the future, for it is obvious that laws passed to bring equality closer to reality seem to come with the explosions of violence." And at last, "Is this where peace, finally, is to be made, or is it the place for the awful opposite?" [72] Williams wrote these comments in 1966, three years before *Sons of Darkness, Sons of Light* was published. It may reassure those who are dismayed by the negativism and hopelessness expressed in Williams's novels to find his protagonists insisting, embittered though they may be, that the violence they prescribe should be practiced in a somewhat controlled manner.

Also reassuring is the fact that *Sons of Darkness, Sons of Light*, unlike the earlier *The Man Who Cried I Am*, ends on an optimistic note. For even though the battle outside rages on, Eugene has forgiven his wife Val for her infidelity and they are reunited physically and spiritually. In defense of his subject matter, form, and vision of life, Williams, in answering the question "What lies ahead for Black Americans?" has stated: "I think the major task of black art is to delineate the political and social situation because it is the most important one; survival depends upon it . . . ." [73] However, cultural definitions and distinctions do not apply to art as easily as they apply to these other areas such as politics.

The Afro-American novel reaches its highest achievement in Ishmael Reed, whose writing is the most unusual of all discussed in this essay. What distinguishes Reed from his predecessors is his "inde-

---

[71] John A. Williams, *Sons of Darkness, Sons of Light* (Boston, 1969), 17.

[72] John A. Williams, "A Postscript Concerning the Times," in *Beyond the Angry Black* (New York, 1966), 197–98.

[73] John A. Williams, "What Lies Ahead for Black Americans?" *Negro Digest* 19 (Nov. 1969), 5.

pendence from Western form." [74] Reed says that sometimes he feels that the condition of the Afro-American writer in this country is so strange that one has to go to the supernatural for an analogy.[75] He calls his work "Neo-Hoo Dooism: Spinetingling melodrammers— the sound of coffin lids opening and the lone black cat down the hall who hasn't been fed for days." [76]

The hero or anti-hero of Reed's first novel, *The Free-Lance Pallbearers*, published in 1967, is Bukka Doopeyduk, a young Negro who is trying to make the grade, against mighty odds, in Harry Sam, a country ruled by the dictator Sam, who thirty years ago "disappeared into the John with a weird ravaging illness." Still very much alive, the dictator rules his country from the John. Bukka, a college dropout, is a dedicated student of the Nazarene manual, under Bishop Nancy Spellman. Bukka has been awarded a golden bedpan for service beyond the call of duty while performing the chores of an assistant's assistant in a psychiatric ward. The chief symbols of this novel all center on excrement. Professor U2 Polygot pushes a ball of manure around with his nose in preparation for his scholarly paper on Kafka's "Metamorphosis." Bishop Eclair Porkchop is the Bishop of Soulsville; Elizah Raven, a budding Black Muslim; and the white Cipher X produces revolutionary theatricals. Bukka's father-in-law who formerly headed the colored Elks sits at home all day long wearing cobwebbed antlers. Bukka becomes a revolutionary by accident and exposes the existing rottenness in Harry Sam.

The title of the novel derives from the words of a delirious and raging patient, whom Mrs. Nurse Rosemary D Camp has assigned to Bukka "to get samples so that we can analyze them." [77] The patient, an eighty-nine-year-old white man who gave his name as Roger Young Ist, is diagnosed as schizoid with paranoid tendencies and is reported to mutter constantly, "The Huns raping the nuns." As Bukka keeps changing the bed and rubbing him down, the old man suddenly rises up, lurches forward, points a long bent finger toward the open door of the room, and screams, "Save me! They're in the door! The Free-Lance Pallbearers are in the door! Look, look! The long frock coats and shiny black boots, the black box! It's them?

---

[74] Ishmael Reed, "Introduction," *19 Necromancers From Now* (Garden City, N. Y., 1970), xvi.

[75] *Ibid.*, xvii.

[76] *Ibid.*, 291.

[77] Ishmael Reed, *The Free-Lance Pallbearers* (Garden City, N. Y., 1967), 57.

They're going to try to take Ol Roger Ist away from here! Please save me, ooooo, save me, no! Get back! Get back! Arra!" [78]

Bukka's surname causes some speculation concerning its origin. The social worker interviewing Bukka and processing his application for an apartment in the Harry Sam Projects, an apartment he needs since he is soon to marry Fannie Mae, asks, "Doopeyduck.... Where dat name come from, kiddo, da Bible or somethin'?" Bukka replies, "No, sir. It came from a second cousin of my mother who did time for strangling a social worker with custom made voodoo gloves." Bukka answers the next question about the nature of his work by saying that he is a "psychiatric technician ... learning about the relationship between the texture and color of feces and certain organic and/or psychological disturbances." [79]

One is not far into the novel, hardly past the first few paragraphs, before he realizes that Reed is exploring, satirically to be sure, the black experience and is sardonically scoring the present situation and scene in this country. The best man at Bukka's wedding has changed from his former pleasant disposition and patriotic stance. "I have rejuvenated myself," he explains, "by joining the Jackal-headed Front. We are going to expose SAM, remove some of these blond wigs from off our women's heads, and bring back rukus juice and chittlins." "You'd better get on the right side, brother," he warns Bukka, "because when the deal goes down, all the backsliding Uncle Toms are going to be mowed down." Elijah is interrupted by the entrance of the Reverend Eclair Porkchop, head of the Church of the Holy Mouth, who upon encountering Elijah in his audience, sneers at him, "O, if it isn't that silly little separatist! I thought you'd be wearing a bone through your nose by now. All of that talk about going back to Africa. What happened? They dispossess your stepladder and five-dollar public-speaking permit?" [80]

Reed's novel is a radical departure from the usual protest novel. Hysterically funny for the most part, Reed's comedy though fantastic is unbearably honest. In an interview Reed was asked, "Your novel has been called satire, has been compared stylistically with a Swiftian approach. But upon reading, it seems that the novel would be easily recognizable by a cat on the corner of any ghetto street as 'the way it is.' Why have the critics treated it only on the level of satire?" Reed replied,

[78] *Ibid.*, 58.
[79] *Ibid.*, 9–10.
[80] *Ibid.*, 12–13.

Because they are afraid of a Renaissance. Fortunately the novel got enough support so that I could appeal to the planet. I didn't have to appeal to any particular group.... The critics are afraid that the black people will have a renaissance and they will break out of this exotic zoo that critics have put them in: one novelist, one playwright, one poet, one opera singer, one mathematician, one scientist, one astronaut. And if they break out of the exotic zoo, and the floodgates open, then what you have is something they can't deal with.

Reed concludes,

You can talk all you want to about what an artist should do, what the artist shouldn't do, 'til the cows come home ding-donging their bells through the pastures. But the Afro-American artist today is an international mind-miner. He's synchrotistic already. He's Afro; he's American, and if he goes to India and does a raga, he's Afro-American-Indian. He's a space cadet, and if you try to put him in a bag you're being dishonest.[81]

II

In the social and political sphere the first major Negro nationalist and "the embodiment of Negro separation" was Dr. Martin Robinson Delany, who not only gave "the early movement a full-fledged theoretical basis" but also acted upon it.

By the time he was forty Delany had proved himself in at least two fields—medicine, being a graduate of Harvard Medical School, and journalism, having founded in 1843 in Pittsburgh one of the first Negro weekly publications, the *Mystery*, which he edited for four years and in which he devoted himself to "the interest and elevation of his race." These two careers, however, were prologue to a still further and greater career in politics. In 1852 he published privately the earliest formulation of "black nationalism" in a book entitled *The Condition, Elevation, Emigration, and Destiny of the Colored People of the United States.* An appendix to this work bore the title of "A Project for an Expedition of Adventure to the Eastern Coast of Africa," in which Delaney, declaring that the Negroes in America were "a nation within a nation," advocated "founding a new Negro nation on the eastern coast of Africa 'for the settlement of colored adventurers from the United States and elsewhere.' "

Born in this country, reared and educated here where "the sacred

[81] Walt Shepherd, "When State Magicians Fail: An Interview with Ishmael Reed," *Nickel Review* 1 (28 Aug.–10 Sept. 1968), 5.

graves" of fathers and mothers are located, the Negroes were, in Delany's words, "aliens to the laws and political privileges of the country." Although the Negroes dearly loved their country, this country despised them, and, according to Delany, "bids us be gone, driving us from her embrace." Clearly one sees then that Delany's "black nationalism" was not based on "a deeply rooted, traditional attachment to another soil and another nation." It was based on the rejection of blacks by a white society.[82]

It is paradoxical that black nationalism in America "arose out of a frustrated American nationalism, a frustration which could only take quasi-nationalists forms rather than form another genuine nationalism." Delany "provided the prototype of a paradox with which his political descendants are still struggling." [83]

Black nationalists in this country have followed one of two courses. Some advocate emigration; others envision an independent black state somewhere within the present boundaries of the United States.[84] In this century Marcus Garvey was the most eloquent spokesman for the former course. Garvey began his organization, Universal Negro Improvement Association, in his native Jamaica in 1914. Two years later he came to this country, where in New York he organized a chapter of the association. At the end of World War I the association enjoyed rapid growth. Garvey and Garveyism were widely popular as his followers responded to his appeal to race pride at a time when Negroes had so little to be proud of. Garvey exalted everything black, insisting that black stood for strength and beauty, not inferiority. Africa, he asserted, had a noble history, and he urged Negroes to be proud of their ancestry. He warned that the only hope for Negroes in Amerca was to flee to Africa and there build up a country of their own. He petitioned the League of Nations for a permit to settle a colony in Africa and to that end negotiated with Liberia. Failing to achieve his goal by peaceful means, he organized the Universal African Legion to drive out the white invaders.[85]

The escapist utopian character of the Garvey movement as an answer to economic deprivation encouraged a large number of former followers of Garvey to join the Father Divine movement during the depression of the 1930s. The Black Muslim movement today is

---

[82] Theodore Draper, "The Father of American Black Nationalism," *New York Review of Books* 14 (12 March 1970), 33–41.

[83] *Ibid.*, 41.

[84] *Ibid.*

[85] Franklin, 489–90.

another example of an extreme Negro nationalist movement. Support for this recent movement comes from the economically deprived lower class. Black Muslims enlist their recruits from the ranks of unemployed and unskilled workers, "for whom automation holds out a bleak future, and for whom the civil rights movement has accomplished nothing to date." [86]

"Black nationalism" is an elusive term meaning different things to the many users of the term. As a viable political movement it does not exist. As an artistic ideal it has always existed in this country from the earliest publication by Phillis Wheatley, "a delicate twelve-year old black girl" who arrived in 1761 on a slave ship which had made the voyage from Africa to Boston harbor,[87] to the latest pronouncement by LeRoi Jones and Eldrige Cleaver. Like Delany most black nationalists, especially those connected with the arts, prefer freedom and equality in the land of their birth instead of emigration to another country.

LeRoi Jones in a brilliant essay entitled "Negro Literature" maintains that "the American Negro has a definable and legitimate historical tradition, no matter how painful, in America," but, Jones goes on, America is the only place such a tradition exists because America is the only place where the American Negro exists. Jones finds it paradoxical that the Negro experience in America is separate from all other experiences, but it is inseparable from "the complete fabric of American life." For the Negro the history of Western culture begins with the arrival of slaves in this country. "It is," Jones avers, "almost as if all Western history before that must be strictly a learned concept. It is only the American experience that can be a persistent cultural catalyst for the Negro," for whom history must be "an emotional attraction." Jones believes that the cultural memory of Africa informs the life of the Negro in this country, but "it is impossible to separate it from its American transformation." Thus, Jones continues, "the Negro writer if he wanted to tap his legitimate cultural tradition should have done it by utilizing the entire spectrum of the American experience from the point of view of the emotional history of the black man in this country: as its victim and its chronicler." The soul of such a man exists "outside the boundaries of commercial diversion or artificial social pretense." This is impos-

[86] Meier, 315.
[87] Richard Wright, "The Literature of the Negro in the United States," in *Black Expression*, 203.

sible without the writer's having "a deep commitment to cultural relevance and intellectual purity."

The Negro writer has always been a social object whether as in the early literature he glorified the concept of white superiority or whether as in the protest literature of the thirties he cried out against it. He never moved himself to a position where he could "propose his own symbols, erect his own personal myths, as any great literature must." Negro literature has always been based on recognized social concepts "within the structure of bourgeois idealistic projections of 'their America,' and an emotional climate that never really existed." The Negro protest novelist invents a protest "quite amenable with the tradition of bourgeois American life" and never reaches the "central core of the America which can cause such protest." Jones sees the intellectual traditions of the white middle class preventing such "exposure of reality," and he insists that "the black imitators reflect this." Jones says such Negro writers in writing on Negro life in America invent that life as well as an America to contain it, and even most of the ones who rebelled against this invented America "were trapped because they had lost all touch with the reality of their experience within the *real* America, either because of the hidden emotional allegiance to the white middle class, or because they did not realize where the reality of their experience lay." [88]

There is a current tendency among American critics (usually from the white establishment) to label the established Negro writer as a spokesman for his race. And there are black writers who think of themselves in such a role. Too, some black writers of today think of themselves as prophets and projectors of the Negro revolution. The avowed purpose of their writing, they insist, is to give blacks a sense of human dignity and to provide them with ideological weapons; motivated by an intense pride in their race these authors celebrate and advocate Black Power and declare themselves not simply writers but black writers. Other black authors reject such a narrow restriction to racial themes and ask to have their work judged on its literary merits and not solely on the basis of its relevance to the struggle of blacks. It has come to be expected of the black writers that in their literature they will confine themselves to their racial situation and that they will all say pretty much the same

[88] LeRoi Jones, "The Myth of a 'Negro Literature,'" in *Black Expression*, 190–97.

things about it. Such unity is more apparent than real. Differences in vision, emphasis, and approaches to their writing give diversity to their writings even when they employ similar themes.

In many areas the Negro writer is urged to catch up with his musical counterpart, to match the examples of cultural genius found in jazz. In this view, the writer in his work is supposed to relate to his people and to be true to his origins. Those holding this view argue not for an economic or social revolution but for a cultural one and warn that the black writer does not have to deny his ethnic origins to achieve universality. Rather, they insist that the black writer's only hope is to turn his back on the decadent values of Western civilization and to do his own thing. They refuse to deny the reality and the power of the slave culture that produced the blues, spirituals, folk songs, work songs, and jazz. The models for much black literature, as we have seen, especially in *Invisible Man* and also in several of the other works, are found primarily in black folk culture, especially in the blues and jazz. One of the functions of any literature is to reconstruct tradition and to give that tradition meaning in light of the manner in which history has moved. It is impossible, like Todd Clifton in *Invisible Man*, to fall outside of history. Black writers in America have explored every aspect of their cultural heritage in their writing; all Americans are much the wiser and our literature is much the richer for it.

BIBLIOGRAPHY

Baldwin, James. *Another Country*. New York: Dial Press, 1962.
———. *The Fire Next Time*. New York: Dial Press, 1963.
———. *Going to Meet the Man*. New York: Dell, 1968.
———. *Go Tell It on the Mountain*. New York: Grosset, 1953.
———. *Tell Me How Long the Train's Been Gone*. New York: Dial Press, 1968.
Baumbach, Jonathan. *The Landscape of Nightmare: Studies in the Contemporary American Novel*. New York: New York University Press, 1965.
Bone, Robert A. *The Negro Novel in America*. New Haven, Conn.: Yale University Press, 1958; rev. ed., 1965.
Draper, Theodore. "The Father of American Black Nationalism." *New York Review of Books*, 14, no. 5 (12 March 1970), 33–41.
Ellison, Ralph. *Invisible Man*. New York: Random, 1952.
Emanuel, James A., and Theodore L. Gross. *Dark Symphony: Negro Literature in America*. New York: Free Press, 1968.

Essien-Udom, E. U. *Black Nationalism: A Search for an Identity In America.* New York: Dell, 1969.

Ford, Nick Aaron. "The Ordeal of Richard Wright." *College English* 15 (November 1953), 87–94.

Franklin, John Hope. *From Slavery to Freedom: A History of Negro Americans.* 3rd ed. New York: Knopf, 1967.

Gayle, Addison, Jr. (ed.). *Black Expression: Essays By and About Black Americans in the Creative Arts.* New York: Weybright and Talley, 1969.

Gloster, Hugh M. *Negro Voices in American Fiction.* Chapel Hill: University of North Carolina Press, 1948; rpt. New York: Russell & Russell, 1965.

Grier, William H., and Price M. Cobbs. *Black Rage.* New York: Bantam Books, 1969.

Hentoff, Nat. *The New Equality.* New York: Viking, 1965.

Hughes, Douglas A. (ed.). *From a Black Perspective: Contemporary Black Essays.* New York: Holt, 1970.

Isaacs, Harold R. *The New World of Negro Americans.* New York: John Day, 1963.

Kearns, Francis E. (ed.). *The Black Experience: An Anthology of American Literature for the 1970s.* New York: Viking, 1970.

Littlejohn, David. *Black on White: A Critical Survey of Writing by American Negroes.* New York: Grossman, 1966; rpt. Viking, 1969.

Malcolm X. *The Autobiography of Malcolm X*, with the assistance of Alex Haley; Introduction by M. S. Handler; Epilogue by Alex Haley. New York: Grove Press, 1966.

Margolies, Edward. *Native Sons: A Critical Study of Twentieth-Century Negro American Authors.* Philadelphia: Lippincott, 1968.

Meier, August. *Negro Thought in America 1880–1915: Racial Ideologies in the Age of Booker T. Washington.* Ann Arbor: University of Michigan Press, 1963; 3d printing, 1968.

Reed, Ishmael. *The Free-Lance Pallbearers.* Garden City, N. Y.: Doubleday, 1967.

———— (ed.). *19 Necromancers From Now: An Anthology of Original American Writing for the 1970s.* Anchor Book. Garden City, N. Y.: Doubleday, 1970.

Richardson, Jack. "The Black Arts." *New York Review of Books* 11, no. 11 (December 1968), 10–13.

Shepherd, Walt. "When State Magicians Fail: An Interview with Ishmael Reed." *Nickel Review* 1, no. 11 (August 1968), 4–6.

Turner, Darwin T. (ed.). *Black American Literature: Essays.* Columbus, Ohio: Merrill, 1969.

————. *Black American Literature: Fiction.* Columbus, Ohio: Merrill, 1969.

————. "Jean Toomer's *Cane*." *Negro Digest* 18, no. 3 (January 1969), 54–61.

————. "*The Outsider*: Revision of an Idea." *CLA Journal* 12 (June 1968), 310–21.

Williams, John A. *The Man Who Cried I Am*. Boston: Little, 1967; rpt. New York: Signet, 1968.

———. "A Postscript Concerning the Times." *Beyond the Angry Black*. New York: Cooper Square Publishers, 1966.

———. *Sons of Darkness, Sons of Light*. Boston: Little, 1969.

———. "What Lies Ahead for Black Americans?" *Negro Digest* 19, no. 1 (November 1969), 5.

Williams, Ronald. "Black Studies: The Work to Come." *Negro Digest* 19, no. 3 (January 1970), 30–35.

Wright, Richard. "How 'Bigger' Was Born." *Saturday Review of Literature* 22 (1 June 1940), 3–4, 17–20.

———. *Native Son*. New York: Harper, 1940; rpt. 1966.

The Conversions of the Jews*

ALLEN GUTTMANN

When the builders of Bay Colony likened themselves to the Israelites of the Old Testament, when they spoke of their settlements at Boston and Salem as a "Wilderness Zion," they could not have known that the Jews of the Diaspora would come, within a generation, to complicate the metaphor that made America the promised land. But come they did, only to discover that acceptance in the New World undid them as persecution in the old had not. Many became Christians. More became converts to the American Way of Life, to the religion of Americanism.

The Sephardic Jews of Spain were expelled in a year remembered for other events of interest to Americans—1492. Many went to Holland, and from Holland to Brazil (newly conquered from Portugal), and from Brazil, in 1654, to New Netherlands, where they received an unenthusiastic welcome. By the end of the eighteenth century, the Sephardim—from 2,000 to 3,000 in number—were a largely acculturated minority committed to what Nathan Glazer has referred to as "dignified Orthodoxy." Some had converted to Christianity but most had adapted their ancestral faith in American conditions.

As early as 1825, however, Jews in Charleston rejected the Orthodoxy of Congregation Beth Elohim and organized the Reformed Society of Israelites. Their statement of principles repudiated rabbinical interpretations of Talmudic law and accepted the Mosaic codes only

* Parts of this essay have previously appeared in "The Ghetto and Beyond" published by *University of Wisconsin Studies.*

as far, in their words, "as they can be adapted to the institutions of the Society in which [we] live and enjoy the blessings of liberty." Their slogan was simple: "America is our Zion and Washington is our Jerusalem." [1]

Reform Judaism in America flourished as Ashkenazic (i.e., German) Jews began to arrive in large numbers. David Einhorn, Kaufmann Kohler, and Isaac Mayer Wise led the way to the Pittsburgh Platform of 1885, the basic document of Reform Judaism in America. The platform was a manifesto that might almost have won the support of William Ellery Channing and Ralph Waldo Emerson: "We recognize in every religion an attempt to grasp the Infinite One, and in every mode . . . of revelation held sacred in any religious system the consciousness of the indwelling of God in man." [2] The Mosaic and rabbinical laws of diet and dress, and even of morals, were rejected insofar as they failed to conform "to the views and habits of modern civilization." [3]

Even as the Reformers extended the "hand of fellowship to all who cooperate with us in the establishment of the reign of truth and righteousness among men," they must have realized that the "views and habits of modern civilization" are often ignoble. Historians and sociologists have shown that Jews converted to the Age of Enterprise as well as to the ideals of the Enlightenment. At their best, American Jews have contributed immensely to the institutionalization of a liberty and equality not available to them elsewhere. At their worst, American Jews have been latecomers to the "great barbecue" of American capitalism, scramblers after the scraps left by Carnegie and Rockefeller and Vanderbilt, greedy greenhorns of the Gilded Age. Many a reformer of traditional Judaism must have wondered—in the din of the marketplace—if the baggage left behind at Ellis Island wasn't better stuff than the shoddy goods bought and sold in Brookline and in Brownsville. But very few have recanted from their metaphoric conversion to America.

As the words of Emma Lazarus on the Statue of Liberty suggest, the story of Americanization is the first great theme in Jewish literature in the new world. The first great name, after Emma Lazarus herself, is certainly that of Abraham Cahan. His collection of stories *The Imported Bridegroom and Other Stories of the New York*

[1] Nathan Glazer, *American Judaism* (Chicago, 1957), 35.
[2] Glazer, 151.
[3] *Ibid.*

Ghetto (1898) and his novel *The Rise of David Levinsky* (1917) are classic accounts of the crisis of ethnic identity confronted by the East-European immigrants as they poured into New York in the 1880s and 1890s.

Twenty-year-old Flora Stroon, heroine of "The Imported Bridegroom," is a modern miss who prefers to read Dickens while her father and his housekeeper pray. Her desire to marry a cultivated man—a doctor, perhaps—receives a blow when her father returns from a visit to the old country. He offers her an "imported" bridegroom, a prodigy of Talmudic lore. "Mister," she tells the bewildered youth, "you had better go. If you think you are going to be my bride groom, you are sadly mistaken," [4] The mistake, however, turns out to be her father's; the pious scholar becomes an *appikoros* ("Epicurean" or atheist), takes to cigarettes, marries Flora in a secular ceremony, and falls in with a group of intellectuals from whose excited concerns Flora feels completely excluded. Her father's pathetic comment sums up the situation: "America has done it all." [5]

A similar fate was encountered by David Levinsky, the hero of Cahan's partially autobiographical novel. When young Levinsky confides in Reb Sender his decision to emigrate, the rabbi is dismayed: "To America! Lord of the World! But one becomes a Gentile there!" [6] Reb Sender was right. David shears off his earlocks and abandons one by one the 613 commandments by which the truly pious Jew regulates his life. "If you are a Jew of the type to which I belong when I came to New York and you attempt to bend your religion to the spirit of your new surroundings, it breaks. It falls to pieces. The very clothes I wore and the very food I ate had a fatal effect on my religious habits." [7] David rises, becomes a millionaire in the garment industry, a freethinker for whom Herbert Spencer's Unknowable replaces the Living God of Abraham and Isaac. His deepest loyalty is to America. David describes a concert where the audience sat apathetically, unmoved by operatic themes and by Yiddish songs. The national anthem brought the Jews enthusiastically to their feet: "It was as if they were saying: 'We are not persecuted under this flag. At last we have found a home.' " [8] It is no exaggera-

---

[4] Abraham Cahan, *The Imported Bridegroom and Other Stories* (New York, 1968), 53.

[5] *Ibid.*

[6] Abraham Cahan, *The Rise of David Levinsky* (New York, 1917), 61.

[7] *Ibid.*, 110.

[8] *Ibid.*, 424.

tion for Melvin M. Tumin, a Princeton sociologist, to speak of American Jews and the "cult of gratitude." [9]

But David Levinsky remembers the old ways too. "I can never forget the days of my misery. I cannot escape from my old self. My past and my present do not comport well. David, the poor lad swinging over a Talmud volume at the Preacher's Synagogue, seems to have more in common with my inner identity than David Levinsky, the well-known cloak-manufacturer." [10] Despite nostalgia and regret, there is no return. Abraham Cahan, whose editorship of the *Jewish Daily Forward* made him the foremost figure in Yiddish journalism, wrote his *Meisterwerk* in English.

A generation later, Meyer Levin, in the one book that insures him a place in our literary history, chronicled the rise of the second-generation Jews of Chicago's West Side. *The Old Bunch*, published in 1937, moves from 1921 to 1934—the years of *The Jazz Singer* and *Show Boat* and Leopold and Loeb and the Lindbergh flight and Samuel Insull and Al Capone and the magnificent mid-Depression symbol of hope, Chicago's Century of Progress World's Fair.

In Levin's book, the older generation speaks Yiddish and fears that bobbed hair is the shortcut to prostitution. The younger generation carelessly leaves the old ways behind as it climbs into the middle class. Doctors, lawyers, dentists, artists, teachers, dry-cleaners, realtors, and part-time bicycle-racers, yes; rabbis and Talmudic scholars, no. *Mitzvot*—God's commandments—are as little regarded as the Volstead Act. Passover becomes a drunken brawl, with paper hats, comic place cards, and a layer cake topped with an effigy of Moses. "Manny picked up a curled streamer that lay near his plate and blew noisily. The red crepe paper shot across the table and dropped over Sam's ear.... The maid brought in an immense, sugar-baked ham." [11] The idealistic lawyer, soon to become a defender of labor leaders and rent-strikers, rushes in disgust from those who have sold their birthright for a mess of *trefa* (nonkosher food). No one can imagine what bothers him. Isn't he, after all, an atheist? *The Old Bunch* differs from Jerome Weidman's *I Can Get It For You Wholesale* (1937) and Budd Schulberg's *What Makes Sammy Run?* (1941) because the earlier novel contains numerous admirable characters as well as a roster of rogues, but none of the books encouraged those

[9] Peter I. Rose (ed.), *The Ghetto and Beyond* (New York, 1969), 69.
[10] Cahan, *Rise of David Levinsky*, 530.
[11] Meyer Levin, *The Old Bunch* (New York, 1937), 484.

who hoped to maintain the traditional wisdom in an urban-industrial age.

A generation later, in 1963, Burt Blechman writes of *The War of Camp Omongo* and charts the continued erosion of Jewish values in the great out-of-doors. The camp is, of course, run for financial profit and sexual exploration. The boys in the camp are wise in the ways of the Age of Eisenhower. "Nobody believes in God. But you still gotta have a religion." [12] When the camp's rabbi misunderstands his purely decorative role and begins to speak of Jehovah, the camp's owner drowns him out with a tape-recorded rendition, by the Marine Corps Band, of "The Stars and Stripes Forever." The creed of Camp Omongo is a parody of Sinai's: "All graven images shall be as follows: Gold for 1st; Silver for 2nd; Bronze for 3rd; and Strontium 90 for the rest . . . . Thou shalt kill for God and country on demand . . . . Thou shalt adulterate the water, pollute the land, and poison the air for the sake of our fathers' pride." [13] Burt Belchman stands in the tradition of those who disbelieve and who are, nonetheless, appalled by the callousness of those who disbelieve.

Philip Roth's collection of stories *Goodbye, Columbus* appeared in 1960. In the title-story we meet the Patimkins, who have risen on kitchen sinks. Business during the war years was phenomenally good. Is not cleanliness more profitable than godliness? Their refrigerators burst with fruit; their trees bear sporting goods. Brenda Patimkin is a paragon of Olympic virtues: she plays tennis, she runs, she rides, she swims. In the pool, she is a long way from the Yiddishe Momma of yesteryear. "I went," says her boyfriend, "to pull her towards me just as she started fluttering up; my hand hooked on to the front of her suit and the cloth pulled away from her. Her breasts swam towards me like two pink-nosed fish and she let me hold them. Then, in a moment, it was the sun who kissed us both, and we were out of the water, too pleased with each other to smile." [14] And, as Leonard Baskin lamented in a recent symposium, "For every poor and huddled *mikvah* [the ritual bath] there is a tenhundred of swimming pools." [15] In this suburban world, the past seems passé indeed.

[12] Burt Blechman, *The War of Camp Omongo* (New York, 1963), 77.
[13] *Ibid.*, 182.
[14] Philip Roth, *Goodbye, Columbus* (Boston, 1959), 17.
[15] Leonard Baskin, "To Wear Blood Stain with Honor," *Judaism* 10 (1961), 294.

In another of Roth's stories, "Eli the Fanatic," the father who attempts to affirm a heritage he never inherited is shocked to discover what that heritage includes: "Sunday mornings I have to drive my kid all the way to Scarsdale to learn Bible stories. And you know what she comes up with . . . that this Abraham in the Bible was going to kill his own kid for a *sacrifice!* You call that religion? Today a guy like that they'd lock him up." [16] When the hero of the story collapses under the strain of his role as go-between in the conflict between suburbia and an Orthodox Yeshiva, he does indeed become a "guy like that" and is indeed locked up. The suburban Jew, for better or for worse, is far closer to his Gentile neighbor than to the vanished world of the East European *shtetl* (i.e., little town). Roth has dramatized what Marshall Sklare, Herbert Gans, and a host of other sociologists have documented—the third-generation Jew of the suburbs may send his children to Sunday school, but he wants no part of the faith for which Abraham was ready to sacrifice his beloved Isaac.

Theoretically, the ultimate consequence of acculturation (the adoption of the culture of the majority) is assimilation (disappearance into the majority). The penultimate step is intermarriage. What prevents the children of nominal Jews from intermarriage with the children of nominal Protestants and Catholics? Very little. From 1908 to 1912, the intermarriage rate for Jews in New York was only 1.17 percent, but sociologists who once stated flatly that 5 percent was the natural limit of the rate of intermarriage now chart rates three times as high. And higher. Where today, in child-centered America, is the parent who will rend his garments and sit *shiva* (i.e., mourn as if dead) for the son who marries a *shiksa* (i.e., Gentile girl)? In his very language, the father of Myron Kaufmann's hero, Richard Amsterdam, betrays his inability to stay the course of Americanization: "All these generations, and now I'm the Last of the Mohicans." [17] Had he called upon the "last of the Just," he might at least have had an alternative to his son's ambitions.

Kaufmann's novel *Remember Me to God* (1957) is one of many commended by sociologists for their insight into the dramatic conflicts brought on by intermarriage. The rabbi of Richard Amsterdam's temple is beloved by his congregation because he cannot speak Yiddish. Richard himself goes to Harvard, mends his manners, and

[16] Roth, *Goodbye, Columbus,* 277.
[17] Myron Kaufmann, *Remember Me to God* (Philadelphia, 1957), 502.

becomes an unscrupulous aspirant to Hasty Pudding. He scorns a lovely Jewish girl in order to whore after a Jezebel from Beacon Hill. His father, an immigrant who worked himself through law school, is pathetic in his inarticulate efforts to prevent the marriage and the conversion to Christianity. No longer aware of his own Jewishness except as instinctive response, he cannot persuade his son to remain a Jew: "I can't explain it.... It's sort of as if that word is me. When I hear the word 'Jew,' I know it means me." [18] He is more dignified, however, even when striking his son and weeping in despair, than Rabbi Budapester, who tells Richard, "It's fun to be a Jew." [19] Budapester borrows from those fashionable literary critics who have ignored the Revelation at Mount Sinai in their vision of the Jew as archetypical victim or Marginal Man. "Jews are Man in the extreme," says Budapester; they "have been at once the most magnificent and the most wretched of peoples, and this is the essence of Man." [20] Richard is unmoved: "I don't want to be anybody's legend.... The trouble with you guys is that you want me to act out your fairy-tale." [21] Rabbi Budapester leaves in a huff—in a Cadillac.

Kaufmann himself, however, remains ambivalent. Complications of the plot prevent Richard's marriage to Wimsy Talbot and the burdens of peoplehood seem to shift to the shoulders of Richard's sister Dorothy. Kaufmann's second novel, *Thy Daughter's Nakedness* (1968), is an unsympathetic portrait of a "liberated" Jewish girl and a spirited defense of her father, an idealistic rabbi who is fired by his philistine congregation.

Paul Shiels, the hero of Neal Oxenhandler's *A Change of Gods* (1962), takes the leap of faithlessness—or of the new faith of romantic love. Attracted by blonde Candy Martin, he marries her in Florence. He is as free of Jewish tradition as she is of Catholic dogma. But motor-scooter and hotel room are false symbols of mobility and freedom. Behind the façade of liberation is the reality of family ties. Paul's family is vulgar and oppressive. Candy's grandfather—a philologist—is austere and devout and determined. Paul must convert to Catholicism. He does become a communicant, is denounced as an Eichmann, and—the plot is complicated—sent to prison. Father and son are eventually reconciled, but the conversion of son to Christian-

[18] *Ibid.*, 428.
[19] *Ibid.*, 529.
[20] *Ibid.*, 538.
[21] *Ibid.*, 540.

ity is for keeps. Paul—like his Damascus-bound namesake—has joined
the ranks of those who pray on Good Friday, until the Vatican
Council shall deem otherwise, for the conversion of the Jews.

The most famous of stories to treat this theme, in this age when
students see little relevance in the New Testament (or in the Old),
is Philip Roth's "The Conversion of the Jews," also in *Goodbye,
Columbus*. Ozzie Freedman, an inquisitive boy, asks the questions
that any intelligent boy wants to ask. How can Jews be the Chosen
People if all men are created equal? How can an omnipotent God
be unable to "let a woman have a baby without having inter-
course"? [22] Rabbi Binder cannot handle questions of this sort. Ozzie
is punished and becomes prudent, but he is one day forced by
Binder's nagging demands to drop his reticence and to reask his
question. When his teacher in a moment of rage and frustration slaps
him, Ozzie flees to the roof of the building and locks the door. The
crowd gathers, the rabbi begs him from the street not to be a martyr,
and his schoolmates—eager for sensation—urge him, "Be a Martin,
be a Martin!" [23] His mother comes and the child becomes the teacher.
Ozzie catechizes them all:

> "Do you believe God can do Anything?" Ozzie leaned his head
> out into the darkness. "Anything?"
> "Oscar, I think—"
> "Tell me you believe God can do Anything."
> There was a second's hesitation. Then: "God can do Anything."
> "Tell me you believe God can make a child without intercourse."
> "He can."
> "Tell me!"
> "God," Rabbi Binder admitted, "can make a child without inter-
> course." [24]

Mrs. Freeman agrees and Ozzie leaps into a safety net. The image is
unmistakably Christian: "right into the center of the yellow net that
glowed in the evening's edge like an overgrown halo." [25] It is a doubly
parabolic descent. The economy of characterization and the simplicity of the fable make the allegorical implications unavoidable. Was
it not written that a child shall teach them?

Paul Shiels and Ozzie Freedman are, of course, unrepresentative.
There are, moreover, Christians who become Jews. Bernard Malamud's Frank Alpine, hero of *The Assistant* (1957) and Philip Roth's

[22] Roth, *Goodbye, Columbus*, 141.
[23] *Ibid.*, 155.
[24] *Ibid.*, 157.
[25] *Ibid.*, 158.

Libby Herz, a central character in *Letting Go* (1962), are fictional voyagers down the improbable path taken by Marilyn Monroe, Elizabeth Taylor, and Sammy Davis, Jr. The real threat to the survival of the Jewish community in America is not from literal conversion to the strange God of the Christians but rather from the pervasive secularism of the modern world.[26] The majority of American Jews are Jews only by the quirks of popular definitions, which hold—contrary to rabbinical laws—that Jews are the children of people who think of themselves as Jews. When asked about his own heritage, Philip Roth spoke for many:

> I cannot find a true and honest place in the history of believers that begins with Abraham, Isaac, and Jacob on the basis of the heroism of these believers or of their humiliations and anguish. I can connect with them and with their descendents [only] as I apprehend their God. And until such time as I do apprehend him, there will continue to exist between myself and those who seek his presence, a question, sometimes spoken, sometimes not, which for all the pain and longing it may engender, for all the disappointment and bewilderment it may produce, cannot be swept away by nostalgia or sentimentality or even by a blind and valiant effort of the will: how are you connected to me as another man is not? [27]

American Jews who have apprehended the God of Abraham and Isaac and Jacob have not ignored the threat of assimilation or been blind to the conversion of Jews to secularism. The American Jews who have remained true to Torah and Talmud have struggled to win converts, not from the Gentiles but from those nominal Jews who have shrugged off the faith of their fathers.

In 1886, only one year after the Reformers' Pittsburgh Platform, Conservative Jews established the Jewish Theological Seminary, the point of departure for the quest for a traditional and historical compromise between Orthodoxy and Reform. The exodus of two million Jews from Eastern Europe saved the Conservative seminary from collapse and enabled the Orthodox to begin, in 1896, their own center of learning, the Rabbi Isaac Elchanan Theological Seminary, now Yeshiva University. The Gordian rapidity with which secularized Jews severed the bonds that bound them to their tradition

[26] It is perhaps significant that Bernard Malamud's novel *The Fixer* (1966), a craftily conventional book, was set in tsarist Russia rather than in the United States or in Nazi Germany. The United States lacked the melodramatic anti-Semitism Malamud needed, whereas Nazi Germany killed the imagination with an overdose of horrific reality.

[27] Philip Roth, "Jewishness and the Younger Intellectuals," *Commentary* 31 (April 1961), 350–51.

brought the leaders of Reform Judaism to second thoughts. They met, therefore, in Columbus, Ohio, in 1937, in order to restore to their creed the centrality of the Torah and a belief in the peoplehood of Israel. In Horace Kallen's philosophy of cultural pluralism, first articulated in *Nation* articles in 1915, Jews anxious to avoid assimilation discovered a rationale by which they hoped to be good Americans and yet maintain their ancestral ways. In the theology of Mordecai Kaplan, in which the religious insights of Judaism were given a more central place than in Kallen's philosophy, many Jews found an extension of Kallen's insights. Although the third and fourth generations continue to drift further and further from Mosaic law and even from any detailed knowledge of Judaism, their elders no longer encourage them.

Within the literary world, the campaign to win "converts" for Judaism has been three-fold: first, the attack on those who defect from or denigrate the Jewish community; second, continued emphasis on the dangers of anti-Semitism; third, an affirmation of the positive aspects of Judaism, the Jewish community, and—especially since 1948—Zionism.

In 1937, Meyer Levin found himself highly unpopular with religiously committed Jews. He wrote in his autobiography that his work was "preached against in the temples and described in some of the Jewish press as a degradation of our people. I received a call from the secretary of the Anti-Defamation League who took me to lunch at one of the downtown Jewish clubs.... The general theme was: Why do you young Jewish writers feel impelled to describe your people in this disgusting manner?" [28] More recently, Edward Adler, Jerome Charyn, Babette Deutsch, Leslie Fiedler, Norman Fruchter, Allen Ginsberg, Herbert Gold, Irving Howe, Alfred Kazin, Philip Roth, Muriel Rukeyser, L. S. Simckes, and Louis Untermeyer have been denounced as anti-Semitic or abused for their aloofness from the Jewish community. Even Norman Podhoretz, editor of *Commentary*, has described difficulties undergone while trying to "do" the modern without undoing the essence of the traditional: "Once ...I nearly caused a riot when I attacked the prosody of a minor Israeli poet by invoking E. E. Cummings as a standard. I was howled down with talk of the blood shed by the six million." [29] Stuart Rosenberg, for example, has alleged that Roth is one of those hateful intellectuals who publish in *Commentary*, one of those whose "criticisms,

[28] Meyer Levin, *In Search* (New York, 1950), 93–94.
[29] Norman Podhoretz, *Doings and Undoings* (New York, 1964), 119.

exaggerated by the self-hate of their alienation, cannot serve as an adequate guide to the true condition of the American Jewish community today." [30] The reference to "self-hating" derives from Theodor Lessing's book *Jewish Self-Hatred* (*Der Jüdische Selbsthass*) (1930), a theory imported into this country by the German-born social psychologist Kurt Lewin in his famous book *Resolving Social Conflicts* (1948). This immensely overworked theory holds that alienated Jews apparently committed to secularism or converted to Christianity are motivated not by any positive values but rather by a hatred of self. These Jews seek neurotically to deny what they know to be their true identity. This theory has two major advantages: it can be applied generally, and it cannot be refuted. (Nor, one should add, can it be proved.)

Recent writers have found the self-hate theory as attractive as writers of the 1920s and 1930s found the Oedipal complex. Meyer Levin has, for instance, accused Budd Schulberg of self-hate because of *What Makes Sammy Run?*, written a novel showing Leopold and Loeb murdering Bobbie Frank because of self-hate, and suggested in *The Fanatic* (1964) that Jewish converts to communism are exemplars of self-hate. Preachments against the "self-hate" of Philip Roth were the missionary's *modus vivendi* before *Portnoy's Complaint* (1969), a book unlikely to disarm Roth's Jewish critics. Like Meyer Levin, Roth has been telephoned and invited to lunch and advised to be more positive. He too has been denounced in the synagogues. Unlike most writers, Roth has braved the fury and answered his detractors: "The question really is: who is going to address men and women like men and women, and who like children? If there are Jews who have begun to find the stories the novelists tell more provocative and pertinent than the sermons of some of the rabbis, perhaps it is because there are regions of feeling and consciousness in them which cannot be reached by the oratory of self-congratulation and self-pity." [31] It was after these remarks appeared in *Commentary*, in 1963, that Roth turned the tables on his critics and wrote *Portnoy's Complaint*, a novel which may well be a parody of the novel of self-hate.

It is the threat of anti-Semitism and the fate of European Jews under Hitler that make understandable the dreary fanaticism of the conventional novels of self-hate. For those who have lived through Auschwitz and Dachau, books that fail to remind us all of the apoca-

[30] Stuart E. Rosenberg, *America Is Different* (New York, 1964), 250.
[31] Philip Roth, "Writing About Jews," *Commentary* 36 (Dec. 1963), 452.

lyptic horror of the concentration camps must seem, at times, utterly irrelevant. American novelists have, however, tended not to attempt dramatizations of the almost unimaginable horror of the concentration camps, a horror which no major American novelist experienced except in imagination. Although Edward Lewis Wallant's *The Pawnbroker* (1961) draws upon Sol Nazerman's memories, Jewish novelists have shied away from situations taken up by European writers (like André Schwartzbart) or diarists (like Anne Frank) or documentary film-makers (like Alain Resnais).

One discovers, therefore, that the novels concerned with anti-Semitism in America are trivial and, in the fashionable social-scientific term, perhaps even counterproductive. Consider, for instance, Arthur Miller's *Focus* (1945), Laura Z. Hobson's *Gentleman's Agreement* (1947), and Irwin Shaw's *The Young Lions* (1948). These novels attempt to demonstrate that Jews and Gentiles are really indistinguishable in their behavior and in their values. Only names are different. But this argument weakens rather than strengthens the demand that Jews affirm their unique and distinctive identity. Ironically, the most impressive novels of anti-Semitism have been Bruce Jay Friedman's *Stern* (1962) and Saul Bellow's *The Victim* (1949), which suggest that the relations between Semite and anti-Semite are somewhat more complicated than those between victim and victimizer. Although no sane observer can deny that instances of anti-Semitism still occur in the United States, there is no reason to doubt the moral suggested by Ivan Gold's story "Taub East" (1963): the defense against anti-Semitism can become almost comically disproportionate in the United States of Arthur Goldberg, Harry Golden, and Barry Goldwater.[32]

The third and most important form of response to the conversion to America is the presentation in literary form of a positive view of Judaism and Jewish life. There is, for instance, the case of Herman Wouk, the best-known of contemporary writers committed to Judaism. Although *Marjorie Morningstar* (1955) is actually an outraged polemic against assimilation, Wouk begins with an attempt at fairness. The attractions of Central Park West and Columbia University are vividly dramatized. Lobster and shrimp entice. Noel Airman, despite his symbolically withered arm (right out of Nathaniel Hawthorne), is sexually irresistible. Marjorie sleeps with Noel: "There

---

[32] The story was collected in *Nickel Miseries* (New York, 1963).

were shocks, ugly uncoverings, pain, incredible humiliation, shock, shock, and it was over." [33] Sexuality without God is a matter of "nasty, squirming, writhing naked bodies." [34] A kindly psychologist helps to restore Marjorie's peace of mind: "Food disciplines are a part of every great religion. Psychologically, they're almost inevitable, and extremely practical." [35] (He does not explain the practical purposes of the rules which restrict women during and after their "unclean" periods.) No wonder that Marjorie abandons Noel to his fate as TV-writer and turns to a young lawyer who manfully survives the traumatic knowledge of Marjorie's sinful past. Marjorie becomes Mrs. Milton Schwartz: "a regular synagogue-goer, active in the Jewish organization of the town; apparently that takes up a lot of her time.... Her husband is active too.... The only remarkable thing about Mrs. Schwartz is that she ever dreamed of being Marjorie Morningstar." [36]

Samuel Astrachan and Chaim Potok are among those who have since the Second World War dramatized conversions to Judaism at a more pervasive level of complexity, but the best of the novels of return continues to be Ludwig Lewisohn's *The Island Within* (1928). Lewisohn himself came to America at the age of seven and pledged his allegiance to his new home. He taught Sunday school, labored in the Methodist church's Epworth League, and described himself as "an American, a Southerner, and a Christian." He took an M.A. at Columbia and discovered that the "host society" did not want Jews—not even converted ones—to teach English literature. He learned also, after getting a job teaching German literature, that Americans with German names were roughly handled in 1917 and 1918. Lewisohn was eventually convinced that the American dream was an illusion and that survival was possible only in Palestine. His autobiographical novel *The Island Within* is the powerful expression of that conviction. Lewisohn shows that the migration of the Levy family from Lithuania to Germany to America is also a movement from Orthodoxy to the most tenuous kind of secularized attachment to Jewishness. American-born Arthur Levy, thinking the attachment to Judaism is completely vanished, marries the agnostic daughter of a Christian minister. "Couldn't one help to destroy all

---

[33] Herman Wouk, *Marjorie Morningstar* (Garden City, N. Y., 1955), 417.
[34] *Ibid.*, 180.
[35] *Ibid.*, 469.
[36] *Ibid.*, 564.

those remnants of man's barbarous past by living as though they had no real existence, by living in the light of reason?" [37] The answer is an emphatic no! Ironically, Arthur Levy, a disciple of Freud, finds himself married to a sexually repressed woman who sublimates her energies into a career as a hack-writer. A distant cousin, Reb Moshe, gradually brings Arthur Levy back to the path he had strayed from. Reading ancestral documents almost a thousand years old, Arthur Levy realizes that Jews are destined to suffer. (The Crusaders massacred the Jews of Speyer and Mainz in 1096; Jews die today in pogroms in Elizavetgrad and Kishinev.) Arthur divorces his wife and returns to his people. Lewisohn himself decided to become an Israeli.

Long before the creation of Israel in 1948, Zionism had become a theme for Jewish writers, especially for those who rejected Judaism but wished nonetheless to maintain the sense of peoplehood which has always been a part of Judaism. Six years before publication of *The Old Bunch*, Meyer Levin turned to the conflicts of Jews and Arabs in the British Mandate of Palestine. *Yehuda* (1931) is a somewhat improbable novel whose hero practices the violin at night after a hard day in the fields of his commune, but it is a better book than *My Father's House*, the simplistic Zionist allegory Levin wrote in 1947. Michael Blankfort, an author whose early works were written from a politically radical point of view, was another who turned to the theme of Zionism. In 1952 he published *The Juggler*, in which Hans Muller comes unwillingly from Germany to Israel, where he eventually accepts his Jewishness. The climactic scene begins when Muller remarks to the heroine, "I have grown fond of your *kibbutz* .... It has made being a Jew not so bad." [38] Equally awkward but more effective—perhaps because derived from the history of General Allenby's remarkable World War I campaign—was Blankfort's more recent novel *Behold the Fire* (1965), which told of Jews who sacrificed their lives in the struggle against Turkish rule. The most popular novel of the genre was, of course, Leon Uris's *Exodus* (1958), a book whose sentimentality was scarcely exaggerated when it was transformed into film. More persuasive were the appeals of Ludwig Lewisohn. "The only Jew who can be loyal to the spirit of America," he wrote in 1939, "is the Zionist." [39] Lewisohn condemned self-hate and then went on to write what ought to be one of the most memorable of appeals:

[37] Ludwig Lewisohn, *The Island Within* (New York, 1928), 237.
[38] Michael Blankfort, *The Juggler* (Boston, 1952), 204.
[39] Ludwig Lewisohn, *The Answer* (New York, 1939), 24.

Escape, escape, anything on any irrelevant periphery. Anything but the center, the heart, the blood. Virgin Spain, the Soviet Fatherland. Anything but the real, the attainable, the given, that for which real work can be done in a world of reality and real sacrifices made and real tears shed and real blood; anything but that to which one is called by nature and unperverted instinct and tradition and where one is wanted and needed and where . . . one can give one's whole heart. Any place but home. Any people except one's own. Any God except the God of one's fathers . . . . Utopia is the opiate of . . . the Jewish people.[40]

Utopia is the opiate of the Jewish people. Or their truest vocation. Perhaps the only category of conversion to rival in importance that of St. Paul was precisely this conversion to radicalism. When seen in perspective, the commitment to Marxism and to the more anarchistic forms of radicalism which flowered in the 1960s will be seen as part of a much more important movement of those alienated from the past and dedicated to the future. The history of political radicalism in America from the anarchism of Emma Goldman and Alexander Berkman through the socialism of Victor Berger and Abraham Cahan and Morris Hillquit to the communism of Herbert Aptheker and Howard Fast and Joseph Freeman and John Gates and Benjamin Gitlow and Mike Gold and Jay Lovestone and Bertram Wolfe and, beyond Marxism, to the exotic rebellions of Abbie Hoffman and Jerry Rubin—the history of political radicalism in America has very largely been the history of Jews doubly alienated from Judaism and from Christendom, apostates from the Mosaic dispensation and from the gospel according to Adam Smith.

If assimilation means a world of Babbitts tenuously tied to the B'nai Brith, if assimilation means a transfer of loyalty from the faith of our fathers to that of our neighbors, if assimilation means removal from Brownsville to Miami Beach, then assimilation is not enough. The task of a writer alienated from traditional Judaism is the secularization of Judaism's historic sense of mission. If the writer departed from the temple is not to lose himself in the lonely crowd, he must labor to bring about the transformation of society. He must create the Zion in which exile can be ended.

For half a century at least, the conversion to utopia has been a major theme of Jewish writers in America. Israel Zangwill, the English novelist, rewrote *Romeo and Juliet* fifty years before Leonard Bernstein set it to music. David Quixano, the hero of *The Melting-Pot*, composes an American symphony, an orchestration of all the

[40] *Ibid.*, 122.

ethnic strains of our nation of nations. He and Vera Revenal break through the barriers of hatred that separated them:

> America is God's Crucible, the great Melting-Pot where all the races of Europe are melting and reforming! Here you stand, good folk, think I, when I see them at Ellis Island, here you stand in your fifty groups, with your fifty languages and histories, and your fifty blood hatreds and rivalries. But you won't be long like that, brothers, for these are the fires of God you've come to—these are the fires of God. A fig for your feuds and vendettas! Germans and Frenchmen, Irishmen and Englishmen, Jews and Russians—into the Crucible with you all! God is making the American! [41]

A generation later, Mike Gold's autobiographical sketch of *Jews without money* ended with an equally millenial vision: "A man on an East Side soap-box, one night, proclaimed that out of the despair, melancholy and helpless rage of millions, a world movement had been born to abolish poverty.... I listened to him.... O' workers' revolution, you brought hope to me, a lonely suicidal boy. You are the true Messiah. You will destroy the East Side when you come, and build there a garden for the human spirit." [42] Even Meyer Levin, whose deepest passion was for Zionism rather than for socialism, wrote in the 1930s of poverty and injustice, of bribed judges and corrupt doctors and a tendency among policemen routinely to beat anyone suspected of communism. When the police, on Memorial Day, 1937, killed ten strikers at the Republic Steel Plant in South Chicago, Levin wrote *Citizens!*, a novel still alive with its author's passionate protest against justice denied in Illinois. In the novel, the doctor-hero, committed only to his family and his career, accidentally witnesses the Memorial Day massacre. He treats the wounded and struggles to keep the police from dragging them from ambulances and hospital beds. He then reads the Chicago papers: "MOB ATTACKS POLICE, 200 INJURED AS STRIKERS CHARGE, STRIKERS DRUGGED TO ASSAULT POLICE." By the end of the novel he had been—in today's jargon—radicalized. He marches in the procession to pay homage to the dead: "As the people approached the wreath, the column narrowed to a single file, and passed slowly, one by one they dropped their dark red flowers, like great swollen drops of blood augmenting the spreading dark pool on the ground." [43]

[41] Israel Zangwill, *The Melting-Pot* (New York, 1910), 37.
[42] Michael Gold, *Jews Without Money* (New York, 1930), 309.
[43] Meyer Levin, *Citizens!* (New York, 1940), 643.

Marxism as a mass movement is finished in the United States. It is common among historians to say that the American consensus has always been too strong for the success of a radical movement. It is perhaps more correct to say that the progressive transformation of America has vindicated the few who prodded the many into reform. Abraham Cahan's decision to vote for FDR was not the betrayal of socialism that it has sometimes been called, nor was Norman Thomas's faint praise for Lyndon Johnson's domestic programs the result of a loss of faith. Although the vision of a truly just and humane society seems at the moment discouragingly distant, we have nonetheless moved a long way in what still seems to some of us the right direction.

This, at any rate, is the judgment of Irving Howe, Lewis Coser, and other spokesmen for democratic socialism. Spokesmen for the New Left are quick to voice their raucus disagreement. Among those dedicated to the romantic radicalism of our time are Paul Goodman and Norman Mailer.

Goodman castigates society's absurdity from the position of a utopian Socialist. "Our society," he writes, "thwarts aptitude and creates stupidity. It corrupts ingenuous patriotism. It corrupts the fine arts. It shackles science. It dampens animal ardor. It discourages the religious convictions of Justification and Vocation, and it dims the sense that there is a Creation. It has no Honor. It has no Community." [44] No community. The United States today lacks the communal sense of a traditional society, lacks, for instance, the closeness and compassion of the world nostalgically recreated by Alfred Kazin in his memoir *A Walker in the City* (1951). Goodman believes that the community can be born from the radical reconstruction of the social system. His book *Communitas* (1960), written with his brother Percival, is a blueprint of the new society, decentralized and humane. His novel *Making Do* (1963) is the dramatic revelation of the possibility of a reasonable love that transcends barriers of class, nation, religion, race, and sex. The novel contains violence and disappointment as well as love, but Goodman refuses to settle for the world as it is. "No," he concludes, " 'The Lord has yet more light and truth to break forth,' as John Robinson said to the Pilgrims embarking toward America." [45] From the Calvinist revolutionaries of the six-

---

[44] Paul Goodman, *Growing Up Absurd* (New York, 1960), 12.
[45] Paul Goodman, *Making Do* (New York, 1963), 276.

teenth century, Goodman draws inspiration for his universalistic vision.[46]

The strange career of Norman Mailer is another sign of the alienated Jewish intellectual's continued dedication to the radical transformation of society. "The sour truth," wrote Mailer in 1959, "is that I am imprisoned with a perception which will settle for nothing less than making a revolution in the consciousness of our time." [47] Mailer's quest in those years of Eisenhower and Kennedy was for the classless society in which the shits will no longer kill us, for the perfect orgasm that will give us the time of our time. *Barbary Shore* (1951), the second of Mailer's novels, was the culmination of what might fairly be called Mailer's Marxist phase. *Barbary Shore* fails as a novel, but who has better described the fascination Trotsky had for some American Jews?

> There was a great man who led us, and I read almost every word he had written, and listened with the passion of the novitiate to each message he sent from the magical center in Mexico . . . . I lived more intensely in the past than I could ever in the present, until the sight of a policeman on his mount became the Petrograd proletariat crawling to fame between the legs of a Cossack's horse.... There never was a revolution to equal it, and never a city more glorious than Petrograd, and for all that period of my life I lived another and braved the ice of winter and the summer flies in Vyborg while across my adopted country of the past, winds of the revolution blew their flame, and all of us suffered hunger while we drank . . . the wine of equality.[48]

But Mailer moved quickly and left "scientific socialism" behind. In 1957, he wrote his widely admired (and condemned) essay "The White Negro," in which Mailer urged his readers to divorce themselves from society in order to achieve "existential" authenticity, in order to surrender themselves to an "incandescent consciousness which the possibilities within death has opened . . . ." [49] In his rage against the dullness of rationalized process, Mailer praised a group of boys who murdered a shopkeeper and thus struck a blow for freedom

---

[46] Saul Bellow, *The Adventures of Augie March* (New York, 1953), 536. The novel ends with a very similar image: "Why I am a sort of Colombus of those near-at-hand and believe you can come to them in this immediate *terra incognita* that spreads out in every gaze. I may well be a flop at this line of endeavor. Colombus too thought he was a flop, probably, when they sent him back in chains. Which didn't prove there was no America."

[47] Norman Mailer, *Advertisements for Myself* (New York, 1959), 17.

[48] Norman Mailer, *Barbary Shore* (New York, 1951), 125–26.

[49] *Advertisements for Myself*, 342.

and significance. This affirmation of the immediate, the spontaneous, the dangerous, and the unknown was, of course, dramatized in Mailer's novel of 1965, *An American Dream*. At some point, however, Mailer turned away from the politics of the "New Left" in order to express his own somewhat middle-aged rejection of the values of "Technology Land." He marched with Paul Goodman and Robert Lowell to the very steps of the Pentagon, but his portrait of the demonstrators was not without ambiguity: "These mad middle-class children with their lobotomies from sin, their nihilistic embezzlement of all middle-class moral funds, their innocence, their lust for apocalypse, their unbelievable indifference to waste.... Yes, these were the troops: middle-class cancer-pushers and drug-gutted flower children." [50] If Norman Mailer is the secular Jew as revolutionary, he is also the reincarnation of Friedrich Nietzsche and the personification of a mood shared by many intellectuals in this present crisis of our civilization.

Goodman and Mailer are, of course, only two writers among many who want to build the new Zion here in the American wasteland. Herbert Gold's best novel, *The Prospect Before Us* (1954), is the epitaph of a stubborn hotel-keeper who defies the prejudices of white America and rents a room to a Negro girl—and dies for love of her. Harvey Swados's stories and essays document the degradation of factory life and debunk the myth of the happy worker. Clancy Sigal's *Going Away* (1961), perhaps the most minutely thorough novelistic criticism of American life since Dos Passos's *USA*, sends its hero driving from Los Angeles to New York in search of that lost world of the 1930s where *unions* meant sit-down strikes rather than racial discrimination and support for war, where *Spain* meant the defense of Madrid from fascism rather than another article in *Holiday*. "I really wanted, while I was on the road, to look at America and try to figure out why it wasn't my country anymore." [51] The 1950s were not the age of political apathy that journalistic myth holds them to have been.

Considering these conversions to Christianity and to secularism, to radicalism and to a rediscovered traditionalism, one can hazard some tentative predictions. I am sure—despite the affluence that fills the land with the Young Women's Hebrew Associations—that traditional Judaism will not disappear from America. There will always be those for whom Abraham and Isaac and the Tables of the Law are

[50] Norman Mailer, *The Armies of the Night* (New York, 1968), 34–35.
[51] Clancy Sigal, *Going Away* (Boston, 1961), 244.

more important than Danny Kaye and Barbra Streisand and ledgers in the black. There will always be those for whom the utopian dream of the brotherhood of man means less than the historical reality of the peoplehood of Israel. But I am also sure that these Jews will decline in number. They will also, if the descent from Ludwig Lewisohn to Herman Wouk is any indication, decline in literary importance. For the great majority of American Jews, the process of secularization seems certain to continue toward assimilation in a more secular if not a more attractive America. The Jewish Book Club of the future will have fifty Edna Ferbers to choose from, and a handful of Allen Ginsbergs to scorn. If present tendencies continue, Negroes are more likely than Jews disproportionately to fill the ranks of dissent and to imagine in novel and in poem another country better than the one we live in now. Paradoxically, the survival in America of a significant and identifiably Jewish literature depends on the unlikely conversion to Judaism of a stiff-necked intractable generation that no longer chooses to be chosen.

BIBLIOGRAPHY

Adler, Edward. *Notes from a Dark Street.* New York: Knopf, 1962.
Antin, Mary. *The Promised Land.* Boston: Houghton, 1912.
Astrachan, Sam. *The Game of Dostoevsky.* New York: Farrar, 1965.
Baron, Sale Wittmayer. *A Social and Religious History of the Jews.* 2nd ed. New York: Columbia University Press, 1952.
Bellow, Saul. *The Adventures of Augie March.* New York: Viking, 1953.
———. *Herzog.* New York: Viking, 1964.
———. *Mosby's Memoirs and Other Stories.* New York: Viking, 1968.
———. *Mr. Sammler's Planet.* New York: Viking, 1970.
———. *The Victim.* New York: Vanguard, 1949.
Berkman, Alexander. *Prison Memoirs of an Anarchist.* London: C. W. Daniel, 1926.
Blankfort, Michael. *Behold the Fire.* New York: New American Library, 1965.
———. *The Brave and the Blind.* Indianapolis: Bobbs-Merrill, 1940.
———. *The Juggler.* Boston: Little, 1952.
Blau, Joseph Leon. *Modern Varieties of Judaism.* New York: Columbia University Press, 1966.
Blechman, Burt. *How Much.* New York: McDowell, Oblensky, 1961.
———. *Stations.* New York: Random, 1964.
———. *The War of Camp Omongo.* New York: Random, 1963.
Cahan, Abraham. *The Imported Bridegroom and Other Stories of the New York Ghetto.* 2nd ed. New York: Garrett Press, 1968.

——. *The Rise of David Levinsky*. New York: Harper, 1917.
——. *Yekl: A Tale of the New York Ghetto*. 2nd ed. New York: Dover, 1969. (1st ed., 1899.)
Charyn, Jerome. *American Scrapbook*. New York: Viking, 1969.
——. *Going to Jerusalem*. New York: Viking, 1967.
——. *Once Upon a Droshky*. New York: McGraw-Hill, 1964.
Cohen, Arthur. *The Carpenter Years*. New York: New American Library, 1967.
Deutsch, Babette. *Coming of Age*. Bloomington: Indiana University Press, 1959.
Eisenberg, Azriel (ed.). *The Golden Land: A Literary Portrait of American Jewry*. New York: Thomas Yoseloff, 1964.
Fiedler, Leslie A. *The Last Jew in America*. New York: Stein and Day, 1966.
——. *No! in Thunder: Essays on Myth and Literature*. Boston: Beacon Press, 1960.
——. *The Return of the Vanishing American*. New York: Stein and Day, 1968.
Friedman, Bruce Jay. *Black Angels*. New York: Simon, 1966.
——. *A Mother's Kisses*. New York: Simon, 1964.
——. *Stern*. New York: Simon, 1962.
Fruchter, Norman. *Coat Upon a Stick*. New York: Simon, 1963.
Glazer, Nathan. *American Judaism*. Chicago: University of Chicago Press, 1957.
Gold, Herbert. *Birth of a Hero*. New York: Viking, 1951.
——. *Fathers*. New York: Random, 1966.
——. *The Great American Jackpot*. New York: Random, 1969.
——. *The Man Who Was Not With It*. Boston: Atlantic-Little, 1956.
——. *The Prospect Before Us*. Cleveland: World Publishing, 1954.
Gold, Ivan. *Nickel Miseries*. New York: Viking, 1963.
——. *Sick Friends*. New York: Dutton, 1969.
Gold, Michael. *Jews Without Money*. New York: Horace Liveright, 1930.
Goldman, Emma. *Living My Life*. Garden City, N.Y.: Garden City Publishing, 1934.
Goodman, Paul. *Growing Up Absurd*. New York: Random, 1960.
——. *Making Do*. New York: Macmillan, 1963.
——, and Percival Goodman. *Communitas*. New York: Vintage Books, 1960.
Gordon, Milton. *Assimilation in American Life*. New York: Oxford University Press, 1964.
Guttmann, Julius. *Philosophies of Judaism*, trans. David W. Silverman. New York: Holt, 1964.
Herberg, Will. *Judaism and Modern Man*. New York: Farrar, 1951.
——. *Protestant, Catholic, Jew*. Anchor Book. Garden City, N.Y.: Doubleday, 1960.
Hobson, Laura Z. *Gentleman's Agreement*. New York: Simon, 1947.
Howe, Irving. *The Decline of the New*. New York: Harcourt, 1970.
——. *Steady Work*. New York: Harcourt, 1970.

Howe, Irving. *A World More Attractive*. New York: Horizon Press, 1963.

Kallen, Horace M. *Culture and Democracy in the United States*. New York: Boni and Liveright, 1924.

Kaplan, Mordecai M. *Judaism as a Civilization*. New York: Thomas Yoseloff, 1957. (1st ed., 1934.)

Kaufmann, Myron. *Remember Me to God*. Philadelphia: Lippincott, 1957.

———. *Thy Daughter's Nakedness*. Philadelphia: Lippincott, 1968.

Kazin, Alfred. *Contemporaries*. Boston: Little, 1962.

———. *Starting Out in the Thirties*. Boston: Little, 1965.

———. *A Walker in the City*. New York: Harcourt, 1951.

Lazarus, Emma. *Songs of a Semite*. New York: American Hebrew, 1882.

Levin, Meyer. *Citizens!* New York: Viking, 1940.

———. *Compulsion*. New York: Simon, 1956.

———. *The Fanatic*. New York: Simon, 1964.

———. *Frankie and Johnny*. New York: John Day, 1930.

———. *The Golden Mountain*. New York: Jonathan Cape and Robert Ballou, 1932.

———. *In Search: An Autobiography*. New York: Horizon Press, 1950.

———. *My Father's House*. New York: Viking, 1947.

———. *The Old Bunch*. New York: Viking, 1937.

———. *Reporter*. New York: John Day, 1929.

———. *The Stronghold*. New York: Simon, 1965.

———. *Yehuda*. New York: Jonathan Cape and Harrison Smith, 1931.

Lewin, Kurt. *Resolving Social Conflicts*. New York: Harper, 1948.

Lewisohn, Ludwig. *An Altar in the Fields*. New York: Harper, 1934.

———. *The American Jew: Character and Destiny*. New York: Farrar, 1950.

———. *Anniversary*. New York: Farrar, 1948.

———. *Breathe Upon These*. Indianapolis: Bobbs-Merrill, 1944.

———. *The Island Within*. New York: Harper, 1928.

———. *The Last Days of Shylock*. New York: Harper, 1931.

———. *Renegade*. Philadelphia: Jewish Publication Society of America, 1942.

———. *This People*. New York: Harper, 1933.

———. *Trumpet of Jubilee*. New York: Harper, 1937.

———. *The Vehement Flame*. New York: Farrar, 1948.

Liptzin, Sol. *The Jew in American Literature*. New York: Bloch, 1966.

Mailer, Norman. *Advertisements for Myself*. New York: Putnam's, 1959.

———. *An American Dream*. New York: Dial Press, 1965.

———. *Cannibals and Christians*. New York: Dial Press, 1966.

———. *The Deer Park*. New York: Putnam's, 1955.

Malamud, Bernard. *The Assistant*. New York: Farrar, 1957.

———. *The Fixer*. New York: Farrar, 1966.

———. *Idiots First*. New York: Farrar, 1963.

———. *The Magic Barrel*. New York: Farrar, 1958.

———. *The Natural*. New York: Farrar, 1952.

———. *A New Life*. New York: Farrar, 1962.

Malin, Irving. *Jews and Americans.* Carbondale: Southern Illinois University Press, 1965.

Miller, Arthur. *After the Fall.* New York: Viking, 1964.

———. *Focus.* New York: Book Find Club, 1945.

———. *I Don't Need You Anymore.* New York: Viking, 1967.

Oxenhandler, Neal. *A Change of Gods.* New York: Harcourt, 1962.

Podhoretz, Norman. *Doings and Undoings.* New York: Farrar, 1964.

———. *Making It.* New York: Random, 1967.

Potak, Chaim. *The Chosen.* New York: Simon, 1967.

———. *The Promise.* New York: Knopf, 1969.

Rischin, Moses. *The Promised City.* Cambridge, Mass.: Harvard University Press, 1962.

Rose, Peter I. (ed.). *The Ghetto and Beyond.* New York: Random, 1969.

Rosenberg, Stuart E. *America Is Different: The Search for a Jewish Identity.* New York: Nelson, 1964.

Roth, Philip. *Goodbye, Columbus.* Boston: Houghton, 1959.

———. *Letting Go.* New York: Random, 1962.

———. *Portnoy's Complaint.* New York: Random, 1969.

———. *When She Was Good.* New York: Random, 1967.

Rukeyser, Muriel. *Water Lily Fire: Poems, 1935–1962.* New York: Macmillan, 1963.

Schulberg, Budd. *What Makes Sammy Run?* New York: Random, 1941.

Schultz, Max F. *Radical Sophistication: Studies in Contemporary Jewish-American Novelists.* Columbus: Ohio State University Press, 1969.

Shaw, Irwin. *The Young Lions.* New York: Random, 1948.

Sherman, C. Bezalel. *The Jew Within American Society.* Detroit: Wayne State University Press, 1965.

Sigal, Clancy. *Going Away.* Boston: Houghton, 1961.

Simckes, L. S. *Seven Days of Mourning.* New York: Houghton, 1963.

Sklare, Marshall (ed.). *The Jews.* Glencoe, Ill.: Free Press, 1958.

Swados, Harvey. *Nights in the Garden of Brooklyn.* Boston: Little, 1961.

———. *A Radical's America.* Boston: Little, 1962.

———. *The Will.* Cleveland: World Publishing, 1963.

Uris, Leon. *Exodus.* New York: Doubleday, 1958.

Wallant, Edward Lewis. *The Pawnbroker.* New York: Macfadden Books, 1962.

———. *The Tenants of Moonbloom.* New York: Popular Library, 1963.

Wirth, Louis. *The Ghetto.* Chicago. Phoenix Books, 1956. (1st ed., 1928.)

Wouk, Herman. *Marjorie Morningstar.* Garden City, N. Y.: Doubleday, 1955.

Zangwill, Israel. *Children of the Ghetto.* New York: Macmillan, 1906.

———. *The Melting-Pot.* New York: Macmillan, 1910.

Cultural Nationalism and its Literary Expression in French-Canadian Fiction

JACQUES COTNAM

Translated by Noël Corbett

In Canada I was made aware as I never had been before of the importance of nationalism as a stimulating force to literature. It was true of most of our own best writers till after the Civil War that they were occupied in one way or another with the attempt to give America an identity—by inventing a legendary past, by idealizing an imperfect present or by prophesying a transcendent future. All these writers had a national mission. But in English-speaking Canada no such mission was felt, because no such independence and no such unity had been achieved.... In French Canada, on the other hand, the literature has kept pace with the nationalist cause, and it is evidently taken more seriously than its English-speaking neighbors take theirs.... One thinks of small nationalities, like Ireland and Hungary, in which the literature has been largely inspired by a movement for national independence and, in turn, has provided an active ferment in the political life of the people.
—Edmund Wilson, *O Canada. An American's Notes on Canadian Culture*

The day is long gone when we could consider literature an inoffensive game. Our entire literary tradition cries out against dilettantism. For us, to write is to live, to defend, and to sustain ourselves.
—Lionel Groulx, *Dix ans d'Action française*

Although there is no question of relating here the complete history of French-Canadian nationalism,[1] it would be nonetheless use-

[1] Books on this subject are so numerous that it would be vain to try to establish an exhaustive list. Moreover, I have already presented a succinct

ful, I think, to sketch its origins and to clarify its initial ambivalence; short of that, I doubt that it would be possible to understand the real meaning of Quebec nationalism today,[2] its political orientation and its literary expression.

First of all, it is vital to remember that, unlike his American counterpart, the French Canadian did not reach full awareness of his distinctive character through opposition to a far-distant mother country, but rather in reaction against a conqueror speaking a language and practicing a religion both of which were foreign to him. Forced by the fortunes of war to give allegiance to an English-speaking Protestant master, he progressively came to seek refuge behind the newly constructed bulwark of "national differences": his language and his religion.

For more than a century and a half, French-Canadian nationalism has, in essence, reflected a desire for survival. Faced with the English

---

bibliography at the end of *Faut-il inventer un nouveau Canada?* (Montreal, 1967), 249–57 and in "Essai de guide bibliographique des études canadiennes-françaises," *L'Enseignement secondaire* (Nov.-Dec. 1967), 318–52.

For more bibliographical detail, see: A. Beaulieu, J. Hamelin, and B. Bernier, *Guide d'histoire du Canada* (Quebec, 1969); F. Dumont and Y. Martin (eds.), *Situation de la recherche sur le Canada français* (Quebec, 1962); N. Story, *The Oxford Companion to Canadian History and Literature* (Toronto, London, and New York, 1967).

For my part, I will simply mention, besides the well-known book by Mason Wade, *The French Canadians*, 2 vols., new ed. (Toronto, 1968), that of R. Cook, *Nationalism and the French Canadian Question* (Toronto, 1967), and the collection of essays that he has published under the title *French Canadian Nationalism* (Toronto, 1969), and *Constitutionalism and Nationalism in Lower Canada* (Toronto, 1969). As for books in French, one may usefully consult the complete works of Lionel Groulx and the books by Michel Brunet: *Canadians et Canadiens* (Montreal, 1954); *La présence anglaise et les Canadiens* (Montreal, 1964); *Les Canadiens après la Conquête* (Montreal, 1969). Finally, I add F. Ouellet, *Histoire économique et sociale du Québec, 1760–1860; structures et conjonctures* (Montreal, 1966). Not to be forgotten are the special issues given over to French Canadian nationalism in *Revue d'Histoire de l'Amérique française* (March 1969), and *Maintenant* (15 Sept. 1967).

[2] In addition to the works mentioned above, consult: J. Berque, *Les Québécois* (Paris, 1967); G. Bergeron, *Le Canada français après deux siècles de patience* (Paris, 1967); M. Bernard, *Le Québec change de visage* (Paris, 1963); M. Chaput, *Pourquoi je suis séparatiste* (Montreal, 1961); A. Dagenais, *Révolution au Québec* (Montreal, 1966); P. Desbarats, *The State of Quebec* (Toronto, 1965); L. Groulx, *Chemins de l'avenir* (Montreal, 1964); D. Johnson, *Egalité ou indépendance* (Montreal, 1965); H. B. Myers, *The Quebec Revolution* (Montreal, 1964); H. Quinn, *The Union Nationale: A Study in Quebec Nationalism* (Toronto, 1963); R. Rumilly, *Le problème national des Canadiens français* (Montreal, 1961); F. Scott and M. Oliver, *Quebec States Her Case* (Toronto, 1964); T. Sloan, *Quebec, the Not-So-Quiet Revolution* (Toronto, 1965); P. Vallières, *Nègres blancs d'Amérique* (Paris, 1969).

presence, the French-Canadian writer, by the simple fact of writing in French, declared himself a militant; wholly devoted to the "national cause," he habitually turned to the past in his efforts to justify that cause and to confirm his "desire for survival." At first a medium of combat,[3] later of resistance, French-Canadian literature would, under such circumstances, cast historians, journalists, and orators in roles of primary importance.[4] As for poets and novelists, they sought their subject matter for the creation of a patriotic, even epic, literature from the history of their forefathers. It was vital that they force a "national spirit" and, to accomplish this task, they turned eagerly to the past, because "the past is patient, and one can do with it what one likes. Especially one can present it in a way that creates an outlet for the nostalgia of those who are dissatisfied with the present."[5]

The French-Canadian had to resist; he had to preserve his identity intact. But what did that mean? However clear the first part of the message might be, the second lent itself to confusion, some preferring to stress the cultural element of that identity, others giving priority to religion. This initial dichotomy explains why French-Canadian nationalism was torn between two opposing but ill-defined poles of attraction, opposites prone to engender internal discord, whose intensity was directly proportionate to the distance separating them. Literature, because of its crucial role as an instrument of survival, necessarily reflects the ambivalence of this self-consciousness.

In the minds of the directors of the Institut Canadien, founded in 1844 to promote development of the arts, letters, and sciences, the French-Canadian was distinguished from his English-speaking compatriots by his cultural affiliations. It was for that reason that the

[3] On the birth of French Canadian letters, the work by S. Marion, *Les Lettres canadiennes d'autrefois*, 9 vols. (Ottawa, 1949–1958), is still worth consulting. In a special issue of *Études françaises* (Aug. 1969), G.-A. Vachon has presented a few texts illustrating this "literature of combat" (1778–1810).

[4] See: L.-A. Bisson, *Le romantisme littéraire au Canada français* (Paris, 1932); P. de Grandpré, *Histoire de la littérature française du Québec*, 4 vols. (Montreal, 1967–1969); G. Sylvestre, *Panorama des lettres canadiennes-françaises* (Quebec, 1964); G. Tougas, *Histoire de la littérature canadienne-française* (Paris, 1964); A. Viatte, *Histoire littéraire de l'Amérique française* (Paris and Quebec, 1954).

[5] H. Straumann, *American Literature in the Twentieth Century*, 3rd rev. ed. (New York, 1965), 62. See: J.-C. Falardeau, *Notre société et son roman* (Montreal, 1967); D.-M. Hayne, "La poésie romantique au Canada français (1860–1890)," in *Archives des lettres canadiennes*, IV (Montreal, 1969); R. Le Moine, "Le roman historique au Canada français," in *Archives des lettres canadiennes*, III (Montreal, 1964); J.-D. Lortie, "Les origines de la poésie au Canada français," in *Archives des lettres canadiennes*, IV.

Institut sought to favor the resumption of cultural relations with France. In his book, whose title *Canada Reconquered by France* is so pregnant with meaning, J.-G. Barthe explained:

> What I dreamed of was the preservation of New France in its national aspect, in its social existence, and in everything that made it an original New World creation. . . . The Institut canadien, a literary, but more particularly a national institution, was created in a spontaneous movement of enthusiasm, to shore up the dikes against the torrent which threatened to carry everything away. I called for a literary reunion, and for the reestablishment of close relationships between us [between France and Canada], only so that this thought, so full of future promise, might reach full bloom, only to hasten the hour when it might bring forth its precious fruits.[6]

Conscious, as they were, that a culture which has no roots in the reality of daily life soon risks losing all its values, leaving behind but a residue of folklore, the directors of the Institut Canadien set out to establish programs of social, political, and economic action as well. That was more than enough to call down upon their heads the wrath of a conservative church eager to anathematize anyone who dared to favor a republican form of government, who dared to support the separation of church and state, who dared to advance liberal ideas, a church which, furthermore, saw heresy in proclaiming a democracy of the people.[7]

Whereas the Institut Canadien took action in the here and now, encouraging its members to take up the challenge of history and life,

---

[6] J.-G. Barthe, *Le Canada reconquis par la France* (Paris, 1855), xvi and xxxi. Unless otherwise indicated, all quoted texts have been translated by N. Corbett.

[7] It is indeed surprising that very few studies deal with the *Institut canadien*. To the best of my knowledge, there exists but a single monograph, by Th. Hudon, S. J., *L'Institut canadien de Montréal et l'affaire Guibord* (Montreal, 1938). However, M. Wade talks at length about the Institut in *The French Canadians*. So does A. Siegfried in *Le Canada. Les deux races* (Paris, 1906). Siegfried's book has been translated under the title: *The Race Question in Canada* (Toronto, 1966).

Let me simply recall here that, in his Encyclical *Quanta Cura et Syllabus Errorum* (1864), Pius IX condemned "the errors characteristic of modern liberalism," particularly socialism, the separation of church and state, and the principle of a democracy of the people. Although the movement of Canadian liberalism has been little more than a pale reflection of European liberalism (see Guido de Ruggiero, *The History of European Liberalism* [London, 1927]), the reactions it has provoked are not dissimilar to those suscitated by liberal ideology in France. For supporting evidence, consult the first two sections of M. Tison-Braun, *La Crise de l'humanisme 1890–1914* (Paris, 1958), and more particularly the chapters entitled: "Individualisme et traditionalisme au XIXe siècle" and "Le procès de l'individu."

the church, for which to be French-Canadian meant above all to be Catholic, withdrew, confining itself introspectively to past and tradition, bending all its efforts to a disregard of day-to-day reality, the better to preach the grandeur of life in the hereafter. That is why, just as it had condemned the Rebellion of 1837 and threatened excommunication for all who might take up arms against the established order, the church would not desist until the day it had Rome condemn the Institut Canadien on the pretext of its having made available to its members books on the *Index* and of seeking cultural relations with an impious France.

For it was indeed impious France which dismayed the church. In concert with the partisans of traditional ideology, the church made a clear distinction between pre- and postrevolutionary France refusing, of course, to recognize anything but the Ancien Régime, whose intellectual and spiritual continuation they sought in the attitude of the French extreme Right. "There exist today two French nations; radical France and conservative France, agnostic France and catholic France, the France that blasphemes and the France that prays. Our France is the second of these." [8]

The distinction is of considerable importance since, without it, one might possibly be tempted to conclude that, while according primacy to the religious identity of the French-Canadian, the church irrevocably closed its eyes to cultural identity. That was certainly not so. The fact remains, however, that the church interpreted this cultural identity according to its own lights, and from an intensely doctrinaire point of view. If, on occasion, it defended the French-Canadian cultural heritage, it was not so much for the intrinsic value of that heritage as it was to build ramparts against the threat of Protestantism, and by extension, of English domination. A French-Canadian was French-speaking, that much was clear; he was also, and above all, a Catholic. "Make no mistake, a French-Canadian who is not catholic is a strange creature, but a French-Canadian who no longer remains a catholic after having been one is a monstrous thing," [9] declared Thomas Chapais.

That the church lost no time laying its hands on the educational

---

[8] Th. Chapais, *Discours et conférences* (Quebec, 1897), 39. One may see this distinction between catholic France and impious France in: A.-B. Routhier, *Causeries du dimanche* (Montreal, 1871); Z. Lacasse, *Dans le camp ennemi* (Montreal, 1893); J. Tardivel, *Mélanges*, 2 vols. (Quebec, 1887; rpt. 1901).

[9] Th. Chapais, *Mélanges de polémique et d'études religieuses, politiques et littéraires* (Quebec, 1905), 87.

system, not only at the elementary but at the secondary and university levels as well, was, given the context, a foregone conclusion. It was vital to form good Catholics and keep them on the pathway to Truth, that is to say, sheltered from Anglo-Saxon Protestantism and materialism.[10] "Our mission, affirmed Mgr. Paquet in 1902, is not to manipulate finances, but to inspire ideas; it is not to light up the factory furnaces, but to tend the luminous flame of religion and thought, spreading its light far and wide." [11] These "ideas," one can well imagine, could only come from the "City of God," for the "City of Light" was no longer obedient to the precepts of Rome.

Since, according to the church hierarchy, the French-Canadian was defined by his religious rather than by his cultural affiliation, it was only natural that religious leaders ask the national literature to reflect this identity as "witness of Christ in America" and to declare the "providential mission of the French-Canadian nation." This was the program set forth as early as 1846, in opposition to that of the Institut Canadien:

> The creation of a national literature answered a need in our society. Separated from France at a time when France was separating herself from God, we have grown up independently, far away from her, and without suffering her revolutions, always following the laws of development that Providence provided for us, conserving the attitudes, the traditions, the spirit of faith, and the social virtues of our forefathers. The France which has lost these values cannot therefore furnish us with all the vital elements of our intellectual life. We must also have our own literature, which can be the expression of our ideas and our customs, and which, in its turn, may play a role in their formation.[12]

Twenty years later, Father H.-R. Casgrain made this program explicit:

> [Our literature] will be religious, the expression of true believers; such will be its characteristic form and expression; otherwise it will not live, but die of inanition. That is the fundamental precondition for its existence; it has no other *raison d'être*; no more than our people have any life-giving principle without religion or faith; the day when we cease to believe, we shall cease to exist.

[10] See Siegfried, *Le Canada*, and A. Buies, *Lettres sur le Canada* (Montreal, 1864).

[11] Mgr. L.-A. Paquet, "Sermon sur la vocation de la race française en Amérique," in *Discours et Allocutions* (Quebec, 1915), 187. See: J. Hulliger, *L'Enseignement social des évêques canadiens de 1891 à 1950* (Montreal, 1958) and W. F. Ryan, *The Clergy and Economic Growth in Quebec (1896–1914)* (Quebec, 1966).

[12] Father Nantel, in *Revue Canadienne* 4 (1846), 773.

... It will not bear the imprint of contemporary realism, that manifestation of impious materialistic thought ....

Fortunately, up till this time, our literature has understood its mission, espousing the doctrines of wisdom, teaching the love of good, admiring what is beautiful, knowing what is true, showing the people how to lead a moral life, opening their souls to all noble feelings, murmuring in their ears, with the names so dearly remembered, the actions which made their lives worthy, crowning all their virtues with its halo, pointing out the paths which lead to eternal life.[13]

It suffices to compare these words with those of J.-G. Barthe to realize the gulf which separated the two ideological currents. For Nantel, and especially for Casgrain, the prime obligation of a national literature was to serve morality; for Barthe, by contrast, it ought rather to be the voice of an original culture. Although, in the first instance as in the second, the past was readily invoked, it was in a different spirit; Casgrain sought refuge in the past whereas Barthe used it as a launching pad. He envisaged present reality as the only foundation for a vibrant future. For Barthe by no means neglected the social or political dimensions of French-Canadian life. To sum up, their glances might for an instant meet in the mirror of the past, but the ultimate objects of their gaze were of a very different nature.

The fact remains that at no time did they lose sight of France. If Nantel and Casgrain turned their backs on France, spurred by the hope of inspiring a national literature, it is clear that they did so for ethical, not for esthetic reasons. As G.-A. Vachon noted, Casgrain himself when setting pen to paper spontaneously reverted to French models.[14] In no sense could such an attitude to the mother country be said to correspond to that of a Poe or an Emerson, for instance. In fact, both Casgrain and Barthe nurtured a feeling of nostalgia for France; all the same, France did not symbolize the same reality for each. It is this feeling of nostalgia that Tougas has neatly labeled by speaking of the "orphan's complex." [15] Perhaps we ought to pity Canadians (in this respect, both English and French-speaking) for never having experienced a war of independence.

From its beginnings down to the present day, French-Canadian literature has remained the literature of men in exile, exile in both

[13] Father H.-R. Casgrain, "Le mouvement littéraire au Canada," *Le Foyer canadien* 4 (1866). See: *Mouvement littéraire de Québec (1860)*, in *Archives des lettres canadiennes*, I (Ottawa, 1961).

[14] G.-A. Vachon, "Aux sources du mythe québécois, l'oeuvre de l'abbé H. R. Casgrain," *Quartier Latin*, 10 March 1966.

[15] G. Tougas, *Littérature canadienne-française contemporaine* (Toronto, 1969), 199.

the temporal and the spatial senses. Torn between America and Europe, the French-Canadian writer remained committed to a ceaseless quest for identity, the question "To be or not to be" habitually presenting itself on the national level.[16] Between this continent and the other, his allegiance was, like that of Henry James, unhappily divided. Let us grant that Guy Sylvestre was right: it is not easy to be an American writing in French in a British country.[17]

In a letter to Father Casgrain, on the twenty-ninth of January 1867, Octave Crémazie lamented:

> The more I think about the fate of Canadian literature, the less chance I give it to leave its mark on history. What Canada lacks is a language of its own. If we spoke Iroquois or Huron, our literature might live. Unfortunately we speak and write in a rather shabby way, it is true, the language of Bossuet and Racine.
>
> Say or do what we wish, we will still be no more, from the literary standpoint, than a mere colony; and if even Canada should some day become an independent country whose flag shines forth in the bright sunlight of all nations, we would still be nothing more than mere literary colonists.[18]

Several would-be Websters said much the same thing; for them, the acquisition of one's own language was the basic prerequisite for a national literature.[19] Without meaning to deny the element of truth that such an affirmation might contain, I think it would be more appropriate, in the case of French-Canadian literature, to lay the responsibility at the doorstep of a closed society, a society impervious to external influences, refractory to progress, and allergic to life it-

---

[16] See: J. Le Moyne, *Convergences*, trans. P. Stratford (Toronto, 1966); G. Marcotte, "Traduit du français," *Les lettres modernes*, Dec. 1966–Jan. 1967, 78–84; P. de Grandpré, "La question des influences," *ibid.*, 109–16.

[17] G. Sylvestre, "Les lettres," *Esquisses du Canada français* (Montreal, 1967), 139. (*Facets of France Canada* [Montreal, 1967].)

[18] Quoted from *Oeuvres complètes de Octave Crémazie* (Montreal, 1882), 39. Incidentally, note that in an article entitled "Le Canada, l'Education et la Société," *Revue des Deux Mondes*, 13 July 1898, Mme. Th. Bentzon supports Crémazie's views. Ch. ab des Halden, on the other hand, takes him to task in *Études de littérature canadienne-française* (Paris, 1904), 114–19.

[19] On this subject, see: D. M. Hayne, "Les grandes options de la littérature canadienne-française," *Études françaises*, Feb. 1965, 68–89. The same article was also published in *Littérature canadienne-française* (Montreal, 1969), 25–52.
At each period of nationalistic fervor, the debate on the appropriateness of a Canadian language is reopened. Following H. Bernard, *Essais critiques* (Montreal, 1929), A. Pelletier, *Carquois* (Montreal, 1931), C.-H. Grignon, *Ombres et clameurs* (Montreal, 1933), and a few others, H. Bélanger has most recently dragged out the question once again in *Place à l'homme, Ecrits du Canada français*, no. 26, 1969.

self. The pivotal error consisted in having turned man away from
the involvement that life normally presupposes, indicating instead
the pathway to heaven; in having sacrificed the normal flowering of
his cultural identity to the exigencies of a religion verging on Jansen-
ism. In a word, in having rendered unto God the things which were
Caesar's.

It is obvious then that there was far too great a tendency to flee
from reality, seeking refuge in a mythical past that writers sought to
resuscitate through a patriotic, moralizing literature, which reached
its zenith in the praise of country life. Despite their valiant attempts
to create a national literature, writers were able to produce only a
nationalistic literature. Barring a very few exceptional cases, it is not
until after the Second World War that we may speak with conviction of the birth of an authentic French-Canadian literature.

The spirit of survival was perpetuated right down to that time;
there is no better way to depict it than by quoting from Louis Hémon's famous novel, *Maria Chapdelaine*:

> Strangers have surrounded us whom it is our pleasure to call for-
> eigners; they have taken into their hands most of the rule, they have
> gathered to themselves much of the wealth; but in this land of Que-
> bec nothing has changed. Nor shall anything change, for we are
> the pledge of it. Concerning ourselves and our destiny but one duty
> have we clearly understood: that we should hold fast—should en-
> dure. And we have held fast, so that, it may be, many centuries hence
> the world will look upon us and say: These people are of a race that
> knows not how to perish.... We are a testimony.
> For thus it is that we must abide in that Province where our fathers
> dwelt, living as they have lived, so to obey the unwritten command
> that once shaped itself in their hearts, that passed to ours, which we
> in turn must hand on to descendants innumerable: In this land of
> Quebec naught shall die and naught shall suffer change....[20]

To remain faithful to the voice of her ancestors, Maria Chapdelaine gives up her chance to follow Lorenzo Surprenant, who holds
out the temptations of the good life in the United States and, with
resignation, she accepts an offer of marriage from Eutrope Gagnon,
a humble French-Canadian peasant. The message of *Maria Chapdelaine* is, indeed, nothing but that of Maurice Barrès's *The Uprooted*
(*Les Déracinés*).

In a more explicit fashion, and with increased intensity, this message was to be taken up again, six years later, in that French-Canadian

[20] Louis Hémon, *Maria Chapdelaine* [1916], trans. W. H. Blake (New York,
1924), 281–83.

novel of "national energy" known as *The Call of the Blood* (*L'Appel de la race*).[21] Not only did its author try to set French-Canadians on guard against the danger of "uprooting" which threatened anyone who betrayed the national cause by marrying an English-Canadian (whether or not he was willing to convert to Catholicism didn't make any difference), but he eloquently took it upon himself to advocate an independent and sovereign Quebec whose name would be Laurentia.

However mediocre—when judged by literary standards—this "novel-cum-manifesto" nonetheless bore witness to a kind of evolution in the nationalistic thinking of French-Canadians. Although by no means rejecting the religious aspect of the French-Canadian identity, Lionel Groulx (a priest) implicitly recognized that this fact alone would hardly suffice, and that it was essential to recall to mind the cultural fact, if a genuine spirit of national survival was to be strongly affirmed. There was, to be sure, no question of subordinating religion to culture. However, according to Father Groulx, to be a French-Canadian was more than to be Catholic; it was to be Catholic and French-speaking.

That is why, although he proclaimed that Rome "gives masters of truth, those who provide rules for great minds, who propound the shining principles without which there can be no firm direction, no intangible foundations, no permanent order, no race assured of its goal," he also considered France as the "immortal mentor," and the French spirit "an incomparable master of clarity, order and finesse, the creator of the world's soundest and most humane civilization, the noblest expression of mental equilibrium and intellectual well-being." [22]

L'Appel de la race echoed with ancestral voices. "Father, I may say that it is on the tomb of my ancestors that my thought has fully matured; down in the old cemetery, I found my true French soul again," confesses Jules de Lantagnac, the hero of *L'Appel de la race*.[23] Whereas, in *Maria Chapdelaine* ancestral voices exhort the heroine to patience and passive resistance, in Lionel Groulx's novel they became much more insistent and invite immediate action. That is what Jules de Lantagnac finally realizes.

[21] L. Groulx, *L'Appel de la race* (Montreal, Bibliothèque de l'Action française, 1922). I quote from the Fides edition published in 1956.

[22] Quoted from J.-L. Roy, in *Maîtres chez nous. Dix ans d'Action française (1917–1927)* (Montreal, 1968), 45.

[23] Groulx, 107.

The son of a simple farmer, Jules had chosen, after his classical studies at a French-Canadian college, to study law at McGill University on the advice of a famous lawyer, George Blackwell. "In this environment, the young man finally lost what little remained to him of his French patriotism. Before long he convinced himself that superiority lay on the side with the largest numbers and the most money; he forgot the Latin ideal and the culture of France; he took on the arrogance of the truly anglicized.... Once admitted to the bar, and finding himself ill at ease among his own people, he set his sights on Ottawa." [24] It was there that he met the one who would soon become his wife, Maud Fletcher, a converted English-Canadian. They had four children who went to English Schools.

> All went well for him until the day when the desire to play a more important role welled up within his heart. It was on the eve of his 43rd birthday. No longer was wealth and fame in legal circles enough to sate his ambition nor his aspirations as a gentleman. He wanted to devote himself to some enterprise of vast proportions, to expand his scope of mind and his style of life. By nature too intelligent to enter politics without preparation, he went back to the books. Convinced that, in Canadian politics, superiority could belong only to the man with a full command of both official languages, he set about to relearn the language of his youth. He chose as French authors his former professors of political science. He read Frédéric Le Play, the Abbé de Tourville, La Tour du Pin, Charles Périn, Charles Gide, Charles Antoine, Count Albert de Mun and a few others. There he got his first shock. He was overwhelmed by these works; he was dazzled by the renewed contact with a kind of order, clarity, and spiritual distinction; it enchanted him. At the same moment, a man entered his life who was to exercise a profound influence: Lantagnac began to visit Father Fabien. Moreover, for some time the lawyer had been experiencing a vague feeling of malaise, the glowing nostalgic embers of a past he thought had been extinguished forever; it stirred him to the very essence of his being. Was he being duped by some illusive genie? He felt that when the love of his race took flight, a vast, barren wasteland had come sweeping into his heart. It seemed as if his very spirit had come unhinged, that his anglo-saxon ideology had begun to ring with the hollow echoes of a creed only half believed. At the same time, he began to have nightmarish thoughts with ominous rumblings of protestantism.[25]

That should suffice amply, I think, to set the tone of the "novel." As one can easily imagine, Jules de Lantagnac returns to the straight

[24] *Ibid.*, 99.
[25] *Ibid.*, 100.

and narrow, and he tries to bring his children with him. "I promised my ancestors that, in their memory, I would bring my children back," he says to Father Fabien.[26]

> "From their mother," continued Lantagnac, "my sons and daughters have received English blood; but through me they have something far more precious; the ancient blood of the Lantagnac courses through their veins, the Lantagnacs who came to New France, the Old World Lantagnacs of Monteil and of Grignan. Forty generations in all. I have sworn to myself. That is the family to which my children will belong! . . .
> "And I want to say something more: the Christian upbringing of my children concerns me above all else. My readings and my studies of late have convinced me that nothing is more significant than that profound affinity which ties the French race to Catholicism. No doubt that is why they call it the universal race. Rivarol wrote of the French language that its genius embraces an essential honesty. For my part, I would add only that this sense of honesty flows from the best Latin and Christian thinkers. I have therefore made up my mind: my children will not continue with their English Protestant training. If at all possible, I will bring them back to the lineage of their forefathers." [27]

Imbued with these freshly acquired convictions, Jules undertakes to reconvert his children to Catholicism and the French tradition in the atmosphere of the family home. Running for office on an independent ticket, he is soon elected as member for an Ottawa county. In a short time, he becomes one of the leading lights of the Franco-Catholic minority in Ontario; it is in this capacity that he prepares to deliver an impassioned speech against Regulation XVII which would abolish the teaching of French in Ontario schools.[28] Now it is Maud's turn to hear *l'appel de la race*. She warns Jules that she will leave him if he persists in his determination to speak for the Franco-Catholic minority. Not knowing which way to turn, Jules seeks counsel of Father Fabien. The priest reassures him without hesitation: patriotic duty comes first! If Maud leaves her husband, she alone will be responsible, affirms the director of conscience. Jules delivers his speech; Maud leaves him, taking with her the two children who have chosen to desert their father.

Despite the author's claims, *L'Appel de la race* was anything but a novel. It was, above all, a manifesto intended to sustain at a fever

26 *Ibid.*, 109.
27 *Ibid.*
28 See M. Wade, *French Canadians*, 608–708.

pitch French-Canadian nationalism; indeed the national fervor had not abated since the beginning of the century. The intransigent attitude, not to say the sheer ill-will displayed by the English-speaking community on the question of teaching French outside Quebec, had raised the hackles of all French Canadians. Their irritation was further exacerbated by the fact that conscription had been used to send them to defend a France whose language they were refused the right to speak anywhere outside of Quebec, and an England for which they nurtured feelings of steadily increasing hostility.[29]

Under such conditions, is it astonishing that French Canadians retrenched themselves within the confines of Quebec province? In truth, the dialectic of Father Groulx boils down to this: Since it is impossible for us to be French Canadians from coast to coast, let us therefore recognize as ours the only territory where we are allowed to be ourselves: "Laurentia." Was that not also the idea given voice by the editors of *L'Action française*, in the very same year as *L'Appel de la race* was published? "To be ourselves, absolutely ourselves, to constitute an independent French state as quickly as Providence will permit, such must henceforth be the motivating force behind all our aspirations, the eternal flame which must never be extinguished."[30]

Forty-six years later, René Levesque, leader of the Parti Québécois, would declare when calling for the political independence and national sovereignty of Quebec:

> We are *Québécois*.
> What that means first and foremost—and if need be, all that it means—is that we are attached to this one corner of the earth where we can be completely ourselves: this Quebec, the only place where we have the unmistakable feeling that "here we can be really at home."
> Being ourselves is essentially a matter of keeping and developing a personality that has survived for three and a half centuries.
> At the core of this personality is the fact that we speak French. Everything else depends on this one essential element and follows from it or leads us infallibly back to it. . . .
> This is how we differ from other men and especially from other North Americans with whom in all other areas we have so much in common. This basic "difference" we cannot surrender. That became impossible a long time ago.[31]

[29] *Ibid.*, 708–80. See also: H. Bourassa, *Hier, Aujourd'hui, Demain* (Montreal, 1916).
[30] *Action française*, Jan. 1922, 24.
[31] R. Levesque, *An Option for Quebec* (Toronto, 1968), 14–15.

Although the goal to be achieved is substantially the same in both instances, it nonetheless follows from premises which are quite different. There is no longer any question of invoking Providence, nor the good counsels of a Father Fabien; neither do we find a determination to be French. To wish to be a Québécois is to make a commitment to the here and now, and to live in it completely, without renouncing one's upbringing or cultural heritage. It is no longer a mere struggle "not to die" as Maria Chapdelaine would have it, but a struggle to live by facing squarely up to North American realities and accepting them. From this new attitude naturally follows the positive character of today's nationalistic thinking—and the new claims it makes. In my view, return to reality is the deeper meaning of the Quiet Revolution (in Quebec, even revolutions have to be quiet) which, for the last decade, has radically transformed the political, social, intellectual, and religious climate of Quebec.

The voice said to Maria Chapdelaine, "but in this land of Quebec nothing has changed. Nor shall anything change, for we are the pledge of it." "It has to change," echoed back the election slogan of Jean Lesage's liberal party which, swept into power in 1960, set the Quiet Revolution in motion. A short while later, another slogan appeared: "Masters in our own house." After having lain dormant beneath the ashes for more than a century, the fire which stirred the minds of 1820 burst forth again, more vigorous than ever before.

In fact, a short thirty years was sufficient to effect this radical transition which, as might be expected, finds itself mirrored in contemporary literature. Besides, it was inevitable that the closed, rigid society of yesteryear should finally open up, or else succumb to total irrelevance. What is truly astonishing is the ease and speed with which the movement of intellectual liberation and emancipation has gained momentum.

Published in March 1934, Jean-Charles Harvey's novel *Sackcloth for Banner* (*Les Demi-civilisés*) [32] bears witness to the initial efforts made to drag "these terribly domesticated people," slumbering away in "this haven of impersonality and deceit, where sanctioned views alone had held sway," out of their century-old state of lethargy.[33] With the obvious intention of exposing the intellectual inertia and the infectious hypocrisy of the petty bourgeoisie composed almost

---

[32] J.-C. Harvey, *Les Demi-civilisés* (Montreal, 1934). This novel has been translated by L. Barette, under the title: *Sackcloth for Banner* (Toronto, 1938). I quote from this translation.
[33] *Ibid.,* 93.

exclusively of "uprooted peasants," Harvey not only tore the veils away from taboo subjects, but he also denounced overtly the "counterfeiters."

In the very first paragraph of his novel, the hero, who prides himself on his supposedly mixed lineage, tells us with a great romantic flourish of his desire to live:

> I am Max Hubert. In my blood, the Norman strain mingles with that of the Highlander, the Marseillais and the Redskin. This hybrid mixture is the battlefield of explosive southern temperament, of the Norseman's ponderous passion, of earnest Scottish sentimentalism and of the adventurous instinct of the *Coureur des bois*. A nature built of levity and reflection, of cynicism and artlessness, of logic and contradiction. No practical judgment, the loftiest scorn for money and its worshippers. Apart from thought, beauty and love—these truly vital elements—nothing really matters to me.[34]

His mother expects him to become a priest, but he has other ideas; he prefers the warmth of feminity to the chill of celibacy. Imbued with idealism, Max sails forth into life, firmly decided to impose his self, to be himself. He quickly discovers that in a closed society where conformity reigns supreme, there is no place for the individual with a personality. A professor to whom he confides his desire for a career in teaching hastens to warn him: " 'I'll gladly recommend you,' he said. 'But, if you ever get in, beware of scoffing too much and being overly independent. All that might imply boldness of character, emancipation from certain principles is taboo at the university, guardian of tradition . . . and of truth.' " [35]

Shortly thereafter, encouraged by a friend, Max becomes a journalist. But—another shock—he finds that society will not tolerate the slightest deviation from conventional ideas. He had written an article "endeavouring to demonstrate that moral liberty is the corner stone of civilization, the underlying condition of the improvement of personality, the foundation of the individual's and, through him, of society's boundless progress." [36] After having submitted his article to a so-called independent newspaper, he sees it refused publication by the editor-in-chief who comments pithily:

> "I mean that you couldn't have set a deadlier trap in my paper's way, even had you tried. I refuse your article. Suppose our subscribers discovered that we harbour a young prig addicted to grammar and

[34] *Ibid.*, 3.
[35] *Ibid.*, 59.
[36] *Ibid.*, 59–60.

common sense and going to the unbecoming extreme of fostering original ideas? I imagine the clamour....

"Ideas, young man, obey the law of supply and demand. Has anyone asked you for your ideas? No? Then keep them. Begin by preparing a market for them, as a business man should always do when opening a territory for a new product.... Besides, you advocate principles which are too clear, simple and elementary to be understood and followed." [37]

Isolated in the midst of this "domesticated herd," Max takes stock of his rebellious nature: "More plainly than ever, I realized that I was a rebel. Whence my rebellion? From a refusal to disown my ego, that ego whose proportions expanded extravagantly when I took scornful or pitying stock of the intellectual inanities in my surroundings." [38]

There is no point in my insisting further on this propagandistic novel which, when all is said and done, has no value other than historical. Perhaps it might be worth adding, nonetheless, that *Sackcloth for Banner* was condemned by the archbishop of Quebec who forbade its reading, sale, or dissemination "on pain of mortal sin." Furthermore, the author's employers were pressured to let him go, in the hope that he would thus be obliged to make amends publicly.

Not only was Harvey a polemicist; he was also a precursor: he struggled to liberate his fellow countrymen from their moral and intellectual servitude by freeing the individual. He was one of the first to call for a breath of fresh air. A staunch nonconformist, Harvey tried hard to sustain this attitude throughout his life, for he struggled to be an authentic human being, in the best tradition of Gide's heroes. Thus, his scorn for counterfeit which, a few years before his death, moved him to denounce what he termed "colonialism of the mind":

Colonialism of the mind so dominates the field of arts and letters that our scribes, however unconsciously, turn their backs upon the marvellous Canadian and North-American reality which is theirs for the taking. We try to be French at any cost, and yet we are no longer Frenchmen. It seems to me that one can love and admire France without contracting a case of Francomania. [39]

Although they eventually won their battle by silencing the "traitor," right-thinking citizens and the apostles of a sterile, retrograde

[37] *Ibid.*, 60–61.
[38] *Ibid.*, 75.
[39] "Témoignage," in *Le roman canadien-français, Archives des lettres canadiennes*, III, p. 278.

nationalism felt themselves threatened all the same. A few years later, say the time it takes a generation to mature, they were menaced much more seriously, and the first call to retreat was sounded.

In any case, the censure of *Sackcloth for Banner* should not astonish us. A closed society, because it feels threatened with extinction if it shows a willingness to relate to the outside world and if it changes its traditional way of life, wants nothing to do with "glorification of the individual." Its sole preoccupation, its sole focus of attention is the "glorification of the race." Such a society willingly sacrifices the individual to the community for, in its view, the former exists only for the sake of the latter. Moreover, that is the reason why what is normally considered to be the unique concern of the individual and his conscience habitually presents itself, in Quebec, in political terms. The present analysis permits us, in my opinion, to better understand the two-pronged ideological question which has enjoyed, and which continues to enjoy currency in French Canada: should we recreate French Canadians as human beings, or human beings as French Canadians? [40]

Given this cultural context, it is easy to understand why *Boss of the River (Menaud, maître-draveur)* [41] would please the community to the same extent that *Sackcloth for Banner* had shocked it (without considering the fact that, from the literary point of view, the two works are not comparable). The kind of liberty that Max Hubert demanded was that of thought, of the individual being; the kind that Menaud wants to conquer is the liberty of his people. "He turned towards his companions who were struggling up behind him. He could see the whole history of his people in that struggle; he saw them crushed by the burden of their conquerors, as, like slaves, they pushed slowly through the lands which had once belonged to their ancestors." [42]

Max wants to impose his being individually; Menaud wants his people to do so collectively. Of course Menaud realizes that before he can liberate his fellows, he must himself be free. But the fact remains that this individual liberty is, in his view, nothing but a means of achieving the broader goal of freedom for the whole community.

---

[40] See Saint-Denys Garneau, *Journal* (Montreal, 1954), 205–10.

[41] F.-A. Savard, *Menaud, maître-draveur* (Quebec, 1937).

[42] Curiously enough, this passage was omitted from Alan Sullivan's translation of *Menaud, maître-draveur* (*Boss of the River*) (Toronto, 1947). On purpose?

... but could one thus spend existence, withdrawn within oneself, letting all around be stripped away without a protest, arguing that it had nothing to do with oneself?

No! that was not the method of one's fathers: from the very first when they were but a fistful they had tramped, paddled, month after month to establish their frontiers; had delegated to each of their sons the duty of maintaining hold on all the land they had so valiantly delimited.

[To defend only one's own possessions, to be concerned solely with what lay within one's fences, to turn a blind eye to the continual encroachments of the conqueror, all such egoism was a betrayal which condemned one to a future of servitude.] [43]

One of nature's free spirits, Menaud is incapable of fighting off the recurring call of liberty; he is of a breed "that the apportioned earth with its tillage and harvests, its cuffs and caresses, had not yet tamed." For him "the true life was that of the forest where one is everywhere at home; far better this than in houses where one choked: it was the mountain—there!—with its manifold retreats, its innumerable trails, all marked with reminders of their forerunners ... : it was there that valiant spirits burned the brightest: thence that freedom would come in a fierce torrent of anger, come like the Sinigolle in springtime." [44]

To possess! To increase! every other instinct was that of death! There was the command of the blood, the rule that rose from the soil, the whole soil that in this fine night of spring announced, "I belong to thee; by the right of the dead of whom I am the sacred monument, I belong to thee: by all the marks of ownership that for three hundred years thine own folk have carved in my body." [45]

"Race," "strangers have surrounded us ... they have taken into their hands most of the rule, they have gathered to themselves much of the wealth," "liberty," "ancestors," just so many *leitmotifs* which, from the beginning of the novel to the end, recur like an incantation. Menaud was bred on *Maria Chapdelaine* and, like Louis Hémon's heroine, he too hears the ancestral voices. These voices are a good deal more insistent here than in Hémon's work or even in Groulx's because, in their lyricism, they seek only to soften the heart and to stir the passions. They call for liberty and encourage revolt.

Menaud is not deaf to this new message; like a savior he turns to

[43] Savard, 109–10. The paragraph in brackets was omitted from the English translation.
[44] *Ibid.*, 14–15.
[45] *Ibid.*, 61.

his fellows and preaches to them. Alas! submissive and obedient, they are incapable of understanding. They will remain prisoners of the "thirty acres" of land they believe to be their own.

> ... then the old fellow began to vent against his own folk all that had accumulated in the worn pouch of his anger—"That bunch of pol- troons," he went on, "who in a common danger have no courage out- side their own back yards! That all should go to the strangers— mountain, field, wood—bah! what does it mean to misers, each crouching over his own board?
>
> "The past!—they smother their dead with fine words, but have given them no heed:—
>
> "Our heroes of old!—they imagine that in boasting about them, they become their rivals:—
>
> "The ancient domain!—they think themselves favoured with leave to exist there as slaves:—" [46]

Seeing his fellows falter, Menaud finds himself alone; his isolation soon gives way to madness. He wanders off into the forest, symbolic in its representation of freedom: "the ambition to protect the rights of others had reduced him to nothing more than an animal in the osiers. But someday he would start out—soon—very soon!" [47] Indeed he would, for there is Lucon, and Marie—Menaud's daughter—who have grasped the meaning of his words. Josime was right when he realized that Menaud's madness was not like another. "To me that sounds like a warning," he predicted.[48]

One year after the publication of *Boss of the River*, Ringuet de- picted, in *Thirty Acres* (*Trente arpents*), the disintegration of an essentially rural and agricultural society, an organism whose funda- mental social structures were the parish church and the family, the priest and the matriarch.[49] All these were the "voice of Quebec" for *Maria Chapdelaine*. *Thirty Acres* struck a new note of warning. The "country of Quebec" had begun to change; it would change even more with the relentless advance of urbanization. The conversion of an agrarian society into an industrial complex necessarily called all traditionally accepted values into question.[50] Then the war and the

---

[46] *Ibid.*, 79–80.

[47] *Ibid.*, 126.

[48] *Ibid.*, 131.

[49] Ringuet, *Trente arpents* (Paris, 1938). Translated by Felix and Dorothea Walter, *Thirty Acres* (Toronto, 1940).

[50] I briefly discussed this social transformation in "Le Québec à l'heure de sa dernière chance," *Culture*, March 1969, 1–19. See also my introduction to *Trentes arpents* (Montreal, 1972). For a study in depth, see: E. Hughes, *French Canada in Transition* (Chicago, 1943); H. Miner, *St. Denis. A*

conscription came to add fresh fuel to nationalistic flames which had never been allowed to die; nor was anyone more eager now than they had been in 1916 to go and get killed in the defense of England.

Nevertheless, the war was, for many, if not a solution, at least an opportunity for social mobility. Jean Lévesque knew how to take full advantage of it in *The Tin Flute (Bonheur d'Occasion)*.[51] For others, the war offered not only work but, in many cases, the possibility of chasing after a star. Basically, everyone was seeking escape. Whether one went to war or tried to climb "the mountain" as in *The Tin Flute*, or "the hill" from *The Town Below (Au pied de la pente douce* [52]), to join hands with the "rich" up top, the departure or the ascent always took on a symbolic dimension: it meant escape. Instead of undertaking the onerous task of changing one's real life circumstances (which would have presupposed at least a modicum of interest in them), everyone crowded his mind with thoughts of escape, by whatever means possible. It was still too early for individual revolt to be transmuted into collective revolution; but that was the course it was taking.[53] What Jean or Florentine in *The Tin Flute* would only have dared to think, their child would probably put into action some twenty years later, following the example of *The Man Who Was Diseased (Le Cassé)*,[54] or Hubert Aquin's characters. "Yesterday, children were dancing around the house. ... Today, they are men ... ready to take up guns in the street." [55]

The work of Roger Lemelin and of Gabrielle Roy is extremely significant, for it marks the beginnings of a period of demystification. The authors of *The Town Below* and *The Tin Flute* are not afraid to unmask the truth and stare it squarely in the face, the former with a good deal of wit and irony, the latter with sorrow and a profound sense of pity. Above all, they succeeded in creating living characters with which their readers could readily identify (something which was hardly the case with their predecessors). Thanks to

French-Canadian Parish (Chicago, 1939); M. Rioux and Y. Martin, *French-Canadian Society* (Toronto, 1964); and Wade, *French Canadians*.

[51] G. Roy, *Bonheur d'Occasion* (Paris, 1945). Translated by Hannah Josephson, *The Tin Flute* (Toronto, 1958).

[52] R. Lemelin, *Au pied de la pente douce* (Montreal, 1944). Translated by S. Putnam, *The Town Below* (New York, 1948).

[53] See: P. Maheu, "De la révolte à la révolution," *Parti Pris* 1 (Oct. 1963).

[54] J. Renaud, *Le Cassé* (Montreal, 1964).

[55] G. Gélinas, *Hier, les enfants dansaient* (Montreal, 1968). Translated by Marvor Moore, *Yesterday the Children Were Dancing* (Toronto, 1966). I have quoted N. Corbett's translation, however.

Lemelin and Roy, the French-Canadian common people acquired the right to speak up and make themselves heard. Awkwardly, to be sure, but people who have remained so long silent and oppressed could hardly be expected to express themselves otherwise; they had to understand the nature of their rebellion before they could talk about it; they had to know themselves before they could declare themselves.

It is perfectly obvious that yesterday's closed society did not open up spontaneously. Although the novels of Harvey, Savard, Ringuet, Lemelin, and Roy were, when seen in retrospect, just so many premonitory signs of a revolution, those who chanted the praises of traditional nationalism and the union of throne and altar were not exactly put to rout. In 1954, you could still read in a Canadian history textbook the words: "After your catechism, your history textbook ought to be the most treasured of all your possessions." [56] (Indeed, after reading this book, one is tempted to ask whether the author wasn't trying in fact to write a catechism.) "All things considered," wrote J.-C. Harvey, "you could hardly expect that a society upon which a form of moral castration had been perpetrated should abandon its prejudices and fears overnight." [57]

The very year that Borduas published his *Total Denial* (*Le Refus Global*), proclaiming "to the common people who cling to the cassocks where alone they may find faith, knowledge, truth, and national wealth, the people who have stood apart from the universal revolution of thought—so rife with risks and dangers," that "the multifaceted reign of terror was over" and in which he affirmed that "the assassination of the present and the future by the past has finally been put to an end," [58] that very year, I repeat, the government of the province of Quebec adopted the fleur de lys as its ensign. Together with the motto of the province: *Je me souviens* ("I have not forgotten"), the fleur de lys, a symbol of the Ancien Régime and the French monarchy, superbly captured the traditional ideology of survival. Two years later, in 1950, the archbishop of Montreal forbade the population to celebrate the centenary of Balzac's death because his books were still on the *Index*. This formal interdiction, it is worth emphasizing, was promulgated in the very same year as the

---

[56] Frères des écoles chrétiennes, *Mon pays* (Montreal, 1954), 7.

[57] Harvey, *Les Demi-civilisés*, 125.

[58] P.-E. Borduas, G. Gauvreau, B. Cormier, F. Sullivan, and F. Leduc, *Le Refus Global* (Quebec, 1948). In his *Histoire de la littérature canadienne-française* Tougas quotes from *Le Refus Global*. My reference is to Tougas, 282.

Cité Libre (the eloquently named periodical founded by Gérard Pelletier and Pierre Elliot Trudeau), one year after the famous asbestos strike which gave Quebec workers a keener appreciation of their own power, and the government an opportunity to display its anti-unionist bias and its total submission to the dictates of foreign financial interests.[59]

Nonetheless, the Quiet Revolution was rolling along under its own steam and could do nothing but gain momentum. In the course of the last twenty years, a particular set of circumstances running all the way from the introduction of television in Quebec in 1952 (if Quebec refused to open its eyes to the world, the world would open them up anyway) right down to General De Gaulle's famous declaration of 1967: "Long live free Quebec," not to mention the establishment of publishing houses such as L'Héxagone (1954), magazines such as *Liberté* (1958) and *Parti Pris* (1963)—1963 also marks the beginning of terrorist activities in Quebec—all contributed to the radical transformation of the political and intellectual climate of the province. This transformation, also mirrored in the creation of a Department of Cultural Affairs (1961) and a Department of Education (1964), is found in every aspect of life in Quebec, most particularly in the literary domain. Adrien Thério did not fail to take this fact into account when he wrote in 1962:

> ... in this country where nothing is supposed to change, the heroes of our novels seem to want to change everything. It is not simply a question of revolt. Rather, it is a matter of destruction. Indeed, in at least half of these novels, we get a very definite feeling that not only does the younger generation fail to understand the ones which preceded, but seems to have made up its mind to humiliate them, to make them suffer for what they have done, and to detach itself from them as completely as it can. This younger generation feels the weight of the past burning and chafing at its shoulders. The young turn against accepted modes of education, against class and religious prejudice, against the hypocrisy of empty rituals, against our jansenist surroundings in which genuine love never really did make its home, against the puritanical mentality which would dash to bits the most innocent expressions of sexual tenderness. Our young heroes ... have just come to realize that, somewhere along the way, they were tricked.[60]

A literature of destruction? Yes, to be sure, the expression suits the mainstream of Quebec literature in the sixties to perfection.

[59] See: Pierre-Elliot Trudeau, *La Grève de l'amiante* (Montreal, 1956).
[60] Adrien Thério, "De la révolte à la destruction," *Livres et auteurs canadiens* (Montreal, 1961), 27.

What was exceptional yesterday and caused a great hue and cry has become today's stock-in-trade and receives a noisy ovation. That is what generally happens when, at long last, a closed society opens its doors; yesterday's taboos are well on their way to becoming the commonplaces of today.

Destruction, demystification, and, one might add: catharsis, for that is indeed what it has been. Whether, like Bessette and Ferron, they had recourse to irony and satire, whether they used caricature following the example of Marie-Claire Blais in *A Season in the Life of Emmanuel* (*Une saison dans la vie d'Emmanuel*), of Ducharme, or of Roch Carrier, whether they gave us an autobiography like that of Claire Martin, contemporary novelists seem incapable of resting until they have denounced traditional society.[61] Moreover, they are not the only ones to work along these lines, because we also find poets and playwrights eager to expose the sickness of the Québécois and to try and exorcise it.

What exactly is this sickness? Whether one explains it in philosophical or political terms, whether one speaks of alienation or colonization, one cannot avoid reaching this conclusion: the sickness of Quebec is a quasi-existential difficulty of being, of imposing one's true self. For more than a century, French Canadians have used every ounce of their energy just to survive, forgetting alas! that not to die is not necessarily synonymous with the will to live. French Canadians have endured life rather than lived it; they put themselves in the service of a hoary past, instead of harnessing the past for their own ends, making themselves masters of the present, where alone the future can be shaped. The narrator of *Le Nez qui voque* declares, "old books are made to be left alone. Many times have I opened old books, and just as many times I have found their pages blank; whenever I open them, a strong, musty odor assails my nostrils and takes hold of my very soul." [62]

To destroy a mythical past is, at the same time, to destroy a false identity.

[61] Gérard Bessette, *La Bagarre* (Montreal, 1958); *Le libraire* (Montreal 1960); *Les Pédagogues* (Montreal 1961); Jacques Ferron, *Contes du pays incertain* (Montreal, 1962); *Contes anglais et autres* (Montreal, 1964); *Papa Boss* (Montreal, 1966); *Le Ciel de Québec* (Montreal, 1969); M.-C. Blais, *Une Saison dans la vie d'Emmanuel* (Montreal, 1965); Réjean Ducharme, *L'Avalée des Avalés* (Paris, 1966); *Le Nez qui voque* (Paris, 1967); Roch Carrier, *Jolis deuils* (Montreal, 1964); *La Guerre, Yes Sir!* (Montreal, 1968); Claire Martin, *Dans un gant de fer* (Montreal, 1965).

[62] Ducharme, *Le Nez qui voque*, p. 103. [This title amounts to a pun based on équivoquer, or to make mistakes.]

I live, I exist beginning with a daily death
I live my death to its last breath gasp . . . day after day
I live with an incurable wound . . . with a boundless
ravaged tenderness . . . with a love changed into hate
I live, I die for a country . . . a dagger plunged through
the heart of its promises, of its passions
and my grief is repulsive to me . . . I cannot speak of it
I am a man ashamed to be a man.
I am a man whose fellows have been violated every one
who can no longer be rational and coherent before other men
till he has cast out the vile abomination . . . of being
French-Canadian.[63]

This will to self-destruction does not correspond, however, to a desire for national suicide. Quite the contrary. Taking his cue from the phoenix, the French-Canadian writer self-destructs only to emerge from the ashes stronger and more optimistic than before, for he believes himself to be, at long last, in possession of an identity. If he turns upon his French-Canadian identity, so rigid under the paralyzing mantle of a history which can do nothing but recall the consequences of a crushing defeat and rationalize his impotence, it is only in order to better affirm his Quebec identity, ripe with future promise and the only prospect he desires to envisage henceforth. "There has never been a French-Canadian literature for the simple reason that there has never been a French Canada. We have never been anything but a few colonists scattered, in isolated outposts, over an immense territory occupied and exploited by foreigners. Those few voices that have spoken out screamed our non-existence to the whole world. Our literature must call itself *québécoise* or it will not call itself anything." [64] A simple play on words? Surely not.

> There are a few of us who reject the term "Canadian writers"; we consider ourselves as Quebec writers and want to be recognized as such.
> . . . Quebec is opposed to Canada just as one fact contrasts with another. Here, the fact is exclusion, contradiction, conflict. We know, because we have lived it daily, that it is not possible for us to be at once Québécois and Canadians; those two conditions negate each other in practice. To affirm ourselves as Québécois means, all in all, to decide our own fate like human beings who belong to a society, to a culture, to a homeland. That is why the terms "Canadians" and "French-Canadians" appear unacceptable to us; they are the very

[63] Paul Chamberland, "Canadiens français," *Les Lettres nouvelles*, Dec. 1966–Jan. 1967, 77.
[64] L. Girouard, "Notre littérature de colonie," *Parti Pris*, Dec. 1963, 30. The issue of Jan. 1965 may be considered as the group's manifesto.

symbols of equivocation and duplicity. Canada is not our country.

... To be *Canadien* really means to be *Canadian;* and to set our-selves the "noble task of building a strong, united Canada" is in itself a tacit invitation to reduce what sets us apart from the others to a mere residue of folklore, local color of the kind tourists love. Thus, there is nothing astonishing in the fact that Quebec which, as a prov-ince, enjoys a certain number of legitimate constitutional powers, should become the magnetic force which keeps French-Canadian life from desintegrating; there is nothing surprising in the fact that this style of life is identified today, in keeping with its decisive orienta-tion, with its birthplace, its maternal home. Our country, from this day hence, is Quebec.[65]

Although undeniably radical, this *prise de position* is no less sig-nificant because it typifies the kind of nationalism which inspires ever-increasing numbers of young writers in contemporary Quebec. Several of them, it goes without saying, have actively joined the ranks of the militant separatists, waiting impatiently for the "pro-chain épisode." [66]

On the literary level, this new attitude of national self-awareness lies at the very source of a creative vitality unprecedented in the short history of letters in Quebec. One would make no mistake in speaking today of a literature which is bubbling over with life.[67]

There is not a single Quebec writer who does not feel, in the very midst of his activity, the terrible process of cultural impoverishment which has victimized his people. For it is his material, the language, which has been damaged. There are a number of us who can no longer tolerate the dishonesty of serenely constructing a work of literature within a linguistic and cultural environment which in fact negates it.[68]

With less clarity perhaps than poetry, the novel takes the measure of this collective effort to give birth to a new type of man.

In this regard, the efforts of novelists of the group *Parti Pris* [69] is particularly revealing. It is they, in effect, who have undertaken to reveal the Quebec man to himself, just as he is—in his full beauty and his total ugliness. (Perhaps it would be more exact to say: just as they see him; or better still: just as they might wish to see him.) On the pretext of realism, and in order to lay bare his alienation,

---

[65] P. Chamberland, "Mise au point," *Les Lettres nouvelles*, Dec. 1966–Jan. 1967, 210–11.

[66] Hubert Aquin, *Prochain Épisode* (Montreal, 1965).

[67] G. Bessette, *Une littérature en ébullition* (Montreal, 1968).

[68] Chamberland, "Canadiens français," 213.

[69] See: Jacques Allard, "Le roman des années 1960 à 1968," *Europe*, Feb.–March 1969, 41–51.

they do not hesitate to use *joual*,[70] the symbol of his cultural deprivation and the mirror of his shame. "To write badly is to descend into
the fires of a hellish way of life, to rescue the Eurydice of our Quebec humanity," [71] says Paul Chamberland. G. Godin, for his part,
explains that the decision to write badly is a decision to portray the
truth. "Good French is the future we all desire for Quebec, but *joual*
is its present." [72] But he adds this qualification:

> To be sure, we do not want *joual* as our "classical language." Far
> from it. Some think that we want to make a language of *joual*. That
> is not so. Those who refuse to make use of *joual* really don't under-
> stand the problem. Of course, in writing magazine and newspapers
> articles, we must use as impeccable a French as we can. *Joual* is noth-
> ing but a literary and stylistic option for novels and short stories. In
> daily usage, we ought to get rid of it. Individually, we have all ob-
> served that this vernacular characterizes the lower classes. By deline-
> ating this characteristic inferiority of a large part of the population,
> we hope that the majority will pull itself together and demand of
> its leaders some true linguistic leadership.[73]

"A literary option," says Godin; I would prefer to speak of a political option. As a matter of fact, in the strictly literary sense, such
an option would finally lead only to an impasse. In reality, to write
joual is to choose a new form of alienation, voluntarily refusing to
face the world, and exigencies of a supranational character. (It would
be quite different, of course, if Quebec had a population of say, a
hundred million, and wielded an uncontested economic supremacy.
But if that were the case, the question wouldn't even crop up.)
Hubert Aquin has understood the weakness of such a "literary option." [74]

The writers of *Parti Pris*, both novelists and poets, have nonetheless made the most important contributions to Quebec's renewed
national consciousness. The work of a Girouard, that of a Renaud, of
a Major, of a Jasmin,[75] all testify to an unprecedented effort to em-

---

[70] Deriving by regular assimilatory channels from standard French *cheval*
(horse), the word *joual—šval > žval > žwal*—is the byword for "badly spoken
Canadian French." It is much broader than "slang" or "argot" and may suggest
a rather rudimentary culture on the part of its user.

[71] P. Chamberland, "Dire ce que je suis," *Parti Pris*, Jan. 1965, 36–37.

[72] G. Godin, "Le joual et nous," *Parti Pris*, Jan. 1965, 19.

[73] G. Godin, "Joual, langue morte ou vivante?" *Le Carabin*, 26 Nov. 1965, 10.

[74] Hubert Aquin, "Littérature et aliénation," *Mosaic*, Fall 1968, 48.

[75] Laurent Girouard, *La Ville inhumaine* (Montreal, 1964); Jacques Renaud,
Le Cassé (Montreal, 1964); André Major, *Le Cabochon* (Montreal, 1964);
Claude Jasmin, *Ethel et le terroriste* (Montreal, 1964); *Pleure pas Germaine*
(Montreal, 1965).

brace the human condition as seen by the Quebec man, and to give him a voice which is undeniably his own. To them goes the credit for having depicted his alienation. To know how to describe things accurately, isn't that an indication one is beginning to master them, to control them? Isn't that one of the first signs of self-liberation?

By doing violence to language and syntax, the novelists of *Parti Pris* have also played the role of harbingers. Gilles Marcotte was probably thinking of some of them when he wrote: "The most significant works from French Canada are those which scorch the earth as they pass, quickly producing a state of sheer desolation, of pure rebirth, where man is challenged to recreate his most fundamental values." [76]

Among the values the writer is "challenged to recreate" is his language. Whether poet or novelist, the young Quebec writer is on the way to rediscovering the power of words. He has just attained the "age of spoken words"; [77] like a child, he delights in reinventing old words, in giving them new meanings. He plays with them, as Réjean Ducharme does so expertly. With Hubert Aquin, Jean Basile, Gérard Bessette, Marie-Claire Blais, Jacques Godbout—Quebec novelists are better and better approximating the style which will give them a name and confer international renown. It would hardly be exaggerating to say that the history of the Quebec novel of the sixties may be succinctly characterized as "a conquest of language, and a victory over words." To convince oneself that this is true, one has only to estimate the distance separating Gérard Bessette's *Not for Every Eye* (1960) from his *Incubation* (1965). As Hubert Aquin has pointed out: "when everything in a society begins to burst open at the seams, it is perhaps predictable and even normal that literature should simultaneously do the same, freeing itself from all formal and social constraints." [78]

Harder and harder to find in 1970 is the Quebec writer who wavers between "the desire to be overhere as far as the substance of the work is concerned, and the need to be overthere for the style." [79]

---

[76] Gilles Marcotte, "Traduit du français," *Les Lettres nouvelles,* Dec. 1966–Jan. 1967, 83.

[77] See: G.-A. Vachon, "L'ère du silence et l'âge de la parole," *Études françaises,* Aug. 1967, 309–21; R. Robidoux, "L'autonomie d'une petite littérature," *Mosaic,* April 1968.

[78] H. Aquin, "Littérature et aliénation," 52.

[79] Jean-Paul Pinsonneault, in *Témoignages des romanciers canadiens-français, Archives des lettres canadiennes,* 3:345. Incidentally, these "témoignages" are interesting from several different viewpoints. They permit us, among other

For he has realized that style and substance are one and the same thing, just as he has understood that, in order to be complete, his being must be entirely indigenous.

Quebec writers do not wish to be French any more that they want to be American (I mean, in the restricted sense of that word). Nor do they aspire to be the "Frenchmen" of America, as General de Gaulle would have it. Just as the Ducharmes and the Godbouts [80] are quick to denounce the glittering attractions of a golden culture bearing the words "made in U. S. A.," so too are they prompt to question the legitimacy of a culture imported directly from France. What would be the point in substituting one kind of cultural and intellectual colonialism for another? The evolution of Jacques Godbout's thinking seems to me, in this respect, to be most revealing. In a statement made to an investigation in 1963, he said:

> We participate without regret in American civilization; we drag our asses around in automobiles "made in U. S. A." I don't see why we should hesitate to borrow from French culture as if it were, and because it is our own.
>   Every student ought to learn that the French literature of Canada begins with Villon; and that no hiatus—not that of the French Revolution, nor even that of Father Combes—will ever suffice to justify our isolationism.[81]

"No hiatus...."; nonetheless, it was only one year later, in 1964, when Jacques Godbout wrote, in his preface to *Knife on the Table* (*Le couteau sur la table*):

> This novel is not a French novel about Canadians but a Canadian novel written in French. This is probably why critics in Canada and France wrote that the French edition of *Knife on the Table* marked another rupture too: the end of a "French literature in America," the beginning of an American literature in French.[82]

"To be ourselves in French." In *Salut Galarneau!*, his most recent novel, Godbout comes a good deal closer to this ideal. The experiences which Galarneau lives through are significant beyond a shadow of a doubt. It is by the very act of writing that this character (in which many Québécois will recognize themselves) reaches a state

---

things, to measure the gap that separates the present generation of Quebec novelists from their predecessors.

[80] See: Ducharme, *Le Nez qui voque*, and Jacques Godbout, *Salut Galarneau!* (Paris, 1967).

[81] J. Godbout, "Témoignage," 373.

[82] J. Godbout, *Le couteau sur la table* (Paris, 1965).

of complete lucidity. *Salut Galarneau!* is in itself a conquest of style and words. Desirous of greater insight and self-awareness, Galarneau shuts himself up in his house and there, alienated from the world, he finishes his book. It is not until the task is completed that he finally consents to leave his retreat. With a symbolic gesture, he takes the manuscript into town so that "all the Joneses of the world may read it." Finally, with full and complete understanding of himself, Galarneau no longer fears to enter relationships with others.

This seems to me to be the destiny of Quebec. As long as the quest for national identity continues, Quebec will not really be able to relate to the world. But the day will come, and I look forward to it with keen anticipation, when we will be able to tell all mankind who and what we are. We will say it in French, but in a French enriched with American insight—just as others have begun to speak, using French as the vehicle for their vibrant African experience.

BIBLIOGRAPHY

[In order to help the reader anxious to acquire a better knowledge of the French-Canadian society and its literature, we have tried in our footnotes to give as complete a list of bibliographical references as possible within the frame of an essay of this nature. Therefore, the following bibliography is solely a complementary list.

Perhaps it should also be pointed out that, in spite of the importance of nationalism in French-Canadian literature, no extensive study has yet been written on that topic. However, many aspects have been analyzed so far. We hope to assist in making the first step toward the required synthesis in a book to be published in the near future.]

Drolet, A. *Bibliographie du roman canadien-française (1900–1950)*. Quebec: Presses de l'Université Laval, 1955.

Dulong, G. *Bibliographie linguistique du Canada français*. Quebec: Presses de l'Université Laval, 1966. The best reference book on questions related to the French language spoken in French-speaking Canada.

Garigue, P. *A Bibliographical Introduction to the Study of French Canada*. Montreal: McGill University, 1956. Very useful in spite of some inaccuracies.

Hare, J. E. *Bibliographie du roman canadien-français (1837–1962)* in *Le roman canadien-français*. Montreal: Fides, 1964. Pp. 375–456. The most complete bibliography of the French-Canadian novel.

Hayne, D., and Tiral, D. M. *Bibliographie critique du roman canadien-français (1837–1900)*. Toronto: University of Toronto Press, 1967. Certainly the best bibliography and the most accurate one for the nineteenth-century French-Canadian novel.

Martin, G. *Bibliographie sommaire du Canada français (1854–1954)*. Quebec: Secrétariat de la province de Québec, 1954.

Story, N. *The Oxford Companion to Canadian History and Literature*. Toronto: Oxford University Press, 1967. One of the most resourceful "companions" to Canadian studies.

Tanghe, R. *Bibliography of Canadian Bibliographies*. Toronto: University of Toronto Press, 1960.

BOOKS RELATED TO THE TOPIC

Angers, P. *Problème de culture au Canada français*. Montreal: Beauchemin, 1959.

L'Avenir du peuple canadien-français. Quebec: Ed. Ferland, 1965.

Corbett, E. M. *Quebec Confronts Canada*. Baltimore: Johns Hopkins Press, 1967.

Dansereau, P. *Contradictions et biculture*. Montreal: Editions du Jour, 1964.

Dumont, F., and Martin, Y. (eds.) *Situation de la recherche sur le Canada français*. Quebec: Presses de l'Université Laval, 1962.

Ethier-Blais, J. *Signets II*. Montreal: Cercle du livre de France, 1967. This book contains important essays dealing with various aspects of French-Canadian cultural nationalism. Blais is one of the most ardent advocates of the French-Canadians' *French* identity.

Falardeau, J.-C. (ed.) *Essais sur le Québec contemporain*. Quebec: Presses de l'Université Laval, 1953.

Grand'Maison, J. *Nationalisme et religion*. Montreal: Beauchemin, 1970. A very interesting book on the real meaning of Quebec's nationalism of today.

Grandpré, P. de. *Dix ans de vie littéraire au Canada français*. Montreal: Beauchemin, 1966.

Jones, R. *Community in Crisis: French-Canadian Nationalism in Perspective*. Toronto: McClelland and Stewart, 1967.

Lemire, M. *Les grands thèmes nationalistes du roman historique canadien-français*. Quebec: Les Presses de l'Université Laval, 1970.

Morton, W. L. *The Canadian Identity*. Toronto: University of Toronto Press, 1961.

Porter, J. *The Vertical Mosaic*. Toronto: University of Toronto Press, 1965.

Quinn, H. F. *The Union Nationale: A Study in Quebec Nationalism*. Toronto: University of Toronto Press, 1963.

Rapport de la Commission royale d'enquête sur l'enseignement dans la Province de Québec. 5 vols. Quebec: Imprimeur de la Reine, 1966.

Report of the Royal Commission on Bilingualism and Biculturalism. Ottawa: Queen's Printer, 1966. Five volumes have been published so far. Certainly the most extensive study on the problems and implications of bilingualism and biculturalism in Canada.

Rioux, M., and Martin, Y. (eds.). *French-Canadian Society*. Toronto: McClelland and Stewart, 1964. Highly recommended introduction to French Canada.

Robert, G. *Aspects de la littérature québécoise.* Montreal: Beauchemin, 1970. Interesting chapters on nationalism and literature in Quebec.

Roy, C. *Pour conserver notre héritage français.* Montreal: Beauchemin, 1937.

Rumilly, R. *Histoire de la province de Québec.* 38 vols. Montreal: Fides, 1941–69.

———. *Le problème national des Canadiens français.* Montreal: Fides, 1961.

Russell, P. (ed.). *Nationalism in Canada.* Toronto: McGraw-Hill, 1966.

Scott, F., and Oliver, M. *Quebec States Her Case.* Toronto: Macmillan, 1964.

Sylvestre, G. (ed.). *Structures sociales du Canada français.* Quebec: Presses de l'Université Laval, 1966.

Wade, M. (ed.). *Canadian Dualism.* Toronto: University of Toronto Press, 1960.

THESES AND DISSERTATIONS

Barcelo, F. "Situation du romancier canadien-français contemporain." Thesis, Université de Montréal, 1963.

Dorsinville, M. "A Comparative Analysis of the Protest Novel in American and French-Canadian Literature." Thesis, University of Sherbrooke, 1968.

Plastre, G. "Une constante de la littérature canadienne-française: le thème de la survivance française dans le roman canadien." Thesis, Université de Montréal, 1954.

Rogers, S. J. "The Philosophical and Literary Background of French-Canadian Nationalism: Garneau to Groulx." Thesis, University of Western Ontario, 1958.

Schoderboeck, A. "The Element of Frustration in the French-Canadian Novel (1940–1954)." Diss. University of Western Ontario, 1958.

Shek, B. Z. "Aspects of Social Realism in the French-Canadian Novel, 1944–1964." Diss. University of Toronto, 1968.

The Third World

THE EMERGING NATIONAL IDENTITIES

III

Contributors to Part III

H. Ernest Lewald, who received his Ph.D. from the University of Minnesota, has taught at Georgia Tech, Carleton College, and Purdue and is presently professor of Romance languages and comparative literature at the University of Tennessee. He has edited several books dealing with Argentine literature and culture: *Diez cuentistas argentinas, Buenos Aires: retrato de una sociedad a traves de su literatura, Argentina: analisis y autoanalisis,* and *Escritores platenses* (with Professor George Smith of the University of California at Santa Barbara). His articles have appeared in such journals as *Books Abroad, Carleton Miscellany, Hispania, Modern Language Journal, Revista Hispanica Moderna, Southern Review,* and *Sur.* The essay in this volume is based on the one appearing in the Symposium on Nationalism featured by *Books Abroad,* Spring 1971.

Seymour Menton holds an M.A. from the Universidad Nacional Autónoma de México and a Ph.D. in Spanish from New York University. He has taught at Dartmouth, the University of Kansas, and the University of San Carlos in Guatemala and was chairman of the Department of Spanish and Portuguese at the University of California, Irvine (1965–1970). A former editor of *Hispania* (1965–1968), he is contributing editor in charge of Central America and the Caribbean for the *Handbook of Latin American Studies.* He was the 1971 president of the American Association of Teachers of Spanish and Portuguese. His list of books includes *Saga de México, Historia crítica de la novela guatemalteca, El cuento hispano-americano,* and *El cuento costarricense.* Among his many articles are "In Search of a Nation: The Twentieth-Century Spanish American Novel" and "La novela de la Revolución Cubana."

GILA RAMRAS-RAUCH teaches Hebrew and world literature at Bar-Ilan University in Israel. She has recently spent two years on a leave of absence during which she taught the modern Hebrew novel in relation to the theme of cultural nationalism at Hofstra and Indiana universities. She is the author of numerous articles, in Hebrew as well as English, that have appeared in Israeli and American publications; the articles show her broad range of interests, from Henry James to Franz Kafka and Lawrence Ferlinghetti. Her international background and multiple cultural experiences have motivated her to analyze the matter of cultural identity within a new state and the Israeli writer's reaction to the cultural dynamics of merging an exiled and native way of life.

SALIH J. ALTOMA holds a B.A. degree from the University of Baghdad and an Ed.D. from Harvard. He has taught Arabic language and literature in Baghdad and, as visiting professor, at Harvard, Princeton, and Columbia. For several years he manned the position of cultural attaché at the Iraqi Embassy in Washington, D. C. Dr. Altoma presently teaches at the University of Indiana in Bloomington. His interests in the fields of literature and education have led to a number of publications, and his text *Modern Arabic Literature,* published by the Ministry of Education in Iraq, has had seven editions thus far. His most recent efforts reveal a keen interest in tracing the impact of social forces, especially in the political field, on the writer in that complex cultural unit known as the Arab World.

GERMAINE BRÉE, agrégée, University of Paris, has been academically active on more campuses in Europe, the United States, and Australia than could be listed easily here. She has been lecturer, guest speaker, recipient of honorary degrees, and, of course, professor. Formerly head of the Department of Romance Languages at New York University, since 1960 she has held the position of professor at the Institute for Research in the Humanities at the University of Wisconsin. Her publications, editorial activities, and research projects are equally impressive. Her studies on such key literary figures as Marcel Proust, André Gide, and Albert Camus and a number of translated editions of outstanding French writers, from Flaubert to Camus, have received critical acclaim. Brée's literary as well as cultural versatility has lately brought her into contact with the francophone literature of former French colonies—literature produced in French by the native Africans in their respective new republics—that has reflected a nationalistic search for identity expressed in terms of language and thought patterns belonging to a European civilization. As a French woman born in Algeria, Germaine Brée is in a unique position to evaluate such literature.

Argentine Literature: National
or European?

H. ERNEST LEWALD

The pitfalls of writing in toto on what is known as Latin America have tripped many a well-intentioned analyst, especially if he looked at his subject with European or North American eyes. Such famous travelers as Count Keyserling, Waldo Frank, and even Spaniards like Miguel Delibes have not done too well in extracting a Latin American essence that would be acceptable to its inhabitants. Instead of one Latin American culture we must consider a Cuban, Mexican, or Chilean one and expect that the artist, writer, or composer will draw from and in turn project a *criollo*, or regional, spirit that forces him to define his particular position within the multiple possibilities of the continent. One could hardly exaggerate the importance of an Indian heritage as well as the influence of the Mexican Revolution on the Mexican writer or artist from 1910 up to the present. At the same time the Indian problem in countries like Guatemala or Ecuador is running an entirely different course, inasmuch as the lack of a pro-Indian revolution has preserved a semi-feudal class structure that in turn prompts the local writer to take issue with his conflicting social scene. *Mister President*, Miguel Angel Asturias's finest novel that was instrumental in bringing the Nobel Prize to this Guatemalan author, could not have been based on contemporary Mexican reality. By the same token, the social consciousness of Castro's Cuba is reflected in the prose of the young writers of this island and must be studied within a unique local context. Obviously, Argentine literature should be examined in reference to this nation's peculiar past and present.

Cultural norms have done their share in playing tricks on the history of many a nation, for better or for worse, as human folly goes. It was not the intention of the Spanish conquerors to till the land upon their arrival in the New World, and they fiercely exterminated the natives of the Caribbean when the latter failed to cooperate. The ensuing importation of African slaves solved the Spaniards' labor problem; it also laid the historical foundation of an African cultural presence in modern Brazil and the West Indies.

By the same token, the huge region comprising the Argentina and Uruguay of today had been totally ignored by the *conquistadores* and colonial administrators in subsequent centuries because the endless plains and rolling grasslands held no promise of precious metals to be mined and showed no large native population that could have been exploited. The pampas were unbelievably empty except for small groups of primitive nomadic Indians and wild ostriches. It followed that the viceroyship of the River Plate did not become established until 1776 and was barely a reality before being abolished a few decades later when the Spanish empire was coming apart at the seams. The Argentine *criollos* encountered little difficulty in declaring their independence from Spain in 1810 and in opening the River Plate to maritime traffic that eliminated the tortuous trade route over the Andes from Panama, a route imposed by the crown in accordance with the interest of the Peruvian viceroyship. But the Argentine *criollos* also embarked on a chaotic and long-lasting civil war that was not truly resolved until the 1870s. Argentina experienced what the Chilean critic Torres Rioseco termed "the romantic upheaval" which clashed with the federalists (*unitarios*), thus creating the decisive struggle over the destiny of Argentina as a modern nation. The losers were the gauchos, those defenders of an autonomous existence who were ruled by a primitive spirit rooted in the ways of the pampas. The policy of their president opponent, Sarmiento, to fertilize the pampas with gaucho blood and to impose a European civilization through the schoolhouse and the bookstore sets the stage for the final act in Argentina's quest to become a modern nation: the landing of millions of Europeans. After 1880 the lifeless pampas and especially the River Plate region became animated with Italians, Spaniards, East Europeans, and even quantities of Syrians and Lebanese. The British proceeded to build a net of railroads and huge terminals that resembled Victoria Station in London, the Italians produced electric power, and the Germans brought their streetcars. Economically integrated into the British Commonwealth, ethnically white and culturally European, the young nation made its final break with indigenous America.

For historian James R. Scobie, the essence of European Argentina is concentrated in what he calls the city-state: greater Buenos Aires with its eight million people, its skyscrapers, subways, docks, factories, Parisian boulevards, sidewalk cafes, the Colon Opera House, and the stylized architecture of Baron Hausmann's Paris.[1] Yet on a cultural level the emerging city-state lacked one essential ingredient for its national survival: that of a proper identity; and no one was more aware of this lack than the writer who by trade had to make the choice of either fashioning a *criollo* literature or echoing European models.

Here, then, begins the search for the spirit of *argentinidad*, which took on larger dimensions as the twentieth century progressed. The hunters for an Argentine essence found but traces on the wind-swept pampas where rested the blanched bones of the last gaucho. Nevertheless, the gaucho, side by side with the liberator San Martín and other historical heroes, today gallops across millions of television screens, part of a wholesale fabrication of symbols and myths that seem necessary to create an Argentine tradition and a national conscience in an amorphous mass society. *Martin Fierro* (1872 and 1879), the gaucho epic by José Hernandez, has become the Argentine *Odyssey*, although it dramatizes the fallacy of a romantic gaucho existence outside of organized society. Martin Fierro, defeated by a hostile nature and not so noble savages in the frontierland south of Buenos Aires, must finally return to make his peace with a Sarmiento-oriented Argentina. Yet, his modern, urbanized admirers feel the need to equate Martin Fierro with the romanticized outsider who doubles as an Argentine myth.

Martin Fierro also became a focal point for the Argentine man of letters. After all, the Argentine intellectual sat in his apartment in Buenos Aires, his back to the ocean, looking at the land from the wrong end of his telescope. Brought up on the best products of European literature and fed on European esthetic and idealistic traditions, he scanned a local *tabula rasa*. As the essays of Scalabrini Ortiz and Eduardo Mallea clearly indicate, the Atlantic is still a very efficient conductor of cultural currents whereas the pampas are not. However, in the twentieth century the Argentine writer clearly visualizes the task of fashioning a literature tied to the land in spite

[1] *Argentina: A City and a Nation* (New York, 1964).

of a superior European heritage; he is, after all, the guardian of a unique culture that remains largely invisible to the average member of modern Argentina's mass society. This uniqueness naturally would be interpreted differently by the individual writer, but it inevitably has to fluctuate between the poles of Europeanism and nativism.

Perhaps the fame of Ricardo Rojas as "dean of Argentine letters" is justified in the light of his role as the initiator of an Argentine identity in the field of literature. In his collections of essays, *The Nationalist Restitution* (1909), *Argentinidad* (1916), and *Eurindia* (1924), he looked for an easy synthesis of what he called "exotismo" and "indianismo," meaning a European and American heritage. What he failed to investigate was the nature of his "indianismo"—Argentina had no Toltec, Maya, or Quechua civilizations to draw from and the regional culture patterns were European. Rojas's sentimental mystique, to quote Professor Martin Stabb in his excellent study *Argentina's Quest for Identity*, left a powerful impact on several important writers who shared his urge to turn away from the city and gaze at the visible and invisible pampas.[2] One could easily name Carlos Alberto Erro, Eduardo Mallea, and Ezequiel Martínez Estrada as writers influenced by Rojas.

Erro, today fairly much eclipsed by the other two, tried to conjure up some telluric forces belonging to earlier Indian life in his *Measure of criollismo (Medida de criollismo)* (1929) and hoped to assimilate these in the national character.[3]

Mallea, the distant but conscious relative of Sarmiento, also tried his hand at Argentine historicity, rejecting visible signs when they conflicted with the invisible Argentina of his idealized remembrances. In his most prominent book of essays, *History of an Argentine Passion (Historia de una pasion argentina)* (1937), Mallea talks of creating a spiritual territory based on his "ethical land." Aloof and aristocratic, Mallea strongly feels that those who let themselves be attracted to the magnetism of technology or an easy materialism "will be bad Argentines; partly because their fathers seemed to have lost already the consciousness of being a true Argentine."[4] In defining their opposite, he draws up a composite picture that bears a certain resemblance to Martin Fierro: "silent, without resentment ... hospitable, generous, disinterested, a friend of nature, simple,

---

[2] *In Quest of Identity: Patterns in the Spanish American Essay of Ideas, 1890–1960* (Chapel Hill, N. C., 1967), 147.

[3] *Ibid.*, 163.

[4] Fifth ed. (Buenos Aires, 1951), 192.

virile, just...." [5] Such an individual understands that one needs more than logic "to comprehend the obscure level of life of an Argentine province and to sense instinctively the natural humanity of provincial gestures...in the midst of a timeless and growing space, in the form of an endless plain, inundated by a dense collective feeling...." [6]

Similarly, Ezequiel Martínez Estrada in *An X-ray of the Pampas* (*La radiografía de la pampa*) (1933) laments the fictitious personality of the Argentine collective character that has lost all contact with the soul of the nation. This Rousseau-like idealism made him reject what he termed the rapaciousness of the Spanish conquerors as well as the money-hungry immigrant of recent times. His deep mistrust of the bourgeois mind and the capitalistic state led him to the idealistic postulates of a Marxism that by now has been crushed by a bureaucratic machinery. Martínez Estrada's brand of ideology prompted a search for a communal spirit quite divorced from any political structure. His treatise on *Martín Fierro* established the gaucho figure as a noble counterpart to the onrushing millions of Europeans ready to pounce upon the virgin land and violate its essence in their greed.

Martínez Estrada's mystic vision left its mark on the younger writers. The most distinguished voice among them is that of H. A. Murena, outstanding novelist and highly original writer of essays who sees his mentor as the cultivator of ontological instead of sociological resources. Thus he coldly rejects all literary symbolization that does not stem from an ontological experience and condemns the writer who makes use of nationalistic figures like the never-vanishing gaucho instead of drawing from contemporary national life forces. For Murena the creation of a nonexperienced past impoverishes the writer's ontological horizon, since he believes true art to be the result of a personal and vital experience, a bridge between the present and the creative impulse. [7] Turning to the cultural role of the writer, Murena bitterly scorns his tradition-hunting for esthetic purposes as something totally artificial. He attributes Argentine nationalism to the lack of an Argentine past; but he also realizes that the time for an organic integration with the land has passed because present-day mass society does not offer its members a common ground to be shared. Murena sees no possibility of an Argentine spirit of brother-

[5] *Ibid.*
[6] *Ibid.*, 93.
[7] *El pecado original de América* (Buenos Aires, 1965), 67 and 74.

hood: "If there is one common denominator, it must be an economic one: money!" Here Murena obviously echoes Martínez Estrada's pessimistic voice in the wilderness.

It profits little to consider the shoutings of the populist and Peronist writers or even the present-day leftist critics who are eager to substitute the rather cosmopolitan level of Argentine fiction with a revolutionary one that would break the "European umbilical cord" in order to draw from an American consciousness and even a pre-Colombian inspiration.[8] Argentina possesses little of the former and none of the latter commodity.

Ernesto Sábato, distinguished literary figure and recognized spokesman for the new generation of Argentine intellectuals, found it relatively simple to reject this political intrusion into a cultural and literary matter.[9] He refused, however, to exclude the existence of an Argentine ontology or its coexistence with the overwhelming presence of European literary thought and techniques.

The whole question of European versus a national literature has found a very original and complex expression in the writings of Jorge Luis Borges, undoubtedly the outstanding literary figure of Argentina and perhaps of the continent in this century. Amazingly enough, his international fame rests largely on a few dozen short stories such as "Tlön, Uqbar, and Orbis Tertius" or "The Babylonian Library." Argentine critics found it fairly easy to tire of what he himself had called "the esthetics of intelligence" and which was transposed into a highly original form of fiction that could well seem esoteric to the average reader. For the committed young Argentines, Borges's labyrinthic formulation of man's universal condition represents a metaphysical exercise; and they accuse him of having turned his back to Argentine reality, of not understanding Peronism, and of having lost an Argentine consciousness.

But Borges's knowledge of literature is too vast and his mental processes are too keen to allow himself to play at a continued and slightly malicious game of dialectics with his readers, to paraphrase the Argentine critic Anderson Imbert.[10] Significantly enough, a number of Argentine critics and writers have made the discovery of at least "two" Borges, one of them fairly unknown to his international public; in fact, a part of the lengthy Festschrift dedicated to him

[8] See, for instance, Pedro Orgambide's *Yo, argentino* (Buenos Aires, 1968), 166–67.
[9] *El escritor y sus fantasmas* (Buenos Aires, 1964), 31–32 and 38.
[10] *History of Latin American Literature* (Detroit, 1963), 482.

and published in French by the Parisian magazine *L'Herne* deals with essays on "the 'two' Borges" written by some of the best Argentine men of letters.[11] Always original, Borges had ironically questioned the doppelgänger motif within himself several years before the publication of *L'Herne* in a dialogue with himself entitled *Borges and I* (1960).

While the "other" Borges appears as an elusive figure not always antithetical to the labyrinth-maker and habitué of the *Thousand and One Nights*, his creative awareness seems clearly connected to an Argentine reality. In "Borges and the Destiny of our National Fiction" Ernesto Sábato sums up the two halves of Borges's essence: one, the manipulator of metaphysical games and hedonistic exercises; and the other, the recreator of the melancholy *porteño* suburb of 1900, the old rustic spirit of manly loyalty and *criollo* courage. Sábato, son of Italian immigrants, strongly disagrees with the statement that "personne n'a moins patrie que Borges," and points to the *criollo* traits in Borges that are identifiable in his mannerisms, an elegant lassitude under the disguise of humbleness, his studied disdain of technical matters, a stoic attitude borrowed from his rural forefathers, and speech patterns that reveal the *criollo viejo*.[12]

Since the beginning of his literary career Borges has consistently refashioned an Argentine past out of a mosaic of personal and vicarious remembrances. At his childhood residence in Adrogué near Buenos Aires the proximity of the pampas left an air of solitude in the forlorn streets, and time must have flowed slowly enough to include at least a recent past. Anderson Imbert did well to observe that in Borges, metaphysics and lyricism are one and the same thing.[13] The most recognized poems of his early volumes, *The Fervor of Buenos Aires* (*El fervor de Buenos Aires*) (1923) and *The San Martin Notebook* (*Cuaderno San Martín*) (1929), are rooted in the metaphysics of the *arrabal porteño*, the city suburb around the turn of the century. The titles are indicative of his mood: "Arrabal," "Unknown Street," "The Guitar," "The Fields at Dusk," or "To the Memory of Colonel Francisco Borges (1833–1874)." The tone is appropriately simple and the imagery tied to the visual range of his childhood:

[11] This number of *L'Herne* was edited by De Roux in 1964 in Paris. Some of the titles are "Les deux Borges" by Ernesto Sábato; "Les deux Borges" by Manuel Durán; "Les Masques de Borges" by Federico Peltzer; and an interview entitled "Les deux Borges" by Nestor Ibarra.

[12] *El escritor y sus fantasmas*, 248–51.

[13] *History of Latin American Literature*, 481.

Mi patria es un latido de guitarra,
unos retratos y una vieja espada,
la oración evidente del sauzal en los atardecerer.

Jactancia de juventud

(My homeland lies in the throbbing guitar,
Some family portraits and an old sword,
And in the prayer of a willow tree's late afternoon.) [14]

Youthful Arrogance

His poem "Dulcia Linquimos Arva" carries a preface, that of "the final *criollo*" who recounts his forefathers with saga-like insistence:

Una amistad hicieron mis abuelos
con esta lejanía
y conquistaron la intimidad de la Pampa.
. . . .
Fueron soldados y estancieros
. . . .
Uno peleó contra los godos,
otro en el Paraguay cansó su espada . . . .

(Soldiers and cattlemen were my forefathers
As they made friends with the horizon
and conquered the essence of the pampas
. . . .
One battled the Gothic warriors
and another wore out his sword in Paraguay . . . .)

But the poem ends on a wistful note, so habitual in Borges's poetry: the realization that he is destined to recollect a remote past through the power of evocation induced by the nostalgic *arrabal* childhood. The last verses are:

Soy un pueblero y ya no sé de esas cosas,
Soy hombre de ciudad, de barrio, de calle:
los tranvías lejanos me ayudan la tristeza
Con esa queja larga que sueltan en las tardes.

(But I'm a townsman and no longer know the past,
a city dweller, in a suburb, on a street
where distant trolley cars voice my deep sadness
in a long whine that overtakes the afternoons.)

The poet's bridge to the pampas and their magical power to materialize an heroic age remain then in the melancholy suburbs of the big city, suburbs still populated with the *orilleros* and *cuchilleros* of 1900 whose epic quality of courage fascinated the precocious reader

[14] The translations into English from Borges's poetry are mine.

of Lewis Carroll and the diligent pupil at a Swiss *lycée*. It cannot be a mere caprice on Borges's part to have busied himself with a number of essays dealing with such subjects as the Argentine language (*El idioma de los argentinos*) (1928); Evaristo Carriego (1930), a sentimental poet of the *arrabal* popular around 1900; Leopoldo Lugones, the author of *The Gaucho Wars*; and the epic *Martín Fierro*, written by a distant relative, José Hernández. Even at the height of his "European" period, some of his most enduring stories express the zeitgeist of Evaristo Carriego's *arrabal*. *The Man from the Pink Corner* (*El hombre de la esquina rosada*) (1935) narrates the ritual of courage, blood, and death in an *arrabal* setting, a ritual that Borges felt compelled to echo in several of his latest stories that make up *Brodie's Report* (*El informe de Brodie*) (1970).

His best story, according to himself, still is *The South* (*El sur*) (1952).[15] In this largely autobiographical piece, we find death complementing a yearning for an epic style of life. Groping blindly in a labyrinth of causality, the protagonist Dahlmann has an accident complicated by a blood infection, suffers through an operation, and travels south for a convalescence in the land of his *criollo*-Germanic forefathers; but Dahlmann is forced by a strange series of circumstances to get off the train in the middle of the pampas and finally to fight a duel under an ominous but open sky. Invited to interpret his story, Borges said:

> When the man is killed, he's not really killed. He died in the hospital, and although that was a dream, a kind of wishful thinking, that was the kind of death he would have liked to have—in the Pampas with a knife in his hand—being stabbed to death. That was what he was looking forward to all the time.[16]

It is not surprising, then, that Borges's "cult of courage" coincides with the hero motif of Germanic mythology, and that Borges should continue to be professor of Old Norse and Anglo-Saxon poetry at the University of Buenos Aires, establishing a paradox to his "universalist" personality, a paradox that could only take place in Argentina, according to Guillermo Ara in his analysis of Borges the man and the writer.[17]

Next to Borges, Eduardo Mallea emerged as the leading Argentine prose writer of the 1930s and 1940s. Curiously enough, there are a

---

[15] "Borges on Borges," an interview with Richard Stern, *The American Scholar* (1969), 456.

[16] *Ibid.*

[17] *Los argentinos y la literatura nacional* (Buenos Aires, 1966), 139.

number of striking parallels in their careers. Both were born at the turn of the century, both are *criollos viejos*, both are steeped in a European literary and cultural tradition and have traveled abroad, both have spent most of their lives moving around the cafes, bookstores, and streets of Buenos Aires and at one time holed up in a waterfront hotel to collaborate on a translation of *The Dubliners* into Spanish; and finally, both have dreamed of a heroic mode that most certainly transcends their existence in the midst of the endless masses of people that swarm through the most Parisian of all Latin American cities.

Over the last decades, Mallea has managed to maintain a well-paced flow of essays, novels, and stories that share such constants as the quest for the spirit of the land, the symbolization of the sterility of modern urban life, the need to re-establish a meaningful level of understanding among his main characters, and the selection of protagonists belonging to an educated elite whose intellect and sensitivity are prerequisites to attaining the almost mystical illumination that is needed to enter Mallea's promised land: the invisible Argentina.

In one of his earliest and most durable volumes, a collection of novelettes and stories entitled *The City Next to the Motionless River* (*La ciudad junto al río inmóvil*) (1936), Mallea conjures up the spirit of an invisible Argentina emanating from the "ethical land." This spirit represents the only salvation for those trapped in the nightmarish city of cement, neon signs, and gasoline fumes where alienated and rootless human beings communicate only their heavy silence, waiting for the day when "the people of Argentina will undergo a rebirth ... from the snow-capped Andes down to Fireland ...." [18] The main characters in *The City Next to the Motionless River* reflect Mallea's existential anguish and alienated condition; most have traveled or studied in Europe and return to Argentina to busy themselves with some artistic or intellectual pursuit without being able to find a meaningful purpose in life. In the story called "Conversation" Mallea's typical husband and wife face each other in the cafes, bars, and restaurants of Buenos Aires—eating, drinking, reading newspapers, and exchanging small talk until one of them cries out in despair: "If I could only find a way to dedicate myself to something." [19] But there is no cause and no chance for a heroic stand, only introspection and self-analysis since Mallea does not allow his characters to be

[18] Preface to *La ciudad junto al río inmóvil*, 3rd ed. (Buenos Aires, 1954), 12.
[19] *Ibid.*, 132.

socially committed. In the story "The Immaturity of Solves" the protagonist is a young man who shares the elegant apartment of an artist and who leads a most comfortable but empty existence. Unable to fully return the love Cristina Ruiz, his companion, offers, he decides to leave her and follow a strange mandate coming from the land, an obscure compulsion that prompts him to divest himself of his urbane shell and European education in order to look for his own origin on the wind-swept pampas.[20]

The Bay of Silence (La bahía del silencio) (1940), perhaps his most successful novel, symbolizes Mallea's Argentine quest and complements it with a "European experience" that allows for the needed confrontation of Argentine and Continental culture. Admittedly the author picked a most Spenglerian moment to visit the Old World. Unfortunately, however, he did not avoid the bait that trapped such nationalistic writers as Raúl Scalabrini Ortiz or Pedro Orgambide, namely, the temptation to reject what the Austrian *Schriftsteller* Hugo von Hofmannsthal had seen as the sum total of a European cultural heritage in favor of postulating a national culture emerging from the *tabula rasa* of the pampas. Thus Martin Tregua, the protagonist of *The Bay of Silence*, proclaims after returning from his European experience: "I have reduced my life to its most elementary level. I only meet with very simple people now. Every day I am getting closer to the silent heart of my country."[21]

The silence of the bay like the silence of the pampas marks the beginning of a creative impulse, the critic Valentín de Pedro tells us; and Mallea's subsequent novels only perpetuate the personal crisis that he bared in the largely autobiographical *History of an Argentine Passion* and that forced him to drain his lifeblood into literary testimonials.[22] His main characters remain shut within their hermetic shells. Agata and Nicanor Cruz in *All Green Shall Perish (Todo verdor percerá)* (1941) agonize within their solitude; Chaves in the novel carrying the same name (1953) embodies an "innate" goodness and strength that he cannot communicate since his "Argentine condition" exists only on the intuitive level. In *The Ship of Ice (La barca de hielo)* (1967) Mallea, not unlike Borges, resurrects family ghosts that lived by the cult of courage and transposes them to the milieu of Buenos Aires around 1900 where a new Chaves—

---

[20] *Ibid.*, 84–91 *passim.*

[21] Second ed. (Buenos Aires, 1945), 584.

[22] "In Search of the Spirit of Our Land," *Nosotros,* 2nd ser., 55: 252–53 and 258.

apparently Mallea's father—appears as the silent spirit of the land.

Quoting from the short-lived but highly influential literary magazine of the 1920s, *Martin Fierro*, the Argentine critic Graciela de
Sola restates the obvious when writing that River Plate literature,
following a nationalistic vogue, acquired a double sickness: the
gaucho and the *arrabal*.[23] Leopoldo Marechal, indirect heir of the
Martin Fierro group, satirized Borges's *arrabal* as well as Mallea's
"ethical land" in his novel *Adán Buenosayres* (1949). However, he
also establishes a personal interpretation of Argentina's destiny
through the odyssey of the Argentine Adam and Adam's archetypal
initiation into the different social and historical worlds that coexist
in and around the River Plate metropolis. Begun in Paris around
1930 and completed only twenty years later, *Adán Buenosayres* is
technically and thematically an overly ambitious and experimental
work and has been resting in the critics' purgatory for a number of
years. No doubt Marechal's association with the Peronist movement
from 1945 to 1955 has done a great deal to tarnish his image with
the literary "establishment." Noé Jitrik, one of the promising
younger critics, judges Marechal quite harshly, alleging that he
"longs for the ancient forms of European expression and laments
their absence in Argentina" while at the same time "the falsification
of our national personality made him an 'Argentine in waiting.'"[24]
Other critics have been kinder. De Sola believes that Marechal uses
the emotive mode to treat the great question of Argentine cultural
identity, in contrast to Mallea who intellectualized on this question
from within his hermetic shell.[25] Adam's archetypal journal is meant
to discover realities that would feed a collective Argentine spirit
instead of an individual imagination. That is why Marechal presents
an intentional caricature of Borges under the disguise of the half-
blind Pereda who hunts for the "newly urbanized yet chemically
pure gaucho" around the city dump and who ecstatically listens to a
gaucho record made for an English department store in Buenos Aires
until his companions accuse him of mental masturbation.[26] Unlike
Borges or Mallea, Marechal possesses a strong populist strain that
reappears in *The Banquet for Severo Arcángelo* (1965), a bizarre

---

[23] "La novela de Latinoamerica: 'Adán Buenosayres,'" *Claves de 'Adán
Buenosayres'* (Mendoza, 1966), 60.

[24] "'Adán Buenosayres': la novela de Marechal," *Contorno* (1955), 42.

[25] "La novela de Latinoamerica," 57.

[26] *Adán Buenosayres* (Buenos Aires, 1965), 132-33.

allegory that includes Argentine social and political dimensions and points to his measure of realism.

In 1961 appeared a lengthy novel, Ernesto Sábato's *About Heroes and Graves (Sobre héroes y tumbas)*, whose continued success has by now made the author an artistic spokesman for a generation that on an average is thirty years younger than he. This success is quite understandable considering that the present-day university student or intellectual reader, who is by and large the descendant of Italian, Spanish, or Jewish immigrants, feels little love for the *criollo viejo* modality and sympathizes with Sábato, the son of simple Italian millers and the challenger of Borges's leadership on the Argentine literary scene.[27]

Following somewhat in Marechal's footsteps, Sábato manipulates mythical themes and independent fictional segments that converge in an amorphous novelistic structure: early Civil War episodes, a subterranean Baudelairean city, the decay of a patrician family, and the prophecy of the common man's era. Alejandra and Fernando belong to the Olmos family, an Argentine House of Atreus that is duly punished for its arrogance, incest, and lack of social awareness. Fernando succumbs to his own chaotic nightmare. Alejandra perishes with her father in a self-willed funeral pyre. Martin, somewhat of an Argentine Parsifal figure who loved Alejandra, decides to leave the city after her tragic death. We see him last as he is urinating onto the silent pampas, next to the truck driver Bucich, the son of humble immigrants, on their way to Patagonia, Argentina's last virgin land. In his closing scene Sábato is able to fuse two contradictory elements: the populist urban man complete with his city slang and lowclass manners, and the lure of the southland where *pampero* winds purify the mind and instill what Martínez Estrada called the primordial spirit of America. It is Bucich, the artless, proletarian giant, who at the end of the novel tells Martin: "Boy, this country of ours is great!" Sábato chose to distill the complexities of his novelistic texture into the wisdom of the *vox populi*.[28]

It is interesting to observe how other South Americans view the Argentine search for a national literature. The Venezuelan critic

[27] In his book of essays, *El uno y el universo*, Sábato called Borges, among other things, a "latinist of porteño slang . . . concocting a mixture of Asia Minor and Palermo, of Chesterton and Evaristo Carriego, of Kafka and Martín Fierro . . ." (p. 27).

[28] See Angela B. Dellepiane's appraisal of Bucich as a key figure in this novel in her excellent study *Ernesto Sábato, el hombre y su obra* (New York, 1968).

Jimenes-Grullos cast an angry look at the River Plate area filled with European immigrants and dismissed Sábato's work as a typical product of a European intellectual who undergoes a bourgeois crisis of conscience filled with bits of Freudianism and some existential anguish. For the Venezuelan, Argentine literary expression has so far been shut off from "indigenous" America since it is being created in a "European tower of Babel" where Sábato presumably occupies one of the top floors.[29]

Since the appearance of *About Heroes and Graves*, Sábato has not produced another novel; however, quite a few women writers, comfortably housed in the "tower of Babel," have explored the question of Argentinism. The most successful novelist in this group is Silvina Bullrich, whose books *A Bourgeois Family* (*Los burgueses*) (1964) and *Tomorrow I'll Say Stop!* (*Mañana digo basta*) (1968) became best-sellers. A member of the upper class and a descendant of *criollos viejos*, Silvina Bullrich knows how to breathe life into the characters that animate her own world and to assure the middle-class reader that he too could live up to their vices, follies, and stupidities. In her presentation of the Argentine oligarchy the novelist focuses on an unavoidable theme, that of the responsibility of the elite to lead the nation on a moral, intellectual, and esthetic level, a responsibility envisioned much earlier by the Uruguayan modernist Rodó in *Ariel* and Ortega y Gasset in *Invertebrate Spain*.[30] Unfortunately Miss Bullrich's Argentine upper class shows no more backbone than Ortega's Spanish counterpart. Moral decay, political corruption, and a lack of civic qualities pervade the highest levels of the nation's public officialdom in *The Saviors of the Country* (*Los salvadores de la patria*) (1965), a most prophetic novel that foreshadowed the military coup of 1968 as a consequence of the intrigues and false vision of the "saviors."

One of the best treatments of myth and reality in the post-Peronist society appeared in Marta Lynch's *To the Winner* (*Al vencedor*) (1965). Technically complex and thematically ambitious, this novel merges such divergent elements as a picaresque urban environment, surrealistic flashbacks, and an archetypally conceived protagonist. Benjamín Díaz, a farm boy who has just finished his military service

---

[29] *Anti-Sábato* (Maracaibo, Venezuela, 1968), 88–89 and 94.

[30] See H. Ernest Lewald's *Argentina: análisis y autoanálisis* (Buenos Aires, 1969), 187–91 on the question of class spirit and social orientation.

in Buenos Aires, represents a rustic Adán Buenosayres who possesses the qualities of Mallea's ideal Argentine: he is honest, generous, manly, selfless, and detached. The picaresque episodes serve to bring him into contact with a gallery of rogues, fools, prostitutes, and zealots, all part of a corrupt and opportunistic society that emerged from the Peronist experience armed with the cynical philosophy of a populism that made allowances for cheating the system and the individual within it. Benjamín, like his famous Mexican forerunner Ixca Cienfuegos in Carlos Fuentes's well-known novel *Where the Air Is Clear*, remains aloof and uncontaminated by all who want to appropriate or misuse his blessed state. His companion Tulio quite obviously symbolizes a Jungean opposite: shrewd, repulsive, effeminate, immoral, and useless. He is a caricature of a blond *gringo*, a parasite who clings to Benjamín even as the latter returns to his home in a far-away province. Benjamín's final act is rather unexpected and perhaps should be interpreted as an archetypal "act of faith." In stabbing his stepmother who emasculated his father and in a Circe-like manner reduced those around her to subhuman beings, Benjamín has removed the Argentine Terrible Mother in a sacrifice worthy of a mythical hero.

On a more sophisticated level, Sara Gallardo has also taken up the theme of "the return of the native," attaching it to the historical task of the elite as postulated by Ortega y Gasset. Actually, Carmen Gándara had earlier utilized this theme and placed it on the unavoidable axis Argentina-Europe in some of her best stories. In her novelette *La Habitada* (1948) the expatriate landowner Felipe finally listens to the voice of the distant pampas and returns from abroad to put his knowledge and talents at the disposition of the land and its people. In *The Greyhounds* (*Los galgos, los galgos*) (1968) Sara Gallardo varies the basic plot to punish the main character, Julian, for having alienated himself from the land and ignoring the loyalty of its rustic inhabitants. Julian goes the way of all good Argentines and makes his pilgrimage to Paris, where he interestingly enough feels more incomprehension toward other Latin Americans than toward Europeans. Yet, in carrying his European experience to its ultimate step, that of physical and spiritual love, he cannot transcend his unique brand of Argentine hermeticism. In the midst of his love affairs Julian's mind reverts to "a translucid sky that sheds beauty, a serene sky that lights up the streets of the old *arrabal* in the South end of Buenos Aires near the old Constitution railroad station, mysterious, transparent, metaphysical. ...." [31] Julian returns to his native land in defeat, a stranger and almost a traitor to his people.

After fifty years, a cycle is completed, and one can almost see blind Borges turning a corner and reciting the verses of *Arrabal* that he published in 1921:

> esta ciudad que yo creí mi pasado
> es mi porvenir, mi presente;
> los años que he vivido en Europa son ilusorios,
> yo he estado siempre (y estaré) en Buenos Aires.

> (The city, seemingly an echo from my past,
> Is but my present and my future;
> The years I've spent in Europe were a dream,
> I have always been and shall remain in Buenos Aires.)

BIBLIOGRAPHY

Anderson Imbert, Enrique. *History of Latin American Literature.* Detroit: Wayne State University Press, 1963.

Ara, Guillermo. *Los argentinos y la literatura nacional.* Buenos Aires: Huemul, 1966.

Borges, Jorge Luis. *Cuaderno San Martín.* Buenos Aires: Proa, 1929.

———. *Evaristo Carriego.* Buenos Aires: Gleizner, 1930.

———. *El fervor de Buenos Aires.* Buenos Aires: Imprenta Serantes, 1923.

———. *Ficciones.* Buenos Aires: Sur, 1944. This collection includes the story "El sur."

———. *El hacedor.* Buenos Aires: Emecé, 1960, Contains "Borges y el otro."

———. *El idioma de los argentinos.* Buenos Aires: Gleizner, 1928.

———. *El informe de Brodie.* Buenos Aires: Emecé, 1970.

Bullrich, Silvina. *Los burgueses.* Buenos Aires: Sudamericana, 1964.

———. *Mañana digo basta.* Buenos Aires: Sudamericana, 1968.

———. *Los salvadores de la patria.* Buenos Aires: Sudamericana, 1965.

Dellepiane, Angela. *Ernesto Sábato, el hombre y su obra.* New York: Las Americas Publishing Company, 1968.

De Roux, Dominique (ed.). Festschrift number dedicated to Jorge Luis Borges. *L'Herne.* Paris, 1964.

Erro, Carlos Alberto. *Medida de criollismo.* Buenos Aires: Porter Hermanos, 1929.

Gallardo, Sara. *Los galgos, los galgos.* Buenos Aires: Sudamericana, 1968.

Gandara, Carmen. "La habitada." *El lugar del diablo.* Buenos Aires: Sudamericana, 1948.

Hernández, José. *Martín Fierro.* Imprenta de la Pampa, 1872.

———. *La vuelta de Martín Fierro.* 1879.

Jimenes-Grullos, Juan Isidro. *Anti-Sábato.* Maracaibo, Venezuela: Universidad de Zulia, 1968.

---

[31] (Buenos Aires, 1968), 213.

Jitrik, Noé. "Adán Buenosayres: la novela de Marechal." *Contorno*, 1955.

Keyserling, Count Hermann. *Meditaciones sudamericanas.* Madrid, Espase-Calpe, 1933.

Lewald, H. Ernest (ed.). *Argentina: análisis y autoanálisis.* Buenos Aires: Sudamericana, 1969.

Lynch, Marta. *Al vencedor.* Buenos Aires: Losada, 1965.

Mallea, Eduardo. *La bahía del silencio.* Buenos Aires: Sudamericana, 1940.

———. *La barca de hielo.* Buenos Aires: Sudamericana, 1967.

———. *Chaves.* Buenos Aires: Losada, 1953.

———. *La ciudad junto al río inmóvil.* Buenos Aires: Sur, 1936.

———. *Historia de una pasión argentina.* Buenos Aires: Sur, 1937.

———. *Todo verdor perecerá.* Buenos Aires: Espasa-Calpe, 1941.

Marechal, Leopoldo. *Adán Buenosayres.* Buenos Aires: Sudamericana, 1949; rpt. 1965.

———. *El banquete de Severo Arcángelo.* Buenos Aires: Sudamericana, 1965.

———. (ed.). *Claves de 'Adán Buenosayres'.* Mendoza, Argentina: Azor, 1966. Contains essays by Julio Cortázar, G. de Sola, and Adolfo Prieto on the novel by Marechal.

Martínez Estrada, Ezequiel. *La cabeza de Goliat.* 2nd ed. Buenos Aires: Emecé, 1947.

———. *Diferencias y semejanzas entre los países de la América Latina.* México: Escuela Nacional de Ciencias Políticas, 1962.

———. *La radiografía de la pampa.* Buenos Aires: Babel, 1933.

Murena, H. A. *El nombre secreto.* Caracas: Monte Avila Editores, 1969.

———. *El pecado original de América.* Buenos Aires: Sudamericana, 1965.

Ocampo, Victoria. *El viajero y una de sus sombras (Keyserling en mis memorias).* Buenos Aires: Sudamericana, 1951.

Onega, Gladys. *La inmigración en la literatura argentina.* Buenos Aires: Piloto, 1967.

Orgambide, Pedro. *Yo, argentino.* Buenos Aires: José Alvarez Editor, 1968.

Rodó, José Enrique. *Ariel.* Montevideo: Imprenta Dornaleche y Reyes, 1900.

Rojas, Ricardo. *Argentinidad.* Buenos Aires: J. Roldán, 1922.

———. *Eurindia.* Buenos Aires: J. Roldán, 1924.

Sábato, Ernesto. *El escritor y sus fantasmas.* Buenos Aires: M. Aguilar, 1964.

———. *Sobre héroes y tumbas.* Buenos Aires: Fabril Financiera, 1961.

———. *El uno y la multitud.* Buenos Aires: Sudamericana, 1945.

Scalabrini Ortiz, Raúl. *El hombre que está solo y espera.* Buenos Aires: Plus Ultra, 1931.

Scobie, James R. *Argentina: A City and a Nation.* New York: Oxford University Press, 1964.

Stabb, Martin S. "Argentina's Quest for Identity." *In Quest of Identity: Patterns in the Spanish American Essay of Ideas, 1890–1960.* Chapel Hill: University of North Carolina Press, 1967.

Torres Rioseco, Arturo. "The Romantic Upheaval." *The Epic of Latin American Literature.* 2nd ed. Berkeley: University of California, 1959.

The Cuban Novel of the Revolution: A Decade of Growing National Consciousness

SEYMOUR MENTON

A study of nineteenth- and twentieth-century Latin America literature reveals a rather high correlation between national consciousness and novelistic production. Nowhere is this better seen
than in Cuba. Prior to the Castro Revolution, Cuba's main contribution to Spanish American literature had been the essays and poetry of
José Martí; the poetry of José María Heredia, Gertrudis Gómez de
Avellaneda, Julián del Casal, and Nicolás Guillén; the short stories
of Hernández Catá and Lino Novás Calvo; and the novels of Gertrudis Avellaneda and Cirilo Villaverde in the nineteenth century
and those of Carlos Loveira, Enrique Labrador Ruiz, and Alejo Carpentier in the twentieth century. Of the novelists, only Carpentier
is of continental stature. By contrast, since the triumph of the Revolution in January 1959, Cubans have published well over fifty novels
and in addition to Carpentier's *Explosion in a Cathedral* (*El siglo de
las luces*) (1962), works by at least three other authors—Cabrera
Infante, Severo Sarduy, and Lezama Lima—have received international acclaim.

Although this phenomenon might have developed as a spontaneous
result of the Revolution, it has been strongly abetted by the avowed
policy of the revolutionary government to make Cuba the cultural
center of all Latin America. To this end, large editions of both
Cuban and Latin American works have been published; annual prizes
in the novel, the short story, the essay, poetry, and the theater have
been periodically awarded by international juries to Cubans and non-

Cubans; the editorial committee of the well-known journal *Casa de las Américas* has included such outstanding authors and critics as the Argentine Julio Cortázar, the Uruguayan Mario Benedetti, the Peruvian Mario Vargas Llosa, and the Mexican Emmanuel Carballo; recent issues of this journal have devoted sections to the new literature of Colombia, Venezuela, Chile, Uruguay, and El Salvador. These foreign contacts along with the revolutionary government's active promotion of literature have resulted in an unprecedented confluence of writers representing various generations who have identified with the Revolution.

A study of the novels written since 1959 reveals a growing awareness of national consciousness in which the Mexican literary evolution from Mariano Azuela's epic chronicle *The Underdogs* (*Los de abajo*) (1915) to the more complex historical panoramas of José Revueltas's *The Stone Knife* (*El luto humano*) (1943), Agustín Yáñez' *The Edge of the Storm* (*Al filo del agua*) (1947), and Carlos Fuentes's *The Death of Artemio Cruz* (*La muerte de Artemio Cruz*) (1962) has been telescoped into less than ten years. From January 1959 to December 1969, three chronologically defined groups of novels are discernible: those published mainly between 1959 and 1960, between 1961 and 1965, and between 1966 and the present.

I

The first group is composed of five works: *Police Station Number 9* (*La novena estación*) (1959) by José Becerra Ortega, *High Noon* (*El sol a plomo*) (1959) by Humberto Arenal, *Bertillón 166* (1960) by José Soler Puig, *Tomorrow Is the 26th* (*Mañana es 26*) (1960) by Hilda Perera, and César Leante's *The Pursued* (*El perseguido*) (1964), which in spite of its date, shares all the characteristics of this group. These novels are short, episodic, and melodramatic accounts of the struggle to overthrow dictator Fulgencio Batista. This immediate problem far overshadows any concern for national consciousness. In fact, the social and racial bias of most of the authors represents a continuation of one of the obstacles to the development of national consciousness in prerevolutionary Cuba.

The action in all five of these novels takes place during the last months of 1958. The triumph of the Revolution appears only in the last chapter of *Tomorrow Is the 26th*. The plots of all five novels unfold in the city: four in Havana and *Bertillón 166* in Santiago. The constant theme of the five novels is the pitiless persecution of the revolutionary conspirators by Batista's henchmen. More than anything else, the writers seem to criticize Batista for the tortures carried out in the last year of his regime.

The revolutionary conspirators in two of the novels belong to the 26th of July Movement; in *High Noon* they are simply members of a movement, and in *Police Station Number 9* and *The Pursued* they belong to another unnamed revolutionary group. In all five novels, the revolutionaries are young; in four, their status as university students is emphasized; in two, they belong to the upper class while in the others they are probably from the middle class. Because of the protagonists' youth, one of the subplots of *Bertillón 166* and *Tomorrow Is the 26th* is the lack of understanding on the part of the parents of the revolutionaries, some of whom had actively participated in the fight against Machado in the early 1930s. Realizing that the fall of Machado did not mark the end of Cuba's ills, they have adopted a cynical attitude in opposition to their children's idealism.

Although the one clear goal of the revolutionaries is to overthrow the Batista regime, three of the novels reveal a small but growing social concern which never reaches the status of a primary theme. In *Police Station Number 9*, the narrator criticizes the government for not having any program to help the poor. In one brief, contrived scene, an old peasant complains to the revolutionary fugitives of the conditions in the sugar cane fields. In *Bertillón 166*, which takes place in Santiago, the revolutionary atmosphere is more intense. Carlos proclaims that he is fighting for a new government for the poor, the workers, the peasants, and the students.[1] The United States is criticized for aiding Batista as well as for controlling the island's economy. *Tomorrow Is the 26th* contains the clearest statement of the ideals of the Revolution in a dialogue between Rafael and his uncle. The young revolutionary sees the need for restructuring the country's economy by instituting an agrarian reform and establishing protective tariffs. Rafael's concern for all of Spanish America and his willingness to compromise his political ideals indicate a marked difference from the other novels: "Cuba is going to solve Spanish America's great dilemma: whether profound economic changes can be carried out through democratic institutions or whether in order to carry out these changes, a dictatorship of the Left is inevitable."[2] In addition to this discussion, the author's socio-

---

[1] José Soler Puig, *Bertillón 166*, 2nd ed. (Havana, 1960), 154.
[2] Hilda Perera, *Mañana es 26* (Havana, 1960), 34.

economic concern is revealed in a peasant's description of his life, which is as gratuitous as that of *Police Station Number 9.*

> Sometimes we ate, sometimes we didn't. Sometimes we had shoes, sometimes we didn't; sometimes we had medicine, sometimes we suffered without it; sometimes we managed to get a piece of meat, sometimes we didn't—and there I am plowing away, tied to the land, look at my hands! I raise my son to the age of 16—and one day they come and take him away for being a revolutionary.[3]

The fact that this peasant's appearance in a Group I novel is so exceptional along with the absence of lower-class characters in general emphasizes the point of view of the early revolutionary writers that the Cuban Revolution was not at first either agrarian or proletarian. In the five novels, the urban masses are either indifferent to the Revolution, or they sympathize with Batista, or they even betray the revolutionaries. Furthermore, four of the authors reveal a racist attitude. In *Police Station Number 9*, the driver for Batista's secret police is a mulatto; in a brief glance at a dance hall, the narrator comments that it is a place where the Chinese and the mestizos go to look for women; police brutality is compared to that of the most savage tribes of Africa. In *High Noon* the informer who reveals the whereabouts of the revolutionary kidnappers is a Negro. In *Bertillón 166*, the Negro Communist senses the distrust of his cohorts because everyone says that the "Negroes go along with Batista." [4] *Tomorrow Is the 26th* is the only one of the five novels where a plot involving the poor is interwoven with the main plot of the upper-class revolutionaries. The original idea of the author seems to have been to contrast the frivolous life of Doña Teresa with the miserable conditions in which her servants live. However, the author herself seems to lose control of her novel as Doña Teresa becomes a revolutionary heroine and her maids are really not mistreated.

This ill-fated attempt to justify the Revolution from the sociological point of view as well as the presentation of some historical figures distinguishes *Tomorrow Is the 26th* as a transitional novel between Group I and II. The final chapter describes the triumphant entry of the revolutionaries into Havana. Fidel Castro, his little son, and Camilo Cienfuegos, "a vigilant Nazarene," are specifically named.

[3] *Ibid.,* 139.
[4] *Bertillón 166*, 44, 126.

II

Whereas the novels of the first group have epigraphs by the now classical José Martí and Jorge Mañach, the first novel of the second group has an epigraph by Jean-Paul Sartre whose visit to Cuba in March 1960 partly inspired the authors of several of the Group II novels. In contrast to the novels of 1959 and 1960 characterized by their romantic heroes who live melodramatically in a short novelistic period of less than a year, the protagonists of the second group of novels are existentialist characters whose anxiety covers the whole prerevolutionary period with the purpose of justifying the social reforms of the Revolution. By placing the Revolution in historical perspective, the authors indicate a distinct awareness of the fact that the overthrow of Batista was not the Revolution's primary goal. The launching of the campaign against illiteracy and the establishment of the Committees for the Defense of the Revolution and Schools of Revolutionary Instruction—all in the latter part of 1960 —indicated that Cubans in all walks of life were being mobilized to create a new nation. Novelists contributed to the effort by portraying the lack of idealism and the anxieties prevalent in prerevolutionary Cuba, particularly in the 1940s and 1950s.

The Search (*La búsqueda*) (1961) by Jaime Sarusky alludes neither to Batista nor to the rebels, but the author gives the impression that he is trying to capture the atmosphere of the old Cuba. The protagonist, a flutist in a dance band, suddenly decides to move up in the world by playing in a symphony orchestra. His failure is a symbolic denunciation of the Cuba of the 1940s inhabited by prostitutes, dope peddlers, police, and mean, selfish people in general.

The Strike (*El descanso*) (1962) by Abelardo Piñeiro is the only novel in which the protagonists are working-class people. The author seems completely familiar with the proletarian environment but he fails artistically in his attempt to blend the social and emotional problems of his characters. The intervention of the police and the role of the courts in thwarting a strike constitute a condemnation of the "Auténtico" [5] governments (1944–1952) without the exact dates' being pinpointed.

Nor are there time limits imposed on the rural world. *Defenseless*

---

[5] Presidents Ramón Grau San Martín (1944–1948) and Carlos Prío Socarrás (1948–1952), who belonged to the Partido Auténtico, were preceded and succeeded by Fulgencio Batista (1934–1944, 1952–1958).

Land (*Tierra inerme*) (1961), the only novel of the land among all
these revolutionary works, although it alludes neither to Batista nor
to Castro, is an attempt to justify the agrarian reform and the Revolution in general. The poor, illiterate, and sick peasants work on the
estate of Clemente Muñoz, but he does not actively exploit them.
Quite the contrary, he treats them rather well. The author, Dora
Alonso, bitterly criticizes the American owners of the nearby cane
field, but they do not appear in the novel except when Mr. Higgins
runs over a poor idiot child without bothering to stop his car.

No Problem (*No hay problema*) (1961) by Edmundo Desnoes
deals with an extended but fixed period, from 1952 to 1958. It begins
with Batista's coup in March and ends with the intensification of
revolutionary activities in the Sierra. Sebastián, whose father is Cuban
and whose mother is American, suffers from the lack of understanding in the corrupt world of Batista's Cuba. Correspondent for
a New York magazine, he is an intelligent and sensitive young man
who cannot communicate with his parents, his friends, his mistresses,
or with himself—among Desnoes's favorite writers are Dostoyevsky,
Franz Kafka, and Pío Baroja. However, in spite of its existentialism,
this work is somewhat related to those of the first group because of
the heroic decision of Sabastián to return from Miami to Cuba in
spite of the tortures he suffered at the hands of Batista's police.

Noel Navarro's *The Days of Our Anguish* (*Los días de nuestra
angustia*) (1962) also seems at first sight to belong to Group I because of its emphasis on police brutality under Batista, but the author's goal is much more all-encompassing. The existentialist title is
a good reflection of the psychic state of the more important characters while the whole structure indicates the author's desire to justify
the Revolution and to place it in historical perspective. The influence
of Dos Passos's *U.S.A.* is seen in the book's sixteen chronological
divisions, in the camera-eye selections, several of which are anti-
United States, and in the biographical sketches of Fidel Castro,
Camilo Cienfuegos, and Ché Guevara. The action takes place in
both the city and country, and the author expresses real social concern.

The Dead Walk Alone (*Los muertos andan solos*), dated January
1962 in Moscow where the author, Juan Arcocha, was working as a
newspaper correspondent, covers the postrevolutionary as well as
the prerevolutionary period. The action apparently begins a few
days before New Year's Day of 1959, but by means of a series of
individual recollections, the author extends his characterization to

the whole prerevolutionary epoch. The nymphomaniac protagonist surrounds herself with a group of young people who are all "walking corpses" because of their lack of idealism. Their lives consist of excursions to Varadero Beach, social gossip, obsessions with the latest United States fashions, and an occasional orgy. The Revolution at first hardly affects their lives, but little by little it dissolves the group. In contrast with the authors of the 1959–1960 novels, Juan Arcocha shows no sign of racial prejudice and displays concern for the lower classes. Scorned by the protagonists, the poor mestizos, mulattos, and Negroes arouse the reader's sympathy. The novel's hero is Luis who succeeds in saving himself by rejecting Rosa the nymphomaniac and embracing the revolutionary-Communist (here equated) cause. In an act of revolutionary comradeship, he helps a half-mulatto, half-Indian soldier to start an expropriated car. Feeling redeemed, he returns home where his wife Esperanza (Hope) has begun to read Communist books in order to better understand the Revolution. This melodramatic ending spoils what is otherwise a fairly good novel.

The next three novels not only justify the Revolution in terms of the past but refer to specific revolutionary events of 1959–1961. José Soler Puig's *In the Year of January* (*En el año de enero*) (1963) records the dialogues and thoughts of representative types near Santiago in the year 1959: the former Batista policeman, the wealthy landowners, the skeptical revolutionary officers, and a team of workers who ultimately take charge of their factory. In Edmundo Desnoes' *The Cataclysm* (*El cataclismo*) (1965), the Revolution is recognized as a cataclysm which affects all Cubans from July 1960 to April 1961. Several alternating plots are interwoven with the expropriation of urban property, the universal participation in the cutting of sugar cane, the guard duty of the "milicianos," the exodus of the "gusanos," [6] and the Bay of Pigs invasion. Whereas Desnoes maintains a somewhat ambiguous attitude toward the Revolution, Daura Olema García's *Volunteer Teacher* (*Maestra voluntaria*), which won the 1962 national prize, is a completely doctrinaire account of the conversion to communism of a volunteer teacher in the Sierra Maestra. The individual is totally subordinated to the group. Even Fidel is no longer considered indispensable. Faith in God is replaced by faith in humanity. The volunteer teachers study the principles of communism and the political economy of the Soviet Union.

---

[6] The derogatory term applied to those who have left Cuba since 1959; literally, "worms."

The group's solidarity is strengthened by the presence of antirevolutionary rebels in the Sierra and the Bay of Pigs invasion.

The greater historical and literary pretensions of the final two novels of Group II indicate the transition to Group III. Lisandro Otero's *The Situation* (*La situación*) (1963) is a Dos Passos-like panoramic presentation of Cuban society in 1951–1952 right before and including Batista's takeover, interspersed with chapters printed in italics that trace the background of some leading families of Havana from the beginning of the twentieth century. The emphasis is on immorality, frivolity, and United States influence. The only real protagonist is Luis Dascal, the typical existentialist character, who senses everything that is wrong about Cuba in 1951 but who feels totally incapable of remedying "la situación." Much more effective in its portrayal of prerevolutionary Cuba and better artistically is José Soler Puig's *The Collapse* (*El derrumbe*) (1964), the author's third and best work. Unlike *The Situation*, this novel concentrates on the life of only one man and fuses rather than separates the different time periods. *The Collapse* also extends its time period up through the triumph of the Revolution. It is a psychological and sociological study of prerevolutionary life in Santiago and the changes wrought by the Revolution. The protagonist's drive to accumulate wealth is equated with his sexual drive, both of which lead him to corruption and immorality. With the triumph of the Revolution, his whole world crumbles. By presenting almost the entire novel through the thoughts of the one protagonist, in whom interior monologues and dialogues from different chronological periods and with different characters are purposely jumbled—*à la* William Faulkner—the author succeeds in humanizing his protagonist so that he is not merely a symbol of the prerevolutionary decadent society. He is clearly an individual who, in spite of his faults, is not totally villainous.

III

In addition to the stimulus provided by the Revolution, the Cuban novel has recently also been inspired by the so-called boom of the Latin American novel in general, which since 1960 has attracted the attention of literary connoisseurs throughout the world, culminating in the awarding of the 1967 Nobel Prize for Literature to Guatemala's Miguel Ángel Asturias. Along with the universally respected Alejo Carpentier, the core of Group III is made up of José Lezama

Lima, Guillermo Cabrera Infante, and Severo Sarduy, the avant-garde novelists whose works indicate an artistic maturity which allows them to experiment with different techniques in the presentation of a variety of national panoramas as well as of themes totally unrelated to either the Revolution or national consciousness. Although Carpentier's *Explosion in a Cathedral* and *Gestures* (*Gestos*) by Sarduy were published in 1962 and 1963 respectively, the group's high point seems to be the 1966–1968 biennium: Lezama Lima's *Paradise* (*Paradiso*) in 1966; in 1967, Cabrera Infante's *Three Trapped Tigers* (*Tres tristes tigres*) and Sarduy's *The Land of the Singers* (*De donde son los cantantes*) along with the less important but also significant *Celestino Before Dawn* (*Celestino antes del alba*) by Reinaldo Arenas, Lisandro Otero's *Urbino's Passion* (*Pasión de Urbino*) and in 1968, *The Children Say Goodbye* (*Los niños se despiden*) by Pablo Armando Fernández.

Interestingly enough, these novelists fall into four distinct literary generations. The oldest and best known of the group is Alejo Carpentier, who was born in 1904. His latest novel, *Explosion in a Cathedral*, was finished by 1959 but it was not published until 1962. Ostensibly a historical novel set in the Caribbean, France, and Spain between the late 1780s and 1808, this artistic creation based on universal myths and archetypes and written in Carpentier's unique baroque style raises some doubts about revolutionary idealism which could well be applied to the Cuban Revolution. This interpretation is supported by Carpentier's penchant for erasing time boundaries as seen in his earlier works, the short story "Like the Night" ("Semejante a la noche") and the novel *The Lost Steps* (*Los pasos perdidos*). Since 1964, Carpentier has been working on *the* novel of the Cuban Revolution, to be called "The Year 59" ("El año 59"), but so far only two chapters have been published: "The Year 59" (1964) and "The Wealthy Guests") ("Los convidados de plata") (1965). Although Müller-Bergh reported in his excellent article in the January–June 1967 issue of the *Revista Iberoamericana* that Carpentier had just finished the novel, the first volume of a trilogy, it has not yet been published. In a letter written in March 1970, the Mexican publishing house Siglo XXI indicated that the novel would not appear for at least another year.

The poet José Lezama Lima, born in 1912, like Carpentier rose to fame in the 1950s but, although he had written some short stories, *Paradiso* was his first novel. Greek mythology as well as philosophy presented in a highly metaphorical language completely overshadow all concern for reality. In keeping with the new novel of Latin America, "language is really the protagonist of this novel." [7] Just as the abstract painters concentrate on the medium to the exclusion of representation, so do the novelists in varying degrees concentrate on the value of the word. Although Lezama Lima does not feel compelled to justify the Revolution in any way, the first part of the novel does present a picture of upper-class society at the turn of the century with its strong ties to the United States.

Although the younger writers were more intimately linked with the gestation of the Revolution, they too are artistically obsessed with their medium. Guillermo Cabrera Infante, born in 1929, first attracted the attention of the literary world in 1960 with the publication of *In Times of Peace as well as War* (*Así en la paz como en la guerra*) in which fifteen one-page vignettes portraying the reign of terror in the last days of the Batista regime alternate with a variety of short stories written between 1950 and 1958 which deal primarily with personal frustrations and the anxieties of the poor. His novel *Three Trapped Tigers* (*Tres tristes tigres*) was awarded the 1964 Seix-Barral prize in Barcelona but was not published until 1967. The first third of this highly experimental novel aims at capturing the flavor of Havana night life, symbolic of the decadent Batista regime in 1958. Beyond that point, the plot, characters, and setting are subordinated to unrestrained experimentation with language. Ingenious puns, plays on names of movie stars and other famous personalities, typographical tricks, and parodies on the styles of various Cuban authors from Martí the Modernist to Guillén the Afro-Cuban all help to create the impression of frivolity and lack of direction that characterized prerevolutionary Cuban life. Although the title *Tres tristes tigres* indicates the author's obsession with linguistic experimentation, the original title, "Scene of Dawn in the Tropics" ("Vista del amanecer en el trópico") is more indicative of the author's prerevolutionary attitude. He has since defected and is now living in London where he is working on a long antirevolutionary novel to be called "Divine Bodies" ("Cuerpos divinos").

In *The Children Say Goodbye* by Cabrera Infante's contemporary, Pablo Armando Fernández (1930), the same commitment to artistic experimentation is linked with official government policy. As in *Paradise* and *Three Trapped Tigers*, character and plot development are subordinated to language: "Nothing is superior to words." [8]

---

[7] Julio Ortega, *La contemplación y la fiesta* (Caracas, 1969), 91.

[8] Pablo Armando Fernández, *Los niños se despiden* (Havana, 1968), 528.

However, the incorporation of the Ten Years' War (1868–1878) into the national heritage, although totally legitimate, was a direct reflection of the celebration of the hundredth anniversary of Cuba's first war of independence and was influential in the novel's being awarded the Casa de las Américas prize. The title of the novel reflects the author's broad vision of Cuba's national roots. The most literal interpretation is that it refers to the many youths who periodically used to emigrate to New York in search of personal gain. More deeply, however, it refers to the creation of a new Cuba by the Revolution. After years of being anchored to its traditions, the new Cuba is taking leave of its parents and is ready to chart its own course. The roots of prerevolutionary Cuba are traced back to the biblical stories of Adam and Eve and Noah's Ark as well as to the Afro-Cuban deities. By a typographical trick of converting 1948 into 1498, the children think of the early Indian inhabitants of Cuba and the Spanish *conquistadores*. Occasional references are made to the sixteenth, seventeenth, and eighteenth centuries, and more frequent allusions are made to the Ten Years' War and the War of Independence (1895–1898), which are regarded as the forerunners of the Revolution of 1959. However, this is not a historical novel by any means. Most of the 547 pages are devoted to the portrayal of life in the imaginary town of Sabanas (Part I) and in New York (Part II), mainly in the 1930s and 1940s. Collages based on the names of movie stars, popular singers, and comic strip characters are one of the author's favorite techniques. New York is presented as the proverbial den of iniquity with gratuitous scenes of sexual perversion. Interspersed among the book's twenty-six chapters are, among other items, seven visions of the Revolutionary Garden of Eden, which culminate in the apotheosis of the new Trinity: the Luz de Yara (1868),[9] the martyr Martí (1895), and Fidel Castro (1959)—"There he is seated on a white horse and his name is Faith and Truth and he judges with justice and he's a fighter." [10]

The fouth generation of writers whose works represent the culmination of a national consciousness under the Revolution is made up of people born in the late 1930s and early 1940s who identify much less than their elders with the era of immorality and injustice of prerevolutionary Cuba and therefore feel less obliged to exorcise the

---

[9] The uprising at Yara on 10 Oct. 1868, with demands for the gradual emancipation of the slaves and universal suffrage, started the Ten Years' War, 1868–1878.

[10] *Los niños se despiden*, 541.

past. Their less tropically exuberant style is both a literary reaction against writers like Lezama Lima and Cabrera Infante and a reflection of the new more dynamic Cuba produced by the Revolution.

Severo Sarduy (1937), now living in Paris where he is associated with the *Tel Quel*[11] group, has published two highly successful novels and is now completing a third one. *Gestures,* published in Barcelona by Seix-Barral in 1963, thematically belongs to Group I. However, its sophisticated artistry has earned it a place in the mainstream of the new Latin American novel. Its 140 pages capture the rhythm of Havana life in the last days of the Batista regime. Exploding bombs alternate with carnival parades, children's games, bus rides, cabaret performances, and politicians' speeches. The characters are all anonymous and are presented through modern film techniques reminiscent of some of Robbe-Grillet's works.

Sarduy's second novel, *The Land of the Singers,* like Carpentier's unpublished "The Year 59," Lezama Lima's *Paradise,* Cabrera Infante's *Three Trapped Tigers,* and Pablo Armando Fernández' *The Children Say Goodbye,* is a highly original vision of Cuba's national components, in this case, its racial components: Spanish, Negro, and Chinese. Although there is no plot, no character development, and no time and space limitations, Sarduy succeeds both in tracing Cuba's roots back to medieval Spain and in capturing the frivolity and corruption of prerevolutionary Cuba. The triumph of the Revolution is symbolized by a religious procession from Santiago to Havana with absurd juxtapositions of subways, helicopters, and snow. In his latest and as yet unpublished novel, *Cobra,* Sarduy seems to have abandoned the theme of Cuba completely. From fragments published in the French journal *Les Lettres Nouvelles* and Venezuela's *Imagen,*[12] the protagonists appear to be members of a modern motorcycle club with no national identification.

The youngest of Cuba's better-known novelists is Reinaldo Arenas (1943), whose two works *Celestino before Dawn* (*Celestino antes del alba*) (1967) and *The Hallucinatory World* (*El mundo alucinante*) (1969) indicate his artistic affiliation with the new Latin American novelists as well as his thematic liberation from the Revolution. The first work presents the sordid life of a poor rural family, but not in the vein of social protest. The narrator is a mentally retarded youngster, reminiscent of Faulkner's character in *The Sound*

[11] *Tel Quel* (1960–), outstanding French literary journal associated with structuralist criticism.

[12] Dec. 1967–Jan. 1968 and 1–15 Oct. 1968, respectively.

and the Fury, who does not distingiush between reality and fantasy. The presence of witches, goblins, talking animals and birds provides the author with complete freedom for linguistic experimentation which both attests to his virtuosity and captures the poignancy of the fairy-tale victim. Arenas's attraction to fantasy is also evident in *The Hallucinatory World,* in which he applies the technique of alternating first-second-and-third-person narrative point of view of Carlos Fuentes's *The Death of Artemio Cruz* to the biography of the extraordinarily fantastic Mexican hero of the War of Independence, Fray Servando Teresa de Mier.

IV

The formal richness of this last group of novels by Carpentier through Arenas plus a subtle antirevolutionary touch in the latest works by Sarduy and Arenas probably indicates that the cycle of the novel of the Cuban Revolution is drawing to a close. From its beginnings in 1959 to its culmination in the late 1960s, the thematic and qualitative differences are enormous. Although no one single work can yet claim to be the most representative novel of the Revolution (Carpentier's unpublished "The Year 59" may or may not live up to expectations), the total novelistic production of the past decade reflects not only official encouragement of the arts but also the development of a strong national consciousness in all sectors of the Cuban population, an experience quite similar to that engendered by the revolutionary Mexican government from the early 1920s, when Minister of Education José Vasconcelos coined the phrase "por mi raza hablará el espíritu" ("Through my people my spirit will express itself") and sponsored the famous murals of Diego Rivera, José Clemente Orozco, and David Alfaro Siqueiros, all architects of a strongly nationalistic cultural movement that was to find a corresponding expression in Mexican literature up to the present.

BIBLIOGRAPHY

Alonso, Dora. *Tierra inerme.* Havana: Casa de las Américas, 1961.
Arcocha, Juan. *Los muertos andan solos.* Havana: Ediciones R., 1962.
Arenal, Humberto. *El sol a plomo.* New York: Las Américas, 1959.
Arenas, Reinaldo. *Celestino antes del alba.* Havana: Ediciones UNEAC, 1967.
———. *El mundo alucinante.* Mexico: Diógenes, 1969.

Becerra Ortega, José. *La novena estación*. Havana: Imprenta "El Siglo XX," 1959.

Cabrera Infante, Guillermo. *Tres tristes tigres*. Barcelona: Seix Barral, 1967.

Carpentier, Alejo. "El año 59." *Casa de las Américas*, Oct.–Nov. 1964.

————. "Los convidados de plata." *Bohemia* 28 (9 July 1965), 28–32.

————. *El siglo de las luces*. Mexico: Compañía General de Ediciones, 1962.

Desnoes, Edmundo. *El cataclismo*. Havana: Ediciones R., 1965.

————. *No Hay problema*. Havana: Ediciones R., 1961.

Fernández, Pablo Armando. *Los niños se despiden*. Havana: Casa de las Américas, 1968.

Leante, César. *El perseguido*. Havana: Ediciones R., 1964.

Lezama Lima, José. *Paradiso*. Havana: Ediciones UNEAC, 1966.

Navarro, Noel. *Los días de nuestra angustia*. Havana: Ediciones R., 1962.

Olema García, Daura. *Maestra voluntaria*. Havana: Casa de las Américas, 1962.

Otero, Lisandro. *Pasión de Urbino*. Havana: Instituto del Libro, 1967.

————. *La situación*. Havana: Casa de las Américas, 1963.

Perera, Hilda. *Mañana es 26*. Havana: Lázaro Hnos., 1960.

Piñeiro, Abelardo. *El descanso*. Havana: Ediciones UNEAC, 1962.

Sarduy, Severo. "Cobra." Fragments published in *Les Lettres Nouvelles* (Paris) (Dec. 1967–Jan. 1968) and *Imagen* (Caracas) 34 (1–15 Oct. 1968).

————. *De donde son los cantantes*. Mexico: Joaquín Mortiz, 1967.

————. *Gestos*. Barcelona: Seix Barral, 1963.

Sarusky, Jaime. *La búsqueda*. Havana: Ediciones R., 1961.

Soler, Puig, José. *Bertillon 166*. 2nd ed. Havana: Casa de las Américas, 1960.

————. *El derrumbe*. Santiago de Cuba: Editora del Consejo Nacional de Universidades, 1964.

————. *En el año de enero*. Havana: Ediciones UNEAC, 1963.

Cultural Nationalism in Israeli Literature

GILA RAMRAS-RAUCH

INTRODUCTION: THE PROBLEMS OF ISRAELI LITERATURE

In speaking of Israeli literature we refer to a secular literature written in a sanctified language, a modern literature using a language which is ancient. It is a modern, secular literature in the sense of voicing current moods, in contemporary modes of expression, but it must use a language laden with religious and historic meaning. This is the dilemma going to the heart of Israeli literature. As a result, the creative framework of the Israeli writer is problem-laden, involving his relation not only to the language to whose use he is born, but also to the land in which he is born. These factors of language and land manifest themselves as problems of time (past or present) and space. It is in relation to these problems that the Israeli writer must constantly define himself. If his existence is completely secular, so that the religious and historic connotations of, e.g., the word "Israel," are entirely outside his spiritual sphere, then the Israeli writer must ask himself what sort of meaning he is to attach to the here-and-now, to a place and a time which, in their deepest significance, transcend their secular actuality. Is the Wailing Wall, for example, a symbol of destruction and exile, of promise and return? Or is it merely an archeological artifact of general interest? Is Mount Sinai the site of the Revelation and the Covenant? Or is it merely a geological entity? These are problems about the land; there are corresponding problems connected with the use of language—which we shall touch upon in due course.

The problematic condition of the Israeli writer begins prior to his time, in the last quarter of the nineteenth century, which was marked by the return of the European Jew (as writer) to the land or to the language of his forefathers. It is a return which is problematic, even paradoxical, since the return is secular, not apocalyptic, whereas the land and language to which he comes are anything but secular. In the nineteenth century, this paradox is immanent in the future development of Israeli literature, raising questions which persist into the present. These are questions pertaining to the very nature of one's existence as an Israeli and to one's *raison d'être* as a writer:

1. What is the relation between the rebirth of the nation and the rebirth and regeneration of man?

2. What is the meaning of the nation? the land? the return?

3. Is the return to the land also a return to one's sources in the past, or is it the secular founding of a modern nation?

4. What are to be the boundaries (physical and spiritual) of Israel? Philosophically (i.e., in formal terms), these are all one question: What is the relation between the here-and-now and eternity? Only in literature (i.e., in terms of content) can we display the differences between these questions.

HEBREW VS. ISRAELI LITERATURE

One fundamental distinction to be made is the distinction between Hebrew and Israeli literature. The distinction begins in a simple way and proceeds to complex and profound differences. The term "Hebrew literature" refers to writers in Hebrew whose mother tongue was either Yiddish (a variant of German) or some other language. The term "Israeli literature" refers to writers whose mother tongue is Hebrew (either because they were born in Israel or came to Israel as small children, prior to or during the Second World War).

This simple distinction regarding the writer's mother tongue involves a many-sided connection to different cultural, social, and religious circumstances. If, for example, the writer of Hebrew literature (in the original generation living in the spiritual as well as geographic Diaspora of late-nineteenth-century Europe) secularized the sacred language as a return to cultural sources, the return to the land was at first only an aspiration for him, and *then* a reality. The modern writer of Israeli literature, on the other hand, is connected to his land as something immediate; he is born to the language. Thus, the disconnection or connection of the language to the land—and the part played by the land in the respective literatures—provide one of the primary bases for the distinction between the Hebrew and the Israeli literatures, and for the characterization of the latter.

The writers covered by the rubric "Hebrew literature" were born and raised in eastern Europe (mainly in Poland or Russia). Their childhood landscape is essentially European, i.e., immersed in the life of the small hamlet (or "*shtetl*," in Yiddish). They were brought up to define themselves as Jews and as participants in the Jewish tradition. Even though their knowledge of Hebrew was deep and was part of their self-definition as Jews, they were brought up not to use Hebrew as a daily language, but reserved it for prayer and religious study. There was no delineation of the self apart from one's membership in the Jewish world and its heritage. (This is the phenomenon of the "collective mentality"—which we shall discuss later.)

The fact that these writers turned to the Hebrew language, rather than confining themselves to Yiddish (or to Russian or Polish), and that they used the holy language to express themselves in a secular manner provides some indication of the many-sided ambiguity of the individual's relation to his tradition. They looked to a return to the language as a spiritual, cultural, and national renewal. Their turn to the secular use of Hebrew may therefore be considered something of a Renaissance.

Under the complex heading of "Hebrew literature" are writers such as Mendele Mocher Sefarim (1836–1917), Mordecai Zeev Feierberg (1874–1899), Uri Nissan Gnessin (1879–1913), and Micha Yosef Berdichevsky (1865–1921), who never lived in Israel; Yosef Chaim Brenner (1881–1921), Chaim Nachman Bialik (1873–1934), and Saul Tchernikovsky (1875–1943), who were born in Europe but who lived and died in Israel. And then there are writers such as Shmuel Yosef Agnon (1888–1970), Gershon Shoffman (1880–   ), and Haim Hazaz (1898–   ), who lived most of their creative lives in Israel. This is the generation of the Renaissance.

In addition, a younger generation of Hebrew literature, the generation of the Realization, also Europe-born, has been, in some complex ways, more open to what might be called "modern" European influences: Uri Zvi Greenberg (1895–   ), Abraham Shlonsky (1900–   ), Yitzhak Shenhar (1907–1957), and Nathan Alterman (1910–1970). Needless to say, there are many other highly significant writers whom we have not mentioned at this point.

The writers covered by the rubric "Israeli literature" were born or raised in Israel, a secular state. The language in which they write is that of their everyday speech, rather than that of the Book. Their version of the "collective mentality" is more national than cultural or religious. Their self-definition is as Israelis more than as Jews. They have a stronger affiliation to the land than to the faith. The main figures are: S. Yizhar (1916–), Moshe Shamir (1921–), Aharon Megged (1920–), Haim Gouri (1923–), Hanoch Bartov (1926–), Yehuda Amichai (1924–), Nissim Aloni (1926–), Aharon Appelfeld (1932–), Avraham B. Yehoshua (1937–).

Accordingly, one can say that there are three generations of writers now living and working in Israel: (1) the older generation of Hebrew literature—the "Renaissance," e.g., Shoffman and Hazaz; (2) the newer generation of Hebrew literature—the "Realization," e.g., Greenberg, Shlonsky, Alterman; and (3) the current generation of Israeli literature, whose work began to appear in the 1940s.

THE PROBLEM OF SECULARIZATION

In the Diaspora (the dispersion of the Jewish people in Europe, from which the Hebrew Renaissance emerged in the late nineteenth century), Judaism's unifying attitude was the hope of redemption and return. Three times daily, prayers were said facing in the direction of Jerusalem. The prayers as constant reiterations of that hope were therefore reminders of the unrootedness of a people.

The existence of that people is thoroughly time-oriented. From the very beginning, its view is that time is the plane on which God manifests His will, and that God's central act is the selection of *this* people as the people to whom He will impart His law. All time is sanctified: every moment of every day is referred to God's will, and to man's interpretation of that will. Finally, God's will is expected to redeem His people and to restore it to Jerusalem, to a condition that will complete and transcend history.

The process of secularization, by which the writers of the Renaissance turned to the secular use of the sacred language, involved the writer's withdrawal from the "collective mentality"—in such a way that the writer severed his connections with the sense of continuity but retained his connections with the present. Accordingly, these writers can be characterized as moving in the direction of greater individualism and yet utilizing the temporal *Weltanschauung* in expressing this individualism. One of the finest examples of this standpoint is Feierberg's short novel *Whither?*[1] This is a novel of a tormented young man who has lost faith in the traditional way as a way to redemption. His inability to find satisfaction in the tradition leaves him with himself alone, a being immersed in a rootless time. His problem is representative of the generation which could neither continue in the tradition of millennia, nor break the bonds with that tradition, nor find a meaningful synthesis between the Judaic and the Western worlds. He cannot go back to the God of his people. Time is no longer redemptive for him. And yet his continued search is a search within a temporal framework, i.e., a search for a meaning which will transcend time.

Whereas Hebrew literature can be characterized by its temporal framework, Israeli literature can be characterized by a spatial aspect. The latter's emphasis is on the here-and-now, without reference to a collective memory; it is an emphasis on the relation between the individual and his environment, the individual set against his landscape. Whereas the sources of Hebrew literature are in the tension between the individual and the collective experience,[2] the Israeli writer is not imbued with a sense of history. His sources are mainly autobiographical—there being for him no problem of defining himself as an individual *vis-à-vis* a historical and spiritual environment. Yet although his outlook regarding his environment is more national than cultural, his persisting problem is that of finding a balance between his national and cultural loyalties.

During and immediately after the War of Independence, in 1948, the writer's concern was solely with the "we" in the present and with Israel's national aspirations—but not at all with the sources of those aspirations in the past. More recently, however, one can detect a trend toward the incorporation of the past into the present. That past includes Israel's broader history as a nation as well as the more proximate experience of the Holocaust (the influence of which we shall discuss below).

The spatial aspect, which may be said to characterize Israeli literature, gives a special importance to the landscape. The land is itself saturated with religious-historic meaning, but the problems of building a modern nation and of giving voice to its national consciousness

---

[1] Mordecai Zeev Feierberg, *Whither?*, trans. Ira Eisenstein (New York, 1959).

[2] See Baruch Kurzweil, *Our Contemporary Literature: Continuity or Revolution?* (published in Hebrew by Schocken Publishing House, Tel-Aviv, 1965), 110.

also tend to stress the relation of the individual to the land. Conceivably, therefore, there could be two sources (religious and secular) of the emphasis on the land in modern Israeli literature. But for the Israeli writer, the land is no longer a redemptive goal in the remote future, but rather a present possession. And yet, paradoxically, that possession derives at least part of its justification from the redemptive (time-oriented) hopes of the past.

The return to the land in our time therefore creates a tension between time and space, as literary elements: the individual writer's relation to historical time and heritage will eventually dictate his relation to site and space. To the individual who is not filled with the sense of time in Israel, the landscape inevitably loses its historic value.

The time-oriented aspect of Hebrew literature has its source in the fact that for the biblical man, the present gets its meaning from the past and the future. Even much later, the traditional Jew is essentially a man-in-the-middle, a link between generations, imparting the meaning of the past to the future—this being an interpretation of time and history in the direction of a unifying heritage and not in the direction of the isolated individual. For the modern Jew, however, a separation is made: one can belong to the Jewish people, yet not serve as bearer of the tradition.[3] His stance is as a part of a didactic continuity, i.e., he is aware of his successive position in the chain of history, but he rejects his position as hander-on of received values.

This in some way illuminates the ambiguous position of the Israeli writer: he is not tied to a continuation of tradition, yet he continues the national existence of his forefathers—by living in the land of his forefathers. Thus, the emphasis on one's connection to the land serves the purpose of cutting one's connection with the redemptive-temporal dimension and of asserting the national dimension! And in this we have the complex phenomenon of a nationalism which ties itself to the most remote past of the people as a nation, but not to the intermediate past with is religious expression.

ISRAEL AND THE DIASPORA

The new generation of Israeli writers, having experienced the creation of a new bond between man and land, considers itself a

---

[3] This view is expressed by Nathan Rotenstreich of the Hebrew University, Jerusalem, in an article in Hebrew, "Historical Consciousness and Jewish Historical Reality," in *Ma'ariv*, 22 April 1969.

"genesis-generation." The older generation of Hebrew writers, having experienced the Diaspora, when Israel was merely a hope based on biblical promise, might be called the "memory-generation." The confrontation between these generations is given expression in their respective literatures; and this repeated confrontation provides the basis for national self-definition in literature. In this process, one question which is constantly being explored is whether the "genesis-generation" has experienced a real national genesis or merely a revival or continuation.

Aharon Megged's short story "The Name" describes touchingly a confrontation between a grandfather—raised in the Diaspora and steeped in memories—and his Israeli-born, genesis-oriented grandchildren.[4] The old man wants their newborn son to be named for a grandson of his who perished in the Holocaust. The baby's mother rejects the suggestion: the name is a ghetto name, ugly and horrible; she would prefer to forget the dreadful past. The baby's father rejects the name because it is suggestive of the Diaspora, an era to which he feels no connection. To the time-haunted old man, "Ties are remembrance," and the attitude of his grandchildren means the cutting of those ties, total death in a very real way. The old man cannot rid himself of bitterness about the past, about the many who were lost. If the child is not to be named for the dead grandson, there will be no memorial, no continuation. He ignores the child, and when the mother leaves with the baby she feels that it is in need of pity, as though it were an orphan.

The Israeli story may be said to evolve out of a problematic incident—as in the story just described. The outlook of the Israeli writer is shaped by a changing reality outside him. He brings with him no fixed ideas, or fixed feelings, about the past. The Hebrew writer, on the other hand, brings with him an already problematic set of convictions and attitudes—framed by his sense of time—and when reality clashes with those convictions, reality becomes even more problematic. It is therefore the Hebrew writer who indulges in ideological self-examination, and this stems from the fact that the present reality which is Israel must be viewed by him in the light of convictions and attitudes acquired in a pre-Israeli (Diaspora) experience.

In "The Sermon," a short story by the Hebrew writer Haim

---

[4] Aharon Megged, "The Name," in *Israeli Stories*, ed. Joel Blocker (New York, 1966). All the stories in this anthology are translated into English.

Hazaz, the protagonist addresses his comrades in a *kibbutz*, or Israeli communal farm.[5] In a meeting devoted to local problems, this pathetically inarticulate individual speaks about the meaning and quintessence of existence in the land of Israel. He maintains that Zionism begins with the wrecking of Judaism, namely, that it is not a direct continuation of Judaism. He regards the history of the Diaspora as a history of suffering and ignominy. But it is easy to understand his disquiet about the new way of life: If a people is shaped by exile, could not the end of exile destroy that people? Here in this treatment of the relation between Diaspora and Homeland, it is the issue and not the incident that takes precedence.

In the writing of S. Y. Agnon, winner of the Nobel Prize for Literature, the use of the particular incident and didactic argument (as literary devices) gives way to an emphasis on complexity and process.* He re-created, in artistic terms, the fullness of Jewish existence in the past as well as the Judaic trauma in the present. One finds in his work the contrasting themes of faith and doubt, destruction and redemption, the literal and the symbolic, innocence and irony, exegesis and the occult, identification and alienation, concealment and disclosure, yearning and repulsion, entrapment and release, fiction and fact, past and present, the holy and the profane—as well as the contrast between Israel and the Diaspora, combining all these themes in a synoptic vision. In present-day Israel, where one's language indicates one's generation and one's primary identification, Agnon utilized every layer of language from the Pentateuch to the present. This makes it possible for us to read his work on the simplest as well as the most complex levels.

The young Israeli can relate to the Diaspora only extrinsically, and in a remote way—either as history or as the experience of his forefathers. Thus, when an Israeli writer looks to the past for subject-matter, he may even focus on the pre-Diaspora era, e.g., the first century B.C., as in Moshe Shamir's novel *King of Flesh and Blood*.

For Agnon, the relation to the Diaspora is far deeper, involving all the themes—literal as well as symbolic—mentioned above. His relation to the Diaspora allows him, therefore, to go beyond it, to universal themes: the home is broken, the key is lost, and man is naked and maimed. Man is driven out of the Eden of faith, into the

---

[5] Haim Hazaz, "The Sermon," in *Israeli Stories*.

* [Editor's note: Agnon died in 1970 after this article was completed. According to the author, the power and influence of Agnon in Hebrew and Israeli literature are without equal.]

macabre annihilating reality. Agnon shows us the Diaspora, spiritual as well as physical, as an exile from grace.

THE WAR OF INDEPENDENCE: 1948

The State of Israel (which was established in 1948) is physically, demologically, and spiritually in the process of becoming. The first generation of Israeli writers, the generation which matured during the war period, is sometimes referred to as the Palmach generation (the word *palmach* refers to underground military brigades operating during the time of the British Mandate). They grew up in the land of Israel in its pre-state days. In addition to their affiliations to language and land, another factor in their growing-up is the youth movement, which provided the ideological framework for their eventual *Weltanschauung*. Despite their various political standpoints, the different factions of the youth movement instilled values common to Zionist, Socialist, and liberalist ideologies. The young were expected to realize and materialize these ideals by joining a *kibbutz*—a collective agricultural settlement.

In 1948, the young generation was called upon to translate national aspirations and national yearnings into reality. Regrettably, the establishment of the state was met by war. This led to a situation in which, for the young, prior values and present reality were not in full accord: the shared experience of the "we"—which was cultivated in the youth movement and implied a mentality of collectivity and belonging—was challenged by the experience of the "I," the experience of fighting as an individual. The war threw the individual back onto his personal responsibility; his sense of belonging to the collectivity was confronted by war, bloodshed, and horror.

One writer who gave voice to the discord between self and reality is S. Yizhar.[6] His typical protagonist is a captive of his sensitivity and his sensibility. He is passive—because activity involves preference, choice, commitment, and irrevocability. Decisiveness and absolute certainty are foreign to him. The time of bliss for Yizhar's protagonist—as for many another Israeli writer—is therefore the period of childhood, before the initiation into adulthood and war. In that period, the landscape and the child are seen to be in complete accord, with open vistas suggesting a world without boundaries.

[6] S. Yizhar, "The Dead and the Living," in *A Whole Loaf*, ed. S. J. Kahn (New York, 1963). An anthology, in English, of stories from Israel. See also S. Yizhar, "The Prisoner," in *Israeli Stories*.

Initiation into reality meant a moment of personal call and ultimately a reassessment of the sense of the belonging of man to land and land to man.

The war raised issues of personal morality: What is to be one's relation to the enemy? to the prisoner? What is to be considered a genuine act of faith and what *mauvaise foi*? Where does justice lie: with one's personal convictions or with collective national need? Yizhar's protagonist does not pass judgment, nor does he undergo an essential change of outlook; the situation is only a stage for his perennial interior monologue, a monologue studded with self-mockery. He tries to escape time and his consciousness. He realizes the irony and ambiguity in reality. Further, he is perpetually aware of his "otherness" in the tension between his self-searching sensitivity and the actions of the others.

Yet this standpoint is by no means the view of all Israeli writers. Moshe Shamir, for example, rejects the separation of the "I" from the "we"—either in literature or in life.[7] Recognizing the tension between the collectivity and the individual as a recurring theme in Israeli literature, he emphasizes the shared experience as a key motif. His protagonists of twenty years ago reflect these feelings: self-assertion rather than self-doubt, action rather than contemplation. They are at one with the call of their time.

Thus, the War of Independence provided for most Israeli writers an initiation into reality and a more complex relation to the land. It also meant the making of history, together with certain ramifications which were problematic for some, but not for others. To most writers it meant an increased self-consciousness as an individual, although not all writers were led to a sense of isolation as a result. In any event, it may be said with some certainty that the experiences of the War of Independence and the subsequent establishment of the State of Israel (two types of event not necessarily connected with any particular literary effect in other literatures) served as the formative crucible for the first generation of Israeli writers.

THE HOLOCAUST

The two major events of Jewish life in the twentieth century are a positive one and a negative one: the establishment of the State of Israel and the Holocaust.

The theme of the Holocaust has been coming up in recent Israeli

[7] In a symposium in *Ma'ariv*, Oct.–Nov. 1968.

prose—in such a way as to raise questions about the individual Israeli's personal relation to Germany and the Germans (past and
present) as well as questions of national self-definition. But there are
even deeper existential questions, both national and individual. Not
enough time has passed to permit the observer to state with certainty
the reasons for this phenomenon. A short survey, however, of the
various trends and treatments of the subject may shed light on this
phenomenon.

There are Israeli writers who experienced the Holocaust at first
hand, and for whom it has been the key motif of their entire output.[8]
Aharon Appelfeld, in his short stories, creates a symbolic vision of
the eternal journey, the endless snowy vista and the delayed spring.[9]
His hollow people are in a no-exit state of being. They are the
messengers and bearers of an apocalyptic horror.

Writers such as Amichai and Ben Amotz share a similar personal
background, without having experienced the Holocaust. This theme
did not appear in their work, either explicitly or implicitly, until
quite recently. Now in their forties, they have returned to the problem of their interrupted youth in Europe: their protagonists return,
belatedly, to the landscapes of their childhoods.

Yehuda Amichai, in his novel *Not of This Time, Not of This
Place*, portrays an Israeli archeologist who, in his life, reaches the
crossroads of self-questioning.[10] Further, the author resorts to the
fictional device of splitting the protagonist's existence, so that he
lives and experiences simultaneously in Jerusalem and in Germany.
He lives in outer and inner time, in a patchwork of imagination and
reality, fantasy and presence.

Dahn Ben Amotz, in his novel *To Remember and Forget*, treats
this theme in a still bolder manner, more realistic, explicit and naked.[11] Written in the first person, the novel depicts a young Israeli
architect, Uri Lam (né Hirsch Lampel), who returns to Frankfurt,
the town of his birth, to collect his German reparations. While de-
spising himself for his lack of integrity and for returning, he redis-
covers his lost home in his love for a German girl. This brings forth
an identity crisis. His self-questioning (am I a Jew or an Israeli?)

[8] Mention must be made of Elie Wiesel, an Israeli who writes in French.

[9] Aharon Appelfeld, *In the Wilderness*, short stories translated from the Hebrew by T. Sandbank, S. Berg, and J. Sloane (Jerusalem, 1965).

[10] Yehuda Amichai, *Not of This Time, Not of This Place*, translated from
the Hebrew by Shlomo Katz (New York, 1968).

[11] Dahn Ben Amotz, *To Remember and Forget* (published in Hebrew by
Amikam, Tel-Aviv, 1968).

and the haunting presence of the past are terminated in his return to Jerusalem with his German wife.

Both novels seem to maintain that a complete self-realization in understanding is impossible without the lost chapter of childhood. It is only a restored contact with the lost landscape of suppressed memories that can complete one's self-portrait—even if these memories are the most painful one can evoke.

A contrasting approach is to evoke, as a deliberate enterprise, one's experiences in the Second World War, as in Hanoch Bartov's novel *The Brigade*.[12] This book deals with the Jewish Brigade of the British army. Specifically, it describes the encounters of a young volunteer with two groups: the desolate Jews and the defeated Germans. This double confrontation leaves the protagonist (and the reader) with an awareness of the limitations of love and hate. Many problems arise: How does the individual avenge the crime committed against others? Can the individual wage a private war? Is the brigade an army of salvation or of retribution? And the answers are shown to have opposed consequences in action. The only certainty is the ineradicable memory of the Holocaust and the frustration of arrested reaction.

There is, in addition, another group of writers concerned with the Holocaust, namely, those who did not experience it directly. Haim Gouri's novel *The Chocolate Deal* is an effort to perceive and understand the Holocaust from this more remote vantage point, i.e., lacking the direct childhood recollection.[13] In the novel, two Jewish refugees return to the scene of their prewar existence in an unnamed city. To one of them, Mordi, the destruction of all remnants of the past means the destruction of the future. Time is at a standstill for him, since it brings no change or continuity. He aspires only to death, as a last act of will. Serenely he withdraws into himself, and death redeems him from a senseless existence. To the other, Rubi, only the world of fantasy can provide a bridge between himself and the present. In a reality devoid of meaning, existence may be possible only outside consciousness, outside reason. Gouri avoids the historical treatment, like many of the other writers in this group. The protagonists are, therefore, the existential and symbolic representatives of the Holocaust.

[12] Hanoch Bartov, *The Brigade*, translated from the Hebrew by S. Segal (New York, 1968).
[13] Haim Gouri, *The Chocolate Deal*, translated from the Hebrew by Seymour Simckes (New York, 1968).

Earlier, we suggested that it was too early to state the reasons for the rise of the Holocaust as a theme in contemporary Israeli prose. The personal experiences of the writers can account for it only in part. In any case, the present interest in areas beyond autobiographical boundaries may point to a quest for a wider historical framework within which to regard the Jew, i.e., for a wider temporal and geographic frame of reference for the Jewish experience.

TRANSITION TO INDIVIDUALISM

The individualistic trend in contemporary Israeli prose has come to the fore only since the early 1960s. The writers of the 1940s and the early 1950s were mainly engulfed in a combination of personal and national ethical problems, a trend which lent a somewhat didactic flavor to their writing. This was an inevitable outcome of their life situation, namely, the proximity of personal to national existence. Thus, their *raison d'être*, both personal and literary, was in a way imposed upon them by the time. Their typical protagonist exists usually against a collective background. His dialogue with this background, expressed in the tension between his being and his action, forms the artistic fabric in which he is revealed. The problem of one's identification as Israeli or Jew was one of the primary concerns of those writers.

Contemporary Israeli writers such as, among others, Avraham B. Yehoshua (b. 1937) and Amos Oz (b. 1939) face problems altogether different from those just described. In a recent interview, Yehoshua has said, "The question of Jewish existence occupied us many years ago, but today it doesn't bother us anymore—as Israelis. We aren't searching for our Jewish identity." Dalia Rabikovitz, a young poetess, says, "The question of belonging [to the Jewish people] doesn't raise any problems. I have no doubt I'm a Jewess. Moreover, here in Israel the Jewish heritage doesn't carry any sense of humiliation as perhaps it still does for Jews abroad. What bothers one more is the Israeli heritage." [14]

The search for roots is a prominent feature in Israeli literature. The question is where to search: In the biblical time? Or in the 2,000-year Diaspora? In the nation when it resides in the land? Or

[14] Both interviews are cited in *Jerusalem Post Weekly*, 3 Feb. 1969. They are part of a collection of 25 interviews with as many Israeli writers, entitled *It's All There in the Book*, ed. Y. Bezalel (published in Hebrew by Hakibbutz Hameuchad, Israel, 1969).

in the nation when it only dreams of residing in the land? Must a nation define itself only in reference to land?[15] More pressingly, must an individual identify himself in this way as well?

It is clear that it is the present rather than the past that will dictate the shape taken by the process of self-definition. The recent concern with the Holocaust as literary material may, perhaps, be seen as an effort to widen the Israeli writer's frame of reference, beyond his immediate time and place, in his quest for self-definition.

Whatever that quest might be, it is accompanied by the young writer's search for self-determination and a noncollective "privacy." Writers now in their thirties lived vicariously through the Second World War, the Holocaust, and the subsequent Ingathering, and experienced directly three wars in Israel, those of 1948, 1956, and 1967. Thus, personal and collective experiences are closely connected. At the same time, the young writer considers himself a man of the twentieth century, open to European and American trends in art, literature, and philosophy. As a result, it is possible to detect a tendency to widen the gap between one's past experience and the here-and-now. This leads to a quest for a deeper and more personal perception of reality. The result is expressed in the symbolism of the personal dream-world—this being one of the means, among others, for the expression of the individual vision.

Nissim Aloni (b. 1926), who shifted from prose to drama, uses motifs of fairy-tale and myth to create a vision of the absurd. An early play of his, *Cruelest of All Is the King*, draws on biblical material and is perhaps the finest Israeli drama of recent times. Yet the world view Aloni seeks is one going beyond the Hebraic or Judaic, approaching the universal.

Amos Oz, in his novel *My Michael*, utilizes the stream-of-consciousness technique, as well as dream and fantasy, to depict a world devoid of any objective correlative.[16] It is an allegorization of reality —of such a kind that to portray its incongruities reveals a depth of

---

[15] According to the small and marginal "Canaanites"—a cultural movement which arose in the early 1950s—land and language are the only genuine sources of identification; they therefore advocate going back to pre-biblical times! Its spokesmen distinguish between the "Hebrew" and the Jew: the former identified with the land, and the latter with the Diaspora. They stress the present and reject completely the idea of the nation as Jewish. The brilliant poetry of J. Ratosh, one of their main figures, evokes pagan myth and the lore indigenous to the region of the Fertile Crescent.

[16] Amos Oz, *My Michael* (published in Hebrew by Am Oved, Tel-Aviv, 1967).

vision entirely personal and removed from all collective awareness.

Simultaneously, a bold attempt is being made to face the complexity of reality in the writing of the novella and the short story. A. B. Yehoshua, one of the most prominent of young Israeli writers, has been powerfully influenced by Kafka and Agnon and is emerging as a writer with a distinct personal idiom. His latest collection of short stories makes use of all the themes and techniques just mentioned: biblical motifs, existential symbol, and even the use of the land as a protagonist.[17]

CONCLUSION

The Israeli writer—like his contemporaries in other cultures—is faced by the twentieth-century verbal crisis regarding the uncertainties of literary form and content. Yet his primary problem comes from his ancient language and his modern land.

Over the millennia, the language has left deposits, like archeological strata, in which are embedded the cultural history of the people. Most of the young writers are acquainted with these sources (especially the Bible), so that the use of a certain word or phrase immediately relates their expression to a certain era in the long history of the national consciousness. Moreover, certain archetypes, symbols, images, motifs, and stories are part of their upbringing and present make-up.

Some of the contemporary writing fuses personal experience with the imagery of the past. Any evocation of the language of the past points simultaneously to the extended national consciousness as well as to an ironic reduction of the sanctified to a personal everyday level. Thus, their language serves to express their ties to and their discontinuities with the past.

Quite different problems are presented to the writer by the fact of his living in modern Israel, where life means change—and this is more often revolutionary than evolutionary, e.g., in the growth and change of population, in the alteration of geographical boundaries. One cannot, in Israel, talk of a totality or reality which is the result of slow, organic growth. This has affected literature, the subject matter as well as the writer's relation toward it.

Basic to the writer's *Weltanschauung* are his belonging to the nation, to the land, and to its language. His relation to Jewish history as

[17] Avraham B. Yehoshua, *Over Against the Woods* (published in Hebrew by Hakibbutz Hameuchad, Israel, 1968).

a whole and to the Jews in the world is more complex; its outcome is in the hand of time.

ACKNOWLEDGMENT

I am indebted to my teacher, Professor Baruch Kurzweil of Bar-Ilan University, Israel, for his deep insights into the problems of Israeli and world literature.

BIBLIOGRAPHY

[Bibliography of Books are in English except where specified.]

SOURCE MATERIALS:

Agnon, Shmuel Yosef. *A Guest for the Night.* New York: Schocken Books, 1968.
———. *Tehilla and Other Israeli Tales.* New York: Abelard-Schuman, 1956.
Amichai, Yehuda. *Not of This Time, Not of This Place.* New York: Harper, 1968.
Appelfeld, Aharon. *In the Wilderness.* Jerusalem: Ah'shav Publ., 1965.
Bartov, Hanoch. *The Brigade.* New York: Holt, 1968.
Ben-Amotz, Dahn. *To Remember and Forget.* Tel-Aviv: Amikam, 1968. In Hebrew.
Blocker, Joel (ed.). *Israeli Stories.* New York: Schocken Books, 1966.
Burnshaw, Stanley, T. Carmi, Ezra Spicehandler (eds.). *The Modern Hebrew Poem Itself.* New York: Holt, 1965. Bilingual.
Kahn, Sholom J. (ed.). *A Whole Loaf.* New York: Grosset, 1963.
Penueli, S. Y., and A. Ukhmani (eds.). *Hebrew Short Stories.* 2 vols. Tel-Aviv: Institute for the Translation of Hebrew Literature and Megiddo Pub., 1965. A collection of Hebrew and Israeli stories.
Rabikovitz, Dalia (ed.). *The New Israeli Writers.* New York: Funk and Wagnalls, 1969.
Spicehandler, Ezra (ed.). *Hebrew Stories.* New York: Bantam Books, 1971. Bilingual. A collection of Hebrew and Israeli stories.
Yehoshua, Avraham B. *Over Against the Woods.* Israel: Hakibbutz Hameuchad, 1968. In Hebrew.
Yizhar, S. *Midnight Convoy and Other Stories.* Jerusalem: Institute for the Translation of Hebrew Literature and Israeli Universities Press, 1969.

SECONDARY MATERIALS:

Band, Arnold J. *Nostalgia and Nightmare—A Study in the Fiction of S. Y. Agnon.* Berkeley: University of California Press, 1968.
Benshalom, Benzion. *Hebrew Literature Between the Two World Wars.* Jerusalem: Youth and Hechalutz Department of Zionist Organization, 1953.

Halkin, Simon. *Modern Hebrew Literature: Trends and Values.* New York: Schocken Books, 1950.

Kurzweil, Baruch. *Between Vision and the Absurd.* Tel-Aviv: Schocken Publishing House, 1966. In Hebrew.

———. *In the Struggle Over the Values of Judaism.* Tel-Aviv: Schocken Publishing House, 1969. In Hebrew.

———. *Our Contemporary Literature: Continuity or Revolution?* Tel-Aviv: Schocken Publishing House, 1965. In Hebrew.

Rabinovich, Isaiah. *Major Trends in Modern Hebrew Fiction.* Chicago: University of Chicago Press, 1968.

Ribalow, Menachem. *The Flowering of Modern Hebrew Literature.* New York: Twayne, 1959.

Wallenrod, Reuben. *The Literature of Modern Israel.* New York: Abelard-Schuman, 1957.

Sociopolitical Themes in the Contemporary Arabic Novel: 1950-1970*

SALIH J. ALTOMA

During the last twenty years, the Arabic novel—hardly half a century old—has emerged as an important literary form recognized both for its diversity of themes and continued artistic development. More and more writers in different Arab countries, notably the U. A. R. (Egypt), have found it the best medium suited for their uncensored reflection on ideas, issues, and events with which they and their society are concerned. Several factors, both intrinsic and extrinsic, have contributed to the flowering of the novel in the post-war years: the gradual technical progress achieved through earlier experimentation, a growing awareness of the various structural elements that enter into the making of a successful novel, and the demands of a widening audience. To these must be added the relative freedom and security with which a novelist can speak through a fictional character in a social or political climate that often stifles open opposition or direct criticism. As a result, not only has the number of novels increased significantly, but through such novels, diverse and sensitive issues have been explored with candidness and courage. A careful reading of selected works by leading Arab novelists (from Egypt, Iraq, Lebanon, and Syria) reveals that their heroes are constantly groping for a meaningful life that their surroundings fail to offer, rebelling against deeply rooted conventions or institutions, satirizing government measures of reform, and pointing to the need for a drastic change in their society's outlook and direction.

* The author wishes to thank Indiana University for providing him with a research grant to undertake this survey.

Perhaps no other Arab novelist has been as comprehensive, skill-ful, and perceptive in his treatment of such issues as the Egyptian writer Najib Mahfuz (1912–   ).

MAHFUZ AND THE QUEST FOR A RATIONAL ORDER

Mahfuz's career as an author of more than twenty fiction works can be divided into three stages: the early stage (1938–1944), deal-ing with ancient Egypt and including three novels; the second (1945–1957), covering modern Egypt before the revolution of 1952; and the third (1961–   ), in which Mahfuz addresses himself to the problems of postrevolutionary Egypt and a variety of universal questions. Central among his themes is the disintegration of familiar frameworks coupled with a quest for seemingly unattainable rational order. The first encounter with such themes takes place in his *New Cairo* (Cairo, 1945), a novel that revolves primarily around the moral bankruptcy of the Egyptian government and high society in the years preceding the Second World War. His principal charac-ters, university students, share a pervasive feeling of contempt for their world but envisage or pursue three different courses of action: the unprincipled conduct of the central protagonist, Mahjub, who views all values and ideologies as absurd; the religious approach sug-gested by Ridwan, who maintains that God's teachings as revealed through Islam are still valid to man's contemporary situation; and secular socialism as proposed by Ali, who underlines the need for a new faith derived essentially from Western sources: science instead of metaphysics, society in place of heaven, and socialism instead of competition or capitalism. However, when the novel comes to an end, the last two solutions—Islamic puritanism and secular socialism —remain confined to the minds of their adherents, yielding no posi-tive social action. Nevertheles, they sustain Ridwan and Ali against the temptations of a decaying society whereas their mutual friend, Mahjub, succumbs to the immoral overtures of a high government official by playing the role of a husband to the official's mistress as a price for a job.

In Mahfuz's later novels, religious and Socialist ideas show greater influence as his characters become actively engaged in opposing the existing order. The trilogy,[1] for example, covering about thirty

---

[1] The trilogy consists of *Bayn Al-Qasrayn* (Cairo, 1956), *Qasr Al-Shawq*, and *Al-Sukkariyya*, both published in Cairo, 1957.

years of Egypt's modern history, traces the evolution of the ideological struggle from the early phases of Egyptian nationalism to Muslim Brotherhood movement and communism. The work begins just after the First World War, when we see Abd Al-Jawad, the head of a middle-class family, secure in his position as a traditional authoritarian father. It concludes after the Second World War with his power greatly diminished and two of his grandsons in jail because of their political activities against the state.

Ironically, the two brothers represent two irreconcilable outlooks: the Muslim Brotherhood, which places total faith in Islam as the only effective means of renewal, and the Marxist revolutionary movement. Both seek solutions for Egypt's ills in movements that encompass other peoples, and both, aware of social injustice, suggest two forms of socialism as a remedy: Islamic and Marxist. Although Mahfuz is noted for his remarkable objectivity in the execution of his plots, only the Marxist is given the opportunity to meditate in his jail on the meaning of his action in a manner that reinforces his faith as the rays of sunlight penetrate his cell.[2]

Mahfuz's novels, up to the end of the second stage, exhibit a Flaubertian preoccupation with detail in delineating types of characters and facets of Egyptian life. However, his latest novels are less concerned with minute details and particulars than with general problems, ideas, or situations with universal dimension. Mahfuz himself has acknowledged this shift in his technique. In his article "My New Direction and the Novel's Future" he states:

> When I was concerned with life and its meaning the approach most suitable to me was realism by which I presented my works for many years. The details whether related to the environment, characters or events were of great importance. This approach reflects life in its totality from which ideas may emerge as by-products. But when ideas and my feelings about them began to occupy my attention neither the environment nor the characters nor the events became necessary. Characters appear like symbols, environment like a modern decor and events are selected on the basis of their contribution to the central ideas.[3]

We can find this change in *The Quail and the Fall* (1962), *The Beggar* (1965), *Chattering on the Nile* (1966), and *The Children of Our Quarter* (1967). Isa of *The Quail*, dismissed from his job after the 1952 revolution, is one of those individuals who has been denied

---

[2] *Al-Sukkariyya*, 385.
[3] *AL KATIB*, no. 35 (Feb. 1964), 22–23.

the opportunity to maintain a positive relationship with his society and thus must endure a life of alienation and exile. A friend suggests that he should look for a job, but the hero regards such an act as one of futility declaring: "In spite of any job we may take, we will remain without action because we are left with no role, and here lies the secret of our feeling of exile." [4] By offering a detailed account of Isa's psychological anguish, the novel seems to plead for a more humane understanding of the individual's acts or feelings and to warn against harsh measures which victimize rather than rehabilitate those accused of wrongdoing.

In *The Beggar*, Mahfuz depicts with skillful symbolism the emotional crisis unleashed by a guilt feeling. As the novel starts, some years after the revolution, we discover that Omar was once a poet and a Socialist. He has, however, given up both poetry, a symbol of his virtuous soul, and his political struggle for personal success and material gain. Through a series of flashbacks containing remarks which suggest disillusionment with the revolution, Omar experiences a soul-searching crisis leading him to withdraw gradually from his job, his family, and life itself. His anguish intensifies upon meeting a friend, Othman, who has served a long political prison term, and he realizes that his friend's commitment remains undiminished. In a number of conversations, Omar's emotional crisis or psychological malady becomes the subject of Othman's sarcastic remarks. His crisis, he is told, is his own making; the search for identity or meaning of existence is irrelevant if we recognize our responsibility toward millions of people, and truth cannot be attained by such emotional upheaval. Othman insists that only by reason, science, and action can a search for truth acquire meaning.[5] Omar's crisis is too severe to permit his return to a normal life, and he goes to the countryside, away from his family and friends, to seek relief for his agonizing condition. But there he experiences nightmarish dreams or visions. In one of these, he is pursued by a character having his son's head and Othman's body, a symbol perhaps of the ideals he betrayed or an invitation to return. He undergoes torturous catharsis and near the end of the novel begins to return to normalcy when he finds himself next to his Socialist friend, who is being led to jail once more for his political activity. The novel ends with a line of verse which the hero remembers vividly: "If you truly want me, why did

[4] *The Quail and the Fall* (1962), 89.
[5] *The Beggar* (1965), 161–62.

you desert me?" By raising such a question, the novel seems to imply that the hero has reached the point of repentance. Perhaps more important, as some critics have suggested, the author wants to impute a similar sense of guilt and responsibility to other Egyptian intellectuals who lose their moral strength in the face of temptations or obstacles.

Mahfuz's concern with man's weakness, his yearning for a better life, his seemingly futile struggle against evil and other universal issues has led him to reenact man's odyssey since Adam's fall in an allegorical but highly controversial novel *The Children of Our Quarter* (published serially in 1959 in Cairo, and as a book in Beirut, 1967). Mahfuz once cryptically remarked in an interview that this work is the antithesis of Swift's *Travels* in the sense that Swift made use of fantasy to criticize reality, whereas he seeks to criticize fantasy by way of reality.[6] His purpose is to achieve a better grasp of man's reality and to sustain our hope. The work captures highlights in man's struggle for the ideal life. The fictional roles played by religion (Judaism, Christianity, and Islam) and science suggest that neither religion nor science alone has succeeded—or is likely to succeed—in offering a lasting solution for man's predicament. The author seems to imply that religious efforts are successful only as long as the heroic self-sacrificing prophets maintain sovereignty over their followers. Once this sovereignty is weakened, man's wickedness reasserts itself and the religion becomes subservient to the selfish interests of the "guardians" in power.

As might be expected, the religious theme dominates Mahfuz's work. Only in the last section does he turn to science, portraying its symbol ʿArafa as being basically concerned with the same objectives of his religious predecessors, though rejecting their magical or metaphysical answer. Scientific wonders, like religious miracles, appear to hold the key to man's ills, but are also misused by the self-centered guardians. Consequently, ʿArafa meets his death as he strives, contrary to the wish of the guardians, to transform his vision into a reality. However distressing the fate of this "new prophet" may be, the seemingly endless futility of man's efforts to cope with his ills is offset by a reassuring tone in the form of rumors about ʿArafa's ultimate triumph with the help of his disciples. Mahfuz does not indicate with certainty how this triumph or how the cure for man's problems can be attained, but he offers hints which suggest that he

[6] *Hiwar* 1, no. 3 (March-April 1963), 72.

is looking for the missing side of his triangle (religion, science, and socialism)—a just sociopolitical order or Sufi socialism under which both religion and science can be fully pursued for the good of man. It is in an atmosphere of such hopeful waiting for salvation that Mahfuz tends to sustain the fruitless efforts of his heroes in their struggle against evil.

THE POLITICAL NOVEL: THE INTERNAL PHASE

As some of Mahfuz's novels indicate, the search for a humane and rational political order recurs as a dominate theme in the Arabic novel, often reflecting the protagonist's impatience with, and criticism of, government measures, sluggish and corrupt bureaucracy, political opportunism, and senseless fratricidal partisan clashes. In his zeal for drastic political reform and his underestimation of archaic but still-powerful values and institutions, the hero frequently vacillates between a feeling of impotence in asserting his vision and a sense of disillusionment. Only occasionally does he emerge triumphant, and then only after enduring frustration and disillusionment from which he cannot completely recover.

A case in point in the main character of *Nothing Matters* (Cairo, 1963) by the Egyptian journalist and novelist Ihsan Abd Al-Quddus (1919–). Obsessed by the need to find a faith that gives meaning to his life, Hilmi follows different paths, but none seems to fulfill his expectations. First, he joins the Muslim Brotherhood, only to discover that it embraces what he regards as fanaticism, hypocrisy, and violence. During his brief association with the movement, he is taught that European civilization is the civilization of atheists and unbelievers; that the Egyptian government or any other government which implements man's laws and discards God-given laws is atheistic; that other political parties are poisoned likewise with atheism; and that it is the obligation of true believers to work for the destruction of both the government and the parties, and for the emergence of an Islamic state that will abide by God's teaching.[7]

Disappointed with this dogma, he turns to a secular Egyptian-oriented party which gradually destroys the foundation of his early religious experience without offering him peace of mind. Finally, he is introduced to materialism as represented by the local Communist

[7] Ihsan Abd Al-Quddus, *Nothing Matters* (Cairo, 1963), 152–53.

party; once more the answers seem far from being adequate. After joining and rejecting all these groups, he comes to the conclusion that each leads only to partial truths and that his task is to search for a faith that encompasses the positive ingredients of all these experiences. The cycle begins with faith in spiritualism, moves to secular nationalism, and ends with disillusionment in materialism. Not yielding to despair, Hilmi adopts a new and vaguely structured belief that combines his faith in God, reason, and individual moral responsibility. Armed with this faith, he, in his capacity as an engineer in a nationalized construction company, attempts to honestly perform his duties. He is caught, however, in a merciless struggle with corruption that infests the revolution's apparatus, leading to his dismissal for stubbornly resisting an ill-planned factory project. The only resort left for him is to write to Nasser, but he gives up the idea, realizing that a leader concerned with the greater issues of the revolution should not be burdened with such an isolated incident.

However, his setback does not last long; the factory constructed against his advice collapses, as he had predicted, and as a result he is reinstated and scandals associated with the project are revealed. But his sense of triumph remains incomplete because he finds that there are still many disloyal spokesmen for the revolution who obstruct an honest implementation of the government's revolutionary decisions. One of these is his friend, Tawfiq, an opportunist who manages to deceive his superiors and maintain his position. In contrast to Hilmi's faith in the ability of the revolution to effect drastic change, Tawfiq views with skepticism the revolution's power to fashion men in its image, as he finds himself in the midst of corrupt officials or party members. He openly questions Hilmi's wisdom, points to the futility of his endeavors, and persists in opportunistic "revolutionary" stance even after Hilmi's triumph. The novel closes with Hilmi's determination to resume his unfinished battle against corruption in spite of two frustrating mentalities: opportunism and indifference.

The rise of opportunists to power has been repeatedly exposed as a symptom of the intellectual's moral bankruptcy and one of the basic evils which revolutionary governments have failed to eradicate. Raouf, one of the central characters in Mahfuz's *The Thief and the Dogs* (1961), is an opportunist editor who once encouraged robbery as an act of patriotism against the establishment. Sa'id, a former associate, takes his teachings literally and is caught and jailed. When he is released, he turns to Raouf as the logical source of assistance. But

Raouf, the editor, not only fails to help his friend resume a normal life but assists in his destruction by publishing informative reports on Sa'id's past.

However, the most detailed account of this symptom appears in Fathi Ghanim's *The Man Who Lost His Shadow*.[8] The novel covers the last years of the old royal regime and the early years of Nasser's rise to power. Yusuf, the chief editor of a leading newspaper in Cairo, rises from a lower middle-class status to his important position through intrigue and hypocrisy. In the process, he severs his ties to the past, including friends and family, and ultimately wins everything—but loses himself. The story is told in four parts and by four characters: Mabruka, a former servant and Yusuf's stepmother; Samia, his mistress, a would-be movie star; Mohammed, his former boss, a corrupt editor whose position Yusuf usurps; and finally Yusuf himself, who sums up his rise to power in an unflattering confession. All tell their stories in the first person, referring to identical events and sometimes repeating identical dialogues. This technique has been criticized as "a device that causes some suspense but ends by diffusing the plot."[9] Nevertheless, the author succeeds in developing an authentic and multidimensional image of opportunism which dehumanizes men and undermines the system it professes to serve, but which seems to survive against all odds. The total picture of the leading influential figures is, however, excessively ugly and uninspiring. As one of the American reviewers observes, "If frustration and unhappiness have on occasion bred compassion and developed character, little of either is evident in this arena of moral squalor where each man, each woman, seems blinder, more predatory than his rival or neighbor."[10]

A sharp contrast to Ghanim's opportunist hero can be found in a partially autobiographical novel by Suhayl Idris, a leading novelist from Lebanon and the editor of the influential literary journal *Al-Adab*. Sami in *Our Burning Fingers* (Beirut, 1962) is the editor of a literary journal and a creative writer who strives to bring into harmonious interplay a variety of his personal interests and responsibilities. As a writer, he is concerned with the artistic quality of his

[8] Fathi Ghanim, *The Man Who Lost His Shadow*, trans. Desmond Stewart (London, 1966).

[9] See the remark made by Harold M. Grutzmacher in *Books Today* of the *Chicago Tribune*, 24 July 1966, 7.

[10] William H. Archer, 'The Man Who Lost His Shadow," *Best Sellers* 26 (1 July 1966), 131.

work; as an editor, he is committed politically and culturally to the Arab cause but is faced with conflicting ideologies and financial problems; and as an individual, he aspires to remain faithful to his wife. Despite financial hardships, his brief teaching experience at a foreign institution suspected for its political activities, and his extramarital adventures, Sami manages to approximate in performance the ideal he set for himself. He seems capable of recovering from setbacks or moral flaws and of pursuing an honest and independent course of action. Central among his virtues is his sense of individual freedom, which is rarely encountered in Arabic novels. Although committed to the Arab revolutionary cause, he refuses to join any political party even if he sympathizes with its ideals because, as he puts it, any partisan commitment is a threat to his freedom of thought and writing. The novel betrays qualities redolent of existentialism which fascinates Idris not only as a doctoral student in Paris but also as a translator and promoter of existentialist works. This tendency is revealed in Sami's continued search for meaning, his moral responsibility, his inquietude, and his insistence on freedom of choice and action.

If Idris displays an understandable tendency to idealize his hero, Ghaib T. Farman, an Iraqi novelist, tends to "deheroize" his characters, including himself, in his novel *Five Voices* (Beirut, 1968). Farman draws on his experience as a journalist to offer what may be called an inside story of some leftist intellectuals in Iraq a few years before the downfall of the royal regime in 1958. His novel explores the feelings, ideas, and personal conduct of five intellectuals: Ibrahim, a lawyer who is editor of an opposition newspaper but, once it is suspended by the government, who retreats into his private world awaiting the day when the paper resumes publication; Sa'id, a journalist (representing the author) whose bent for public service is overshadowed by his weakness and who chooses to flee the country rather than defy persecution; a second journalist and a poet, Sharif, whose obsession with sex in conduct and poetry strikes a discordant note in his professed political ideology; Hamid, a bank employee who poses as a progressive but whose performance displays irresponsibility and indifference, whether in relation to his family or public issues; and Abd Al-Khaliq, a government employee who, despite his seemingly mature and far-sighted vision, loses faith when his people fail to seize golden opportunities for popular action against the regime. With these ambivalent characters, the novelist attempts to capture the climate of restlessness, frustration, and boredom that characterized Iraq prior to the 1958 revolution, but, as the Lebanese novelist Suhayl Idris remarked, Farman's characters do not suggest that a revolution is in the making. This is due not so much to a lack of fidelity in the portrayal as to the narrow choice of characters. Farman's characters belong to a political ideology which expresses faith in evolution rather than revolution, and rejects, on the whole, acts of violence or conspiracy. Consequently, they are overtaken by a mood of resignation and helplessness in the face of a repressive political system.

One of the novels that deal sympathetically with Arab aspirations for unity is *Tshombe* (Beirut, 1965) by the Syrian novelist Adib Nahwi. Tshombe's role as a separatist in Congo's politics in the early sixties is contemptuously used to characterize the conduct of the separatist in Nahwi's work. The story, set in an ancient quarter in Aleppo during Syria's secession in 1961 from the short-lived union with Egypt, describes the agony of the characters as they see their cherished hope of unity shattered, and as their spirit of resistance is gradually subdued by the separatist regime. Most Arabic novels revolve around intellectuals; in contrast, Nahwi's heroes are members of the working class, unpretentious men who are deeply patriotic. Nahwi has chosen a style of language that is well-suited to his characters. It is highly colloquial and rich with folkloric imagery and phrases. Al-Haj Saayaat, an old man and the civilian chief of the quarter, appears to be cooperating with the separatist regime as an informer. By assuming such a dishonorable role, he exposes himself to public scorn and humiliation, but the novel reveals near its end that he is actually a Unionist and loyal party member. He has been deliberately chosen by the Unionist party to act as a traitor so that he can shelter in his house a party leader sought by the regime and carry on, without government suspicion, important party activities. In his endurance of daily insults, Al-Haj offers an eloquent testimony of man's capacity for self-sacrifice in the service of an ideal. When his wife pleads that he put an end to their suffering by revealing his true patriotic role, he refuses to do so and entertains the hope, in a pathetic monologue, that his redemption when the Union is restored is not far off.

THE EXTERNAL PHASE

Characters involved in actions against foreign occupation or domination have not been given primary treatment in the postwar novels. Nevertheless, reference should be made to several attempts to depict Arab resistance to external dangers. *There is a Man in Our House* (Cairo, 1957) by Ihsan Abd Al-Quddus in the story of Ibrahim, a self-denying patriot—reminiscent of the Egyptian commandos or *fedayeen* in the early fifties—who repeatedly risks his life in an attempt to bring about his country's liberation. He attacks British soldiers, assassinates a leading politician viewed as an enemy agent, is imprisoned, escapes, and finally meets death in a suicidal attack on a British camp in Cairo. But what seems to stand out as a positive feature is not only Ibrahim's patriotic spirit or his willingness to sacrifice himself, but also the redeeming effect his conduct has on a number of apathetic and morally weak characters whom he meets while seeking shelter in their house. The transition from a morally corrupt individual ready to act as an informer to a man of principle, the shift from complete indifference to political awareness and commitment are well described. The novel does contain elements of overoptimism, romantic patriotism, and a measure of artificiality in contriving happy endings for several characters, but the overall portrayal of individual rather than collective heroism and the political tension in Egypt before the revolution of 1952 is unmistakably authentic.

The tragic conflict in Palestine has been a source of inspiration for Arab poets for more than fifty years, but only recently have the fiction writers made it their theme. During the last twenty years, a small number of novels and numerous short stories have sought to bring out the various issues and consequences of the Arab-Israeli conflict: the injustice done the Palestinians in the creation of Israel, their attempts to defend or regain their rights, their suffering in the refugee camps, their humiliating effort to find livelihood in different parts of the Arab world, and the corruption of the regimes which have failed to effectively face the Israeli challenge. But very few of these attempts have successfully treated the basic issues involved. Yusuf Al-Sibaai, a former Egyptian military officer and a prolific writer of sentimental novels, has tried in *The Road of the Return* (Cairo, 1958) to stress the negative aspects that led to the Arab defeat in 1948. He ended up, however, with a melodramatic story of men who are only incidentally concerned with the war. Jabra I. Jabra, a leading novelist and critic from Palestine, is more successful in suggesting the mood of angry and disappointed Palestinians and other Arab intellectuals in his novel *Hunters in a Narrow Street* (London, 1960). The Palestinian conflict, however, is treated only as a secondary theme, out of which transpires a self-critical image, as the following remark suggests: "Dishonesty right and left, within and without.... Our papers find in Palestine a rich source of material to fill up their columns. It's repetitious, uninformed, hotheaded, high-worded and the people are sick of it. But how else can we prove to them we're patriotic?" [11] Perhaps a more thorough and mature treatment of the Palestinians' predicament is offered by two young novelists, Ghassan Kanafani, a Palestinian, and Halim Barakaat, a Lebanese. The former has thus far published three novels on the subject: *Men Under the Sun* (Beirut, 1963), *What is Left For You* (Beirut, 1966), and *Returning to Jaffa* (Beirut, 1970).

The central theme of *Men Under the Sun* is the futility or immorality of self-centered solutions in the context of a national predicament. The novel's three Palestinian refugees set out on a journey to Kuwait, the oil-rich Arab state on the Persian Gulf. Since they are displaced individuals without a country and without legal papers, they resort to illegal means to cross national borders. After dehumanizing bargains with smugglers in Basrah, Iraq, they resign themselves to a dangerous scheme by which they hope to enter Kuwait. They meet a Palestinian driver who offers to hide them in his truck's empty water tank at border posts, where he stops to process his papers. The refugees begin their desert journey on a hot summer day, survive the tank's suffocating heat at the first stop, but meet their deaths at the Kuwaiti border. As if to underline the futility of their effort, an absurd situation causes their deaths. The driver, who became impotent during the Palestinian war of 1948, is delayed at the custom's office by remarks about his sexual adventures. Thus a few minutes pass beyond the margin of safety set for his victims' endurance in the tank; he returns to his truck only to discover that they are dead. The novel ends on a note implying irresponsibility on the part of the Palestinians themselves; the driver wonders, after burying his victims, why they failed to knock on the tank's walls, and why they did not speak out.

Kanafani's technique is full of symbolism which alludes to both the predicament of the Palestinians and the complicity of different parties in their continued suffering.

Halim Barakaat (1933–   ) attacks with pitiless candor his people's weaknesses and guilt in two novels devoted to the Palestinian tragedy. *Six Days* (Beirut, 1961) is the story—told in the form of a

---

[11] Jabra I. Jabra, *Hunters in a Narrow Street* (London, 1960), 27.

six-day diary—of a small Arab town as it struggles with the enemy's ultimatum to either surrender or be completely wiped out. Given six days to make up its mind, the town accepts the option made by Suhayl, the hero, death or triumph, and begins hasty and inept preparations for resistance. Suhayl, a Christian intellectual, constantly brings home the point that his people have failed in their encounter with external enemies because they have failed to correct their shortcomings from within. Primarily through his eyes, we see irreconcilable patterns of behavior: a Westernized girl next to a woman covered by a thick veil, the selfishness of characters who seek to escape or seize upon the opportunity to acquire wealth, the disorganized or emotional nature of the townspeople's efforts, and betrayal by a character posing as a patriot. The story ends with the expected enemy triumph, but not before two instances of heroic resistance occur. Suhayl's fighting comrades-at-arms reveal unwavering loyalty to their ideals, and Suhayl himself refuses to compromise with the enemy when arrested, or to act with indifference toward a seemingly hopeless situation. Both instances emanate from an individual, rather than collective, spirit to fight.

Barakaat's gloomy social settings stress the urgent need for a fresh and honest examination not only of political and social ills, but also of the manner in which they have been treated. In order to bring about a radical transformation of the society's conditions and outlook, a faithful leader capable of performing such act is needed. Suhayl in *Six Days* makes a comparison between the Flying Dutchman searching for a faithful woman, and his people who, like the Dutchman, are sailing helplessly. Barakaat turns this motif into a major theme in his second novel, *The Return of the Flier to the Sea* (Beirut, 1969).

The central part of the novel, a six-day diary, unravels the inner feelings and thoughts of the characters as they live the events of the June 1967 war. Ramzi, a university professor and a Palestinian in exile for twenty years, wonders whether the new encounter with the enemy will terminate his exile. Emotionally, he is sustained by a sense of confidence, but intellectually he realizes that reality does not support his hope and confidence. Through his monologue and discussions with others, he gradually develops the view that his country is backward, disjointed, and lacks both planning and a realistic vision of the future. He attacks the idea of unity among the Arabs as a myth, pointing to the fact that Arabs live in their shells, detached from each other. Neither genuine cooperation nor coordination exists among the Arabs—as states, as groups, or as individuals. He feels that the revolutions, which are regarded as a positive development, have failed to bring about basic changes. As for students, teachers, and intellectuals in general, Ramzi finds them totally unprepared to perform in the present crisis, and incapable of any act except killing time, like the rest of the people, reading newspapers, listening to the radio and TV stations, or exhausting their vitality in senseless emotional outburst. They are partly to blame because they have failed to make proper use of their potential, but the schools, universities, and the various governments are primarily responsible. They have failed to prepare these intellectuals for such a crisis by barring them from free participation in the transformation of their society, or by wasting their resourcefulness. He recalls that thousands of experts, technicians, and specialists are paralyzed for one reason or another: for example, persecution, improper placement, and lack of encouragement or incentives.

The other important point in this self-critical appraisal is related to the unrealistic assessment the Arab makes of forces at work in his society or elsewhere, and the deceptive and illusionary world which he helps in shaping or to which he falls victim. This becomes very clear as Ramzi listens to exaggerated accounts of the war and the news of Arab armies advancing in the enemy's territory, while in fact, the Arab defeat was determined or predicted on the first day of the war.

Although Ramzi seems more concerned with the faults of Arab society, he does not absolve the West of responsibility for the creation of Israel or the problem of the refugees, and for entertaining an unrealistic assessment of the Arabs' determination to regain their right. The West and the Zionists suffer from a number of myths or false assumptions: that the Arabs will give up their fight; that once the refugees are forced to settle elsewhere, the tension will be removed; and that the more frequently the Arabs are defeated militarily, the greater will be their willingness to compromise. To the protagonist, these claims are completely false and will generate a more militant response on the part of the Arabs.

Therefore, it is not surprising that he sees, in the aftermath of the war, the *fedayeen* as the only hopeful sign which restores to the Arab his pride and his faith in the future. Ironically, Ramzi finds in Western voices the best means to express his anger against the West, and his faith in the ultimate triumph of his people: T. S. Eliot, the

Flying Dutchman, Dante, American civil rights songs, and Dylan Thomas, who, in his poem, "Death Shall Have No Dominion," seems to reflect the Arab mood of defeat and defiance. By so doing, Barakaat seems to suggest that his people are not basically anti-West, that once the causes of tension are removed, mutually beneficial Arab-Western relationships will be restored.

THE NOVEL AND WOMAN'S SEARCH FOR EMANCIPATION

In spite of the significant progress that Arab women have made in the last twenty years, they are still engaged in a painful search for identity and a meaningful role and position in a highly traditional and conservative society. It was natural for the postwar novels to turn increasingly to the various issues involved in this search. But the novelists, both male and female, have rarely succeeded in providing a rich and inspiring picture of the feminine protagonist. Perhaps this is mainly because they have not yet evolved a clear vision of what position or role a woman should have in her society and her relationship with the other sex.

Representative of this uncertainty is the hero of *Meeting There* (Cairo, 1961) by Tharwat Abaza (Egypt); Abbas rejects his father's world of traditional values and espouses progressive Western ideas. He has premarital relations with a girl whom he promises to marry, but looks suspiciously at his sister's talking alone to one of his relatives. Later, he backs out of his promises to his girlfriend, casting doubt on her integrity and her moral ability to act as his faithful wife. After having endured adverse consequences of his break with traditions, Abbas realizes that his self-fulfillment can be attained only by restoring his ties with his father's world. This he achieves by marrying, in accordance with traditional procedures, one of his relatives who holds that woman's proper place is in her own house.

A more consistent but less drastic norm of man-woman relationship is encountered in Suhayl Idris's autobiographical novel *Al-Khandaq Al-Ghamiq* (Beirut, 1958). Set in one of Beirut's traditional quarters known as "Al-Khandaq Al-Ghamiq," the story provides an excellent example of the process of change through which an urban middle-class family goes. Sami, the son of a religious father, attends a religious school, but within a four-year span he gradually emancipates himself from his father's traditional worldview. He asserts,

among other things, his right to pursue a secular education and his
freedom to associate with the other sex. Then he comes to his sister's
aid in her conflict with the same world that he rejects and acts as an
instrument to her discovery of the world beyond the family's limits.
He introduces her to a trusted friend of his, and stands behind her
when she decides to put aside the veil, symbolic of the barrier that
has stood between woman and her society. Both Sami and his sister
succeed in their rebellious efforts, but they do not resolve, nor do
they face, other more sensitive issues such as premarital relationships
or the extent of woman's freedom to participate in public life.

Some of the sensitive problems that women face in their professional life are reflected in *The Vice* (Cairo, 1962?) by Yusuf
Idris (1927–). Journalistic and didactic in nature, the work
sketches the tragic experience of Sana, one of five girls newly appointed to jobs in a government office where all the other employees
are men. It is a hostile, hypocritical, and corrupt atmosphere. Sana's
efforts to perform her duties as a morally responsible public servant,
although briberies are constantly committed in her office and immoral overtures are made, succeed only temporarily. Ultimately, she
is trapped into accepting a bribe and then succumbs to other immoral acts.

In contrast to this example of woman's quick fall before the temptation or corruption of the outside world, Ameena of *I Am Free*
(Cairo, 1954) by Ihsan Abd Al-Quddus is an extraordinary woman.
Since childhood, she has stubbornly pursued an independent course
of action and resisted immoral traps. As is customary with this
author's technique, the novel begins with a prefatory note: "There
is no such thing as freedom. The most free amongst us is a slave to
the principles in which he believes and the objective for which he
strives. We seek freedom in order to place it in the service of our
aims. Before you seek freedom ask yourself: To what aim shall I
give my freedom?" [12] Ameena, obsessed with a desire to maintain her
freedom—"freedom from the house, from conventions, from the
East, from her need for men, all men" [13]—reaches a point where she
discovers that her vision of freedom is leading nowhere, and that
freedom without commitment is nothing but emptiness. After a
period of soul-searching, she begins a new phase of her life in which
she commits herself to the service of one of her childhood friends,

[12] Ihsan Abd Al-Quddus, *I Am Free* (Cairo, 1954), 13.
[13] *Ibid.*, 148.

who is noted for his moral character and lofty patriotic principles. By becoming committed to her friend and his ideals, and thus restricting her freedom, she believes that she has not given up her freedom; rather she has placed it in the service of a new faith and a true love. For Ameena it is now immaterial whether her relationship with her friend (which lasts eight years) is consummated in marriage in the traditional sense. What is more important and rewarding is that she has demonstrated her ability, as a woman, to pursue her chosen course of action without yielding to established norms of behavior. The plot borders on the unbelievable, at least in its Egyptian context, but does develop a sympathetic view of the basic questions which the Arab woman has to resolve in her struggle for equal rights.

The attempts of male novelists to deal with woman's search for emancipation often suffer from excessive sentimentality, artificiality, or failure to understand the feminine nature.

However, several promising young women have taken up various aspects of this subject in the postwar years: Jadhibiyya Sidqi, Sufi Abdullah (Egypt), Daisy Al-Ameer (Iraq), Samira Azzam (Palestine), Ghada Al-Samman, Colette Khuri (Syria), and Layla Baalabakki (Lebanon).

Perhaps the best examples are those written by Khuri and Baalabakki.[14] Lina of Baalabakki's novel *I Live* (Beirut, 1958) is an extreme example of a woman disenchanted with her existence as she seeks to find meaning for her life and asserts her individuality despite the restrictions of a conservative society. Describing the rebellious mood of her generation in a lecture with the suggestive title, *We, Without Masks* (Beirut, 1959), Baalabakki stresses the need for freedom as the motivating force. "We are more cruel," she declares, "more violent, more miserable than the youth of America and Europe because we are still enduring a battle to gain our freedom, as individuals, a state and people whereas they practice freedom."

She does not hesitate to confront her audience with a basic grievance—women's restricted association with men. "Here they teach us," she complains, "to be ashamed of our bodies, to fight every feeling which ties us to the other sex; then we waste days torn by

---

[14] These remarks on Khuri and Baalabakki are taken from my paper on "Islam and Westernization in Modern Arabic Fiction" published in the *Yearbook of Comparative and General Literature* 20 (1971), 81–88.

anxiety. How shall I see him? Where shall I see him? And what shall I do if someone surprises me while talking with him in the street?" [15]

Despite her attempts to escape established mores, the heroine of *I Live* fails in her quest for self-fulfillment. She discovers that she, in her zealous obsession with freedom, is denied the support of the antitraditional elements of her society. Even her chosen hero, Baha, a Marxist, seems unprepared to marry her, primarily because he, like other traditionalists, has reservations about the morality of her free conduct. Having failed to consummate her will in life, she attempts to commit suicide in a gesture of defiance, but she fails and is compelled to return to her family's house which she so much despised. The young novelist seeks to underline, among other things, not only the absurdity of tradition but also the hypocrisy and dishonesty concealed by an antitraditional façade.

Another woman novelist, Kulit (Colette) Suhayl Al-Khuri, a Christian from Syria, has addressed herself to the predicament of the Arab woman in a number of novels and short stories including *Days With Him* (Beirut, 1959) and *One Night* (Beirut, 1961). In contrast to Baalabakki's sweeping condemnation of society, Al-Khuri presents a more mature and reasoned plea for understanding women's legitimate feelings and aspirations. The rebellious girl of *Days With Him*, Reem, manages with some success to work her way and assert her personality in a man's society, assuming a fairly independent role whether in relation to her association with men, work, or other matters. She is impressed, like the novel's other protagonist Ziyad, who is a Western-oriented musician, by women's life in the West, but she refuses to go all the way with Ziyad in emulating Western women. A vaguely defined norm of conduct which does not completely disregard Eastern values, particularly in the area of male-female relationships, is suggested. Stress is placed on women's right to pursue their education, to work, and to maintain an open association with men. The dilemma she faces stems from a variety of factors: a stagnant society that is not ready to recognize such rights, half-hearted support given by Western-oriented individuals, and the failure of educated women to stand collectively and consistently for their own rights. Therefore, it is natural that any individual act of defiance will result in unpleasant consequences if not complete disappointment. But Reem, partly because of her sympathetic understanding of her society and her resilience, manages to effect a posi-

[15] Layla Baalabakki, *We, Without Masks* (Beirut, 1959), 20–21.

tive change in Ziyad's outlook and to pursue a course that spares her self-destruction.

THE NOVEL AND THE PEASANT

Most Arab novelists have been preoccupied primarily with the problems of the city, the intelligentsia, the emancipation and education of women, and various aspects of urban life. In only a relatively small number of novels does the *fellah*, the peasant, assume a central role. One would expect to find a larger number, especially since *Zaynab* (Cairo, 1914), regarded as the first successful novel in Arabic, brought into focus the plight of the Egyptian *fellah* not only in its plot, but also by alluding anonymously to its author as "an Egyptian fellah." [16] Among the best peasant-oriented novels are *The Earth* (Cario, 1954) [17] and *The Peasant* (Cairo, 1967?) by the Egyptian writer Abd Al-Rahman Al-Sharqawi.

The Earth, set in prerevolutionary Egypt, provides a rich though slow-moving picture of the peasants' constant struggle against an unsympathetic authority, the ineffectiveness of their spontaneous actions, their intense love for the soil, and their often exploited fatalism and simplicity. In delineating the central position of the land in the peasant's life, Sharqawi uses a variety of devices: his description of peasant action, dialogue, and interior monologue. Examples include such passages as: "In a surge of violent feelings to protect the land, to give it water, the villagers set upon each other, beating and being beaten without thought or care: as if they were strangers to each other . . . as if each could do anything, however terrible, to his brother—do anything to obtain water." [18] Or a peasant girl's remark: "Those who have no soil have nothing, not even honor" in response to a suggestion that a landless young man might approach her for marriage. But some of the most revealing passages are those related to the insensitivity of the village's preacher, Sheikh Shinnawi, as he repeatedly injects God or Quranic verses into the peasants' deliberation on their practical problems:

> Sheikh Shinnawi asked everyone to join him in the chapter of the Koran called *Ya-Seen*, as a way of invoking God's vengeance on

[16] Written by M. H. Haykal (1889–1956), a prominent figure in Egyptian politics for more than thirty years, the work was intended to express the author's patriotic pride in Egypt and his romantic admiration for the primitive.

[17] Translated as *Egyptian Earth* by Desmond Stewart (London, 1962).

[18] Abd Al-Rahman Al-Sharqawi, *The Earth* (Cairo, 1954), Stewart's translation, p. 122.

the men from the Irrigation Department. At this Abdul Hadi could keep silent no longer. He asked with ironical politeness that the reverent Sheikh should either think of something better or keep his mouth shut and let others do the thinking.[19]

On another occasion, the sheikh announces in a Friday sermon that the village's water crisis is divine punishment, and when some of the restless farmers interrupt to protest his irrelevant explanation, he rants angrily about hell, punishment, blasphemy, and other religious matters. Again Abdul Hadi, one of the central characters, finds himself compelled to reject the sheikh's insinuation, reflecting in a monologue on the wretchedness of farmers hired as serfs and the affluence of landlords who escape God's wrath in spite of their impious acts.

> "Perhaps if the Sheikh himself owned some land," Abdul Hadi thought, "perhaps if he had mixed his sweat with the earth, and perhaps if he had seen the tender maize shoots wilting like dying children, perhaps then he would have understood . . . would have not equated the action of the Government with the wrath of God. But the Sheikh was not a farmer. He was, with his preaching, more like a man who had something to sell, and provided he could sell it, let the earth perish with thirst!"[20]

By such comments or thoughts, the novelist develops a negative, though familiar, image of the traditional religious leader who, in his approach to temporal problems, lacks perceptiveness, enthusiasm, and a genuine sense of self-denial. But, more important, he seems to imply that disenchantment with religion has spread from urban centers to the countryside.

In *The Peasant*, Sharqawi's second novel using the *fellah* as a central character, the author revisits his village in the postrevolutionary era to describe the effect of changes precipitated by the new revolutionary regime. In a balanced and critical approach, the novel succeeds in bringing out—with complete candor—the virtues and abuses of the Socialist measures. The language and the attitudes of the peasants are permeated with a new class awareness that restores to them a sense of pride and self-respect and inspires them to stand against those who would impede the process of socialization. The villains turn out to be none other than the individuals in charge of the local apparatus of the Socialist Union, including its secretary and the head of the Cooperative Society (described as a former land-

[19] *Ibid.*, 53–54.
[20] *Ibid.*, 65.

lord); various government officials on both local and national levels who protect each other to maintain their vested interest; and the village's sheikh who identifies himself with those in power—until they are defeated. Only after a series of humiliating episodes of investigation and torture do the peasants succeed in defeating their opponents by electing their own representatives to the Cooperative Society and the local Socialist Union.

The novel uses familiar techniques associated with Socialist Realism in its emphasis on the peasants' faith and perseverance in their patriotic struggle, the ultimate triumph of their cause, and the downfall of dishonest and self-centered bureaucrats. Although the work betrays antireligious overtones, the religious nature of the peasantry reasserts itself when they exhaust, without success, all legal means to secure the release of their imprisoned spokesmen. The narrator is besieged by the villagers to pray on their behalf at the shrines of several Muslim saints in Cairo. He hesitates, having the intellectual's lack of faith, then decides to honor their request. At the shrines he is surprised by the number of people who have come to voice their grievances and seek salvation through spiritual channels. He then raises a question which casts doubts on the success of the existing system: "Is it an act of piety that drives these people to God's saints or is it their loss of faith in God's creatures?" [21] Paradoxically, the happy news of the peasants' triumph becomes known only after the narrator performs his spiritual pilgrimage.

Relatively minor works based on a similar or related theme include *The Hands, the Earth and the Water* (Baghdad, 1948) by the leading Iraqi novelist Dhunnun Ayyub (1908–   ). This is the story of three idealistic intellectuals who undertake an agricultural project aimed at improving the peasant's economic conditions. Their efforts, however, run into a frustrating clash with the neighboring landlords, the apathy of the peasants and their fear of reprisals if they participate in the project, and hostile or indifferent government officials. As the French orientalist Jacques Berque [22] points out, Ayyub's work is a documentary on the feudal regime which was dominant in Iraq before 1958 and serves to underline the antithesis that exists between the peasants and their descendants, the more intellectual elements, who aspire to return to their roots.

The preceding survey has attempted to indicate the wide range of issues and problems with which most Arab novelists have been

[21] Abd Al-Rahman Al-Sharqawi, *The Peasant* (Cairo, 1967?), 248.
[22] "Iraq Society in Literature," *New Outlook* I, no. 6 (January 1958), 58–59.

preoccupied during the last twenty years. Admittedly, there is a pronounced emphasis on particular regional, political, or social problems as compared to universal themes, as there is a tendency among the novelists surveyed to bring forth a gloomy picture of conditions in their society especially under earlier regimes. By so doing, not only do they seem to aim at projecting the traditional socio-political system as totally incapable of reform, but also suggest, with a large measure of candor, that changes which "revolutionary" regimes or movements have brought about are not adequate or effective. However, in addressing themselves to postrevolutionary settings, they tend to infuse the predicament of their heroes with a tone of sympathy or a sense of identification with the new system as noted, for example, in Sharqawi's *Peasant* and Abd Al-Quddus's *Nothing Matters* and some of Mahfuz's works. Although it is too early to generalize, one can detect an evolving pattern which marks the novelists' portrayal of postrevolutionary settings in contrast to that of the prerevolutionary era, a pattern that includes, among its ingredients, the hero's ambivalent attitude toward his reality, or the "system" which determines his fate.

A SELECTIVE BIBLIOGRAPHY

TRANSLATIONS AND ANTHOLOGIES

Ghanim, Fathi. *The Man Who Lost His Shadow*, trans. D. Stewart. London, 1966.

Al-Hakim, T. *Bird of the East*, trans. R. B. Winder. Beirut, 1966.

———. *Maze of Justice*, trans. A. Eban. London, 1947.

Husayn, Taha. *An Egyptian Childhood*, trans. E. H. Paxton. London, 1932.

———. *The Stream of Days*, trans. Hilary Wayment. Vol. 1. London, 1948.

Johnson-Davis, D. *Modern Arabic Short Stories*. London, 1967.

Mahfouz, N. *Midaq Alley*, trans. T. Le Gassick. Beirut, 1966.

Manzaloui, Mahmoud. *Arabic Writing Today: The Short Story*. Cairo, 1968.

Salih, Tayyeb. *Season of Migration to the North*, trans. D. Johnson-Davis. London, 1969.

———. *The Wedding of Zein*, trans. D. Johnson-Davis. London, 1968.

Sharqawi, A. R. *Egyptian Earth*, trans. D. Stewart. London, 1962.

STUDIES

Abadir, Akef, and Roger Allen. "Nagib Mahfuz, His World of Literature." *The Arab World* 16 (Sept.–Oct. 1970), 7–14; 16 (Nov.–Dec. 1970), 9–20, 17 (Aug.–Sept. 1971), 7–18.

Altoma, Salih J. "Westernization and Islam in Modern Arabic Fiction." *Yearbook of Comparative and General Literature* 20 (1971), 81–88.

Awad, Louis. "Literary Schools and Socialist Literature." *Political and Social Thought in the Contemporary Middle East,* ed. Kemal H. Karpat. New York, 1968. Pp. 175–84.

Badawi, M. W. "The Lamp of Umm Hashim: The Egyptian Intellectual Between East and West." *Journal of Arabic Literature* 1 (1970), 145–61.

Cowan, David. "Literary Trends in Egypt Since 1952." *Egypt Since the Revolution,* ed. P. J. Vatikiotis. New York, 1968. Pp. 162–77.

Gabrieli, F. "Contemporary Arabic Fiction." *Middle Eastern Studies* 2 (1965), 79–84.

Khulusi, S. A. "Modern Arabic Fiction with Special Reference to Iraq." *Islamic Culture* 30 (1956), 199–210.

Le Gassick, Trevor. "A Malaise in Cairo: Three Contemporary Egyptian Authors." *Middle East Journal* 21 (1967), 145–56.

———. "Najib Mahfouz' Trilogy." *Middle East Forum* 39 (Feb. 1963), 31–34.

Milson, Menahem. "Nagib Mahfuz and the Quest for Meaning." *Arabica* 17 (1970), 177–86.

———. "Some Aspects of the Modern Egyptian Novel." *Muslim World* 60 (1970), 237–46.

———. "Taha Husayn's The Tree of Misery: A Literary Expression of Cultural Change." *Asian and African Studies* 3 (1967), 69–99.

Sfeir, George N. "The Contemporary Arabic Novel." *Daedalus* 95 (1966), 941–60. Reprinted in *Fiction in Several Languages,* ed. Henry Peyre (New York, 1968), 60–79.

Sherif, Nur. "The Thief and the Hounds by Naguib Mahfouz." *About Arabic Books* (Beirut, 1970), 74–81.

Somekh, S. "Zaᶜbalawi—Author, Theme and Technique." *Journal of Arabic Literature* 1 (1970), 24–35.

Vatikiotis, P. J. "The Corruption of Futuwwa: A Consideration of Despair in Nagib Mahfūz's Awlād Hāritnā." *Middle Eastern Studies* 7 (1971), 169–84.

———. "The Sad Millenarian: An Examination of Awlād Hāratinā." *Middle Eastern Studies* 7 (1971), 49–61.

Senghor's Africanism
and the Francophone Mode

GERMAINE BRÉE

When I was younger, I would gladly have come forward as the spokesman for all Africa, or at least for "Négritude." By now experience has taught me the diversity of Negroes and Africans and it would be presumptuous of me to speak in the name of either.
—PRESIDENT LÉOPOLD SEDAR SÉNGHOR, *Africa Report*, February 1967

If, for Africa, 1960 was the "year of destiny," for many Africans it was also the beginning of a long and difficult process of national construction. It opened the decade in which some forty new African nations acquired sovereignty. What "nationalism" had meant in the years of the struggle for independence could no longer apply to their postindependence situation. Among the men who most articulately and consistently voiced the feelings and the concepts that so deeply marked the emerging new values and who helped to shape their course, President Léopold Sédar Senghor of Sénégal is a figure who stands apart. From the year 1934, when he founded, with Aimé Césaire of Martinique and Leon Damas of Guyana, the review *L'étudiant noir*, to the present, when he presides over the destiny of the Republic of Sénégal, he seems single-mindedly to have followed a straight itinerary as poet, literary critic, spokesman for francophone Black Africa, and statesman. A figure of quiet dignity, less flamboyant than his more eloquent and dramatic friend Aimé Césaire, yet a man possessed by an inner vision, his work as poet and essayist so far has received little attention in this country. His literary output is considerable and varied: six collections of poems published between 1945 and 1961; a number of articles, prefaces, translations, and essays that cover a wide range of topics: [1] studies in linguistics, literary criticism, definitions of cultural problems, political discussions of topical issues. From none of these, however brief or purely ceremonial, has Africa ever been absent, much as it has never been absent from Senghor's effort to make explicit and define those traits of the "black personality" evoked by the word "Négritude."

In his introduction to the first volume of his collected prose writings, *Liberté I: Négritude et humanisme*, alluding to that title and to the title of a further volume *The Concept of Nation and the African view of Socialism* (*Nation et voie africaine du socialisme*), President Senghor remarked: "Everything the author has written, for twenty-five years, constitutes only *variations* on these four particular themes," i.e., Négritude, humanism, nationalism, and socialism. "In fact, since his years in the 'Quartier latin,' the author has been preoccupied only by those four ideas, which truly became an *obsession*. They explain his life and his work, even when he speaks of French poetry in the sixteenth century." [2] It seems to have been that obsession which first really "informed," as Gide would have said, the poet in Senghor, sending him back to the poetic forms alive in the oral literature of his people; the poet in turn then "informed" the statesman. One can, in a sense, organize the four obsessive themes in a kind of circular interdependence with the concept of Négritude at the dynamic core determining the content of the three others. Senghor's thesis concerning the particular non-Marxist form of socialism through which the new nations of Africa could best be organized rests upon his vision of the humanistic aspirations peculiar to black Africans, expressed in their art and literature as well as in their social organization. These all reveal the cultural values cherished, values which bear the stamp of and perpetuate a characteristic affectivity. Art in all its forms is the expression of that affectivity. Poetic speech or song is central then to the life of the community.

---

[1] A 1964 volume of 445 pages, *Liberté I*, subtitled *Négritude et humanisme* (Paris) collected 58 addresses and essays given between 1937 and 1963 of particular interest to our topic, as are also the longer essay *Nation et voie africaine du socialisme*, *Présence Africaine* (Paris, 1961) and the 50-page essay *Pierre Teilhard de Chardin et la politique africaine* (Paris, 1962). Armand Guibert has written a good introduction to Senghor's personality and work for the Senghor volume in the *Poètes d'aujourd'hui*, Seghers Séries (vol. 82). For a biography of President Senghor, see Milcent Ernest and Sordet Monique, *Léopold Sédar Senghor*, Seghers Séries (Paris, 1964).

[2] Preface to *Négritude et humanisme*, 7.

Very early in his career, Senghor defined his role as poet in relation to his people and to their traditions. He was to be the Dyâli, the singer poet, who among the Serère tribes—to which Senghor belongs—celebrates the greatness of a high personage; but the personage, for Senghor, was to be no single human being but a people. "Notre noblesse nouvelle est non de dominer notre peuple, mais d'être son rythme et son coeur.... Non d'être la tête du peuple mais bien sa bouche et sa trompette." [3] (Our new nobility is not to dominate our people, but to be its rhythm and its heart.... Not to be the head of the people but in truth its mouth and trumpet.)

And again, in a formal song, as poet addressing the maidens among his people:

> Mais je ne suis pas votre honneur, pas le Lion
>   téméraire, le Lion vert qui rugit l'honneur du
>   Sénégal
>   • • • • • •
> Je ne suis pas le Conducteur. Jamais tracé sillon
>   ni dogme comme le Fondateur
> La ville aux quatre portes, jamais proféré mot
>   à graver sur la pierre.
> Je dis bien: je suis le Dyâli. [4]

(I am not your honor, not the audacious Lion, the green Lion who roars out the honor of Senegal.... I am not the Leader. Never traced Furrow, or dogma as the Founder [traced]. The city with the four doors, never proffered a word to engrave on stone. I say in truth: I am the Dyâli.)

To that people in a fervent and prophetic prayer addressed to the "Elephant of Mbissel," one of the legendary mediators between men and the powers of the cosmos, he dedicated his life, words, and action:

> Grant that I may die for the quarrel of my people, and if need be
>   in the odor of powder and cannon.
> Preserve and root in my liberated heart the primordial love of that
>   people
> Make of me your Master of language; but now, appoint me its ambassador. [5]

For Senghor, literature and art can only be, as he himself has indicated, "functional, collective and committed." Political action and

---

[3] "Poème liminaire," *Hosties noires in Poèmes* (Paris, 1964), 55–62. The poem is dedicated to L. G. Damas. The translations are mine.
[4] "L'Absente," *Ethiopiques* (Paris, 1956), 23.
[5] "Le retour de l'Enfant prodigue," *Chants d'ombre* (Paris, 1964), 47–51.

poetry cannot be separated. Yet rare in Senghor's verse are the militant themes, the cries of revolt that we have come to associate with the rich vein of literary expression characteristic of the black "renaissance," and more particularly of the Martiniquean poet Aimé Césaire. The poet in Senghor's world is a courtly figure; he celebrates, illustrates, praises; and by naming he rekindles in the memory and imagination of his people the noble legends, myths, and achievements of the common past. In his introduction to the Seghers anthology of Senghor's poems, Armand Guibert questioned the appropriateness of one of Senghor's poems, entitled "Chaka," a "Dramatic poem for several voices" dedicated to the "Bantu martyrs of South Africa" and included in *Ethiopique*. A Zulu warrior and tyrant, sometimes known as the Black Napoleon of Africa, Chaka had conquered vast stretches of South African territory, which he had plunged into a blood bath, eventually massacring his own mother and fiancée. The Bantu epic had already been sung by an African poet, Thomas Mofolo, and translated into French in 1940. Guibert's objection to Senghor's interpretation of Chaka's revolt was that it glorified and justified unwarranted and bestial butchery. Understandably, the reproach mistakes the particular role of the poet as Senghor sees it. In the figure of Chaka, "pinned to the ground by three spears" and about to die, it is not the historic chieftain Senghor evokes, but the passion of a whole people incarnated in the proud figure of the man who sacrificed his private love for a woman to his revolt against the white invader, his vocation as poet to his role as leader. The poem, a dirge for the martyred Bantu, is the transmutation of the man, his renaissance beyond defeat as the "poet," the annunciator of a new dawn for his oppressed race. It is, Senghor believes, the poet's task "to prophesy, to awaken declining hope, to announce the final victory and the renaissance," [6] rather than to denounce. The personal sense of poetry as a perpetual recall of man's highest dignity bestowing upon men's acts the aura of beauty, hence meaning, sets Senghor apart among his black contemporaries and links him to a French poet he admires, St. John Perse.

When "on the morning of August 20, 1960" the Senegalese nation was born and Senghor became its first president, few had been his references to that nation as such. The allusion in the poem just quoted is an exception. When in *Black Hosts* (*Hosties noires*) he speaks to and for the Senegalese soldiers killed or made prisoner in

[6] *Négritude et humanisme*, 326.

France—"the Senegalese prisoners obscurely lying on the soil of France" [7]—whose destiny he shares, or when he recalls the family home, it is without a trace of exclusiveness.

> For we are here, gathered together, different in color—
> There are those whose color is like roasted coffee, others like golden bananas others like rice fields,
> Divers in features, costumes, customs, language: but deep in the eyes the same chart of suffering in the shadow of long feverish eyelashes:
> Kaffir, Kabyl, Somali, Moor, Fân
> Fôn, Bambara, Bobo, Mandiago....

Around the Africans, Senghor then gathers all the oppressed:

> Here is the miner of the Asturias, the Liverpool docker, the Jew thrown out of Germany, and Dupont and Dupuis and all the lads from Saint-Denis. [8]

One among the anonymous soldiers designated by the French as the Senegalese *tirailleurs* ("sharpshooters"), Senghor merges into the group of all his brothers alive and dead the 500,000 men thrown by France into its battlefields; they in turn draw around them all their African brothers, and beyond them all the oppressed, the infantrymen in all the armies of the world, including those of France, to which Senghor remained loyal in her defeat. This merging of the poet's own individual situation with the great mass of humanity through ever-widening circles is characteristic of Senghor's poems, reflecting his natural inclination to reach out and gather all others into the circle of his poem. Senghor's "peuple" then people the earth; through the mediation of his own situation, seen through French eyes as a black from the colonial territory of Sénégal, the privileged boy from the royal Sérère tribe becomes brother to all exploited human beings on this earth. Black Africa is then the mediator, conferring upon the poet the gift of social innocence, the mission of liberator. It becomes the spiritual homeland of the "wretched" of the earth, and the African is thus today, whether he knows it or not, a man charged with a mission. When Senghor speaks as he sometimes does of an "African nation," he is referring to that Africa as much as to the geographical and complex continent itself. It is a "seamless" whole that wipes out all frontiers: between the self and the other; between Senghor the privileged Sérère poet and the

---

[7] *Hosties noires* in *Poèmes*, 61.
[8] "A l'appel de la Race de Saba," *Hosties noires,* 19.

men of his own tribe; between the Sérère and the Senegalese; between the Senegalese and the other blacks; between the blacks and the whites.

Time and time again, in congresses and conferences, African leaders have voiced their concern for the need to develop among Africans a sense of the whole, a feeling that each African and all Africans belong to a single community. For Senghor himself, that is the first meaning of the word "nation," the corollary being that the community must insure the full and harmonious development of the potentialities of each of its members, more simply stated, their happiness. In Senghor's terms, one is not "within" a community but "of" a community. It was the sense of that community that first released the poet in Senghor, and it was the poet's vision that the political activist and statesman voiced and struggled to bring into being, at least potentially, within the bounds of political reality. "Négritude" he defined and redefined in terms of the developing African situation which carried him along in its momentum. It seems to have been his way of maintaining his own goal and sense of purpose in the surge of events.

The word first expressed his sense of his own separate identity with regard to the French culture he had so eagerly absorbed, and his bonds with French-speaking blacks of whatever origin. Négritude also accompanied his active partisanship, among his own people as well as the French, for the creation of an independent French Black African group of nations, within a French Commonwealth, with equal rights for all its citizens. Consciously a *métis* ("half breed") culturally, he first rehabilitated and sought out the African component in his "métissage," namely, the Négritude through which, acceding to his own inner kingdom, he simultaneously transcended the mental and more especially spiritual provincialisms of what he sometimes called the "hexagone." Borrowed from the abstract political jargon of the time—when the concept of the French Commonwealth was superseding the concept of a colonial empire—the word, in Senghor's use of it, took on the quality of an ideogram, a quality he most particularly attributes to the use of images in African languages: it quietly relegated French power to its geographic limits. Used by a man who was never inclined to attack French culture indiscriminately, who rather pointed only to the vast areas of its self-deceits—it was as powerful a form of demystification as the virulent denunciations of white humanity. The distinctions between the purveyor of culture and the receiver, between the superior civilized colonizer and the inferior colonized blacks were quietly dismissed.

In his famous and influential preface to Senghor's *Anthology of the New Black and Madagascan Poetry* (*Anthologie de la nouvelle poésie nègre et malgache*) (1948), Sartre dramatically defined the common source of inspiration for black lyricism in terms of the black revolt against the white image imposed upon the blacks by colonial masters, itself the obverse of the deified mask of himself created by the white to hide his real face from himself. Desecration, denunciation, and destruction of the white image, and celebration of all things black were then the natural means of liberation from the constraining judgment of the "Other," and with them the concomitant and necessary violence. But whether prose or poetry, such forms of exorcism are rare in Senghor's writing. Rather, with regard to the European man, we find a stern accounting, more specifically for his mercantilism and his disregard for the suffering he inflicts. This is the theme of the postwar "Prière de paix," the last poem in *Black Hosts*, written to be spoken to the accompaniment of the great church organs. It is an indictment of the Europeans' murderous waste of human lives over the centuries, but a prayer too for their pardon, and a fervent plea for God's aid in crushing "the serpent of hatred that rears its head in my heart, the serpent I had thought was dead."

There was a time, admittedly, recorded in poems like "Le retour de l'Enfant Prodigue" ("The Return of the Prodigal Son") when, in his Parisian "exile," he rejected all things French, the French language among them. It was, he later rather humorously remarked in a speech addressed to his Sorbonne masters, necessary "pour les besoins de ma thèse." [9] But his Négritude was not, as Sartre would have it, a mere by-product of the white man's presence. Senghor, as we shall see, could stand his own ground. Curiously, and revealingly, Senghor does not shun the word "white" in his poems, nor does he equate it with forms of evil. It generally appears quite naturally among the gamut of colors he uses; when on one occasion in the poem "Chaka," "the white voice" is the voice of the accuser, it is not necessarily the voice of the white. The "return to the sources" for him was the rediscovery of his cultural inheritance as a son of the Sérère clan. It involved a new awareness of the forms of its oral literature, the integration of words, song, and dance. This was a time

[9] *Négritude et humanisme*, 225.

when he translated the poems of the village poetess, Marône. And it was the time when he found his own idiom as Sérère poet, writing in the French language. Senghor's poems, in the main, elaborate upon the suggestions of that oral tradition. Many of them are songs, formally designed and modulated according to diverse poetic purposes or intentions: a "taga," for the celebration of a human being or specific action; a "way" or ode; an elegy or satire. Each of these he writes for accompaniment by specific instruments, tam-tams extraordinary in their diversification: dyoung-dyoung or royal tam-tam of Sine, gorong, mbalakh, ndeundere, sabar, talmblatt and tama; balafong (xylophone); khalam (guitar); rîti (viola); flute or modern jazz orchestra. It is not by chance then that the "Prayer for peace" was written for organ music. The theme of the return to the sources was indeed more than a thesis; it was a necessary prelude to the poet's discovery of his own idiom.

Senghor, in fact, loves literature too deeply to renounce the pleasures and sustenance it offers. Corneille, Lautréamont, Rimbaud, Péguy, Claudel, and "le grand Hugo" are among the masters who opened up to him worlds of thought and poetry, and he once called French "the language of the Gods"; that is to say, French considered in its literary, "universalizing" usage. Of the contemporary French poets, the one to whom he is most drawn, whose conception of poetry and the poet's mission most clearly approximated his own, is St. John Perse, the West Indian Creole poet. Perse's idiom moved him more deeply than that of his friend Aimé Césaire. Politically and intellectually, the thinker who most deeply influenced Senghor—besides Marx, with whom he felt that same affinity—was the Jesuit ethnologist and philosopher, Teilhard de Chardin.[10] St. John Perse is a "cosmic poet" who celebrates the epic of man's spiritual odyssey on this planet, apparent in the often tempestuous course of the civilizations he temporarily sets up, and in the inventions or "sea-marks" that chart his course in the uncharted stretches of space and time. The poet, according to St. John Perse, is he who records the adventure, each great poem itself a "sea-mark," at one and the same time the story of its own emergence and of the creation of the world, poetry itself being the eruption of the word that merges world and consciousness, the singer with the surge. Poetry is then the advent or incarnation of the spiritual in the material that gives all things, sweep-

[10] Senghor's essay on Teilhard de Chardin contains what amounts to an intellectual history of the various phases and connotations acquired over the years by the word "Négritude."

ing through space and time, a transcendental unity and human meaning. To see things whole is perhaps the gift of the poet; it is certainly the essential need of the human being in Senghor's world.

For Teilhard de Chardin, too, man must be considered as a "cosmic phenomenon" within the spatio-temporal cosmos whose basic substance is matter and which on a vast scale is organized in complex systems whose effects are described scientifically in the quanta and relativity theories of scientists. What Teilhard sought to demonstrate, and Senghor found so deeply congenial intellectually, was the theory of the slow emergence within ever more complex living organisms of a factor of "indetermination," hence of freedom, culminating in the "life-consciousness" of men, which is to say, their capacity for reflection. To reflect as Teilhard notes, and Senghor emphasizes, is totally to interiorize time and space and to "think" them in general, not merely immediate, terms. More specifically, Teilhard saw as a corollary to his view of the evolutionary process, the continued evolution of human beings in terms of their consequent ability to organize societies and civilizations on an ever larger scale, and their progressive totalization and socialization, moving, if they should choose to make a positive use of their freedom, toward a "panhuman convergence" outside time and space in a center of centers of super-being, God.

It would be idle, and beyond the scope of this paper, to pursue further this too-sketchy recall of a complex hypothesis, theoretically based on specific scientific concepts and considered by many as highly controversial. The brief outline merely stresses the extent to which Senghor has been and has remained open and receptive, intellectually as well as affectively, to such modes of thought that aim at totality and that refuse to cordon off intellectual disciplines or groups of men, whether in terms of scientific knowledge, rationality, or race. Brought up within the Catholic faith, he never relinquished its ideal of catholicity. He early rejected the concept of "nation" as "the object of a sort of cult," or as the "idealization of a social and political régime," [11] and immediately after the war he forged the "mot d'ordre" for himself and his peers: "to assimilate, not to be assimilated."

This first signification of Négritude was easily extended to all black African peoples; thence, as political events accelerated and accumulated it was further stretched to fit Senghor's new awareness

[11] *Négritude et humanisme*, 46.

of a more complex continental African pattern termed "Africanity," including the area shared with the nonblack Arabs in Northern Africa. Africanity itself was to be understood only within the larger perspective of Teilhard's "panhumanism." Rather than rejecting or condemning any group of men, Senghor defines and differentiates their "situation." He does not judge or condemn them, perhaps because to judge or condemn is to separate.

Quite naturally, nonetheless, after 1960, allusions to the Senegalese nation are more numerous and scattered throughout Senghor's prose writing, for the most part in speeches in which he speaks officially for the country he represents: "For us, Senegalese," "For this reason, my country, Sénégal," "the Senegalese people," "we Senegalese," "Senegalese literature," "the Senegalese élite." [12] But seldom is the word dissociated from a larger frame of reference including Negro-African, Black Africa, Africanity, and from the theme of a future to be created in common, a nation to be constructed by all; a nation "in the making." President Senghor, whose country comprises somewhat less than four million people belonging to three main ethnic groups speaking different languages, has a strong political sense of the problems of national unity, yet he constantly eschews an appeal to what he once termed "micro nationalism." He is always ready, in words at least, to wipe out boundaries created by the white man's "interdiction and segregations," as is shown in his early attempt at federation with neighboring Mali, destined to failure. And indeed, the political boundaries of his country, as is the case in ex-colonial Africa, are artificial units carved out according to the hazards of conquests and of European concepts of colonial administration. The African "homeland" of his Paris days, not the political unit of any one country, was the primary reality for Senghor, and it was upon the moral and spiritual features of that homeland that he wanted the spiritual unity of Senegal to rest. For, in his eyes, unlike the Europeans imprisoned within their respective frontiers, Africans had first become conscious of their common identity within the seamless whole of the continent. For Senghor, access to the "political kingdom" was not gained by the access of each former colonial entity to independence. This was only a first step toward the interdependence subsumed in the bond of Négritude. Senghor embodied this belief in the national hymn he wrote for his people:

> Sénégal, nous faisons nôtre ton grand dessein
> Rassembler les poussins à l'abri des milans

[12] *Ibid.*, 308, 318, 320, 356, 369, and 386.

Pour en faire de l'est à l'ouest du nord au sud
Dressé, un seul peuple sans couture
Mais un peuple tourné vers tous les vents du monde.

(Senegal, we make ours your great purpose to gather together and
shelter the chickens from the hawks, to make arise from east to west
and north to south a single seamless people, a people turned toward
all the winds of the world.)

The hymn calls into brotherly union, by name, the different peoples of the continent, and beyond them the white man himself. "The
Bantu is a brother and the Arab and the White." To equate Senghor's
concept of Négritude with either racism or nationalism as we understand them is to misunderstand the connotations the word took on
in its relation to a complex personal experience and a deeply subjective view of human reality. Today, the history of the intellectual
and political movement connected with the term Négritude is well-
known. It has been told in the carefully documented study by Lilyan
Kesteloot, *Black Francophone Writers* (*Les écrivains noirs de langue
française*), now in its third edition (Brussels, 1965). The word was
first used in print in Aimé Césaire's *Journal of a Native's Return*
(*Cahier d'un retour au pays natal*) (1939), one of the great poems
of our time, whose immense impact upon the francophone young
Africans and sympathizers can hardly be overestimated at present.
Senghor too had taken the road back from France to his native land,
to "Négritude refound." But his is the "return of the Prodigal Son,"
carried out with a passion that made him "prey to burning lava of
an inner volcano." It was predominantly Césaire's fierce indictment
of white culture that made the word "Négritude" the rallying cry
in his denunciation of the manner in which France had debased the
300,000 black inhabitants of his island making of them "a vanquished
people." Négritude, then, could be viewed as an account of his attempted evasion from their misery, and his final identification with
and commitment to them. The bitter revolt was uniquely Césaire's,
but its counterpart within the poem itself, the dream of the absent
African homeland, was most certainly Senghor's. "When I came to
know Senghor," Césaire said, "I called myself African." Revolt and
exile are Césaire's great themes.

Senghor's sense of himself as African crystallized around quite different images, the memory of a childhood "royal" in its wonder,
happiness, and freedom. It produced a recurrent image in his poetry,
which sometimes emigrates into his prose, what he would perhaps
call rather than a symbol an "ideogram": "le Royaume d'Enfance,"

the Childhood Kingdom. At the heart of "le Royaume d'Enfance" is the memory of a happy childhood in a prosperous family in the Sérère village of Djilar. "Almost all the people and things they evoke," he wrote of his poems, "are from my small region, a few Sérère villages lost among the *tanns*, the woods, the *bolongs*, and the fields. I need only name them to live once again the *Royaume d'Enfance* [*The Kingdom of Childhood*]." [13]

Senghor's personal quest for what he has called the "Grail-Négritude" always leads back to that kingdom from which both his poems and his political vision and action draw their substance. Because of it the Senegalese sharpshooter, shivering and abandoned in his prisoner-of-war camp, is kin to the legendary *quelwár* or nobleman of the great legendary kingdoms of the past. The poet will clad him again in this ancestral nobility through the nobility of language, he whom "the merchants and bankers proscribed from the Nation," as they proscribed the volunteer Senghor and "upon the honor of [his] arms, engraved 'mercenary.' " [14] No bitterness touches the "Royaume d'Enfance" which knew nothing of colonialism, harking back to the "ancient kingdom of Sine." In an early poem *Joal* (*Songs of the Shade*) Senghor recalls the fabulous visits to his father's house of the last of Sine's kings, Koumba N'Dofène. [15] As a small boy in his native village of Djilos, Senghor left the cultural confines of his home to listen to the tales and legends told him by his mother's brother; and along with black mythology, he absorbed a sense of participation of all things and beings in the cosmic whole, including the presence of the "blood" of the common Ancestor in his own veins that linked him to the wide community of the family.

It was during the Paris "exile" that Senghor made the passionate discovery of Frobenius and the group of ethnologists who described the present and past civilizations of Africa and reversed the European image of the primitive black barbarian, whereupon the "Royaume d'Enfance" became the very incarnation of Négritude, giving it a peculiarly Senghorian coloring. Adapting Frobenius's thesis concerning the unity of the Negro-African world, Senghor saw in it an archetype, a model of African civilization, that made it the very essence of Négritude. For him the word designates "the configura-

---

[13] *Tann:* flatlands flooded at high tide. *Bolong:* inlets or channels. For a short glossary of Sérère terms used in Senghor's poems see *Nocturnes*.

[14] "Le Retour de l'Enfant prodigue," 74.

[15] The kingdom of Sine disappeared in 1925, absorbed into the territory of the colony of Sénégal.

tion of cultural values of the Black world as they are expressed in the life, institutions and works of the Blacks" [16] but seen in the perspective of their "absence," the perspective of exile and memory. This too is the perspective of poetry.

In a 1963 preface, "Black Dominion" ("Domaine noir"), to a volume called *African Africa (Afrique Africaine)* [17] illustrating diverse aspects of Africa, Senghor, drawing upon the work of many ethnologists, fully developed his theory of black sensitivity, constantly turning to his own "pays du Sine" and to its pastoral civilization for a relevant example. The Negro he defines as "l'homme de la nature," a "thinking man" but one who thinks "forms and colors and more especially odors, sounds and rhythms" without "filtering intermediaries." [18] To this physical and mystical sense of the earth he attributes the black esthetic of art as a synthesis of all media—dance, music, language, sculptured mask—actively involving all the sensory apparatus of the human body in the act of creation, which is in fact the symbolic act of liberation from domination by the material forces of the cosmos. The same sense of physical participation links mother and son, the mother through whom the "flame of life" is transmitted with the blood of the ancestor. The African family he notes is the "microcosm, the first cell that through extension is reproduced by all the concentric circles which form the different levels of society, village, tribe, kingdom, empire," a harmonious community which colonialism disrupted, whose central concern was the integration of each member into the spiritual whole and the concern that he bring to the whole, as individual, the full participation which is the measure of a man's freedom and his share in the perpetual re-creation of the integral spiritual whole and its liberation from domination by the inhuman powers of the cosmos.

For Senghor, the outer social configuration then corresponds to a cosmic, spiritual, and mystical design which reproduces the natural expansive movement of his own sensitivity apparent in his poems. Quite clearly, he has incorporated into that design the mystical spiritual community of the Christian church, to which Senghor nonetheless addressed the reproach that it had "torn from [his] too loving heart the chains that linked him to the pulse of the world." [19] For Senghor, the social pattern of the African clan thus idealized is itself

---

[16] *Négritude et humanisme*, 3.
[17] Ed. Michel Huet (Lausanne, 1963).
[18] *Ibid.*, 8.
[19] "Le Retour de l'Enfant prodigue," 50.

an "ideogram," the inscription in a concrete social organization of the central African concern with the wholeness of the human being, suggesting, beyond it, an archetype. In spirit, it reflects the harmony of innocence and timeless order of the "Royaume d'Enfance." "Domaine noir" was published in 1963, the year Senghor also wrote the preface to *Négritude et humanisme*, the articles the volume contains being in a sense a record of his public pronouncements over more than a quarter of a century. The central theme running through the book is "the conquest of freedom"—his own, one feels, and his people's, a conquest whose several stages he recalls as "the recovery, affirmation and illustration of the collective personalities of the Black people, of 'Negritude.' " [20] The "illustration" is manifest in all forms of culture, poetry, and political institutions alike. Consciously and carefully, in his *The Concept of Nation and the African View of Socialism*, Senghor defined "nation" in terms both of the archetype and of the political and social realities of Africa. The nation he distinguishes from a Barrèsian *patrie*; the *patrie* is the heritage transmitted by the ancestors, "a land, blood, a language or at least a dialect, mores, customs, folklore, art, a culture rooted in the soil and expressed in a race," [21] precisely the concept often equated with nationalism. The nation is then the next higher circle in the African design: a "voluntary" creation or "restructuration" of the individuals formed by the *patrie* conceived on a larger scale in terms of the common virtues to which each *patrie* had attuned their emotions. The nation then, like the clan, is created anew each day in the "souls" of its members. The state is the means whereby the inner creation is in fact incarnated. Marx is then, as Senghor had noted when discussing the ideas in Teilhard de Chardin, turned upside down, and modern African socialism wedded to the "collective personality of the Black peoples, of 'Négritude.' " [22] The "new Negro" and "new nation" is a new incarnation and conscious recreation of the African humanistic civilization in terms of the modern environment.

Over the years, Senghor tirelessly fulfilled his role as intellectual, within the design he had formulated for it: the task of the intellectual was to reiterate the black values "in their truth and excellence," engraving as it were, ever more deeply, the image of "virtues rediscovered," [23] those virtues once obscured by the foreign conqueror.

[20] *Négritude et humanisme*, 3.
[21] *Nation et voie du socialisme*, 22–23.
[22] *Négritude et humanisme*, 322.
[23] *Ibid.*, 139.

This is the realm of all culture, in relation to a civilization as such, and thereby, specific though it is, no culture need exclude another. As the nation transcends but does not negate the *patrie*, so culture transcends but does not negate a civilization. It is in his definition of the "virtues rediscovered" that Senghor comes full circle back to the "imaginary continent" within himself. To Négritude he attributes the African peasant's "mystical sense of the earth" which makes "the healthiest and strongest people" and the gift of emotion, "the royal domain of the Negro," [24] which is also the key to the "realm of art and poetry," that ultimate aspiration of all culture which is to allow men "to produce works of beauty and to enjoy them." To the European he allots reason as against imagination for the African, discursive knowledge as against unitary vision, science as against art and the freedom attained by the black; a political freedom to be sure, but in part also the freedom acquired with the sense of his own creativity in the practice of his art.

Négritude of late has been under attack, as witnessed in a debate recorded in *Africa Report* [25] and entitled "A Dialogue on Cultures" that engaged two Africans, Joseph O. Okpatu and Tapan lo Liyong, anglophone Africans studying in the United States. Accusing African intellectuals of "speaking in the ears and microphones of the Western world," Okpatu charged that they had failed in their mission which was first and primarily to communicate with their own people, a failure which foreboded in the future an insurrection of the masses against the "sophisticated elite": "an uprising of those we often call 'the masses,' in which everything must go—our intellectualism, our academicism, our sophistication and any other absurdity in which we dress ourselves today." The remedy: "a reunion with the main body of our fellow-Africans." One might have thought that this "return to the sources" was an echo by a younger generation, of the Paris groups' rediscovery in exile of the African "soul of the ethnologists." For Okpatu, Négritude is merely a "once useful anachronism," a myth with a certain degree of political efficacity, tailored to the needs of an alienated elite:

> an examination of "Négritude" (despite the political role it played, largely through the enthusiasm of those who misunderstood its implications) and of all our cultural, social and political behavior re-

[24] *Ibid.,* 19 and 24.
[25] Joseph O. Okpatu and Tapan lo Liyong, "A Dialogue on Cultures," *Africa Report,* Oct. 1968, 13–20.

veals the fact that African intellectuals carry on their existence in purely Western terms. "Négritude" was never addressed to the Black "masses" of Africa. Its language, its implications were all aimed at a dialogue with the White; it was and is a statement made to the Western world about Africa.

Facts hardly bear this out entirely. As one leafs through the speeches Senghor addressed to his fellow Africans, it is evident that his attention focused on the Sérère peasants and their folklore. True only in part, it overlooks the fact that for Senghor at least, and for Césaire, Négritude is, too, a dialogue of complex personalities with themselves. How large was the part drawn from ethnologists of dream and imagination in the creation of a "noble" past, a precolonial Africa, "cradle" of humanity, animator of the ancient civilization of Egypt rich in mighty kingdoms and innocent of crime which the poems of Senghor allow us to glimpse? How alien to the mass of his countrymen is this vision? The verdict is difficult to assess.

Taban lo Liyong's counterappeal to Africans to "stretch" their minds spiritually rejects the "return to the masses" theme of Okpatu. His is an eloquent appeal to Africans to "forget the African [they] are supposed to be," to assimilate all the knowledge, wherever they may find it, needed to become a twentieth-century man, eschewing ignorance of the masses. He might, one feels, have been drawn to Senghor's vision of the creation of a new African man, emerging into the ever-larger circle of a humanity moving toward the truly seamless planetary panhumanism, in fact, taking the lead over a less liberated, less truly humanistic Europe. Yet he too finds fault with Négritude: "Nationalistically inspired slogans such as 'Négritude' and the African personality have inhibited [the African students'] participation in other peoples' cultures," glamorizing a "medieval peasant 'Négritude' " inappropriate in the modern world.[26] President Senghor here seems directly under attack, although, by quoting the words we placed at the head of this article, Liyong disassociates him

---

[26] The counterpart in Anglophone Africa of the concept of Négritude, which has never been uncritically received there. Liyong invokes Fanon, the West Indian writer, psychiatrist, and revolutionary who fought in the Algerian War of Independence and showed great concern for the rise of tribalism and regionalism in postindependence Africa: "African unity takes off the mask and crumbles into regionalism inside the hollow shell of nationality itself," surely a danger Senghor had sought to obviate in his definition of the new African concept of "nation." See Ruth Schacter Morgenthau, "Frantz Fanon: Five Years Later," *Africa Report*, May 1966, 69–71.

from the partisans of Négritude under attack: "When I was younger, I would gladly have come forward as the spokesman for all Africa, or at least for 'Négritude.' By now, experience has taught me the diversity of Negroes and Africans and it would be presumptuous of me to speak in the name of either." The avowal is not without its tinge of melancholy. It was made the year following the First World Festival of Negro Art held in Dakar under the patronage of President Senghor himself. Its purpose had been highly Senghorian, "the defense and illustration of 'Négritude,' " and it proposed to proceed to "the elaboration of a new humanism, which [would] include all of humanity, on the whole of our planet." It was at the festival, despite its unquestionable success, that the whole concept of Négritude came under attack.[27]

No one more clearly than Senghor himself has diagnosed the mythical quality of a vision, poetic in essence, and created out of the very absence of the reality that engendered it: "Here he is, today's poet, grey in winter in a grey hotel room. How could he not think of the 'Royaume d'Enfance,' of the Promised Land of the future in the nothingness of the present time? How could he not sing 'Négritude arise'?" For Senghor, clearly, the black is the poet, not the political or the racial figure, and Africa the inner continent of his longing. The "continent of the imagination" bridged the present that negated it. For Senghor the political and the poetic vision were one; and he lived to see the unity of these visions in part realized through his own action. The potential contradictions and immediate practical incompatibilities within the dream have perhaps now become apparent; yet it would seem that a goal was set and a personal credo faithfully lived. "We lived," wrote the Guadeloupean poet Paul Niger, "on an unreal 'négritie' [negrity] built on the theories of sociologists and other scholars who study men behind plate-glass windows." [28] This could not be the case with Senghor who, even if he renounced his role as spokesman for all Africa or Négritude, could still combine in the fine balance of his love of beauty, imagination, and concrete practical sense, in a time of violence, his total fidelity to his own inner universe and his dedication to a people, his, and yet linked to all humanity.

---

[27] For an account of the festival see Newall Flather, "Impressions of the Dakar Festival," *Africa Report*, May 1966, 57–60.

[28] Lilyan Kesteloot, *Les écrivains noirs de langue française* (Brussels, 1965), 253.

BIBLIOGRAPHY

Africa Report, Feb. 1967, 46.

Césaire, Aimé. Cahier d'un retour au pays natal. 2nd ed. Paris, 1956.

Ernest, Milcent, and Sordet Monique. Léopold Sédar Senghor. Seghers Séries. Paris, 1964.

Flather, Newall. "Impressions of the Dakar Festival." Africa Report, May 1966, 57–60.

Irele, Abiola. "Negritude, Literature and Ideology." Journal of Modern African Studies 3, no. 4 (Dec. 1965).

Kesteloot, Lilyan. Les écrivains noirs de langue française. 3rd ed. Brussels, 1965.

Melore, Thomas, "De la Négritude dans la littérature negro-africaine." Présence Africaine. Paris, 1962.

Morgenthau, Ruth Schacter. "Frantz Fanon: Five Years Later." Africa Report, May 1966, 69–71.

Okpatu, Joseph O., and Tapan lo Liyong. "A Dialogue on Cultures." Africa Report, Oct. 1968, 13–20.

Sartre, Jean-Paul. "Orphée noir." Preface to Anthologie de la nouvelle poésie nègre et malgache de langue française. Paris, 1948.

Seller, Eric. "Negritude: Statics or Dynamics?" L'Esprit Createur 10, no. 3 (Fall 1970).

Senghor, Léopold Sédar. Afrique Africaine, ed. Michel Huet. Lausanne, 1963.

———. Anthologie de la nouvelle poésie nègre et malgache. Paris, 1948.

———. Chants d'ombre. Paris, 1964.

———. Ethiopiques. Paris, 1956.

———. Liberté I: Négritude et humanisme. Paris, 1964.

———. "Le Retour de l'Enfant prodique." Chants d'ombre. Paris, 1964.

———. Nation et voie africaine du socialisme. Présence Africaine, Paris, 1961.

———. Pierre Teilhard de Chardin et la politique africaine. Paris, 1962.

———. "Poème liminaire," Hosties noires in Poèmes. Paris, 1964. Pp. 55–62.

Index

The Cry of Home was manually composed on the Linotype, printed letterpress, and sewn and bound by Kingsport Press, Kingsport, Tennessee.

The book was designed by Jim Billingsley. Janson type was used exclusively. The paper on which the book is printed bears the watermark of the S. D. Warren Company and was developed for an effective life of at least three hundred years.

THE UNIVERSITY OF TENNESSEE PRESS
KNOXVILLE